P9-CDC-971

THE
GILBERT AND SULLIVAN
COMPANION

by the same author

THE WIT OF MUSIC
THE PROMS

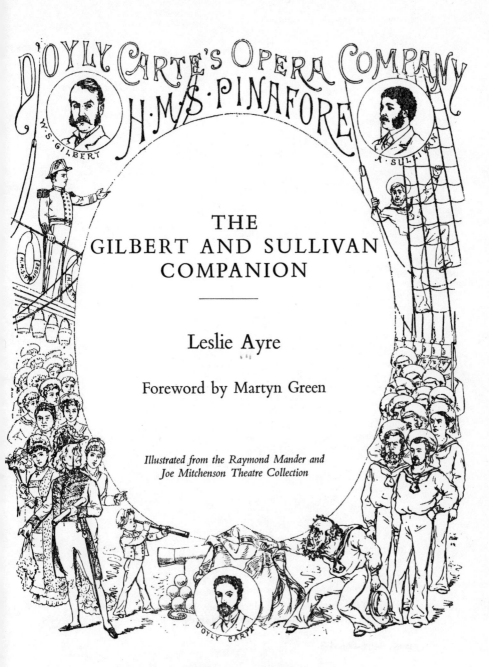

THE
GILBERT AND SULLIVAN
COMPANION

Leslie Ayre

Foreword by Martyn Green

Illustrated from the Raymond Mander and
Joe Mitchenson Theatre Collection

DODD, MEAD & COMPANY
NEW YORK

To Olga and Carl

Foreword

> First you're born and I'll be bound you
> Find a dozen strangers round you.
> 'Hallo!' cries the new born baby,
>   'Where's my parents? Which may they be?'
> *Utopia, Ltd.*

The young Princess Victoria was just seventeen, living quietly and decorously at Kensington Palace. Studying her music, with emphasis on Italian Opera and Beethoven, and reading, among the lighter works, the novels of Sir Walter Scott and probably a new serialised novel by Charles Dickens, *Pickwick Papers*, she was blissfully unaware that in less than a year she would be hauled out of bed in the early hours of the morning to be told that she had ascended the throne of England. She was equally unaware of the birth of a baby to a retired naval surgeon and his young wife. Even if she had been made aware of the latter fact it would not have given her any concern. It was to be many years before she became cognizant of the baby's existence. It was also many years later before the one-time baby told the interviewer, 'Date of birth: 18th November 1836. Place of birth: 17 Southampton Street, Strand, in the house of my grandfather, who had known Dr Johnson, Garrick, Reynolds, and who was the last man in London, I believe, to wear Hessian boots and a pigtail. I was named William, after my father, and Schwenck after someone or other else, I suppose!'

There is no record, to my knowledge, of Arthur Seymour Sullivan having made any similar statement. It is known, however, that he was not named Arthur after his father, his father's name being Thomas, as was his grandfather's. His uncle's name was John, and there is not a Seymour among his immediate relatives. The choice of given names was, in its way, a source of some embarrassment to Sullivan in so far as he would eschew the use of his initials for obvious reasons! So much has already been written about the great triumvirate—Gilbert, Sullivan and Carte—that it is difficult to write a foreword to a 'new' work on the subject let alone to write the work itself—Edith A. Brown, Arthur Lawrence, Saxe Wyndham, Sir Arthur Quiller-Couch, Sir Alexander Mackenzie, Messrs Cellier and Bridgeman, Isaac Goldman, Messrs Sydney Dark and Roland Grey, Hesketh Pearson, W. A. Darlington, Deems Taylor, Lord Robert Cecil (in a foreword to *The Savoy Series of World Classics*), even I myself have attempted some marginal notes in a volume called *A Treasury of Gilbert and Sullivan*. After that 'little list' what can there be left to say that is 'new'? As Gilbert himself *might* have said, in a paraphrase of Winston Churchill in 1941, and of himself in 1885: 'I often wonder, in my artless Gilbertian way, how it is that so many managed to write so much about so few!'

But Gilbert was not a modest man by any means. He had a great opinion of, and a great belief in, W. S. Gilbert and W. S. Gilbert's talents. To Gilbert, Gilbert was the alpha and omega of dramatists. I don't think, for a moment, he ever doubted that he, together with Sullivan and Carte, would be the subject of a biographer. After the opening of *The Gondoliers*, he wrote to Sir Arthur, 'I must thank you for the magnificent work you have put into the piece. *It gives one the chance of shining, right through the twentieth century, with a reflected light*'! (The italics and the exclamation mark are mine.) The letter was written eleven years before the twentieth century was born.

I am consumed with admiration for Leslie Ayre. His re-telling of the stories leading up to and during the various productions is factual and simply told, and his appendices or dictionary type of listing, with short biographical notes of the actors and actresses who, over the years, have appeared in the Savoy Operas, and explanations of various quotes from the works themselves are a mine of information. He has refrained from including any legendary or misleading information, or coming to personal conclusions that are as erroneous as they are ludicrous, such as one biographer did when, among other things, he accused Gilbert of being a prude. The word 'prude' is defined by the dictionary—the Oxford Dictionary, of course!—as being: 'One that maintains or affects extreme propriety of speech or behaviour, especially in regard to relations of the sexes: demure or prim. Usually applied adversely.' As I have said earlier, Gilbert was not a modest man, and very far from being demure or prim. He was one of the most down-to-earth men of his time. He had a biting tongue and a satirical wit, and yet, withal, he was a gentleman. But he was no prude.

6

The Savoy Operas, though some have fared better than others, have been popular throughout the length and breadth of the world and have been translated into many languages, including American and Australian, not to mention German, Japanese and, I believe, Chinese. I am frequently asked two questions. Which collaborator was the greatest and what is the secret of their continued charm and popularity? The first is simple to answer. Without Gilbert and without Sullivan there would have been no Savoy Operas. Each was a master in his own field and remains a master today. Gilbert is still quoted, and Sullivan is still whistled, sung and hummed. Each was great, and neither was the greater. The second question is probably answered best by this little true story.

Some years ago, at the invitation of Danny Kaye, I was attending a matinée at London's Palladium where Danny was taking over the second half of the program. As the curtain came down a young boy seated in front of me—he was about thirteen or fourteen years of age—was asked by his companion, who may have been his mother but whom I presumed to be an aunt, what he thought of the show and of Danny Kaye in particular.

'I liked it,' he said. 'He reminds me of Gilbert and Sullivan.' Neither the boy nor his companion knew who was sitting behind them, but his reply so intrigued me that I would have given myself away and asked him why he was so reminded had not the lady forestalled me. The boy then said: 'It is the sort of show to which a boy can take his parents without feeling embarrassed.'

I have tried to think of a better answer but cannot.

Martyn Green,
New York, April 1972

Key

To avoid constant repetition of titles of the operas, the following abbreviations are used throughout:

Cox and Box	(C)
Thespis	(T)
Trial by Jury	(J)
The Sorcerer	(S)
HMS Pinafore	(HMS)
The Pirates of Penzance	(PP)
Patience	(P)
Iolanthe	(I)
Princess Ida	(PI)
The Mikado	(M)
Ruddigore	(R)
The Yeomen of the Guard	(Y)
The Gondoliers	(G)
Utopia, Limited	(U)
The Grand Duke	(D)

Acknowledgments

I am sincerely grateful to Miss Bridget D'Oyly Carte for her kindness in reading the manuscript of the book and making many valuable suggestions. My thanks are due also to Mr Frederic Lloyd, the general manager, Mr Albert Truelove, the secretary, and many past and present members of the D'Oyly Carte Opera Company for their ready assistance.

Messrs Chappell & Co. Ltd publish the vocal scores of *Trial by Jury*, *The Pirates of Penzance*, *Patience*, *Iolanthe*, *Princess Ida*, *The Mikado*, *Ruddigore*, *The Yeomen of the Guard*, *The Gondoliers*, *Utopia, Limited* and *The Grand Duke*. Those of *The Sorcerer* and *HMS Pinafore* are published by Messrs J. B. Cramer & Co. Ltd and that of *Cox and Box* by Messrs Boosey and Hawkes. The libretti of the operas—spoken dialogue and lyrics—are published by Oxford University Press as *The Savoy Operas*, with text prepared under the guidance of Miss Bridget D'Oyly Carte and with introductions by her and by David Cecil and notes by Derek Hudson. *The Savoy Operas* are also published by Messrs Macmillan & Co. Ltd. Libretti of separate operas are published by the publishers of the vocal scores.

The following books may be selected from the extensive bibliography as being of particular value, and several of them are referred to in the text:

The D'Oyly Carte Opera Company in Gilbert and Sullivan Opera: a Record of Productions, 1875–1961 compiled by Cyril Rollins and R. John Witts (Michael Joseph, 1962); *The Gilbert and Sullivan Book* by Leslie Baily (Cassell, 1952, Spring Books, 1966); *Gilbert, Sullivan and D'Oyly Carte* by Francis Cellier and Cunningham Bridgeman (Pitman, 1927); *The Story of Gilbert and Sullivan* by Isaac Goldberg (John Murray, 1929); *Gilbert and Sullivan Opera* by H. M. Walbrook (F. V. White, 1922); *A Picture History of Gilbert and Sullivan* by Raymond Mander and Joe Mitchenson

(Vista Books, 1962); *First Night Gilbert and Sullivan* by Reginald Allen (Heritage Press, New York); *Gilbert and Sullivan* by Hesketh Pearson (Hamish Hamilton, 1935, Penguin Books, 1950); *Gilbert and Sullivan* by Arthur Jacobs (Parrish, 1957); *A Gilbert and Sullivan Dictionary* by George E. Dunns (Allen & Unwin, 1936); *Sullivan* by H. Saxe Wyndham (Kegan Paul, 1926); *Sir Arthur Sullivan* by Arthur Lawrence (James Bowden, 1899); *W. S. Gilbert: His Life and Letters* by Sidney Dark and Rowland Grey (Methuen, 1923); *Sir Arthur Sullivan: His Life, Letters and Diaries* by Herbert Sullivan and Newman Flower (Cassell, 1927); *Composers of Operetta* by Gervase Hughes (Macmillan, 1962); *Thespis: A Gilbert and Sullivan Enigma* by Terence Rees (Dillon's University Bookshop, 1964); *Gilbert and Sullivan Opera* by Audrey Williamson (Rockliff, 1955); *London's Lost Theatres of the 19th Century* by Erroll Sherson (John Lane, 1925); *Secrets of a Savoyard* by Sir Henry Lytton (Jarrolds, 1921). *Brewer's Dictionary of Phrase and Fable* (Cassell, 1968) has proved valuable in checking several of Gilbert's allusions.

Preface

It was clearly a moment of crisis. One of the young secretaries in my office came rushing into my room in a state of wild alarm. 'You must do something about it,' she insisted. 'You must ring up the D'Oyly Carte people at once and stop it or things will never be the same again.'

What had happened was that her favourite artist was leaving the D'Oyly Carte Opera Company. The outlook was bleak, for there could be no one else like him. In a fatherly kind of way I pointed out that this sort of thing had happened before, but that, even though it was true that there would be no other artist exactly like Mr So-and-so, the Gilbert and Sullivan operas would probably survive. Yet she had my sympathy. There was a time—a few years ago now—when I was convinced that there would be no future without such artists as, for instance, Bertha Lewis, Winifred Lawson, Henry Lytton, Leo Sheffield and Darrell Fancourt. These were the people who introduced me to these wonderful operas, and affection for them remains firmly in the heart.

Yet, though I am not so long in the tooth as to be able to go back to Grossmith, it is reasonable to suppose that Lytton was quite unlike him. Certainly Martyn Green differed greatly from Lytton and Peter Pratt was no carbon copy of Martyn Green any more than is John Reed of Peter Pratt. For within the framework and the tradition, each artist brings something of himself to the particular role. All are part of the life-stream of the operas. So you will find in this book many names. All those who first played the roles are here and many others who, through the years, have carried on the succession. Since *Trial by Jury* first delighted London in 1875 great numbers of artists have played the various parts in the operas and I beg you, if your own particular favourite is absent, not to prepare for me some punishment with boiling oil in it.

Though many distinguished artists have contributed their talents through the years, William Schwenck Gilbert and Arthur Seymour Sullivan, that 'pair of sparkling guys' (in the phrase of the late Stephen Williams), remain the dominant figures. The sheer strength of their works has never been more clearly demonstrated than in the years since the copyright in Gilbert's libretti expired at the end of 1961, that in Sullivan's music having run out eleven years earlier.

As the time for the expiry of the Gilbert copyright approached, voices were raised in alarm at the possible fate of the operas. Thrown unprotected on the world, they would surely suffer a terrible mauling at the hands of the vandals! This great English heritage might even be destroyed altogether! Leading articles in many newspapers expressed the most serious misgivings and it was even suggested that a special Bill should be placed before Parliament for the protection of the operas. But it was not by any means everyone who took such a pessimistic view. There were those—Miss Bridget D'Oyly Carte notable among them—who firmly believed that the intrinsic merit of the operas would carry them triumphantly through whatever might lie ahead. Of that time, I personally recall deriving considerable confidence from looking at a set of coloured prints, hanging on the wall of my flat. They represent characters from a burlesque called *Carmen Up-to-Data*, presented in London at the beginning of this century. Escamillo, the bullfighter, is a shapely young woman in tight trousers and many of the dragoons are girls. Yet Bizet's *Carmen* is still played round the world because it is a masterpiece. *Carmen Up-to-Data* was just another show.

In fact, nothing ghastly has happened. The position of the D'Oyly Carte Opera Company—whose presentations of the operas through the years have not by any means remained as static as some people think—was strengthened by the formation of a Trust, and the company is as popular as ever it was, both in Britain and in America. There have been other professional productions—different but worthy—by, for instance, Sadler's Wells Opera, Scottish Opera, and Tyrone Guthrie. The Gilbert and Sullivan for All organisation, which gives concert performances and some staged productions, grows in strength and, far from taking liberties, depends largely on the original prompt books. It just happens that Gilbert and Sullivan knew what they were about and wrote very good pieces.

Leslie Ayre

The Gilbert—Sullivan Partnership

The Fateful Meeting In the autumn of 1869 Queen Victoria had not long ago celebrated her fiftieth birthday and had been on the throne for thirty-two years, the last eight of them as a widow. Mr W. E. Gladstone, her Prime Minister but not her favourite man, had just completed his first year of office. Alfred Tennyson, the Poet Laureate, was in the midst of *Idylls of the King*. The public were enjoying a new novel, *Lorna Doone*, by R. D. Blackmore, and had had the opportunity of reading all the novels of Charles Dickens except *The Mystery of Edwin Drood* on which he was now working and which was to be uncompleted on his death the following year.

John Everett Millais, the one-time boy prodigy, had abandoned the precepts of the Pre-Raphaelite Brotherhood and was painting fashionably and lucratively; Holman Hunt was engaged on one of his visits to the Holy Land, busily depicting Biblical subjects; and Burne-Jones was painting in the 'greenery-yallery, Grosvenor Gallery' manner.

In the musical world the 'oratorio industry' was in full swing and so was the drawing-room ballad. Joseph Barnby, William Sterndale Bennett and Julius Benedict were familiar names. Edward Elgar was a lad of twelve. The strains of Johann Strauss's 'Blue Danube' had reached London. Wagner's *Das Rheingold* had had its first performance in Munich, Verdi was a vigorous fifty-six and Berlioz had just died.

Michael Costa, Italian-born conductor settled in London, had just been knighted for his long service at the Royal Opera House, Covent Garden, where Adelina Patti, Therese Tietjens and Charles Santley were winning applause. There were Promenade Concerts in London but Henry Wood, who was to give the term new significance, was at the moment uttering baby-cries over a shop off Oxford Street. Incidentally, as a very young man he was to play a part in the Gilbert and Sullivan story, assisting at the first rehearsals of *The Yeomen of the Guard*.

The lighter musical theatre in London was not in a healthy state, consisting largely of entertainments which the boys-about-town would attend but to which they would not dream of taking auntie. Rather more tasteful than these—but not much more—were the adaptations of operettas by Offenbach and others, adaptations which, in the process of translation, alteration and presentation, had had most of their original Parisian charm removed and replaced by crudity and boorish horseplay.

But there *were* oases even in the desert of light entertainment, places where the shows, carefully planned to suit a family audience, were guaranteed not to bring a blush to the most innocent cheek. There were not many of them but one successful purveyor of such blameless entertainment was Thomas German Reed, who had the double satisfaction of feeling that he was doing something worthwhile and also of observing that his bank balance was looking quite healthy on it. He was well equipped for the path on which he had embarked, being not only a musician and an experienced man of the theatre but also an astute businessman. He saw that there was a public for wholesome entertainment and he proceeded skilfully to fill the gap.

German Reed's early venture was to present a variety of entertainments, such as ballad concerts by distinguished singers, dramatic readings by Charles Dickens, and songs at the piano by a young artist called George Grossmith in a hall in Long Acre. Things went well and German Reed moved into more ambitious premises in the lower part of Regent Street, premises to which he gave the dignified name of the Royal Gallery of Illustration. To further emphasise the sobriety of the establishment, he arranged that the music was usually provided by a piano or harmonium, than which there could hardly be a more proper and homely instrument.

Though the diversions at the Royal Gallery of Illustration may not seem particularly exciting to-day, German Reed did in fact attract artists of talent who were happy to have their work presented there. One of these was the gifted musician, Frederic Clay, whom some people will still remember as the composer of such ballads, once immensely popular as 'She Wandered Down the Mountain Side', 'Sands o' Dee' and 'I'll Sing Thee Songs of Araby'. But he also wrote a number of operettas of quality, one of which, *Constance*, was presented at Covent Garden.

In 1869, when he was thirty-one, Clay was working on a show for German Reed called *Ages Ago*. His collaborator, two years older than himself [William Schwenck Gilbert] had already had considerable success as a dramatist, showing a sharp appreciation of a good theatrical idea and a sense of economy which would not permit him to waste it. Thus *Ages Ago* had as its big scene the coming-to-life of the family portraits in a picture-gallery, a device Gilbert was to revive with telling effect eighteen years later in *Ruddigore*.

One of Clay's closest friends was the brilliant young musician, Arthur Seymour Sullivan, who, though only twenty-seven, was already something of a darling in the world of 'serious' music. Sullivan, on his part, had for Clay the greatest regard and affection, which were to persist through the years. What, then, could be more natural than that Clay should suggest that his young friend, Arthur Sullivan, might like to come along to a rehearsal of *Ages Ago* at the Royal Gallery of Illustration and meet his interesting and talented collaborator? Whether or not he had in mind that Gilbert and Sullivan could work successfully together, one does not know. After all, Sullivan, the serious composer, *had* written the music for a jolly romp called *Cox and Box* and, for German Reed, an operetta, *The Contrabandista*. Anyhow, by bringing the two together, Fred Clay, while losing the collaboration of the most gifted librettist of the day, was to lay the foundation for something unique in the history of the English stage.

And so it was that, during a break in rehearsal at the Royal Gallery of Illustration, Clay introduced Mr Sullivan to Mr Gilbert.

It was no doubt an amiable meeting but, immediately after the exchange of compliments, Gilbert, with an air of the utmost gravity, had a serious problem to place before the distinguished young composer: 'My friend Fred Clay and I have been discussing a technical point on which you may be able to throw some light. My contention is that if a musician who is a master of all his instruments has a musical theme to express, he can express it as readily upon the simple tetrachord of Mercury, in which, as we all know, there are no diatonic intervals whatever, as upon the more elaborate disdiapason with the three tetrachords and the redundant note which, as I need not remind a composer of your distinction, embraces in its perfect consonance all the single, double and inverted chords.'

According to Gilbert years afterwards, Sullivan thought for a few seconds and then said that he would not answer off-hand but would think it over and let him know. It is difficult to believe that Sullivan was fooled by the pseudo-technical claptrap. Most probably he was somewhat taken aback by this extraordinary man and was merely being polite.

Gilbert was in fact working at the time on a blank-verse comedy, *The Palace of Truth*, in which one of the characters talked pretentious musical rubbish. In order to provide suitable speeches, he had dug out various terms and phrases from the *Encyclopaedia Britannica* and strung them together. It was one of these speeches, changed from blank verse into prose, that he inflicted upon Sullivan. Gilbert never did get an answer from Sullivan. 'He must still be thinking about it,' he once said.

The important thing for future generations was that contact had been established, even though it did not produce immediate results. Thomas German Reed, however, did nearly achieve the distinction of being the first impresario to present a Gilbert and Sullivan opera, for he certainly saw the potentialities. He got so far as to write to Sullivan, suggesting that he might compose the music for a new Gilbert piece *Our Island Home*, but Sullivan was not at that time prepared to take up the idea and German Reed wrote the music himself.

Though Gilbert and Sullivan had not yet worked together, their names had by now appeared for the first time on the same vocal score: *Ages Ago*. Written by W. S. Gilbert. Music by Frederic Clay. Dedicated to Arthur Sullivan.'

And what of Frederic Clay? After the portentous introduction, he and Gilbert worked together on several pieces, among them *The Gentleman in Black*, *Happy Arcadia* and *Princess Toto*, before Gilbert concentrated on his collaboration with Sullivan. Clay, whose friendship with Sullivan remained firm through the years, went out to New York in advance of the presentation of *HMS Pinafore* there. It was while on the way home from the first night of his own opera, *The Golden Ring*, at the Alhambra Theatre, London, in 1889, that he was suddenly paralysed by a stroke. He died at Great Marlow at the age of fifty-one, while his friend Sullivan was completing the score of *The Gondoliers*. Sullivan, greatly distressed at his death, said of him: 'Fred Clay was one of the most brilliant and gifted of men and like a brother to me.'

Gilbert Before Sullivan It was a somewhat winding path that carried Gilbert to the meeting with Sullivan at the Royal Gallery of Illustration and at an early stage it led him into an episode of comedy-drama. When only two years old he accompanied his parents on holiday to Italy and, while they were staying near Naples, he was taken out for an airing by his nurse. Up to them came two plausible gentlemen who said that they had been sent by Gilbert, Senior, with the request that they should take the child back to him at once. The young woman yielded up Master Gilbert —and in due course his father received a demand for a ransom of twenty-five pounds, which was promptly paid and the child recovered. In the light of subsequent events he was cheap at the price!

William Schwenck Gilbert—his second name, which he heartily disliked, was the surname of his godmother—was born at No. 17 Southampton Street, Strand, London, on November 18, 1836, of parents in reasonably comfortable circumstances. Whatever else he may have inherited from his father, a naval surgeon who took to writing late in life, he certainly acquired his fiery temper. On one occasion, Gilbert, Senior, walked into a branch of W. H. Smith, demanded all the copies of one of his novels and tore them to shreds because the proofs had not been properly corrected—an action entirely worthy of his son.

Two other characteristics may possibly be traced to Gilbert's upbringing. He had an abiding interest in matters nautical, as evidenced in the *Bab Ballads* as well as in the operas, and there was his strange and often cruel attitude in the operas towards women who were plain or who had committed the unpardonable sin of being unmarried and no longer young. It is possible that his youthful observation of the cat-and-dog affair that his parents made of marriage had some influence on his outlook. Yet his own marriage in 1867 to Lucy Blois Turner, when she was seventeen and he thirty-one, was the start of a long and happy companionship which ended only in his death.

He went to school in Boulogne and later to Great Ealing School, where his dramatic sense first started to show itself in little plays written for performance at the school. He subsequently attended King's College. The next stage in his career was described in some detail by himself:

'When I was nineteen years old, the Crimean War was at its height, and commissions in the Royal Artillery were thrown open to competitive examination. So I gave up all idea of Oxford, took my B.A. degree at the University of London, and read for the examination for direct commissions, which was to be held at Christmas, 1856. The limit of age was twenty and as, at the date of the examination, I should have been six weeks over that age, I applied for and obtained from Lord Panmure, the then Secretary of State for War, a dispensation for this excess and worked away with a will. But the war came to a rather abrupt and unexpected end and, no more officers being required, the examination was indefinitely postponed. Among the blessings of peace

may be reckoned certain comedies, operas, farces and extrava-
ganzas which, if the war had lasted another six weeks, would in
all probability never have been written. I had no taste for a line
regiment, so I obtained, by competitive examination, an assistant
clerkship in the Education Department of the Privy Council
Office, in which ill-organised and ill-governed office I spent four
uncomfortable years.

'Coming unexpectedly into a capital sum of £300, I resolved
to emancipate myself from the detestable thraldom of this baleful
office; and on the happiest day of my life I sent in my resignation.
With £100 I paid my call to the Bar (I had previously entered
myself as a student at the Inner Temple), with another £100 I
obtained access to a conveyancer's chambers, and with the third
£100 I furnished a set of chambers of my own, and began life
afresh as a barrister-at-law.' (Article contributed by Gilbert to
the magazine, *The Theatre*, 1883.)

His first brief as a lawyer did not exactly bring him celebrity.
Of his unsuccessful defence of a woman, he said: 'No sooner had
the learned judge pronounced sentence than the poor soul stooped
down and, taking off a heavy boot, flung it at my head as a reward
for my eloquence on her behalf, accompanying the assault with a
torrent of invective against my abilities as a counsel, and my line
of defence. The language in which her oration was couched was
perfectly shocking. The boot missed me but hit a reporter on the
head, and to this fact I am disposed to attribute the unfavourable
light in which my search for a defence was placed in two or three
of the leading daily papers next morning.'

His activities on the northern circuit, with some appearances at
the Old Bailey, were not a financial success. In his first two years
he earned £75 and during his four years at the Bar he averaged
only five clients a year.

But he was active in other directions. A familiar picture shows
him as an officer in the militia, looking very proud of himself in
the kilted uniform of the 3rd Battalion, The Gordon Highlanders.
(His mother was a Scot.) And he was writing.

His first published work was a commission from the singer,
Mlle Parepa, to prepare an English translation of the 'Laughing
Song' from Auber's opera, *Manon Lescaut*. Mlle Parepa, who later
married Carl Rosa of operatic fame, duly sang Gilbert's version in
a Promenade Concert conducted by Alfred Mellon at Covent
Garden. Like most young authors Gilbert confessed to the thrill of
watching his neighbours reading his words in their programmes.

Significantly Gilbert's first professional play had a pseudo-magical theme, for he was always interested in such subjects, often to the near-despair of Sullivan. Called *Dulcamara, or The Little Duck and the Great Quack*, it was a burlesque on Donizetti's opera *L'Elisir d'Amore* and, written in ten days and rehearsed in a week, it was presented with some success at the St James's Theatre in December 1866. Burlesque on opera was very much in his line at this time and he followed up with treatments of Donizetti's *The Daughter of the Regiment*, under the title *La Vivandière*, Balfe's *The Bohemian Girl* (*Merry Zingara*) and Meyerbeer's *Robert the Devil*, the last-named for the opening of the Gaiety Theatre.

He also wrote some theatrical criticism, one of the pieces he noticed being *Cox and Box*, the one-acter which Sullivan wrote with F. C. Burnand. He took the view that Sullivan's music was too good and unsuitable for the playlet.

Of great importance for his own future collaboration with Sullivan were the lively poems, illustrated by his apt sketches, which he had for some years been contributing to the paper *Fun* and which are still celebrated as *The Bab Ballads*, source of many of the ideas for his opera libretti.

Sullivan Before Gilbert Sullivan differed in almost everything from Gilbert, in nature, background and personality. As a result the collaboration was a source of constant friction.

Sullivan was undoubtedly the gentler and more naturally amiable personality of the two, with a greater anxiety to get along with people, particularly the 'best people'. Perpetually hankering after applying himself more exclusively to writing the sort of music which he considered worthy of his talents, he yet needed the money which his successful association with Gilbert brought in—money to spend in maintaining his social position and in enjoying the fascination of the tables at Monte Carlo. He really wanted it both ways—the prestige of the 'serious' composer and the comfortable income of the more popular entertainer. As Gilbert expressed it at a time when Sullivan was protesting that he wished to free himself from the partnership in order to concentrate on his own music: 'He is like a man who sits on a stove and then complains that his backside is burning.'

Though of humble origin, Sullivan never had any difficulty in making friends nor of gaining entry and maintaining his associations in society. These things happened naturally and almost without effort on his part. For from his boyhood days he had the gifts of talent and high intelligence, good looks and irresistible charm.

Men enjoyed his company and women wanted to mother him. He moved as easily in Royal circles as in any other. Prince Albert was so pleased with his solo singing as a boy soprano that he tipped him with half a sovereign and, in later years, Queen Victoria herself thought of him in the same terms as her beloved Mendelssohn and suggested to him that he must write a Grand Opera. It is little wonder that with all his acclaim in the musical world—acclaim that came to him very early in his career—it often seemed to him that he was wasting his time and talents in writing operetta.

There was never much money around in the house at No. 8 Bolwell Terrace, Lambeth, not far from Lambeth Walk, where Arthur Seymour Sullivan was born on May 13, 1842, just over five years after Gilbert. But the absence of material benefits was compensated by the wealth of mutual affection that filled the household, the affection of his mother, who was of Italian origin, of his Irish father, and of his elder brother Frederic.

True, he lacked one gift with which to face the battle of life—the gift of good health. From an early age he suffered from a serious liver complaint and throughout his working career he had to endure periods of excruciating pain. Some of his gayest and apparently most carefree music was written at such times, the composer stretching out in agony on a settee between the spells of actual writing.

Young Arthur never seems to have had any doubt that music was to be the dominant factor in his life, though he would certainly have expressed incredulity if someone had forecast the *nature* of the music that was to bring him lasting fame. He wrote his first anthem, 'By the Waters of Babylon', when he was eight. There was music around him from the start. Thomas Sullivan, his father, was bandmaster at the Royal Military College, Sandhurst, before taking up a post at Kneller Hall, and from a tender age Arthur could play nearly all the wind instruments. When he was twelve he entered upon a happy time as a chorister at the Chapel Royal, where he became 'first boy' two years later. Before reaching that eminence, however, he had published his first composition, a sacred song called 'O Israel', and had won the Mendelssohn Scholarship to the Royal Academy of Music, a scholarship which was twice renewed before he went to study in Leipzig, where his fellow-students included Grieg and Carl Rosa and where he met Franz Liszt.

Though he worked diligently in Leipzig, Arthur found time to write long letters to his father in London about the progress of his musical studies. It was in Leipzig that he enjoyed his first big success as a composer when, at the age of eighteen, he heard his music for *The Tempest* performed, a success which was repeated when the work was given the following year at the Crystal Palace, London. For some time after his return to London he worked hard not only at his composition, but also as organist at St Michael's, Chester Square, and St Peter's, Cranley Gardens. His compositions about this time included 'Princess of Wales March', an opera *The Sapphire Necklace* (with, it seems, an abysmal libretto and mercifully never produced), a ballet *L'Ile Enchantée*, presented at Covent Garden, and the Symphony in E. At this time too he suffered a severe personal blow with the death of his beloved father. It came when he had just been invited to write a work for the Norwich Festival, a commission which he found very difficult indeed to carry out in the midst of his sorrow. But in due course it was completed and performed—*In Memoriam*, to the memory of his father.

Sullivan had struck up a close friendship with George Grove, later Sir George Grove of *Dictionary of Music and Musicians* fame, and in 1867 they set off together for Vienna in the hope of unearthing some lost manuscripts of Schubert. At first their search was fruitless but, when they were about to give up, they came upon their treasure, covered in dust, in a cupboard—the complete music for *Rosamunde*. Understandably, they forgot their dignity as distinguished English musicians and celebrated with a game of leapfrog together.

In the same year Sullivan was drawn for the first time into the field of lighter music when he collaborated with F. C. Burnand in that one-act frolic *Cox and Box*, presented at Moray Lodge, Kensington, and later by Thomas German Reed at the Royal Gallery of Illustration. With Burnand, too, he wrote a full-length comic opera, *The Contrabandista*, commissioned by German Reed for the St George's Hall and seventeen years later given in a revised form at the Savoy Theatre with the title *The Chieftain*.

Thus Sullivan was already well acquainted with German Reed when he went with Frederic Clay to the Royal Gallery of Illustration for that first meeting with Gilbert. He was also flushed with the success of his oratorio, *The Prodigal Son*, which had just been performed at the Worcester Festival.

Thespis One year before their first meeting, a new theatre, the Gaiety, had been opened under the management of the enterprising John Hollingshead. In the bill for the opening night there were three pieces, one of them called *Robert the Devil: or The Nun, the Dun and the Son of a Gun*, written by W. S. Gilbert; and sitting in the fashionable audience on that first night was the distinguished young composer Arthur Sullivan, blissfully unaware that in this same theatre his partnership with Gilbert was to have its beginning.

In the two years after the Royal Gallery of Illustration meeting Sullivan enhanced his reputation with a number of works, among them the overture *Di Ballo*, which still appears from time to time in concert programmes, incidental music to Shakespeare's *The Merchant of Venice* and a number of hymns, including 'It Came upon the midnight clear' and 'Onward Christian Soldiers'. Gilbert poured forth a steady flow of plays, including *The Princess* (which later developed into *Princess Ida*), *Great Expectations* and *Pygmalion and Galatea*.

At this time John Hollingshead had gathered round him a group of players who appeared regularly for him in his presentations at the Gaiety, artists such as the well-known comic actor J. L. Toole, Nelly Farren, Constance Loseby and Annie Tremaine, and as Christmas, 1871, approached he was looking round for a suitably gay new piece. It occurred to him that it would be a good idea and would attract plenty of publicity and interest if he could bring together the witty and successful playwright W. S. Gilbert and the distinguished musician Arthur Sullivan. Where Thomas German Reed had failed, John Hollingshead succeeded, for they accepted his invitation.

Gilbert had a piece—or probably the preliminary draft—ready for Hollingshead, who passed it on to Sullivan, who was quite happy to set it to music. The preparation and presentation of *Thespis* seem to have been done in a rush. Gilbert said in later years that it was put together in three weeks, with one week's rehearsal. He later amended this to five weeks which, in any case, was not very long. *Thespis; or The Gods Grown Old* was duly presented on Boxing Night, 1871, running for ninety minutes as an after-piece to H. J. Byron's *Dearer Than Life*. It was produced by Gilbert, who had already learned a good deal about stagecraft from writer-producer T. W. Robertson, and one of the features of the production— immensely important in later years—was the imaginative use of the chorus, who had to play an active part in the performance rather than merely standing around and looking decorative. Many of Hollingshead's contract artists took part as well as Frederic Sullivan, the composer's brother, who was to score a great success in the subsequent *Trial by Jury*.

Nelly Farren as Mercury wore a tight-fitting silver suit and from several ladies in the company there was a liberal display of leg, consistent with Gaiety policy but not on any account to be followed in the later Gilbert and Sullivan operas. *Thespis* ran for sixty-four performances although subsequently Gilbert referred to it as a failure. Certainly it was if compared with, say, *The Mikado*. But Terence Rees in his exhaustive study, *Thespis: A Gilbert and Sullivan Enigma*, contends that it was much more successful than many latter-day commentators believe. He points out, for instance, that *Thespis* outlived five of the nine major pantomimes in London at the time.

Thespis does remain an enigma, for the musical score disappeared and was never published. When asked about it later, Sullivan jokingly replied that he had kept the tunes for use in other operas. This is certainly true of the chorus, 'Climbing over rocky mountain', which turns up in *The Pirates of Penzance*, but whether or not other tunes now familiar to us first appeared in *Thespis* we do not know. The only other surviving number from the opera is Sparkeion's song 'Little maid of Arcadee', which was published separately.

Trial by Jury—and Richard D'Oyly Carte Whatever the truth about the success or failure of *Thespis*, the usually astute John Hollingshead evidently did not think it worth while to pursue his association with Gilbert and Sullivan as a team. Indeed, *Thespis* seems to have been merely an episode for all concerned. Sullivan resumed the path of 'serious' music with a *Te Deum* for the recovery of the Prince of Wales from illness, an oratorio *The Light of the World*, and incidental music for Shakespeare's *The Merry Wives of Windsor*. Gilbert pursued the way of the successful playwright with such pieces as *Happy Arcadia*, *The Wicked World*, *The Wedding March*, *The Happy Land*, *Charity*, *Sweethearts*, *Topsy-Turvydom* and *Broken Hearts*. Each was very busy, completely independent of the other, though they did write a couple of songs together, 'Sweethearts' and 'The Distant Shore'.

But waiting in the wings, so to speak, was a man who, in these circumstances at any rate, showed more perception than had John Hollingshead.

Richard D'Oyly Carte was well equipped for the mission which he dreamed of from a very early age—no less than to establish English comic opera in a theatre of its own. But he combined just the right gifts for the task. Brought up with a musical family background, he possessed artistic ability of his own and was also a shrewd man of business and a brilliant organiser. It is said that because of his smooth manner he was nicknamed 'Oily Carte'.

His father, also Richard, was the inventor of a new kind of flute, an example of which is to be seen in a collection of musical instruments on exhibition at the Victoria and Albert Museum. He was also founder of *The Musical Dictionary*. He was married to a Welsh girl, daughter of the Rev. Thomas Jones, of the Royal Chapel, Whitehall, descendant of the old Norman family of D'Oyly or D'Ouilly.

Young Richard D'Oyly Carte, born in Soho on May 3, 1844, studied at London University, as had Gilbert before him, and then went into the London business in which his father was a partner— Rudall, Carte and Co., musical instrument makers. But it was not long before he launched out with his own concert and lecture agency in Craig's Court, Charing Cross, building up a strong connection which embraced people like Adelina Patti, the famed tenor Mario, Matthew Arnold and later Oscar Wilde. He was a trained musician and in his early twenties was composing songs and operettas.

In the 1870's the Royalty Theatre in Soho was leased by Mme Selina Dolaro so that she might present and appear in operettas by Offenbach and others. Richard D'Oyly Carte became her manager. They decided to present one of Offenbach's shorter operettas, *La Périchole*, preceded by a piece with the resounding if bewildering title of *Cryptoconchoidsyphonostomata* or, rather more understandably, *While It's to be Had*. But the bill was still on the short side and D'Oyly Carte, looking round for a suitable third piece for inclusion, happened to encounter Gilbert and at once suggested that he might write something, perhaps renewing his brief collaboration with Sullivan.

As it happened Gilbert had recently looked out a ballad he had written for the paper *Fun* and had put it into dramatic form with the idea that it should be set to music by Carl Rosa, who that same year founded the Carl Rosa Opera Company. The main soprano part was to have been sung by Mme Parepa-Rosa, Carl Rosa's wife—the same Mme Parepa for whom the young Gilbert had made the English translation from *Manon Lescaut*. But Mme Parepa had died suddenly and the project had been abandoned. Now Gilbert suggested the piece to Carte, who liked it and asked Gilbert to put it up to Sullivan.

One does not think of Gilbert as being a man who had many qualms about his own ability, but it does seem that it was with a good deal of trepidation that he called upon Sullivan and read the little piece over to him. He felt that Sullivan, deeply involved with his 'serious' music, was bored by this trifle—though in fact Sullivan recorded later that he had been curled up with laughter at Gilbert's comical treatment of the episode in the solemn setting of a court

24

of law. Preparations took only three weeks and the little after-piece, *Trial by Jury*, made an immediate hit in March, 1875, one of the major personal successes being scored by Fred Sullivan, the composer's elder brother, in the role of the Learned Judge.

Trial became the main attraction of the bill and, after *La Périchole* had been taken off, was still running in company with *La Fille de Madame Angot*. It registered 131 performances in this first run and would have gone on longer but for the death of Fred Sullivan, to the deep distress of his brother.

This work has several distinctive features. It is the only Gilbert and Sullivan piece in one act and the only one in which the music runs straight through without breaks for spoken dialogue. It fore-shadows many things to come in the imaginative handling of the chorus, for instance, and the Judge's Song in which he reviews the stages by which he reached his present eminence. And it was the first of the Gilbert and Sullivan works which are still played.

The Sorcerer The success of *Trial by Jury* encouraged D'Oyly Carte in his ambition to create a theatre devoted to the presentation of English comic opera, though at this stage he had only prospects and no money and so had to make do with a lease on the Opera Comique. But it was a move in the right direction. The Comedy Opera Company was formed with Carte as manager, and Gilbert and Sullivan were approached for a new piece.

Never one to waste an idea and always fascinated by 'magical' themes, Gilbert went back to one of his own stories for the plot of the new opera, based on the workings of a love philtre. The presentation of *The Sorcerer*, the first two-act Gilbert and Sullivan opera, is of particular interest in that in the casting of it they laid the foundation of a company of regular players for whom many roles in subsequent operas were to be specifically written. George Grossmith, Rutland Barrington and Richard Temple now appeared for them for the first time. *The Sorcerer* had a run of 178 performances at the Opera Comique.

In the interval of more than two years between the productions of *Trial by Jury* and *The Sorcerer*, Sullivan had written another comic piece called *The Zoo* which was presented at the St James's Theatre. The score was never published but Sullivan is thought to have used some of the music in later works with Gilbert. Gilbert, on his part, had written two or three pieces, among them *Princess Toto* with Fred Clay.

But Richard D'Oyly Carte was asking for more—and Messrs

Gilbert and Sullivan came up with what, after some initial difficulty, proved to be a winner.

HMS Pinafore The subject for the next opera came naturally enough for Gilbert. With a father who was a naval surgeon he was familiar with the jargon of the sea from his boyhood days and, indeed, throughout the operas nautical terms and allusions keep popping up. Having decided upon his subject, which Sullivan accepted enthusiastically, he set about ensuring authenticity of detail in the setting by a visit to Portsmouth for a careful examination of the deck of HMS Victory. From his sketches he reproduced the scene in a model at his home.

Into the cast came a newcomer, the mezzo-soprano Jessie Bond, who was eventually to establish herself as one of the most popular of Savoyards. *Pinafore* was produced at the Opera Comique on May 25, 1878, and had a first-night reception which promised well for its future. But London found itself in the midst of a heat wave and business in the theatres generally fell away, with *Pinafore* no exception. The directors of the Comedy Opera Company, nervous about the safety of their money, worked themselves into a state of panic and on several occasions posted up backstage notices of closure of the show. These were, however, taken down and the cast voluntarily accepted cuts in salary in order to keep the piece running.

Quite suddenly business was given an enormous boost at, of all places, the Royal Opera House, Covent Garden. Sullivan was at that time conductor of the Promenade Concerts there, and in one programme he included an arrangement of some of the *Pinafore* music by Hamilton Clarke for orchestra and brass band. It scored an immediate success, was encored whenever it was played—and the situation at the Opera Comique was entirely changed. *Pinafore* sailed on triumphantly for 571 performances.

As in the case of many of the operas, Gilbert adapted ideas from his own *Bab Ballads* in writing the libretto. 'The Bumboat Woman's Story', 'Captain Reece', 'The Baby's Vengeance', 'General John', 'Lieutenant-Colonel Flare', 'Joe Golightly' and 'Little Oliver' all provided him with material from which *Pinafore* grew. Sullivan wrote the seemingly carefree music while torn with pain from his constant liver complaint.

The tunes were whistled by the errand-boys and the catchphrase 'What, *never?*' . . . 'Hardly ever!' swept Britain and America. There was even the puzzled German who, as recorded by Arthur Lawrence in *Sir Arthur Sullivan*, lamented with a combination of bewilderment and exasperation, 'Dot "Pinafore" expression vas a noosence. Auf you tole a feller sometings, he speaks noding von blame English. He says, "Vot, hardly, sometimes, nefer!" Vot kind of language is dose?'

In the absence of any copyright agreement between the United States and Britain, pirated versions of the opera broke out like a rash in America and, indeed, one newspaper commented: 'At present there are forty-two companies playing "Pinafore" about the country. Companies formed after six p.m. yesterday are not included.' The originators of the work found it difficult to combat this wholesale piracy but, deciding at any rate to show how the piece *ought* to be presented, they put on a company of their own in New York and took the town by storm. The difference in the style of presentation was enthusiastically noted by the Press and Gilbert, in a speech from the stage, dryly commented, without direct reference to the pirated versions: 'It has been our purpose to produce something that should be innocent but not imbecile.'

Nor was everything peaceful at home. Those directors of the Comedy Opera Company who had taken fright in the early days and had wanted to take the piece off now made a ruthless bid to grab a greater share of the profits of success. They took action which resulted in the fantastic Battle of the Opera Comique. During an actual performance they assembled a gang of toughs and launched an assault on the theatre with the idea of seizing the scenery and properties in order to put on their own production elsewhere. A pitched battle followed with the audience in a state of near-panic, and the attackers were thrown back. The directors did in fact present their own production of *Pinafore* at the Aquarium Theatre and later the Olympic but failed to gain the support of the public, who rallied to the authentic production which was still playing nearby. The matter went to the courts, resulting in a legal ruling which forbade the rebellious directors from presenting the works of Gilbert and Sullivan. It was the end of the Comedy Opera Company which went into liquidation. Gilbert, Sullivan and Carte formed their own association for the presentation of the operas. Gilbert celebrated appropriately with the purchase of a yacht.

The Pirates of Penzance While *HMS Pinafore* was still running at the Opera Comique, plans were going ahead for the next Gilbert and Sullivan opera. Whether or not the idea for the piece was put into Gilbert's head by the experiences of American 'piracy' is not known, but not only were pirates featured in the libretto but elaborate steps were also taken to combat piracy on the other side of the Atlantic.

The collaborators were in America in connection with their New York production of *Pinafore* and they decided to forestall the pirate promoters by carrying out the next operation in reverse—that is to say, to hold the first night of their new opera *in America*. The final writing of the work was done in New York. Sullivan, a very sick man at this stage, had prepared his musical sketches for the work while in England but had inadvertently left much of his material behind. He found himself having to rewrite a great part of the score from memory and in fact the overture was completed with Alfred Cellier in the early hours of the day of production. Rehearsals were carried out with guards on the theatre so that no unauthorised person should be able to find out what was going on.

Things were not made easier when the orchestra, recruited in America, pointed out that there was so much music in the piece that it was more like grand opera and they therefore demanded higher rates of pay. Sullivan bluffed them out of it by saying that if they refused to play he would have the Covent Garden Orchestra brought over from England and even that, as a last resort, the piece would go on with himself at the piano and Alfred Cellier playing a harmonium. He admitted afterwards that all this *was* bluff—but it saved the situation.

The Pirates of Penzance in due course opened at the Fifth Avenue Theatre, New York, on December 31, 1879, before a highly enthusiastic audience—and, to strengthen the defence against unauthorised productions, four companies were despatched to various parts of the United States.

But there was also the question of the protection of the British copyright and for this purpose a single scratch performance was staged on December 30 to coincide as nearly as possible with the American première. It must have been a most weird and bewildering affair. A D'Oyly Carte company was playing *Pinafore* at Torquay at the time and was sent over to the Bijou Theatre, Paignton, for the single 'copyright' performance. Directing the strange operation was Helen Lenoir, stage name of Helen Cowper Black, a brilliant business-woman who was then D'Oyly Carte's secretary and later became his second wife. The score of *Pirates* had been sent over piecemeal from America and was probably incomplete, the cast wore their *Pinafore* costumes (the policemen were dressed as sailors) and many of them carried their sheets of music on the stage because they had not had time to learn their parts and had had only one rehearsal. But the copyright was officially established.

It was not until April 3, 1880, that the 'New and Original Melo-Dramatic Opera' had its London première at the Opera Comique, where it ran for 363 performances. On the opening night it was preceded by a short curtain-raiser, *In the Sulks*, with music by Alfred Cellier.

Patience—and the Savoy Theatre D'Oyly Carte was now approaching the realisation of his dream. By the time the next opera had reached the planning stage, building work was in full swing on the new Savoy Theatre in the Strand. But for the moment the Opera Comique was still the centre of Carte's theatrical activity. What was the new opera to be about?

Gilbert once more thumbed through the *Bab Ballads* and came upon a piece called 'The Rival Curates', which set him thinking of an opera on similar lines. He could certainly have got plenty of fun out of it but it occurred to him that, whereas it had been all very well to write lightheartedly on, for instance, a legal or a naval theme, the Church might prove to be somewhat dangerous ground. But at this time the 'aesthetic movement', personified by people like Oscar Wilde, Rossetti, Burne-Jones and Whistler, was at its height. Surely its more absurd extravagances would provide ample scope. The rival curates became rival aesthetes, and Reginald Bunthorne and Archibald Grosvenor were born in Gilbert's mind.

This was all very well from the London point of view. But there was also the American production to consider and, as the aesthetic craze had not yet crossed the Atlantic, the Americans could hardly be expected to appreciate to the full a piece which satirised its excesses. The shrewd Richard D'Oyly Carte came up with the answer by despatching Oscar Wilde, with his fluting voice, knee breeches, floppy ties and a lily in his hand, on an extensive lecture tour of the States. The Americans very soon knew all about the craze of aestheticism.

Sullivan, as was usual with him, left the writing of the music until the last moment and in ten days did the orchestration, the score arriving bit by bit at the Opera Comique after the rehearsals of *Patience* had begun.

Gilbert himself did the designs for the 'aesthetic costumes' in the production, which opened with great success on April 23, 1881, preceded on the first night by Alfred Cellier's piece, *In the Sulks*. To avoid any suggestion of plagiarism on Gilbert's part [since, shortly before the opening of *Patience*, F. C. Burnand had written a skit on aestheticism called *The Colonel*,] a special announcement was made: 'The Management considers it advisable to state that the Libretto of this Opera was completed in November last.'

In the music which Sullivan sent along in the last-minute rush of

29

rehearsals, there was one song which has never been heard. It was a tenor solo for the Duke of Dunstable and it would seem that the orchestra's part came along in the ordinary way, while the melody was written out on a separate piece of paper and handed to the Scottish tenor, Durward Lely, who was singing the role of the Duke. Eventually, however, it was decided not to use the song at all. The orchestration still exists but the melody has been lost.

Patience ran merrily along and became the talk of London, arousing much speculation as to the originals of Bunthorne and Grosvenor. Dante Gabriel Rossetti became firmly convinced that Bunthorne was a skit on himself but, for fear of being laughed at in the theatre, carefully avoided going to see the piece. He eventually sent along a friend who assured him that Bunthorne was nothing like him!

By now the new Savoy Theatre, the first theatre in the world to be lit throughout by electric light, was ready and the highly successful *Patience* was transferred for the fashionable opening on October 10, 1881. In all, the opera had a run of 578 performances. When it went out on tour, an explanatory statement was issued: 'In satirising the excesses of these so-called aesthetes, the authors of *Patience* have not desired to cast ridicule on the true aesthetic spirit, but only to attack the unmanly oddities which masquerade in its likeness.'

Iolanthe It was back again to the *Bab Ballads* for Gilbert when the time came to devise the plot for the next opera and, as with *Patience*, his train of thought started off with the idea of a curate. Just as 'The Rival Curates' had become rival aesthetes, so did 'The Fairy Curate' of another ballad become Strephon, the Arcadian shepherd, half fairy and half mortal, in *Iolanthe*. Always with the eventual stage picture very much in his mind, Gilbert no doubt recalled with satisfaction the colourful effect produced in *Patience* by introducing the dragoons in their uniforms. For colour in *Iolanthe* he has the magnificent robes of the Peers and, for full measure, the uniforms of a band of the Brigade of Guards for their first entrance.

Since it happened that Sir Henry Irving owned the rights in a play called *Iolanthe*, D'Oyly Carte had to come to an arrangement with him for the use of the title.

Sullivan produced for the piece a score which combined idyllic charm with stirring tunes and yet it was written at a time of severe emotional stress. Just when he was embarking on it, he was stricken by the death of his mother whom he adored and had to force himself by sheer effort of will to settle down to work. But he did have some measure of compensation in the company of Mrs Ronalds, a beautiful American woman who was separated from her husband and whose close friendship with Sullivan lasted until the composer's death.

There was a slight contretemps during the rehearsals of *Iolanthe*. Splendid moustaches were much favoured by the men of the day and, when Gilbert ordered that the 'Peers' must shave off their treasured appendages, the chorus promptly threatened to go on strike. But eventually Gilbert talked them round—with the exception of one. He was sacked.

Elaborate precautions were taken to protect the new opera from piracy. The greatest secrecy was observed during the preparation of the production and, as an additional measure, the word *Iolanthe* was never used during rehearsal. Wherever it would have occurred the artists were instructed to say or sing the words 'Come Perola'. At the last moment they were told that on the opening night they were to substitute the name 'Iolanthe' and, when one of them pointed out to Sullivan that it would now be difficult for them to make the change, he cheerfully replied, 'Oh, just sing the music and use any name that comes into your head. No one will notice anything wrong—except Gilbert, and he won't be there!' He knew that, as was his custom, Gilbert would be nervously strolling outside the theatre until the final curtain.

Iolanthe opened simultaneously in London and New York on November 25, 1882, and the audiences were treated to another theatrical innovation. For the first time electric light was used as a part of stage costume, battery-operated lights gleaming in the fairies' hair.

The piece was warmly received in both centres—but the cheering audience in London little knew that just before coming to the theatre the conductor, Arthur Sullivan, had received the news that through the bankruptcy of a firm of stockbrokers he had lost all his savings.

Princess Ida In 1847 Tennyson had published a long poem, 'The Princess', about the foundation of a college for women. The general subject of the education of women was much in the air in the middle of the last century and Gilbert—as part, one might suppose, of his peculiar attitude towards women—tended to sneer at the whole idea. Women of the forbidding, scholastic type had no appeal for him whatsoever. It was a subject after his own heart for the purpose of parody, and a play of a skittish nature and bearing the same title as Tennyson's poem was duly presented at the Olympic Theatre in 1870.

When the time came to produce an opera to follow *Iolanthe*, Gilbert went not this time to the *Bab Ballads* but to his play about the education of women, changing the title to *Princess Ida*—'a respectful Operatic Perversion of Tennyson's "Princess".'

The period of preparation of the work was not auspicious. Sullivan had recently been knighted at Windsor Castle and it seems probable that Gilbert was irritated by the fact that, whereas one member of the partnership was now *Sir* Arthur, the other remained *Mister* Gilbert. Sullivan on his part was in very poor physical shape, his liver complaint causing him the severest pain and exhaustion. He collapsed during rehearsal, while part of the opera still remained to be composed, but he struggled on, forcing himself to complete his task. It was only by injections from his doctor and copious draughts of black coffee that he managed to get himself to the Savoy Theatre to conduct the first performance of *Princess Ida* on January 5, 1884. But he fainted as soon as it was over and lay ill for some time at his home in Victoria Street.

There are several distinctive features in *Princess Ida*. It is the only one of the operas written in blank verse and the only one in three acts, originally described as 'in a prologue and two acts'. In it, too, Gilbert breaks his usual rule against men dressing as women and permits Hilarion, Cyril and Florian to don the academic robes of the women's college. The piece had a run of 246 performances, a considerable drop on what the partnership had come to expect.

The Mikado Sitting in his study in Harrington Gardens, Kensington, Gilbert was racking his brains in the effort to find a suitable idea for an opera to follow *Princess Ida*. He was not in the easiest frame of mind. *Ida* had not really caught the fancy of the public and business at the box-office was sagging. Relations between composer and librettist had recently been strained almost to breaking point—and Gilbert's gout was giving him hell.

The trouble between Gilbert and Sullivan had blown up when D'Oyly Carte, realising that *Princess Ida* was not settling down into a run comparable with those of its immediate predecessors, had decided that a new opera must be got on the stocks as soon as possible and, in accordance with the agreement among the three of them, had written to composer and librettist, giving the requisite six months' notice for the production of the next work. Sullivan's reaction came as a shock. He had reached the stage when he wanted to have done with comic opera and to concentrate on what he regarded as his more important work. There had, of course, been hints of this before, but now he wrote with firmness and seemingly with finality.

His attitude provoked a bitter correspondence. 'With *Princess Ida*,' he wrote to Gilbert, 'I have come to the end of my tether— the end of my capability in that kind of piece. My tunes are in danger of becoming mere repetitions of my former pieces. . . . I have looked upon the words as being of such importance that I have been continually keeping down the music in order that not one should be lost . . . the music is never allowed to arise and speak for itself.'

Gilbert expressed hurt amazement at what he regarded as Sullivan's slurs on the quality of his libretti but he did call upon Sullivan with a suggestion for a new work. This, however, did not help matters at all, for his plot hinged upon the taking of a magic lozenge with powers of transformation—an idea which Sullivan had rejected some years earlier, just the kind of fantastic, supernatural theme from which he wanted to escape.

There were further acid exchanges between them, though Gilbert did suggest, in what would seem to have been a genuine attempt to save their friendship, that Sullivan might care to sever their association temporarily and write one work with another librettist. With D'Oyly Carte always trying to heal the breach, neither of the two really seemed to want to make a final break.

And so Gilbert found himself still searching for an idea which would prove acceptable to his partner and enable their old association to continue. It was then that there occurred an incident almost as dramatic as anything he could invent. A Japanese executioner's sword, hanging on the wall, suddenly became dislodged and clattered to the floor—and it was as though it jolted Gilbert's racing thoughts into a single channel.

In Knightsbridge, not far from his home, there was in progress at the time a Japanese exhibition—a Japanese Village, inhabited by real Japanese folk, geisha girls and all. London was in the midst of a Japanese craze; to be interested in Japanese art and customs was the 'done thing' in fashionable circles. Yes, that was it—a Japanese opera! Gilbert set about at once planning his characters to suit the particular talents and personalities of the leading players who had already served him so well at the Savoy.

Sullivan was well pleased with the draft of the libretto and produced music that is not only among his most delightful but also strangely apt in that its charms take away such bitter taste as might be induced by the libretto's stress upon torture and execution.

C

Gilbert was as meticulous as ever about the details of his production. In the case of *Pinafore* he had gone to HMS Victory at Portsmouth in search of authenticity. In that of *The Mikado* he went not to Japan but more conveniently to Knightsbridge, where he found those who could instruct his cast in matters of deportment and the correct handling of a fan. The programme duly carried the announcement: 'The Management desires to acknowledge the valuable assistance afforded by the Directors and Native Inhabitants of the Japanese Village, Knightsbridge.' And in the opera itself when Ko-Ko is asked where Nanki-Poo has gone, he promptly replies: 'Knightsbridge!'—though the name of some other nearby place of topical interest has later been substituted, a procedure sanctioned by Gilbert in his lifetime. Perhaps as a good-luck charm, the sword which had fallen so dramatically from Gilbert's wall was carried by George Grossmith (Ko-Ko) on the opening night.

That opening night, on March 14, 1885, was a triumph—and the opera which had been born out of so much stress and uncertainty ran for 672 performances, the longest run of any Savoy opera, and is still the most popular of them all.

It is, incidentally, strange to recall that during rehearsal Gilbert suddenly had doubts about the wisdom of including the Mikado's song, 'My object all sublime', and even went so far as to announce that he had decided to cut it out altogether. His reason is difficult to understand, but fortunately the chorus realised what a loss it would be and, gathering round Gilbert, they begged him to retain it. How right they were has been amply proved through the years.

Those years have, however, brought about some alterations in the text for reasons of changing taste or of comprehensibility. In 1948, for instance, there appeared in *The Times* this letter from Rupert D'Oyly Carte:

'We found recently in America that much objection was taken by coloured persons to a word used twice in *The Mikado*, a word which I will not quote but which your readers may easily guess. Many protests and letters were received, and we consulted the witty writer on whose shoulders the lyrical mantle of Gilbert may be said to have fallen. He made several alternative suggestions, one of which we adopted in America, and it seems well to continue doing so in the British Empire. Gilbert would surely have approved, and the alteration will be heard during our season at Sadler's Wells.'

At the time when Gilbert wrote *The Mikado* Nigger Minstrels were a highly popular form of entertainment. In later years, however, the word has acquired an unsavoury and insulting connotation. One of the uses of it to which Mr D'Oyly Carte referred was in the Mikado's song and the other in Ko-Ko's 'little list'. Sir Alan Herbert confirmed for me that it was to him that D'Oyly Carte went for suggested alternatives. The original version in the Mikado's song had it that the lady 'who pinches her figger is blacked like a nigger with permanent walnut juice,' which Sir Alan transformed into 'is painted with vigour and permanent walnut juice.' In Ko-Ko's song, 'nigger serenader' became 'banjo serenader.'

In one recording of the opera you may hear Donald Adams, as the Mikado, singing a 'wrong' word—'*with* permanent walnut juice' instead of '*and* permanent walnut juice.' In this case it was Sir Malcolm Sargent, conducting the recording, who insisted that the word should be 'with'—though 'and' was the word which A. P. H. wrote, making a much more effective line.

After the enormous opening success of *The Mikado* in London there came the question of its American presentation. Two impresarios, a Mr Stetson of the Fifth Avenue Theatre and a Mr Duff of the Standard Theatre, were in negotiation with D'Oyly Carte for the American première in New York and Carte clinched with the former. But Mr Duff was not prepared to allow matters to rest there. Carte heard that he was planning to get in first with a 'pirate' production and so laid his own plans with the thoroughness and secrecy of a military operation. First he bought up all the Japanese costumes then available in London and Paris and gathered together a company which he rehearsed on the pretext that they were to tour the provinces in this country. Only when everything was ready did he call them together at the Savoy Theatre and tell them in the strictest confidence that they were going to New York. Their cabins in the Cunard liner all bore fictitious names and Carte himself travelled as 'Mr Henry Chapman.' He caught his opponent completely by surprise. *The Mikado* had scored a smash hit in New York almost before Mr Duff had started rehearsals.

The work, though sung in English, was enthusiastically received the following year in Berlin and Vienna and soon afterwards it was given in a German translation in America. By the turn of the century it had been presented on the Continent in Hungarian, Russian, French, Swedish, Croatian, Danish, Italian and Czech.

Through the years Sullivan's music has continued to delight and Gilbert's words to entertain audiences in the theatre, but during the D'Oyly Carte's 1906-7 season there occurred an episode which aroused roars of laughter *outside* the theatre. It was at the expense of the Lord Chamberlain who, in case the work might give offence and seriously impair international relations, banned performances of *The Mikado* in this country during the visit to London of Prince Fushimi of Japan. As the Press gleefully pointed out the authorities had failed to appreciate the whole essence of the thing—that, though the opera was set in a Japan that did not exist and never had existed, Gilbert's satire was directed not at Japan but at essentially *English* customs and institutions!

Ruddigore It was a busy and successful period for Sullivan, though not by any means calculated to calm his growing restlessness over his dual position as widely-acclaimed 'serious' musician and as the partner in the *The Mikado* triumph. He enjoyed the dignity of his knighthood and was out and about with his friends in high society. He had just been appointed conductor of the Philharmonic Society and his large-scale oratorio, *The Golden Legend*, a setting of a poem by Longfellow, scored an enormous success at the Leeds Festival, prompting Queen Victoria to suggest to him that he really ought to write a grand opera. No wonder he found it difficult to adjust his thoughts to the writing of a new comic opera, as D'Oyly Carte required.

But Gilbert, who had been generous in his congratulations to Sullivan about the success of *The Golden Legend*, was getting down to his part of the task and for his idea he went back to that early piece of his, *Ages Ago*, which had been in rehearsal at the Royal Gallery of Illustration when Fred Clay had first introduced him to Sullivan. The scene in which the portraits of the ancestors stepped out of their picture-frames became the most spectacularly effective episode in the new opera. Despite the many distractions Sullivan did in fact settle down to work on *Ruddigore* and it appears that he finished the score without the frantic last-minute rush that had marked many of the previous productions.

Ruddigore opened at the Savoy Theatre on January 22, 1887, three nights after *The Mikado* had completed its splendid run of 672 performances. It was written as a skit on the more bloodthirsty melodramas of the time and its deliberately melodramatic title caused trouble from the start. The piece opened as *Ruddygore* but, as a concession to those critics who found the title distasteful, the change to *Ruddigore* was made after a few nights. And there was Gilbert's sharp and irritated rejoiner to a friend whom he met in the street and who inquired how 'Bloodygore' was going: 'It's *Ruddigore*,' said Gilbert. 'Oh, it's the same thing,' insisted the friend. 'Is it?' retorted Gilbert. 'Then I suppose that if I say I admire your ruddy countenance, it means I like your bloody cheek!'

Electric light always seemed to be coming in for new applications at the Savoy Theatre in those days. The theatre itself had been the first to be lit throughout by electricity and in Act II of *Iolanthe* electric light had been used for the first time as part of stage costume. Now, in *Ruddigore*, a problem arose for Sullivan whose baton could not be seen during the black-out preceding the moment when the ancestors stepped out of their picture-frames. So a special baton was devised—a transparent tube through which passed a platinum wire which glowed when a battery was switched on. Gilbert, by the way, was not happy about Sullivan's ghost music for that scene, which he thought might have been treated more humorously.

The piece was in the main well received on the opening night, though there were some boos from those who found it so very different from *The Mikado*. Gilbert bitterly commented that, instead of having the title *Ruddigore, or The Witch's Curse*, it might have been called *Ruddigore, or Not So Good As The Mikado*. Neither Gilbert nor Sullivan was satisfied with the finale to the opera and some alterations were made after the first night.

Indeed, that opening was far from uneventful. To Gilbert's amazement there were complaints from some French sources that Dick Dauntless's references to the 'darned Mounseer' and the 'poor Parley-Voo' constituted an insult to their national pride. And a few nights later George Grossmith fell ill and into his place as Robin Oakapple stepped his understudy, a young man called H. Henri, who later was to become one of the most famed of Savoyards under his real name – Henry A. Lytton.

Ruddigore kept going for 288 nights, quite a respectable run, if not on the spectacular scale of *The Mikado*. Years afterwards, Gilbert commented: 'We are credited – or discredited with one conspicuous failure, *Ruddigore, or The Witch's Curse*. Well, it ran for eight months and, with the sale of the libretto, put £7,000 into my pocket. It is not generally known that, bending before the storm of Press execration aroused by its awful title, we were within an ace of changing it from *Ruddigore, or the Witch's Curse* to *Kensington Gore, or Robin and Richard were Two Pretty Men*.'

The Yeomen of the Guard It was a rather less dramatic circumstance than the falling of the Japanese sword from the wall that guided Gilbert into writing an opera centred at the Tower of London. Nothing more romantic than an advertisement for the Tower Furnishing Company, observed as he waited for a train on Uxbridge station, turned his thoughts in that direction. From the visual point of view it was just the sort of idea that appealed to him for, as noticed previously, he never missed an opportunity of introducing colourful costumes into his scenes.

Some such promising idea was sorely needed at this stage, for the Sullivan-Gilbert relationship was strained almost to breaking point. Sullivan's *The Golden Legend*, after a poor first performance, had been received with immense acclaim when presented a second time. A commissioned ode in celebration of Queen Victoria's Jubilee was much in his mind and he was feeling less and less sympathetic towards Gilbert's whimsical plots. Would he never escape from writing music which, as he contended, was always subservient to the words? However, D'Oyly Carte, that persistent and fortunately often successful go-between, brought Sullivan to the point of agreeing to hear the librettist's latest ideas.

Far from helping matters, the meeting served only to irritate Sullivan the more. For with Sullivan determined to get involved only in a plot with situations arising out of the relationships between reasonably credible people, Gilbert came up with his old favourite, his 'King Charles' Head', the plot about a fantastic lozenge with magical properties. This was a tactless move and yet there seems no doubt that it was Gilbert – and of course D'Oyly Carte – who tried desperately to hold the partnership together at such a time as this. Fiery-tempered though he was and full of confidence in his own powers as a dramatist, he was far less inclined than Sullivan to allow the partnership to waver and collapse.

Realising his mis-judgment, Gilbert now showed the essence of tact in his handling of the new subject. For he proceeded to write the most 'serious' of all the operas, coming much nearer to grand opera than ever before. Indeed, in later days he spoke of it as 'a step in the direction of serious opera.' The title he first considered was the obvious one, simply *The Tower of London* but, perhaps thinking that people are more appealing than things in a title, this became *The Tower Warden* then *The Beefeater* and finally *The Yeomen of the Guard*. A preliminary germ of an idea seems to have come from a *Bab Ballad* called 'Annie Protheroe', in which a girl falls in love with the public headsman, who reads out to her his 'favourable notices, all pasted in a book.'

Sullivan, though delighted with the outline of the piece which Gilbert sent to him, still wavered about his future course, and these doubts were accentuated by the success of Alfred Cellier's operetta *Dorothy* at the Gaiety Theatre, where it eventually exceeded the original run of *The Mikado*, setting him wondering whether there might not now be others who could outpace them in the field of light opera. This brought another flare-up from Gilbert who not unreasonably pointed out that the great success of *The Mikado* had not suddenly induced every other management to go out of business. Why, then, should the Savoy team throw in their hands just because someone else had scored a success?

Anyhow, Sullivan applied himself diligently to the writing of the music for the *Yeomen*, with Gilbert, it would seem, going out of his way to be co-operative in supplying lyrics which he thought would appeal to the composer. Sullivan was duly inspired to produce a splendid score, though not without some difficulty – strange as this might seem in the case of music which appears to flow so easily. The lovely ballad 'Is Life a Boon?' and Jack Point's 'I have a song to sing, O,' for instance, caused the composer a good deal of trouble.

Neither composer nor librettist seems to have felt confident about the success of the piece, Sullivan nagged by doubts as to whether he should have taken it on at all and Gilbert wondering if he had gone too far in his concessions to seriousness. He spent one of the jumpiest nights of his career not merely walking about on the Thames Embankment but, it is said, going so far as to watch somebody else's play in another theatre while the *Yeoman* was being seen by the Savoy audience for the first time.

There was one important change in the Savoy team for the *Yeomen*. Rutland Barrington had departed for a brief and not highly successful career in management – he returned for *The Gondoliers* – and into the role which would have been his came the comedy actor W. H. Denny. And Jack Point was the last of the famed series of roles originated by George Grossmith before he left the company, never to return.

On its presentation at the Savoy Theatre on October 3, 1888, the *Yeomen* was well received by public and Press and embarked on a run of 423 performances. Despite their initial doubts, both Gilbert and Sullivan considered it later to be the best work they had done together. Yet it was not enough to bridge the personal breach that was ever widening between them.

The Gondoliers Though *The Gondoliers* turned out to be the happiest and sunniest of all the operas, its conception was a case of sunshine breaking through the storm clouds. Again, Gilbert was doing his best to hold the partnership together. In the *Yeomen* he had moved as far as he felt practicable towards a 'serious' work. He felt that he could go no further in that direction but in his libretto for *The Gondoliers* he made sure that, while writing a lighthearted piece, he was giving the composer ample scope.

The creation of the work was preceded by squabbling of the bitterest sort. Sullivan was hankering more and more after writing a grand opera – after all, no less a person than Queen Victoria had suggested that he should do just that. But he knew well that it was the Savoy partnership which brought in the money for his enjoyment of life in high society. He did, however, suggest that Gilbert might care to write the libretto for his grand opera – a suggestion which Gilbert turned down, while pointing out that he saw no reason why Sullivan, while getting his grand opera off his chest, should not also compose another Savoy opera. The clash became fiercer with Sullivan suggesting that his music had always been subservient to Gilbert's words, and Gilbert asserting that grand opera was a form in which the librettist was always swamped by the composer.

The situation reached crisis when Sullivan wrote to D'Oyly Carte, complaining of the time-wasting way in which Gilbert dominated rehearsals so that, apart from the purely musical sessions, he, Sullivan, was reduced to 'a cipher in the theatre'. Carte showed the letter to Gilbert and there was the inevitable flare-up.

Yet it was again the activities of D'Oyly Carte, with his wife Helen playing a very prominent part in the peacemaking negotiations, which brought about a compromise between the two, without undue loss of face on the part of either.

Carte had embarked upon the building of the Royal English Opera House at the top of Shaftesbury Avenue – the Palace Theatre, as we now know it – and what better man could be found to write the opening work than the fashionable composer, Sir Arthur Sullivan? Gilbert's earlier suggestion became a fact. Sullivan did embark on a grand opera, *Ivanhoe*, while at the same time working on the score of a new Savoy opera, *The Gondoliers*. He was delighted by Gilbert's gay libretto and set to work with a will, though deeply grieved by the death of his old friend, Frederic Clay.

Presented at the Savoy on December 7, 1889, *The Gondoliers* scored an immediate triumph and started on a run of 554 performances, again not as long as *The Mikado* but still very satisfactory. Here Gilbert and Sullivan were back in their gayest mood, the mood in which their audiences loved them.

Meanwhile Sullivan's opera *Ivanhoe*, with a libretto by Julian Sturgis, was presented at Carte's new Royal English Opera House on January 31, 1891, with the Prince of Wales and the Duke and Duchess of Edinburgh in the audience, a dazzling first night. The work was presented with two casts of equal status so that it could run continuously for six nights a week. One particular song out of t, 'Ho! Jolly Jenkin,' caught the public's fancy and was for years sung at concerts and in the home. In recent times it has become rather the habit to write off *Ivanhoe* as a failure, but in fact it had a continuous run of 155 consecutive performances, a truly remarkable record for a grand opera. It was revived for two performances in Sir Thomas Beecham's season at the Royal Opera House, Covent Garden, in 1910, conducted by Percy Pitt. But despite this D'Oyly Carte's overall scheme failed and the Royal English Opera House became the Palace Theatre in 1892.

The Closing Stages There were mutual congratulations about the triumph of *The Gondoliers*. Gilbert said of Sullivan's score: 'It gives one the chance of shining right through the twentieth century with a reflected light.' Sullivan brushed aside the suggestion of 'reflected light' and insisted: 'In such a perfect book as *The Gondoliers* you shine with an individual brilliancy which no other writer can hope to attain.' But the atmosphere of amiability did not last long, and *The Gondoliers* had been running for only a few months when the storm broke. It took the form of the famous 'carpet quarrel'.

It has sometimes been suggested that Gilbert and Sullivan 'fell out over a carpet' but in fact this was only an episode, though a serious one, in the strained relationship between two men of utterly different temperaments. It started when Gilbert asked Carte for detailed accounts of the cost of putting on *The Gondoliers* and was staggered to see that the figure was £4,500. Among the details to which he took particular objection was £500 for new carpets for the auditorium. He at once tackled Carte about it and insisted that there should be an entirely new agreement among the three of them. Carte, however, contended that this could surely wait until the next opera was coming along.

It would seem that Gilbert at first thought that he would have the wholehearted support of Sullivan in his clash with Carte. But he was mistaken. Sullivan, no doubt, did not wish to upset D'Oyly Carte at a time when his grand opera *Ivanhoe* was at last to be produced at the new opera house and, in any case, he was very much closer personally to Carte than to Gilbert. This aggravated Gilbert's fury and he vowed that he would never write another libretto for Carte and also insisted that none of his existing works should be presented at the Savoy Theatre again after Christmas of that year. Eventually he went so far as to take the matter to court in actions against Carte and Sullivan and the public had the unpleasant spectacle of an open wrangle among people who had in the past given them so much joy. The case ended in an uneasy compromise in an atmosphere of such bitterness that it seemed that any further collaboration was out of the question.

After the run of *The Gondoliers* Carte put on several other pieces at the Savoy, among them *Haddon Hall*, with a book by Sydney Grundy and music by Sullivan and with a cast including several favourite Savoyards such as Rosina Brandram, Courtice Pounds and W. H. Denny. It came off after 204 performances and was followed by a piece called *Jane Annie*, with book by J. M. Barrie and Conan Doyle and music by Ernest Ford.

Meanwhile Gilbert was not idle. A burlesque on *Hamlet* entitled *Rosencrantz and Guildenstern* was presented at the Vaudeville Theatre; a comic opera, *The Mountebanks*, with music by Alfred Cellier, had a run of 229 performances at the Lyric; and *Haste to the Wedding*, with music by George Grossmith, was given at the Criterion.

It seems probable that both Gilbert and Sullivan were hankering after a renewal of the old association, but each had his pride. Their friends wanted to see them together again and so undoubtedly did D'Oyly Carte. Eventually there was an exchange of letters between them, resulting in Gilbert calling at the composer's flat for a handshake and a chat amid 'a cloud of smoke', as Sullivan put it. They agreed that neither must ever again refer to the recent unhappy events. Whether or not they decided then and there to collaborate in another opera is not known. In any event, Fate almost put paid to any further collaboration for Sullivan nearly died before the next opera was written.

While the composer was on one of his visits to the Riviera, writing the music for *Haddon Hall*, his long-standing liver complaint struck him down more fiercely than ever before. He lingered on the brink of death but rallied enough to be brought back to London, there to make a slow recovery. The gout-beset Gilbert applied himself to writing another comic opera, calling it *Utopia (Limited)*, and engaging in vigorous satire of cherished English institutions, including the somewhat dangerous topic of a Royal drawing-room.

The atmosphere was generally amiable with a good deal of give-and-take between the two during the writing of *Utopia*, in the rehearsals of which Gilbert was so severely afflicted by his gout that he had to hobble around on crutches. For the first time in the history of the operas it was agreed to admit the Press to the dress rehearsal, Gilbert contending that some of the adverse notices in the past were due to the critics not fully understanding the works at a single hearing. *Utopia (Limited)* opened at the Savoy on October 7,

1893 – the title being changed to *Utopia, Limited* after the first few nights – and had a run of 245 performances.

Not the least cause of the audience's pleasure on the first night of *Utopia* was the sight of Gilbert and Sullivan standing side by side on the stage of the Savoy at the end of the performance and warmly shaking hands. There had been much to enjoy in this latest elaborately-staged piece.

After the comparatively brief run of *Utopia*, Sullivan and F. C. Burnand revised their old operetta, *The Contrabandista*, and, under the title *The Chieftain*, it was presented at the Savoy but with no great success. In the same year, 1894, there was presented at the Lyric Theatre a comic opera, *His Excellency*, with a book by Gilbert and music by F. Osmond Carr. It had a run of 116 performances.

Eventually, on March 7, 1896, the last Gilbert and Sullivan opera, *The Grand Duke*, was presented at the Savoy. But the old magic was sadly missing and the piece petered out after 123 performances. It became clear that there never would be a new *Mikado* or *Gondoliers*.

Sullivan busied himself in other fields. The year 1897 saw the Diamond Jubilee of Queen Victoria and Sullivan appropriately marked the occasion with a ballet, *Victoria and Merrie England*, presented at the Alhambra Theatre, and also a 'Festival Te Deum'. For the Savoy in 1898 he wrote *The Beauty Stone* with Arthur Pinero and Comyns Carr and, for the same theatre the following year, *The Rose of Persia* with Basil Hood.

His frail health had been further undermined by a severe attack of bronchitis while holidaying in Switzerland, but back at his flat in Victoria Street he struggled to get on with the music for *The Emerald Isle*, another collaboration with Basil Hood. But on November 22, 1900, he died, at the age of fifty-eight. The music for *The Emerald Isle* was completed by Edward German and the piece was presented at the Savoy the following year.

As Sullivan's funeral procession passed along the Thames Embankment on the way to his burial at St Paul's Cathedral, Richard D'Oyly Carte was lying desperately ill at his home in the Adelphi. He died on April 3, 1901, aged fifty-six.

In the years that followed the production of *The Grand Duke*, Gilbert wrote a play *The Fairy's Dilemma*, produced at the Garrick Theatre in 1904; a comic opera, *Fallen Fairies* with music by Edward German in 1909; and a one-act piece, *The Hooligan* in 1911.

But the years and his state of health were compelling him to take life more gently. At his home at Grim's Dyke, Harrow Weald, he was the mellowing country squire, sitting from time to time on the local Bench. He had been knighted in 1907.

He had not seen Sullivan since November, 1898, when at a revival of *The Sorcerer* at the Savoy Theatre, they had stood bowing to the audience from opposite sides of the stage but had left the theatre without speaking to each other.

On a sunny day in 1911 – May 29 – two girls, friends of the Gilberts, were swimming in the lake at Grim's Dyke when one of them got into difficulties and called out for help. Gilbert at once dived in and helped the girl to struggle to safety. But the effort was too much for his weak heart. He was dead when his body was recovered from the bottom of the lake.

Though the famous partnership had often been a stormy one, Gilbert had always spoken generously about Sullivan after the composer's death:

'It is a source of gratification to me to reflect that the rift that parted us for a time was completely bridged over, and that, at the time of Sir Arthur Sullivan's lamented death, the most cordial relations existed between us.'

'With Sullivan I never had to do that fatal thing – explain a joke.'

'My old friend and invaluable co-worker, Arthur Sullivan, whose untimely death, in the fullness of his powers, extinguished the class of opera with which his name was so honourably associated – a composer of the rarest genius, and who, because he was a composer of the rarest genius, was as modest and as unassuming as a neophyte should be but seldom is.'

'I remember all he has done for me in allowing his genius to shed some of its lustre upon my humble name.'

The truth was, of course, that neither one nor the other was the sole architect of success. That success was the triumph of the extraordinary combination of diverse talents and personalities we know as Gilbert-and-Sullivan.

The Operas

THESPIS	Gaiety Theatre	December 26, 1871
TRIAL BY JURY	Royalty Theatre	March 25, 1875
THE SORCERER	Opera Comique	November 17, 1877
HMS PINAFORE	Opera Comique	May 25, 1878
THE PIRATES OF PENZANCE	Opera Comique	April 3, 1880

(Bijou Theatre, Paignton, December 30, 1879; Fifth Avenue Theatre, New York, December 31, 1879)

PATIENCE	Opera Comique	April 23, 1881
	Savoy Theatre	October 10, 1881
IOLANTHE	Savoy Theatre	November 25, 1882
PRINCESS IDA	Savoy Theatre	January 5, 1884
THE MIKADO	Savoy Theatre	March 14, 1885
RUDDIGORE	Savoy Theatre	January 22, 1887
THE YEOMEN OF THE GUARD	Savoy Theatre	October 3, 1888
THE GONDOLIERS	Savoy Theatre	December 7, 1889
UTOPIA, LIMITED	Savoy Theatre	October 7, 1893
THE GRAND DUKE	Savoy Theatre	March 7, 1896

Abbott, Margery Joining the D'Oyly Carte chorus in 1934, Margery Abbott was soon singing some of the smaller parts. In 1937 she was singing Celia (I), Lady Psyche (PI) and Zorah (R) and in the following two years added Plaintiff (J), Aline (S), Rose Maybud (R), Casilda (G), Patience and Yum-Yum (M). She was with the company until 1946.

'About a century since' Song by the Notary, with chorus (D).

Abudah 'Our Abudah chests, each containing a patent Hag who comes out and prophesies disasters, with spring complete, are strongly recommended.'—John Wellington Wells (S). The reference is to Abudah, a Baghdad merchant who, in Ridley's *Tales of the Genii*, was haunted nightly by an old hag. Thackeray makes an allusion to him.

Aceldama Bunthorne (P) recites: 'Oh, to be wafted away/From this black Aceldama of sorrow.' The Aramaic word means 'the field of blood' and is used figuratively for a place of great slaughter. There are two Biblical references to the Aceldama (Matthew XXVII, 8, and Acts I, 19) as the Potter's Field, near Jerusalem, bought with the betrayal money paid to Judas and used as a burying-place for strangers. Years later it was used as such by Christians during the Crusades.

Actors Gilbert, who was himself a good amateur actor, knew exactly what he wanted from his players. He would not permit additional gags or stage 'business' without his permission and he detested *over*-acting. As he said to Henry A. Lytton: 'Always leave a little to the audience's imagination. Leave it to them to see and enjoy the point of a joke. I am sure you are intelligent but, believe me, there are many in the audience who are more intelligent than you!' What to do with the hands is a problem for many actors and, as he related in *The Secrets of a Savoyard*, Lytton once asked Gilbert for advice. 'Cut them off at the wrists, Lytton, and forget you've got any hands!' was the brisk reply. Of one showy actor he remarked: 'Poor fellow, he has all the faults of an actor without being one.' And when a man who had been playing Falstaff and was perspiring freely under his heavy make-up asked Gilbert what he thought of the performance, he received the enthusiastic reply: 'I think your pores act marvellously, my dear fellow.'

On a night when Gilbert had been appalled by the poor performance of an actor in a straight play, he was induced to go backstage to see the artists. On entering this particular actor's dressing-room, he patted him enthusiastically on the shoulder and declared, 'My dear fellow, *good* isn't the word!'

And there was the actor who approached him and said, 'My name is Such, but I act as Granville.' To which Gilbert retorted, 'I wish your name was Granville and you acted as such.'

'Rule a Grand Duchy? Why, my good girl, for ten years past I've ruled a theatrical company! A man who can do that can rule anything!'—Ernest Dummkopf (D).

Ada (PI) Ada, the girl graduate, was first played by Miss Twyman.

Adams, Donald Sitting in front during a performance, Donald Adams's wife heard a neighbour remark: 'He's really quite nimble for his age.' It is true that many Gilbert and Sullivan artists find themselves playing roles much older than themselves. Donald Adams, a member of the D'Oyly Carte Company for seventeen years and principal bass for fifteen, started the practice early. Born in Bristol, he was a chorister at Bristol Cathedral, where at the age of sixteen he played Thomas à Becket in T. S. Eliot's play *Murder in the Cathedral*. His early intention was to be a straight actor and he was broadcasting in plays when still at school. In the Army during the War, he was for the last two years of his service resident producer of the Army Repertory Theatre at Catterick Camp. His first professional engagement was in a play at the Embassy Theatre, Swiss Cottage, London, in 1949, followed by two years as leading man in Great Yarmouth Repertory Company, pantomime, member of a vocal quartet called 'The Regal Four'—and the Irish washerwomen Mrs Ginnochie with Lucan and McShane ('Old Mother Riley and her daughter Kitty') on the music-halls! It was while they were playing at Chelsea Palace that Arthur Lucan suggested that Donald Adams should combine his acting and singing and apply to the D'Oyly Carte Company. He joined the chorus of the company, singing also some small parts, and the following season he played Colonel Calverley (P) and understudied twenty-six roles. He became principal bass in 1953, his main roles being Dick Deadeye (HMS), Pirate King (PP), Colonel Calverley (P), Earl of Mountararat (I), Arac (PI), Mikado, Sir Roderic Murgatroyd (R) and Sergeant Meryll (Y). He made his last appearance with D'Oyly Carte in San Francisco in January 1969, when he left to concentrate on Gilbert and Sullivan for All, which he had founded in 1963. Favourite role: Pirate King (PP) 'because it's every schoolboy's idea of a Pirate King, a good part to act, with some fine mock-Verdi to sing.' Favourite aria: The Ghosts' High Noon (R).

Adrian, Max The Irish-born actor Max Adrian, who had scored a big success in a one-man show as Bernard Shaw at the Edinburgh Festival and later in London, followed up at the King's Lynn Festival, Norfolk, in July 1969, with the world première of another solo programme in which he presented both Gilbert and Sullivan. Unlike his technique in the earlier show Adrian did not make up as either Gilbert or Sullivan but, in a script prepared by himself, conveyed the two vastly different characters entirely by voice and manner, with a few interpolations as Richard D'Oyly Carte. The Queen Mother, who drove over from Sandringham to enjoy Adrian's remarkable feat of memory and characterisation, told him afterwards that she had first made the acquaintance of the operas when her mother and father used to sing some of the songs at the piano.

Aestheticism 'There is a transcendentality of delirium—an acute accentuation of supremest ecstasy—which the earthy might easily mistake for indigestion. But it is *not* indigestion—it is aesthetic transfiguration!'—Lady Jane (P).

'My eyes are open; I droop despairingly; I am soulfully intense; I am limp and I cling!'—Lady Jane (P).

'After sailing to this island' Duet for Tessa and Gianetta (G).

Agamemnon 'It is confidently predicted that my appearance as King Agamemnon, in a Louis Quatorze wig, will mark an epoch in the theatrical annals of Pfennig Halbfennig.'—Ludwig (D). In Greek legend, Agamemnon, King of Mycenae, led the Greeks at the siege of Troy. On his return from the war he was murdered by his wife, Clytemnestra.

Age 'My experience is that old age is the happiest time in a man's life. The worst of it is, there's so little of it.'—W. S. Gilbert.

At a late stage in his career, Gilbert wrote in a letter quoted by Leslie Baily (*The Gilbert and Sullivan Book*): 'I am a crumbling man —a magnificent ruin, no doubt, but still a ruin—and like all ruins I look best by moonlight. Give me a sprig of ivy and an owl under my arm and Tintern Abbey would not be in it with me.'

'Ah! gallant soldier, brave and true' Duet for Princess Zara and Captain Fitzbattleaxe (U).

'Ah, leave me not to pine' Mabel's ballad (PP).

'Ah, pity me, my comrades true' Julia Jellicoe's song in the finale to the first act (D).

Ahrimanes 'Or you or I must yield up his life to Ahrimanes.' —John Wellington Wells (S). In Zoroastrian theology, Ahrimanes was the spiritual enemy of mankind and in eternal conflict with Ormuzd, the angel of light and goodness.

'Alas! I waver to and fro!' Trio for Phoebe, Leonard and Sergeant Meryll (Y).

Alexis (S) *Tenor* Officer in the Grenadier Guards and son of Sir Marmaduke Pointdextre, originally played by George Bentham, a member of Her Majesty's Opera Company.

Alhambra del Bolero, Don (G) *Bass-baritone* There is a macabre touch of the dentist's waiting-room about Don Alhambra's reply when asked whether he ought not to go and put out of her suspense an old woman who is languishing in the torture-chamber. 'Oh no—there's no hurry—she's all right,' he says. 'She has all the illustrated papers.' The Grand Inquisitor was first played by W. H. Denny.

Aline (S) *Soprano* Daughter of Lady Sangazure. Alice May was the original player.

'All is prepar'd for sealing and for signing' Ensemble for Aline, Alexis, Lawyer and Chorus (S).

Alliteration 'Ha! Friend Jailer! Jailer that wast—jailer that never shalt be more! Jailer that jailed not, or that jailed, if jail he did, so unjailerly that 'twas but jerry-jailing or jailing in joke—though no joke to him who, by unjailerlike jailing, did so jeopardise his jailership. Come, take heart, smile, laugh, wink, twinkle, thou tormentor that tormentest none—thou racker that rackest not—thou pincher out of place—come, take heart, and be merry as I am!'—Jack Point to Wilfred Shadbolt (Y).

'No sicklying taint of sorrow overlies the lucid lake of liquid love, upon which, hand in hand, Aline and I are to float into eternity!'—Alexis (S).

'I have loved you with a Florentine fourteenth-century frenzy for full fifteen years!'—Archibald Grosvenor (P).

'To sit in solemn silence in a dull, dark dock,
In a pestilential prison, with a life-long lock,
Awaiting the sensation of a short, sharp shock
From a cheap and chippy chopper on a big, black block '—(M).

'Although of native maids the cream' Duet for Nekaya and Kalyba about their English upbringing (U).

Amaranthine 'Quivering on amaranthine asphodel.'—Reginald Bunthorne (P). An amaranth is an imaginary purple flower which never fades and the name is also applied to the flower known as love-lies-bleeding. Amaranthine means never-fading.

Amaryllis 'So come, Amaryllis.' (R) The name, which appears in the pastorals of Theocritus and Virgil, is associated with a rustic sweetheart. Milton's 'Lycidas' contains the line: 'To sport with Amaryllis in the shade.'

Amateur Performances Two early amateur performances are mentioned by Leslie Baily (*The Gilbert and Sullivan Book*). *HMS Pinafore* was given by students of Columbia College at the Union League Theatre, New York, on April 28 and 29, 1879, and by the Harmonists' Choral Society at the Drill Hall, Kingston-on-Thames, Surrey, on April 30 of the same year.

And on September 23, 1879, there was a highly unusual amateur performance of *Pinafore* aboard HMS Wolverene while she was stationed at Sydney. Leading roles were played by an able-bodied seaman and a private of marines and the chorus was composed of sailors and marines serving in the vessel.

Anacreon 'You should read Anacreon.'—Lady Psyche (PI). The reference is to the Greek lyric poet (563–478 BC) who wrote chiefly of love, wine, dancing and general enjoyment.

Ancestors (R) Apart from Sir Roderic, the Murgatroyd ancestors who step from their frames in the picture-gallery are Sir Rupert, Sir Jasper, Sir Lionel, Sir Conrad, Sir Desmond, Sir Gilbert and Sir Mervyn. They were originally played by Messrs S. Price, H. Charles, Trevor, P. Burbank, Tuer, J. Wilbraham and Cox.

Andersen 'It seems that she's a fairy/From Andersen's lib*rary*.'—Lord Chancellor (I). Hans Christian Andersen, the famed Danish writer of fairy tales, lived from 1805 until 1875 and was thus a contemporary of Gilbert.

Angela, The Lady (P) *Mezzo-soprano* Jessie Bond was the original player of this 'rapturous maiden'.

Apollo (T) An aged Olympian, played by Frederic Sullivan, the composer's brother.

Aquinas, Thomas Colonel Calverley (P) refers to the theologian born near Naples in 1227. He died in 1274 and was canonised in 1323.

Arac (PI) *Bass-baritone* Richard Temple was the first artist to play Arac, one of King Gama's three sons.

Arcadia 'Peckham an Arcadian Vale.'—Counsel for Plaintiff (J). According to Virgil, Arcadia was a district of the Peloponnesis in Greece, where all was happiness and pastoral simplicity.

Aristophanes 'I know the croaking chorus from *The Frogs* of Aristophanes.'—Major-General Stanley (PP). *The Frogs* is one of the best-known plays of the Athenian comic dramatist (c. 445–385 BC).

Art Galleries 'I will give them all to the Nation, and nobody shall ever look upon their faces again!' Sir Despard Murgatroyd's threatened revenge on the family portraits (R).

Arthur, King 'I know our mythic history, King Arthur's and Sir Caradoc's.'—Major-General Stanley (PP).

'As before you we defile' Opening chorus to the second act (D).

'As escort for the prisoner' Trio for Fairfax and two Yeomen, leading to the final ensemble of the first act, 'All frenzied with despair I rave' (Y).

'As in a month you've got to die' Solo for Pooh-Bah in the finale to the first act (M).

Asinorum pons 'For that *asinorum pons* I have crossed without assistance.'—King Paramount (U). For the sake of scansion Gilbert has reversed *pons asinorum* ('bridge of asses'), the nickname given to the fifth proposition of Euclid, Bk 1.

'As o'er our penny roll we sing' Duet for the Baroness and Rudolph (D).

Asphodel 'Quivering on amaranthine asphodel.'—Reginald Bunthorne (P). A kind of lily, the asphodel in mythology was an immortal flower that grew in the Elysian Fields.

'As pure and blameless peasant' Robin Oakapple's solo after he has been revealed as Sir Ruthven Murgatroyd (R).

'As some day it may happen that a victim must be found' Ko-Ko's song about the people he's got on his little list—'they'll none of 'em be missed.' In performance the opportunity is usually taken to pop in a few topical allusions here!

'At the outset I may mention it's my sovereign intention' Song for Ludwig, with chorus (D).

Attic 'In the period Socratic every dining-room was Attic (which suggests an architecture of a topsy-turvy kind).'—Ludwig (D). The pun is on the word for Athenian.

Augarde, Amy Many theatregoers of the older generation will still remember Amy Augarde who for many years played in a great number of musicals and operettas in London and on tour. Born in London in 1868, she made her first stage appearance in the D'Oyly Carte chorus when she was only sixteen and went to New York with the company the following year. At the Savoy Theatre she understudied Jessie Bond, sometimes playing the role of Mad Margaret (R) in the original production. She also played Hebe in the first revival of *Pinafore* at the Savoy. In 1888 she appeared as Lydia in Alfred Cellier's *Dorothy* at the Lyric Theatre. A most versatile artist, she also played Principal Boy in a 'Dick Whittington' pantomime at the Adelphi.

Aurora 'As Aurora gilds the day.'—Sir Marmaduke Pointdextre (S). In Greek mythology the 'rosy-fingered' goddess Aurora pioneers the rising of the sun.

'Away, Remorse! Compunction, hence!' Robin Oakapple's recitative and song—'The title's uncommonly dear at the price!' (R).

Ayldon, John After understudying Donald Adams for some time, John Ayldon succeeded to the principal bass-baritone roles with the D'Oyly Carte Company in January 1969. A Londoner, he was educated there and in San Francisco, where he spent four years and had his first theatrical experience in school shows and in some professional productions. Returning to England in 1958, he had his introduction to Gilbert and Sullivan when a local society was short of a policeman for *The Pirates of Penzance*. He was with this local company for six years, playing principal roles, before being invited to audition for the D'Oyly Carte chorus, which he joined in 1967. His leading roles now are Bouncer (C), Sir Marmaduke Pointdextre (S), Dick Deadeye (HMS), Pirate King (PP), Colonel Calverley (P), Lord Mountararat (I), Arac (PI), Mikado, Sir Roderic Murgatroyd (R) and Sergeant Meryll (Y). The theatre is his principal hobby as well as his profession but he is also fond of music in general and is a keen Dickensian.

The 3 sons of Gama MESSRS TEMPLE. GREY & LUGG

BUNTHORNE

Bab Ballads In a speech in 1906, Gilbert declared: 'I am anxious to avow my indebtedness to the author of the Bab Ballads, from which I have so unblushingly cribbed. I can only hope that, like Shakespeare, I may be held to have so far improved upon the original stories as to have justified the thefts that I committed.' He was, of course, the author of the ballads, most of them written for the paper *Fun* and illustrated by himself. They were later published in two series, *Bab Ballads: Much Sound and Little Sense*, 1869, and *More Bab Ballads*, 1873. His acknowledgment of his 'indebtedness' is apt, for he drew on many ideas from the ballads in writing his libretti. The title 'Bab' was taken from Gilbert's pet-name as a child.

Bailey 'At the Bailey and Middlesex Sessions' and 'At the Sessions or Ancient Bailey.'—Learned Judge (J). The Old Bailey in the City of London is the Central Criminal Court.

Baker, George Though not a Savoyard in the strict sense of having worked with the D'Oyly Carte Opera Company in the theatre, George Baker is an authority on the operas and particularly on the delivery of the patter songs, of which he has made many recordings. And it all came about in the first place by accident. Born in Birkenhead in February 1885, he went on to study at the Royal College of Music and began his career as an organist and choirmaster. He made his first stage appearance as Sir Francis Drake in a revue, *Now's the Time*, at the Alhambra Theatre in 1915 and through the years has made a great number of appearances in the musical theatre and on the concert platform in Britain and abroad. 'It was indeed sheer accident that introduced me to the Gilbert and Sullivan roles,' he told me. 'When HMV and Rupert D'Oyly Carte first reached agreement about recording the operas, I was under contract to HMV and rather famed for my clarity of enunciation. The agreement was reached on the understanding that I would sing the Grossmith and other roles and D'Oyly Carte on his part insisted that the roles should be studied with J. M. Gordon, the famed stage director who had worked with Gilbert, and that he should be at all rehearsals and recording sessions. Thus, I was able to get the authoritative rendering of the pieces straight from Gilbert by way of J. M. Gordon. The first complete recording was made in November 1917—*The Mikado*, in which I sang Ko-Ko and Pish-Tush and other bits and pieces. Since then I have made a great number of recordings of the operas, the last being in December 1962, when I sang Robin Oakapple in *Ruddigore*.' George Baker was amply justified in his comment: 'Not a bad run!'

Baker, Mildred The original Olga (D).

Baring 'The shares are a penny, and ever so many are taken by Rothschild and Baring.'—Lord Chancellor (I). Two brothers, John and Francis Baring, sons of an immigrant cloth manufacturer from Germany, founded the firm of merchant bankers in London in 1770.

Baritones Principal baritone roles in the operas are: Learned Judge and Counsel for Plaintiff (J); Dr Daly and John Wellington Wells (S); Sir Joseph Porter, Captain Corcoran and Bill Bobstay (HMS); Major-General Stanley and Samuel (PP); Colonel Calverley, Major Murgatroyd, Reginald Bunthorne and Archibald Grosvenor (P); Lord Chancellor, Earl of Mountararat and Strephon (I); King Gama, Florian and Guron (PI); Ko-Ko and Pish-Tush (M); Robin Oakapple (R); Jack Point and Second Yeoman (Y); Duke of Plaza-Toro, Giuseppe and Antonio (G); Scaphio, Phantis, Tarara, Calynx, Lord Dramaleigh, Sir Bailey Barre and Mr Blushington (U); Rudolph, Ben Hashbaz and Herald (D).

Barnett, Alice The roles of Lady Jane (P) and Queen of the Fairies (I) were first played by Alice Barnett, who had played Ruth in the first performance of *The Pirates of Penzance* in New York.

Baroness von Krankenfeldt (D) *Contralto* Rosina Brandram was the first artist to play the role.

Barre, Sir Bailey, QC, MP (U) *Baritone* Enes Blackmore was the first artist to play the role.

Barrington, Rutland Many of the leading baritone roles in the operas were first played by Rutland Barrington—Dr Daly (S), Captain Corcoran (HMS), Sergeant of Police in the London production (PP), Archibald Grosvenor (P), Earl of Mountararat (I), King Hildebrand (PI), Pooh-Bah (M), Sir Despard Murgatroyd (R), Giuseppe (G), King Paramount (U) and Rudolph (D). He later added other roles, notably Wilfred Shadbolt (Y) and Don Alhambra (G). Barrington's real name was George Rutland Fleet. He was born at Penge in 1853 and educated at Merchant Taylors School. He made his first stage appearance in a straight play at the Olympic Theatre at the age of twenty-one and, like George Grossmith, toured with Mrs Howard Paul's entertainment for two years before joining D'Oyly Carte in the role of Dr Daly. Barrington, again like Grossmith, was not at all sure that he would be suitable for the part. He was a stolid, serious sort of individual and indeed there were those who questioned Gilbert's wisdom in selecting him for a singing part in comic opera. But Gilbert knew what he was about. 'He's a staid, solid swine, and that's what I want,' he said—and his judgment was in keeping with his view that comedy is most effective when played seriously, with the artist simply allowing the lines to have their effect without straining for laughs.

As well as playing the Gilbert and Sullivan roles, Barrington appeared in many musicals under George Edwardes' management. He left D'Oyly Carte after *Ruddigore* and went into management—not very successfully—at the St James's Theatre, where he produced Gilbert's play, *Brantingham Hall*, but returned to the Savoy for *The Gondoliers*. He also toured the halls, played Falstaff at His Majesty's and wrote several plays, including *Bartonmere Towers*, produced at the Savoy in 1893, and a version of Kingsley's *The Water Babies*, produced at the Garrick in 1902. Barrington sparked off one of Gilbert's quips during an early rehearsal of *Pinafore*, with scenery and properties just roughly knocked together. Gilbert required him to sit pensively on one of the ship's skylights but, when Barrington lowered his considerable weight into position, the whole affair collapsed under him. 'No,' said Gilbert, 'that's *ex*pensively.' Barrington was pursued for many years by the effects of a notice written by one critic after the first night of *The Sorcerer*, in which he created the role of the parson, Dr Daly: 'Mr Barrington is wonderful. He always manages to sing one-sixteenth of a tone flat; it's so like a vicar.' Much later, D'Oyly Carte came round to him and said: 'Barrington, what's the matter? Someone has just come out of the stalls and says you are singing in tune. It will never do.' Barrington died in 1922 at the age of 69.

Basingstoke 'I sometimes think that if we could hit upon some word for you to use whenever I am about to relapse—some word that teems with hidden meaning—like 'Basingstoke'—it might recall me to my saner self.'—Mad Margaret (R).

Basses Principal bass roles in the operas are: Foreman of the Jury and Usher (J); Notary (S); Dick Deadeye and Bob Beckett (HMS); Sergeant of Police (PP); Go-To (M); Old Adam Goodheart (R); Giorgio (G).

Bass-baritones The dividing line between the low voices is often very narrow but the following roles can be placed in the bass-baritone category: Sir Marmaduke Pointdextre (S); Pirate King (PP); Private Willis (I); King Hildebrand, Arac and Scynthius (PI); Mikado and Pooh-Bah (M); Sir Despard Murgatroyd and Sir Roderic Murgatroyd (R); Sir Richard Cholmondeley, Sergeant Meryll and Wilfred Shadbolt (Y); Don Alhambra (G); King Paramount, Captain Sir E. Corcoran and Mr Goldbury (U); Ludwig and the Prince of Monte Carlo (D).

Battle's roar is over, The Duet for Richard Dauntless and Rose Maybud (R).

Beadle of Burlington Two explanations have been given of Colonel Calverley's (P) reference, that he is (a) the official who presided at London's fashionable Burlington Arcade in Piccadilly or (b) Erastus F. Beadle, of Burlington, New York, pioneer of cheap literature in the United States.

Beckett, Bob (HMS) *Bass* The Boatswain's Mate, or Carpenter, was originally played by Mr Dymott.

Belgrave Square 'Hearts just as pure and fair may beat in Belgrave Square' (I). Built in 1845, Belgrave Square is cited here by Gilbert to indicate fashionable life in London.

Bell, May The original player of the role of Melene (U).

Ben Hashbaz (D) *Baritone* Ben Hashbaz, the costumier, was first played by C. H. Workman.

Bentham, George The first artist to play Alexis (S). He was with Her Majesty's Opera Company.

Bernard, Annie The original Inez (G), Annie Bernard had also sung Katisha (M) in some performances of the first production. Her other roles were Lady Sangazure (S), Little Buttercup (HMS), Lady Jane (P), Fairy Queen (I), Dame Carruthers (Y), Duchess of Plaza-Toro (G) and Lady Sophy (U).

Bertha (D) *Mezzo-soprano* Jessie Rose was the first artist to play Bertha, a member of Dummkopf's theatrical company.

Bethell, Anna Joining D'Oyly Carte in 1909, Anna Bethell played Kate (PP), Lady Saphir (P), Leila (I) and Chloe (PI) for three years. In a later period with the company, from 1921 until 1939, she played Mrs Partlet (S), Lady Saphir, Leila, Chloe and Inez (G). In 1947-8 she was stage director. Anna Bethell, who was married to Sydney Granville, died in 1969.

'Big bombs, small bombs, great guns and little ones!' Duet for Rudolph and Ludwig in the finale to the first act (D).

Billington, Fred Though he did not create any of the parts, Fred Billington was famed in the 'Pooh-Bah roles' during 38 years with D'Oyly Carte, starting in 1879, when he sang Bill Bobstay and Dick Deadeye (HMS). In the single 'copyright' performance of *Pirates* at Paignton later that year, he played the Sergeant of Police. Billington died in November 1917, while on a tour in which he played the Sergeant of Police, King Hildebrand (PI), Pooh-Bah (M), Wilfred Shadbolt (Y) and Don Alhambra (G).

Binnacle Light 'Let your heart be your compass, with a clear conscience for your binnacle light.'—Richard Dauntless (R). The binnacle is the container for the ship's compass.

Bismarck 'Genius of Bismarck devising a plan'—Colonel Calverley (P) refers to the famous German Chancellor, known as the 'Iron Chancellor' (1815–98).

Blackmore, Hugh Enes Joining D'Oyly Carte to create the part of Sir Bailey Barre (U), Blackmore sang with the company for 29 years, his roles including Captain Fitzbattleaxe (U), Ralph Rackstraw (HMS), Duke of Dunstable (P), Marco (G), Nanki-Poo (M), Dummkopf (D), Leonard Meryll (Y), Luiz (G) and Cyril (PI).

Blanche, Lady (PI) *Contralto* Rosina Brandram was the original player of Lady Blanche, the professor of abstract science.

Blushington, Mr (U) *Baritone* Herbert Ralland was the first artist to play the county councillor.

Bobstay, Bill (HMS) *Baritone* Boatswain, originally played by Fred Clifton, he resembles Dick Deadeye in one sense only—that Gilbert chose a nautical term for his surname.

'Bold-faced ranger (Perfect stranger)' Lady Sophy's lecture about the etiquette of courtship in the English manner (U).

Bonaparte Napoleon comes in for a reference by Lord Mount-ararat (I): 'When Wellington thrashed Bonaparte . . .'

Bond, Jessie 'The Savoy is not the same without you,' wrote Gilbert to Jessie Bond after she had left the D'Oyly Carte Company. He undoubtedly had great regard for her, even though he could exclaim, 'You little fool!' when she told him that she was going to marry and leave the company. To which the lively Jessie replied, 'I have often heard you say you don't like old women. I shall be old soon. Will you provide for me? Well, I am going to a man who will.' And hers was a happy marriage.

She was the original player of a long list of mezzo-soprano parts —Hebe (HMS), Lady Angela (P), Iolanthe, Melissa (PI), Pitti-Sing (M), Mad Margaret (R), Phoebe Meryll (Y) and Tessa (G). Gilbert wrote the role of Iolanthe specifically with her in mind and, when he gave her the part of Phoebe, he said (as she recalled in *The Life and Reminiscences of Jessie Bond*, as told by herself to Ethel Macgeorge, 1930) 'Here you are, Jessie. You needn't act this. It's you.'

Jessie Bond was born in Camden Town, the daughter of a piano-maker. Her parents intended her to be a professional pianist.

They moved to Liverpool and at the age of eight Jessie played a Beethoven sonata at a concert there. When she was seventeen she joined the Liverpool Choral Society, happened to meet Santley and went to study at the Royal Academy of Music with Manuel Garcia. It was when she was singing in a concert at St George's Hall that Richard D'Oyly Carte heard her and suggested concert engagements for her. *The Sorcerer* was running at the time and when the following opera, *HMS Pinafore*, was being prepared, Jessie was offered the part of Hebe, thus starting an association with Gilbert and Sullivan which continued until 1891, after which she sometimes returned for revivals and also played in musical comedy. Her favourite role was Mad Margaret. Jessie Bond died at Worthing in 1942, at the age of eighty-nine.

Bond, Neva The first artist to play the role of Isabel (PP) in the London production.

Booth, Webster Though this distinguished tenor made his name on the concert platform, in musicals and in duets with his wife Anne Ziegler, it was with D'Oyly Carte that he first stepped on to a stage. Born in Birmingham, he was twenty-two when he joined the chorus and appeared under the name of Leslie W. Booth as First Yeoman (Y) at the Theatre Royal, Brighton, in 1924. He was with the company for four years but, long after he had left, he was seen in the film, *The Story of Gilbert and Sullivan*, which included excerpts from the operas and which had its première in 1953.

Botticelli 'How Botticellian!'—Lady Saphir (P). Sandro Botticelli (c. 1445–1510), the great painter of the Italian Renaissance, one of whose best-known pictures is 'Primavera'.

Boucicault 'The pathos of Paddy, as rendered by Boucicault.'— Colonel Calverley (P). The Irish dramatist, Dion Boucicault (1822–90) wrote or adapted about 140 plays, the most successful of which was *The Colleen Bawn*, produced at the Adelphi Theatre in 1860 and running for 360 nights. Gilbert almost certainly saw it. Boucicault's daughter, Nina, was the first of the long line of actresses to play Barrie's Peter Pan.

Bovill, Frederick The first artist to sing Pish-Tush (M).

Bowdler 'But, if you will be advised, You will get them Bowdlerised!'—Lady Psyche (PI). In 1818 Thomas Bowdler brought out an edition of Shakespeare in which 'those words and expressions are omitted which cannot with propriety be read aloud in a family.' Lady Psyche suggests that the young ladies of the college should read the classics in similar editions.

Bowley, George The first artist to play the Solicitor (P).

Boyd, Mr The original Second Citizen (Y).

Bracy, Henry The original player of Hilarion (PI).

Braham, Leonora She was born in 1853 and originated the roles of Patience, Phyllis (I), Princess Ida, Yum-Yum (M) and Rose Maybud (R). She had made her first stage appearance in a St

George's Hall revival of Gilbert's piece *Ages Ago*, the original production of which had been in rehearsal at the Royal Gallery of Illustration when Gilbert was first introduced to Sullivan by the composer Frederic Clay. It is said that Gilbert's idea for the Three Little Maids (M) came about through the fact that his three leading ladies of the time—Leonora Braham, Jessie Bond and Sybil Grey— were all petite. Leonora Braham died in 1931.

'Braid the raven hair' Pitti-Sing and the chorus, assisting Yum-Yum in her bridal toilet (M).

Brandram, Rosina The first artist to play many of the 'forbidding' women of the operas, Rosina Brandram was the original Lady Blanche (PI), Katisha (M), Dame Hannah (R), Dame Carruthers (Y), Duchess of Plaza-Toro (G), Lady Sophy (U) and Baroness von Krakenfeldt (D). Her other roles included Little Buttercup (HMS), Ruth (PP), Lady Jane (P) and Fairy Queen (I), and she was the only principal to appear in every original production at the Savoy Theatre. Gilbert later spoke of her as 'Rosina of the glorious voice that rolled out as full-bodied Burgundy rolled down; Rosina, whose dismal doom it was to represent undesirable old ladies of sixty-five, but who, with all the resources of the perruquier and the make-up box, could never succeed in looking more than an attractive eight-and-twenty—it was her only failure.' Rosina Brandram died in 1907, at the age of sixty-one.

Briercliffe, Nellie In her first season with D'Oyly Carte in 1915, Nellie Briercliffe sang a number of principal parts, Hebe (HMS), Edith (PP), Angela (P), Iolanthe, Melissa (PI), Pitti-Sing (M), Phoebe (Y) and Tessa (G). She added Constance (S) in the following season and left the company in 1920, returning for one season in 1929, when her roles included Mad Margaret (R). She died in 1966.

'Brightly dawns our wedding day' Madrigal: Yum-Yum, Pitti-Sing, Nanki-Poo and Pish-Tush (M).

'British tar is a soaring soul, A' Glee for Ralph Rackstraw, Boatswain, Boatswain's Mate and Chorus (HMS).

Broad, John Though born and brought up in Hampshire, John Broad had his musical and dramatic training in Birmingham, where he studied for four years at the School of Music under Rene Soames and Frederick Sharp, and for three years at St Peter's College,

Birmingham, where he became chairman of the Dramatic Society and directed several major college productions. He was also a founder member of the Capricorn Youth Theatre and took leading roles in their productions at the Nuffield Theatre, Southampton. His baritone roles with the D'Oyly Carte Company include the Notary (S), Guron (PI) and Lieutenant of the Tower (Y).

'Broken every promise plighted' Julia's song (D).

Bromley, Nelly She was twenty-five when she became the first artist to play the role of the Plaintiff (J). She died in 1939 at the age of eighty-nine.

Brownlow, Wallace The first artist to play the Lieutenant of the Tower (Y) and Luiz (G).

Bunthorne, Reginald (P) *Baritone* The role of the 'fleshly poet' was originally played by George Grossmith.

Bunthorne's Bride Alternative title of *Patience*.

Bunthorne's Solicitor (P) George Bowley was the original player of the part.

'Buon'giorno, signorine!' Duet for Marco and Giuseppe on their first entrance, with chorus of girls (G).

Buttercup, Little (HMS) *Contralto* Just as, perhaps, a big man might be nicknamed 'Tich', so is Mrs Cripps, the Portsmouth bumboat woman of impressive proportions and uncertain age, called 'Little Buttercup' by the crew of 'Pinafore'—'Though I could never tell why,' as she herself says. Far from being little, she is described *en passant* by Captain Corcoran as 'a plump and pleasing person'. The waltz-time song with which she introduces herself has a prominent place in the score—it is used an an entr'acte and it also turns up in the finale. The role was first played by Henriette Everard.

'By the mystic regulation' Ludwig's song, with chorus (D).

Caesar Julius Caesar (102–44 BC) comes into Colonel Calverley's list of the qualities of a Heavy Dragoon: 'The genius strategic of Caesar or Hannibal' (P).

Calverley, Colonel (P) *Baritone* Richard Temple was the original player of the officer of the Dragoon Guards, who has the elaborate patter-song, enumerating the varied qualities that go to the making of 'that popular mystery known to the world as a Heavy Dragoon.'

Calynx (U) *Baritone* The Utopian Vice-Chamberlain was first played by Bowden Haswell.

Camberwell 'Camberwell became a bower.'—Counsel for the Plaintiff (J). District of south-east London.

Capital Punishment 'Our logical Mikado, seeing no moral difference between the dignified judge who condemns a criminal to die, and the industrious mechanic who carries out the sentence, has rolled the two offices into one, and every judge is now his own executioner.'—Pooh-Bah (M).

Caradoc, Sir 'I know our mythic history, King Arthur's and Sir Caradoc's.'—Major-General Stanley (PP). One of King Arthur's Knights of the Round Table, Sir Caradoc had the distinction of being the only one whose wife could wear 'the mantle of matrimonial fidelity.'

'Carefully on tiptoe stealing' Ensemble as Ralph Rackstraw and Josephine prepare to elope, leading to 'He is an Englishman!' (HMS).

Carleton, E. The original Viscount Mentone (D).

Carruthers, Dame (Y) *Contralto* The housekeeper of the Tower of London, who sets her cap at Sergeant Meryll, and gets him, reluctantly on his part, was originally played by Rosina Brandram.

Cartoons 'In the cartoons of a comic paper, the size of your nose always varies inversely as the square of your popularity.'—King Paramount (U).

Casilda (G) *Soprano* The Duchess of Plaza-Toro's daughter, in love with Luiz, was originally played by Decima Moore.

Castle Adamant Alternative title of *Princess Ida*

Catchy-catchies 'Men are grown-up catchy-catchies.'—Captain Corcoran (HMS). Babies.

Cecil, Sylvia As well as 'officially' singing Plaintiff (J), Ella (P) and Fiametta (G), Sylvia Cecil made occasional appearances as Princess Ida, Yum-Yum (M) and Elsie Maynard (Y) in her first season with D'Oyly Carte in 1918. In the two following seasons she was confirmed in these roles and added Casilda (G) and Rose Maybud (R). She was away from the company until 1929, when she appeared in one season in which her new roles included Josephine (HMS) and Gianetta (G). Back with the company in 1935-7, Sylvia Cecil went with them on their American tour and, with Derek Oldham, was invited to sing the duet 'Prithee, pretty maiden' (Patience and Archibald Grosvenor) at a White House party before the Presidential Inauguration of Franklin D. Roosevelt, a keen Gilbert and Sullivan enthusiast.

Celia (I) *Soprano* One of the leading fairies, Celia was first played by Miss Fortescue.

Cellier, Alfred and François Born in London in 1844, the son of a French teacher, Alfred Cellier made the acquaintance of Sullivan early in life. Both were choristers at the Chapel Royal, St James's, and for a time, when Sullivan was 'first boy' there, Cellier fagged for him. They were joint conductors of Promenade Concerts at Covent Garden. Apart from his work with the Savoy operas, Cellier was a gifted composer in his own right, his most successful work being the light opera *Dorothy*, which had a run of more than

900 performances. His other works included *The Mountebanks*, with a libretto by Gilbert, and both he and his brother wrote also some curtain-raisers to precede the shorter Savoy operas. In his early years he was a church organist. He conducted Gilbert and Sullivan operas at the Opera Comique and Savoy for five years and later represented their interests in the United States and Australia. He died in 1891.

Alfred's younger brother François, who was also a chorister at the Chapel Royal, was associated with the D'Oyly Carte Company as conductor for 35 years. He was born in 1849 and died in 1914. The well-known West End actor Frank Cellier was François's son.

Censor It was a matter of pride and principle on the part of Gilbert that he would on no account write or present anything that could be regarded as in any way improper. But he had no love for the censor and enjoyed quoting instances of the absurdities that arose through that official's search for 'irreverent[1] words in manuscripts submitted for his approval. An early piece of his own was a dramatisation of Dickens's *Great Expectations*, in which the convict, Magwitch, said to Pip: 'Here you are, in chambers fit for a Lord.' Gilbert vowed that the word 'Lord' had been struck out and 'Heaven' substituted!

There is a dig at the censor in *Utopia, Limited*: 'Are you aware that the Lord Chamberlain, who has his own views as to the best means of elevating the national drama, has declined to license any play that is not in blank verse and three hundred years old—as in England?'—Phantis.

In 1909 Gilbert gave his views about the censorship of plays to a Joint Select Committee of the House of Lords and House of Commons. Others whose opinions were included in a Blue Book, subsequently published, were William Archer, Bernard Shaw, Granville Barker, J. M. Barrie, Forbes Robertson, John Galsworthy, Laurence Housman, Beerbohm Tree, A. B. Walkley, Gilbert Murray, Lena Ashwell, George Alexander, George Edwardes, the Speaker of the House of Commons, Oswald Stoll, the Bishop of Southwark, Hall Caine, Israel Zangwill, Squire Bancroft, Arthur Pinero and G. K. Chesterton. Not a bad cast. The Blue Book cost 3s. 3d. or 16 new pence.

It was not until 1968 that the Lord Chamberlain's censorship of plays was abolished in Britain.

Chard, Kate The original player of Lady Psyche (PI).

Charity 'A few gifts, dear aunt, for deserving villagers. Lo, here is some peppermint rock for old gaffer Gadderby, a set of false teeth for pretty little Ruth Rowbottom, and a pound of snuff for the poor orphan girl on the hill.'—Rose Maybud (R).

Chassepôt rifle 'When I can tell at sight a chassepôt rifle from a javelin.'—Major-General Stanley (PP). Named after its inventor, the rifle was used by the French in the Franco-Prussian War of 1870. The more familiar Mauser has later been substituted for chassepôt in the text.

'Cheerily carols the lark' Mad Margaret's scena, including the ballad 'To a garden full of posies.' (R).

Children's Companies In 1879–80, Richard D'Oyly Carte presented *HMS Pinafore* for a matinees-only run of 78 performances at the Opera Comique with a cast entirely composed of children. They later toured and then came back for a further 28 matinees. There was some slight raising of eyebrows that a child, playing Captain Corcoran, should be required to say, 'Why, damme, it's too bad!' There were also matinee performances of *The Pirates of Penzance* by a children's company at the Savoy Theatre in 1884–5, followed by a short tour.

Chloe 'Come, Chloe and Phyllis.' (R) The name of Chloe, the shepherdess in Longus's romance, *Daphnis and Chloe*, is used by poets for a rustic sweetheart.

Chloe (PI) *Soprano* Chloe, the girl graduate, was first played by Miss Heathcote.

Cholmondeley, Sir Richard (Y) *Bass-baritone* The Lieutenant of the Tower of London was originally played by Wallace Brownlow.

Choregus 'Accept as the choregus of the early Attic stage.'—Ludwig (D). The leader of the chorus in the ancient Greek drama.

Chorus One can hardly overestimate the importance of Gilbert's then revolutionary handling of the chorus in his conception and production of the operas, his transformation of them from a decorative but faceless assembly, providing a mere background to the proceedings, into *people* with some reason for being there and with an active part to play in the scene. He developed this idea right from the start, the Plaintiff in *Trial by Jury* appearing in court attended by her bridesmaids in full rig. True, his reasons for bringing on the chorus were often—well, Gilbertian—as, for instance, Sir Joseph Porter (HMS) insisting on travelling around accompanied by 'his sisters and his cousins and his aunts' or Major-General Stanley (PP) with his attendant assembly of daughters! But they were at any rate somebodies, with a definite place in the topsy-turvy scheme of things. Just how deliberate all this was is shown by a programme note in the early opera, *The Sorcerer*: 'Produced under the personal direction of Messrs. Gilbert and Sullivan, special attention having been paid to the Departments of Chorus and Orchestra.'

The significance of Gilbert's approach to this matter was apparent to Sullivan from the time of *Thespis*, the first opera the two wrote together. As he said in later years (*Sir Arthur Sullivan* by Arthur Lawrence): 'Until Gilbert took the matter in hand, choruses were dummy concerns and were practically nothing more than a part of the stage setting. It was in *Thespis* that Gilbert began to carry out his expressed determination to get the chorus to play its proper part in the performance. At this moment it seems difficult to realise that the idea of the chorus being anything more than a sort of stage audience was at that time a tremendous novelty.'

'For Heaven's sake wear your coronets as if you were used to them!' said Gilbert to the chorus of Peers before the first performance of *Iolanthe*, in his anxiety to get them to behave naturally and not as though they were on their way to a fancy-dress ball. But his insistence on the importance of the chorus and his determination to get the stage picture just as he wanted it sometimes provoked brisk exchanges with people on the stage. Taking exception to some detail of his direction, one of the principals at a rehearsal was moved to protest: 'Really, Mr Gilbert, why should I stand here. I'm not a chorus girl.' 'No, madam,' said Gilbert, 'Your voice is not strong enough, or you would be.'

Gilbert was, however, equally adroit at smoothing out the various little contretemps that arose at rehearsal. Arthur Lawrence has a story of an exchange between Gilbert and one of the chorus during rehearsal: 'One day a girl came up to us crying, and Gilbert asked her the cause of it. She said that Miss X, one of the costumiers' assistants, had been very rude and had said to her, "You are no better than you ought to be." Gilbert immediately looked very sympathetic and said to her, "Well, you are not, are you, my dear," to which she replied promptly, "Why, of course not, Mr Gilbert!" "Ah, then that's all right!" he said, and she went away perfectly comforted.'

Sullivan on his part, fully appreciating the care with which Gilbert wrote for and produced the chorus, gave them much attractive music to sing.

Chronos 'Oh, Chronos, Chronos, this is too bad of you!'— Archibald Grosvenor (P). The Greek word for Time.

Cimmerian 'The Cimmerian darkness of tangible despair.'— Ralph Rackstraw (HMS). Homer refers to the Cimmerians as dwellers in a land without sunshine.

Circe 'Lady Circe's Piggy-wigs.'—Hilarion (PI). In Greek mythology Circe was a sorceress who, when Ulysses landed on her island, turned his companions into pigs.

City of London Festival In the first of the City Festivals (1962), *The Yeomen of the Guard* was presented in the open air in the actual setting of the Tower of London and the production was repeated in the Festivals of 1964 and 1966. A particularly attractive feature of Anthony Besch's production was the way in which he used the greensward surrounding the Tower so that, while the overture was being played, the townsfolk could be seen strolling or running into the scene. The cast included John Carol Case (Lieutenant of the Tower), Thomas Round (Colonel Fairfax), Bryan Drake (Sergeant Meryll), John Wakefield (Leonard Meryll), John Cameron (Jack Point), Kenneth Sandford (Wilfred Shadbolt), Ann Dowdall (Elsie Maynard), Anne Pashley (Phoebe), Johanna Peters (Dame Carruthers) and Sylvia Gray (Kate). The townsfolk were members of the New Opera Company Chorus and of the various operatic societies in the City of London. The designer was Peter Rice and the conductor Lawrence Leonard.

Clifford, Grahame During World War II Grahame Clifford sang the leading comedy roles for the D'Oyly Carte Company— Sir Joseph Porter (HMS), Major-General Stanley (PP), Bunthorne (P), Lord Chancellor (I), Ko-Ko (M), Robin Oakapple (R), Jack Point (Y) and the Duke of Plaza-Toro (G). On returning from service in 1946, Martyn Green resumed the roles he had been singing before the war. Grahame Clifford joined Covent Garden Opera, newly formed in 1947, and with them sang a number of roles, including Papageno (*Magic Flute*), Faninal (*Rosenkavalier*), Ping (*Turandot*), Beckmesser (*Mastersingers*), Benoit (*Bohème*) and Alberich (*Ring*).

Clifton, Fred The roles of the Notary (S) and Bill Bobstay (HMS) were first played by Fred Clifton, who also played the Sergeant of Police in D'Oyly Carte's first presentation of the *Pirates* in New York.

'Climbing over rocky mountain' Entrance of the girls (PP), first used in the early *Thespis*.

Cole, Annie The original Vittoria (G), Annie Cole also sang Hebe (HMS), Pitti-Sing (M), Phoebe (Y) and Tessa (G).

Colocynth 'The amorous colocynth.'—Reginald Bunthorne (P). A bitter Asiatic gourd.

Cologne 'Oh! fetch some water from far Cologne!'—Counsel for the Plaintiff (J). The perfumed spirit known as Eau de Cologne.

Comedy Opera Company Ltd *The Sorcerer* and *HMS Pinafore* were first presented by the Comedy Opera Company, which was formed in 1876 with Richard D'Oyly Carte, lessee of the Opera Comique, as manager. The company disintegrated after disagreements resulting in the extraordinary 'Battle of the Opera Comique' in which the directors tried to seize the *Pinafore* scenery and properties for presentation in another theatre. Gilbert, Sullivan and Carte formed their own partnership in 1879. Incidentally, the directors of the Comedy Opera Company had vigorously opposed the recruitment of George Grossmith to the cast of *The Sorcerer*!

'Come hither, all you people' Opening to the finale of the first act (D).

'Comes a train of little ladies' Chorus of girls as Yum-Yum, Peep-Bo and Pitti-Sing make their first entrance with their schoolfellows (M).

'Comes the broken flower' Chorus of bridesmaids (J).

'Comes the pretty young bride, a-blushing, timidly shrinking' Women's chorus at the opening to the finale of the opera (Y).

Command Performances Though Queen Victoria gave Sullivan much encouragement as a 'serious' composer, it was *The Gondoliers* which she commanded to be presented before her at Windsor Castle.

The performance took place on March 6, 1891, most of the principal parts being played by the artists who had created them at the Savoy Theatre. The Queen was evidently well pleased, for later the same year, when she was staying at Balmoral Castle, she commanded the D'Oyly Carte touring company to present *The Mikado* there. The principal players on this occasion included Rose Hervey (Yum-Yum), Haidee Crofton (Pitti-Sing), Alice Pennington (Peep-Bo), Kate Forster (Katisha), Fred Billington (Pooh-Bah), George Thorne (Ko-Ko), Tom Redmond (Mikado), Richard Clarke (Nanki-Poo) and J. J. Fitzgibbon (Pish-Tush).

By an unfortunate oversight, the programme for the Windsor Castle performance of *The Gondoliers* omitted any mention of Gilbert's name. As he wrote years afterwards: 'When *The Gondoliers* was commanded at Windsor by her late Majesty, the piece was described as "by Sir Arthur Sullivan" on a programme which contained the name of the wig-maker in bold type! And I had to pay £87 10s. as my share of sending the piece down to Windsor, besides forfeiting my share of the night's profits at the Savoy!'

'Complicated gentleman allow me to present, A' Princess Zara's solo about Sir Bailey Barre, Q.C., M.P. (U).

Conies 'I've chickens and conies.'—Little Buttercup (HMS). Cony or coney is a word for a rabbit.

Constance (S) *Soprano* The role of Constance, daughter of Mrs Partlet, was first played by Giulia Warwick, a member of the Carl Rosa Opera Company who later became a professor of singing at the Guildhall School of Music.

Contraltos Principal contralto roles in the operas are: Lady Sangazure and Mrs Partlet (S); Little Buttercup (HMS); Ruth (PP); Lady Jane (P); Queen of the Fairies (I); Lady Blanche (PI); Katisha (M); Dame Hannah (R); Dame Carruthers (Y); Duchess of Plaza-Toro and Inez (G); Lady Sophy (U); Baroness von Krakenfeldt (D).

Conundrum Jack Point: 'Before proceeding to a more serious topic, can you tell me, sir, why a cook's brain-pan is like an over-wound clock?'
Lieutenant: 'A truce to this fooling—follow me.'
Point: 'Just my luck; my best conundrum wasted!'
One wonders whether Gilbert ever did have an answer to Jack's conundrum.

Conversation 'They say that in England the conversation of the very meanest is a coruscation of impromptu epigram!'—Calynx, the Utopian Vice-Chamberlain (U).

Cook, George Born in Coventry, George Cook joined the Royal Navy during World War II and afterwards was persuaded by his parents, both of them enthusiasts, to join an amateur operatic society. He became fascinated by the Gilbert and Sullivan roles he played and, after further training, he joined D'Oyly Carte in 1953 as a chorister and later singing several principal bass-baritone roles. George Cook has an unusual and, as it happens, very apt hobby. Japanese fans being in short supply a few years ago, he studied the art of fan-making and to-day not only supplies all those used in the company's productions of *The Mikado* but also provides them for almost every amateur production of the opera throughout the country. He married Marian Martin, a member of the company, which he left in August, 1969.

Copyright 'It seemed to be their opinion that a free and independent American citizen ought not to be robbed of his rights of robbing somebody else,' said Sullivan bitterly of the early 'pirate' performances of the operas in the United States, where some of Gilbert's straight plays had already been similarly presented. Of copyright in general, Gilbert expressed the view: 'It is a shameful thing that copyright should expire. It ought to be freehold, like land.' According to the law, however, copyright expires fifty years after the death of the author or composer—at the end of 1950 in the case of Sullivan's music and at the end of 1961 for Gilbert's libretti.

Coram, Elsie With D'Oyly Carte from 1914 until 1922, Elsie Coram played a number of leading roles, including Plaintiff (J), Lady Ella (P), Phyllis (I), Sacharissa and Lady Psyche (PI), Yum-Yum and Peep-Bo (M), and Casilda (G).

Corcoran, Captain (HMS) *Baritone* Commander of HMS Pinafore, originally played by Rutland Barrington. He has the famous catchphrase 'What, *never?*' . . . 'Hardly ever!' which became so maddeningly familiar that, so the story goes, one newspaper editor ruled that it must never be used in his paper. 'What, *never?*' innocently asked one of the staff. 'Well,' groaned the editor, 'hardly ever.' One of the oddities about Captain Corcoran is the question of his age. As it is eventually revealed that he and Ralph Rackstraw were mixed up as babies, one would expect them to be much of an age, whereas Corcoran appears as a much older man. In a Gilbertian situation, however, one need not worry unduly about such a matter!

Corcoran, Captain Sir Edward, KCB, RN (U) *Bass-baritone*
Lawrence Gridley was the first artist to play the role.

Cornucopia 'Cornucopia is each in his mental fertility.' (U). In mythology, the child Zeus was fed on goat's milk by Amalthea, daughter of the King of Crete. Gratefully he presented her afterwards with a goat's horn, to which he had given the power of bestowing abundance of all things desired by the possessor. Thus the cornucopia, sometimes called Amalthea's horn, is the horn of plenty.

Coronal 'Time weaves my coronal!'—Lady Blanche (PI). A coronal is a crown or wreath.

Counsel for the Plaintiff (J) *Baritone* The original was Mr Hollingsworth.

Coutts 'The Aristocrat who banks with Coutts.'—Marco Palmieri (G). The banking house originated in a goldsmith's and moneylender's business in the Strand in about 1690 and was later given the name of Coutts's Bank after James and Thomas Coutts had greatly developed the business. It was taken over by the National Provincial Bank in 1919.

Cowley, William Appointed associate conductor and chorus master of D'Oyly Carte in 1970, William Cowley was born in Douglas, Isle of Man, where he studied music and appeared professionally as accompanist and as flugel-horn and cornet player in brass bands. He conducted choirs and operatic performances before joining D'Oyly Carte.

COX AND BOX Though this lively little piece is not *Gilbert* and Sullivan, it finds its place here for several reasons. It marked Sullivan's first departure from the 'serious' music by which he was then known. It was the means whereby Sullivan's name first appeared on a playbill and, when German Reed revived it at his Royal Gallery of Illustration, the names of Gilbert and Sullivan first appeared on a bill together. It was presented with a piece by Gilbert called *No Cards*.

Cox and Box came about through a street meeting between Sullivan and F. C. Burnand, prominent *Punch* writer and later its editor, who said that he had been working on a version of a farce called *Box and Cox* by J. Maddison Morton for private presentation among friends and wondered whether Sullivan would write the music for it. Sullivan at once agreed and, with the names of the original title reversed, it had its private performance in 1867, with George du Maurier, who later wrote the novel *Trilby*, playing the part of Box. There was a charity performance at the Adelphi Theatre, organised by the *Punch* staff for a former colleague, and in 1869 German Reed presented it for a run at the Royal Gallery of Illustration. Meanwhile, Sullivan and Burnand had collaborated in *The Contrabandista*, put on by German Reed at the St George's Opera House. It is played from time to time by D'Oyly Carte with one of the shorter operas.

Cox and Box, which has the sub-title *The Long-Lost Brothers*, is described as a 'triumviretta in one act'. The scene is a lodging-house run by a crafty old soldier called Bouncer, who lets off the same room to two different men, one a journeyman hatter called Cox, who works during the day, and the other a journeyman printer called Box, who works at night. Whenever the situation seems to be getting awkward, as it does when Cox is given a day off from work, Bouncer's device is to burst into songs of a military nature in recollection of his Army days.

After a brisk overture Bouncer regales the not-very-enchanted Cox with a martial 'Rataplan' but Cox, whose wood and coals have a way of mysteriously disappearing, is getting suspicious and, when Bouncer is trying to beat a tactful retreat, endeavours to detain him in the duet 'Stay, Bouncer, Stay'. It is Cox who departs and in comes Box, who is also becoming suspicious about the various goings-on. But he sings himself to sleep with a lullaby which is rather charming, even though it has the absurd first line 'Hushed is the bacon on the grid.' In due course Cox and Box meet and there is a duet, 'Who are you, sir?' which becomes a trio when Bouncer bursts in with a vigorous 'Rataplan' in the effort to divert attention. Forced into a corner, he agrees to get ready another little room.

Left alone, Box and Cox decide that they may as well put up with each other for the time being and they join in a duet serenade 'The Buttercup'. When they fall to talking about themselves, Box tells how he was about to be married but, deciding to get out of it on the ground of unworthiness, was threatened with an action for breach of promise. So he decided to do a disappearing act by leaving a bundle of clothes on the edge of a cliff, with a note addressed to his Penelope Ann. The name at once rings a bell with Cox and a little questioning reveals that she is the same Penelope Ann to whom *he* is engaged. There is nothing else for it. They call for Bouncer to send in a brace of pistols but he brings instead a note which he had forgotten to give to Cox. It is from Penelope Ann, telling him that she now intends to marry a Mr Knox. Cox and Box decide that their plights have so much in common that they must be long-lost brothers, a fact which is at once proved when they find that *neither* has a strawberry mark on his left arm! And so to a gay finale, 'My hand upon it,' with Bouncer joining them in 'Rataplan'.

Crichton 'A Crichton of early romance.'—Robin Oakapple (R). The reference is to the Admirable Crichton, the name given to James Crichton, 16th-century Scottish traveller and scholar. He also established a reputation as a swordsman in Spain, where he was eventually killed in a street brawl.

'Criminal cried, as he dropped him down, The' Trio for Ko-Ko, Pitti-Sing and Pooh-Bah, in which they 'describe' the execution that never took place (M).

Cripps, Mrs (HMS) *Contralto* Better known as Little Buttercup, the Portsmouth bumboat woman.

Criticism Though Gilbert was decidedly testy about criticism of his own work, he was forthright enough about other people's efforts when he used to write criticism as a young man. For instance: 'With every disposition to deal gently with a very charming young lady, it is impossible to say that Miss Bateman's appearance in this lively little piece is at all calculated to advance her professional reputation. It is really time that the truth were spoken about this young lady; she is not and, as far as we can form an opinion, never will be a great actress. . . . It is only fair to Miss Bateman to state that that dismal actor Mr. Jordan was playing in the same piece, and it is impossible to say how much his depressing presence may have told upon the animal spirits of the audience.'

The young Sullivan, too, had strong views. As a 15-year-old chorister he wrote home: 'I enjoyed the Philharmonic very much —all except Rubinstein. [This was the Russian composer-pianist

Anton Rubinstein, who visited London in 1857.] He has wonderful strength in the wrists, and particularly so in octave passages, but there is a good deal of claptrap about him. As for his composition, it was a disgrace to the Philharmonic. I never heard such wretched nonsensical rubbish; not two bars of melody or harmony throughout. . . .'

Giving evidence in a court case, Gilbert agreed that he preferred to read unfavourable criticism of his plays. As he explained, 'I know how good I am, but I do not know how bad I am.'

The phrase 'funny without being vulgar' is usually credited to Gilbert in criticism of Sir Herbert Tree as Hamlet. Bernard Shaw, however, informed Hesketh Pearson (*Gilbert and Sullivan*) that Gilbert had told him that Tree himself had invented it and fathered it upon Gilbert.

Gilbert does not seem to have had a very high regard for Shakespeare. As he once put it to George Grossmith: 'If you promise me faithfully not to mention this to a single person, not even to your best friend, I don't think Shakespeare rollicking.' On another occasion he demonstrated the obscurity of Shakespeare by quoting: 'I would as lief be thrust through a quicket hedge as cry Pooh to a callow throstle.' His companion proceeded to explain its meaning but admitted that he could not recall which play the quotation came from. Said Gilbert: 'I've just invented it—and jolly good Shakespeare too!'

As witness in a court action, he said of one branch of entertainment: 'I call it bad and the managers call it musical comedy.'

Somebody asked Gilbert if he had been to see Irving in *Faust*. 'I go to the pantomime,' said Gilbert, 'only at Christmas.'

Cross, Emily As Miss Everard had been hurt in an accident, Emily Cross became the first artist to play the role of Ruth (PP) in the London production.

Cuneiform 'I can write a washing bill in Babylonic cuneiform.'— Major-General Stanley (PP). An ancient form of impressed script.

Cymon (T) Member of a travelling theatrical company, played by Miss L. Wilson.

Cyril (PI) *Tenor* Durward Lely was the first artist to play the role of Cyril, one of Hilarion's friends.

Cytherian 'Never doubting that for Cytherian posies he would gather aught but roses.'—Mad Margaret (R). In mythology, Cythera, off the Peloponnese, was the island where Aphrodite, the Greek Venus, rose from the sea.

YE GREENERY-YALLERY GROSVENOR GALLERY ONE

Daly, Dr (S) *Baritone* Vicar of Ploverleigh, originally played by Rutland Barrington, the first of his series of leading roles in the operas.

'Dance a cachucha, fandango, bolero' Chorus and dance (G).

Dances¹ Dance a cachucha, fandango, bolero.'—(G) All are lively Spanish dances.
  'Now a gavotte perform sedately.'—Duke of Plaza-Toro (G). An old dance in 4/4 time.
  Jack Point (Y) has his own specialities: 'We can dance you saraband, gondolet, carole, Pimpernel, or Jumping Joan.' The most familiar of these is the saraband, Spanish in origin and written in triple time. The carole was a dance accompanied by a song.
  'That is one of our blameless dances.'—The reformed Mad Margaret (R).

Daphne (T) Member of a travelling theatrical company, played by Annie Tremaine, one of the Gaiety company and formerly on the music-halls. In her later career she was with the Carl Rosa Opera Company under the name of Madame Amadi.

Daphnephoric 'With a Daphnephoric bound.'—Chorus of maidens (P). In mythology Daphne, daughter of the river-god, fled from the love of Apollo and was turned into a laurel tree.

Darnton, Leo An artist whose smile was as attractive as his tenor voice, Leo Darnton joined D'Oyly Carte as a principal in 1920, singing Duke of Dunstable (P), Tolloller (I), Cyril (PI), Nanki-Poo (M) and Leonard Meryll (Y). In the following few years he added Box (C), Defendent (J), Ralph Rackstraw (HMS), Richard Dauntless (R) and Fairfax (Y).

Darwin 'Darwinian Man, though well-behaved, at best is only a monkey shaved!'—Lady Psyche (PI). Charles Darwin's *The Descent of Man*, which caused a sensation, was published in 1871, just thirteen years before the first performance of *Princess Ida*.

Dauntless, Richard (R) *Tenor* Dick Dauntless, the forthright foster-brother of Robin Oakapple, was originally played by the Scottish tenor Durward Lely. It was Lely who, during rehearsal, casually suggested that, after his first entrance and his song about the encounter with the 'darned Mounseer,' Richard might dance a hornpipe. Gilbert immediately seized upon the idea and sent Lely off to a dancing master. Since then every Dick Dauntless has had to learn to execute a sprightly hornpipe.

Davies, Aileen Joining D'Oyly Carte in 1923, Aileen Davies at once played several of the smaller roles. Two years later she took over such leading mezzo-soprano parts as Hebe (HMS), Angela (P), Iolanthe, Mad Margaret (R), Phoebe (Y) and Tessa (G), adding Pitti-Sing (M) the following year. She was with the company until 1928.

Deadeye, Dick (HMS) *Bass* One is tempted to wonder how Dick, with his ugly twisted form, ever managed to get into the Queen's Navee in the first place. Any idea that he got that way in the course of service before the mast is discredited out of his own mouth. Agreeing that you can't expect a chap with a name like Dick Deadeye to be a popular character, he declares, 'From such a face and form as mine the noblest sentiments sound like the black utterances of a depraved imagination. It is human nature—I am resigned.' Gilbert picked for him not only a name which is sinister in sound but also one which has a nautical flavour. A deadeye in shipping parlance is a wooden block used for tightening or extending the shrouds of a ship. The role of Dick Deadeye, able seaman (!), was first played by Richard Temple.

Dean, John He was with D'Oyly Carte for twenty-one years, singing leading tenor roles for the greater part of that time. He went into the chorus in 1925 and two years later sang his first small part, First Yeoman (Y). There followed Defendant (J), Francesco (G), Luiz (G), Box (C), Earl Tolloller (I), Cyril (PI), Nanki-Poo (M), Leonard Meryll (Y), Frederic (PP), Duke of Dunstable (P), Richard

Dauntless (R), Fairfax (Y), Ralph Rackstraw (HMS), to which he added Marco (G) just before the war. He left the company in 1946.

'Dear father, why leave your bed' Mabel's solo at the opening of the second act (PP).

'Dear friends, take pity on my lot' Ensemble for Constance, Notary, Aline, Alexis and Chorus (S).

'Death to the invader' Opening chorus to the third act (PI).

Defendant (J) *Tenor* The original was Walter H. Fisher.

Defoe Daniel Defoe (1660–1731) is mentioned in Colonel Calverley's song (P). His most famous character is referred to by the Duke of Plaza-Toro: 'Though Robinson Crusoe would jib at their wearing apparel.' (G).

Della Cruscan 'You are not Della Cruscan. You are not even Early English.'—Lady Jane (P). The Della Cruscans, a group of affected young English poets in 18th-century Florence, took their name from the Accademia della Crusca, founded for the purification of the Italian language.

Denny, W. H. The original Wilfred Shadbolt (Y), Don Alhambra (G) and Schaphio (U), Denny was born in Birmingham in 1853 and had a great deal of stage experience before joining D'Oyly Carte for the first performance of *The Yeomen of the Guard* in 1888.

Designers From the earliest days of the D'Oyly Carte Company, first-class artists have been engaged for the scenery and costumes. Gilbert, himself a gifted artist, did detailed sketches for costumes for *Patience, Iolanthe, Princess Ida* and *Ruddigore*. Between the two world wars, Rupert D'Oyly Carte presented new productions of fourteen operas, artists involved being Hugo Rumbold (*Patience*), Percy Anderson (*Pirates, Yeomen, Trial, Ruddigore* and *Princess Ida*), Norman Wilkinson (*Iolanthe*), Charles Ricketts (*Mikado* and *Gondoliers*), George Sheringham (*Patience, Pinafore, Pirates* and *Iolanthe*) and Peter Goffin (*Yeomen*). Since World War II, a new look has been given to the operas by Peter Goffin (*Ruddigore, Mikado* and *Patience*), James Wade (*Princess Ida*), Stephen Bundy (*Gondoliers*), Luciana Arrighi and John Stoddart (*Gondoliers*) and Disley Jones (*Mikado*).

In connection with their season at the Royal Festival Hall, in 1971, the D'Oyly Carte Company put on the most comprehensive exhibition of stage and costume designs they had ever presented. The development of the visual side of the productions was interestingly outlined:

The three partners in the original productions of the Savoy Operas were, each in his own way, perfectionists. The books and music of the operas bear witness to this for two of the partners, but the important part played by Richard D'Oyly Carte—and later Rupert, his son—in the visual aspects of the operas is less well known. His employment of the best theatrical designers of the period established a tradition which is still in force to-day.

The designs of the earliest date are very different from those of to-day or even of the operas' middle years. The difference is not so much one of accuracy to a given period but of the way in which this is presented and of the less defined lines of the actual drawings, some of which are sufficiently vague in detail to constitute a real difficulty to the dressmaker. The details are sometimes blurred to make an attractive drawing somewhat difficult to reproduce in actuality. They are, in fact, attractive but rather imprecise working drawings. This can be explained by the fact that the designers of the earliest period were often closely connected with a professional costumier and even, in some instances, a part of such a firm. A comparison between the designs of Wilhelm in 1893 and of Percy Anderson's later designs in the early twenties with those of Charles Ricketts or Peter Goffin will show this difference of approach very clearly.

The earlier drawings are delightful dresses but are not an interpretation of character; those of the later designers are not only lovely in themselves but also illustrate the character for which they are designed. In the earlier designs the emphasis is on charm rather than on characterisation but, all the same, they must have made enchanting ensembles. The operas' later designers—Hugo Rumbold, Charles Ricketts, George Sheringham, Peter Goffin and Luciana Arrighi—have all been preoccupied with designs which were not only lovely in themselves but also viable interpretations of the actual characters and scenes.

Diana (T) An aged Olympian, played by Mrs H. Leigh.

Dickens Sullivan was a friend of the famous novelist who, when the composer was still very young, predicted a great future for him. On one occasion, Dickens acted as his guide on a tour of

Paris. Gilbert makes two references to Dickens: 'Narrative powers of Dickens and Thackeray'—Colonel Calverley (P); 'An Earl of Thackeray and p'r'aps a Duke of Dickens'—King Paramount (U).

Dickson, Muriel Known in the company as 'Poppy', she joined D'Oyly Carte in 1927 and, after several small parts, played the Plaintiff (J) in 1930. The following year she moved into a long line of major roles—Josephine (HMS), Mabel (PP), Patience, Phyllis (I), Lady Psyche (PI), Yum-Yum (M), Rose Maybud (R), Elsie Maynard (Y) and Gianetta (G). She added Aline (S) and Princess Ida in 1932 and remained with the company until 1935.

'Didst thou not, oh, Leonard Meryll' Couplets sung by the chorus of Yeomen about Leonard's courage (Y).

'Die is cast, The' Lisa's song in the finale to the first act (D).

Dionysiac 'Dionysiac or Bacchic.'—(D). Dionysus is the Greek name and Bacchus the Latin for the God of Wine.

Dithyrambic revels 'The dithyrambic revels of those undecorous days.'—(D). A dithyramb is an ancient Greek hymn to the God of Wine.

Dixon, Beryl A member of the D'Oyly Carte Company from 1951 until 1960, Beryl Dixon sang Peep-Bo (M) in her first season and later added Lady Angela (P), Leila (I), Melissa (PI), Ruth (R), Phoebe (Y) and Tessa (G).

D'Orsay 'The dash of a D'Orsay, divested of quackery.'—Colonel Calverley (P). Count D'Orsay (1801–52), a French dandy, lived in London for some years, his house in Kensington becoming famed as an intellectual and social centre.

Dow, Clara When Sadler's Wells Opera presented *Iolanthe* in 1962, Clara Dow was an honoured guest—understandably, for she was one of the last direct links with Gilbert. Born at King's Lynn in 1883, she sang in oratorio and in concerts after her studies at the Royal College of Music. As she used to tell, she began singing principal parts with D'Oyly Carte after, one day at rehearsal, Gilbert had been listening to an artist from the Carl Rosa Company singing beautifully but with indifferent diction. 'I didn't sit up all night for my words to be distorted by this damned Italian method!' he burst out. The singer left the stage in tears and Clara Dow was called from the chorus to continue the song. She sang her first principal part in 1907 and continued as a leading artist until 1914, her roles including Josephine (HMS), Mabel (PP), Patience, Phyllis (I), Princess Ida, Yum-Yum (M), Elsie Maynard (Y), her favourite part, Gianetta and Casilda (G). Clara Dow, who died at Epsom in 1969, was enthusiastically producing amateur societies into the 1960's.

Dow, Gerard 'I can tell undoubted Raphaels from Gerard Dows and Zoffanies.'—Major-General Stanley (PP). The reference is to Gerhard Dou (1613–75), a portrait and genre painter of Leyden and one-time pupil of Rembrandt.

D'Oyly Carte Island Richard D'Oyly Carte, a great lover of the Thames, lived for many years in Adelphi Terrace, near the Embankment and the Savoy Theatre. One of the social events of the Savoy company was their annual trip up the river, to the accompaniment of much feasting and singing. It was on one of these outings that Sullivan, at the steering wheel, nearly rammed a punt, apologising with the quip: 'I always thought I was a good contrapuntalist!' In earlier days, D'Oyly Carte had often spent summer holidays, camping and exploring the upper reaches of the Thames with his two sons, Lucas and Rupert. Eventually, in 1888, the year of *The Yeomen of the Guard*, he built himself a house on Eyot Island, near Shepperton Lock.

D'Oyly Carte Opera Company After the disintegration of the Comedy Opera Company through disagreements among the board of directors during the run of *HMS Pinafore* at the Opera Comique, Richard D'Oyly Carte entered into a new partnership with Gilbert and Sullivan in 1879 and for some time the company was billed as Mr D'Oyly Carte's Opera Company. D'Oyly Carte married as his second wife, Helen Lenoir, his secretary and general factotum and a woman of remarkable intelligence, imagination and abounding energy. On his death in 1901 Mrs D'Oyly Carte took over the direction of the company, managing the Savoy Theatre until 1909 and continuing to direct the opera company's touring activities until her death in 1913, when she was succeeded by her step-son, Rupert, as the sole director of affairs. Rupert D'Oyly Carte controlled the company for 35 years until his death in 1948 at the age of seventy-two. His only son had been killed in a car accident in Switzerland some years earlier and the direction of the company passed to Rupert's daughter, Miss Bridget D'Oyly Carte. As the time for the expiry of the copyright in the Gilbert and Sullivan operas approached, there was much speculation about the future of the company, but the position was made clear in a statement issued early in 1961: 'When the copyright in the Gilbert and Sullivan operas ends on December 31, 1961, the world-famous D'Oyly Carte Opera Company will continue touring in Great Britain and abroad under the auspices of the D'Oyly Carte Opera Trust. Bridget D'Oyly Carte has generously given her rights in the operas and in the existing company to a Trust which she will endow and of which she will be an active member. Her gifts will include the whole of her opera organisation; all stage settings and band parts; the benefit of all her contracts; and her gramophone record, film and television rights. Thus, under the auspices of the Trust, the company that sprang from the original Gilbert, Sullivan and D'Oyly Carte partnership, and whose amazing story of success and popularity is unique in theatrical history, will go on in the future to serve the great audiences on both sides of the world that love to see and hear their performances.'

Dragons (Reluctant) There is a good deal of blood and thunder in the operas, or at any rate, there is plenty of colourful talk about such matters. Indeed, it is all talk. Nobody gets hurt. True, the 'humane' Mikado derives evident satisfaction from discussion of the details of torture and execution, but most of the others involved in situations of violence show a distinct reluctance. The 'execution' of Nanki-Poo (M), described with such a wealth of corroborative detail by Ko-Ko, Pitti-Sing and Pooh-Bah, never took place. The Lord High Executioner himself admits: 'You don't suppose that, as a humane man, I'd have accepted the post if I hadn't thought the duties were purely nominal? I can't kill anything!' Wilfred Shadbolt, revelling in the titles of Head Jailer and Assistant Tormentor, can boast: 'In the nice regulation of a thumbscrew—in the hundredth part of a single revolution lieth all the difference between stony reticence and a torrent of impulsive unbosoming that the pen can scarcely follow. Ha! ha! I am a mad wag.' But he has confessed earlier: 'I didn't become a head-jailer because I like head-jailing. I didn't become an assistant-tormentor because I like assistant-tormenting.' And Wilfred's dramatic 'shooting' of Fairfax is as imaginary as the 'execution' of Nanki-Poo. There was never a less efficient lot of wrongdoers than the Pirates (PP), as Frederic frankly tells them: 'You are too tender-hearted. For instance, you make a point of never attacking a weaker party than yourselves, and when you attack a stronger party you invariably get thrashed. . . .

Then, again, you make a point of never attacking an orphan!' With all their 'Tarantara!' the Police, setting out to exterminate the Pirates, are in no hurry for a fight. Even the Sergeant points out that the reason why a policeman's lot is not a happy one is that 'Our feelings with difficulty we smother, when constabulary duty's to be done.'

Gilbert undoubtedly enjoyed the melodramatic and in his private affairs could breathe fire when occasion demanded, but in later years, when he was living the life of a country gentleman, he confessed, in the manner of Ko-Ko: 'I have never wittingly killed a beetle.'

Dramaleigh, Lord (U) *Baritone* The British Lord Chamberlain was first played by Scott Russell.

Dramatists It was from T. W. Robertson, experienced man of the theatre, that Gilbert learned much about the art of the dramatist and particularly about the art of theatrical production. But he always had a workmanlike approach to the job, tending to deprecate its importance as an intellectual exercise: 'It does not call for the highest order of intellect—it demands shrewdness of observation, a nimble brain, a faculty for expressing oneself concisely, a sense of balance both in the construction of plots and in the construction of sentences.' He received £30 for his first play, *Dulcamara*, and, once the deal was safely concluded, the manager offered him a piece of advice: 'Never sell a play like that so cheaply again.' Gilbert took his advice to heart. He was always money-conscious, which is not the same as saying that he was mean. He was rather as Shaw was in later years, insistent that the artist, like any other skilled workman, should be fully rewarded for his efforts. The 'romantic' idea of the artist starving in a garret had no appeal for him whatsoever.

Drinking But there's a distinction decided—
    A difference truly immense—
    When the drink that you drink is provided, provided,
    At somebody else's expense.'
               —Baroness von Krankenfeldt (D)
After a man had given him offence, Gilbert contemplated inviting him to dinner: 'I have an avenging sherry at one-and-nine which I think will astonish his digestion.'

Drummond-Grant, Ann Though she later became noted in the leading contralto roles, Ann Drummond-Grant, who died in 1959, first sang as a soprano. She had played in amateur productions and in grand opera and musical comedy before joining D'Oyly Carte in 1933, remaining for five years, during the last few months of which she became a principal, singing Plaintiff (J), Celia (I), Psyche (PI), Zorah (R), Fiametta (G), Josephine (HMS), Elsie Maynard (Y), Patience, Aline (S) and Phyllis (I). After leaving the company she played in operettas such as *Waltzes from Vienna* and in summer shows, but in 1950 she returned to the company and the following year took over the principal contralto roles from Ella Halman. Ann Drummond-Grant was married to Isidore Godfrey, D'Oyly Carte's musical director.

Dummkopf, Ernest (D) *Tenor* The theatrical manager was first played by Charles Kenningham.

Dunstable, Lieut. the Duke of (P) *Tenor* This officer of the Dragoon Guards was originally played by Durward Lely.

Dymott, Mr The first artist to play Bob Beckett (HMS).

'Eagle high in cloudland soaring' Unaccompanied chorus (U).

Easton, Florence The original player of the role of Phylla (U).

Edith (PP) *Mezzo-soprano* Julia Gwynne was the first to play the role in the London production.

Editors 'The Editor of a scurrilous paper can stand a good deal—he takes a private thrashing as a matter of course—it's considered in his salary—but no gentleman likes to be publicly flogged.'—Scaphio (U).

In writing this, Gilbert may have had in mind an episode in the life of his own father who one day stormed into the office of a weekly review, demanding to see the editor. He was asked the nature of his business. 'To thrash him!' he roared. Though Gilbert seems to have inherited his fiery temper from his father, the same cannot be said of his literary leanings. Indeed, the reverse appears to have been the case. Gilbert, Senior, took to writing novels late in life. As his son said of him: 'My father never had an exaggerated idea of my abilities. He thought that if I could write, anybody could, and forthwith he began to do so.'

Elburn, Beatrice Joining the D'Oyly Carte chorus in 1924, Beatrice Elburn was soon singing the roles of Kate (PP), Sacharissa (PI), Leila (I), Peep-Bo (M), Ruth (R) and Giulia (G). Later she sang Lady Angela (P), Iolanthe, Margaret (R) and Tessa (G) before leaving the company in 1930.

Ella, The Lady (P) *Soprano* This 'rapturous maiden' was originally played by Miss Fortescue.

Ellison, Jon Born in Whitchurch, Shropshire, Jon Ellison sang for seven years as boy soprano at St Alkmund's Church there, trained with John Bratby at Wistaston, Cheshire, and continued his studies at the Guildhall School of Music and Drama. In 1951 he won the solo baritone prize at Llangollen International Eisteddfod and has appeared on television and the concert platform and in pantomime. His principal baritone roles with D'Oyly Carte include the Usher (J), Bosun (HMS), Solicitor (P), Scynthius (PI) and Old Adam (R). He is married to Joy Mornay, a former member of the D'Oyly Carte Company. His hobbies include the keeping of pet turtles.

Eloquence 'In me there meet a combination of antipathetic elements which are at eternal war with one another. Driven hither by objective influences—thither by subjective emotions—wafted one moment into blazing day, by mocking hope—plunged the next into the Cimmerian darkness of tangible despair, I am but a living ganglion of irreconcilable antagonisms,' declares the humble sailor, Ralph Rackstraw. (Josephine: 'His simple eloquence goes to my heart'.) (HMS).

Elsa (D) *Mezzo-soprano* Ethel Wilson was the first artist to play Elsa, a member of Dummkopf's theatrical company.

Elysian Fields 'What's the use of yearning for Elysian Fields when you know you can't get 'em, and would only let 'em out on building leases if you had 'em?'—Reginald Bunthorne (P).
  'The sudden transition is simply Elysian.' (R).
  The Elysian Fields were the abode of the blessed in Greek mythology.

Emetical 'Your placidity emetical.'—Lady Jane (P). In modern parlance, sick-making.

Encores Many people will remember when the D'Oyly Carte Company used to give almost unlimited encores. They happened automatically, to the delight of more 'traditional' members of the audience and the irritation of some others. In more recent years the practice has become much more flexible, the encores being geared to the circumstances of the evening. As can be imagined, the change, while satisfying some opera-goers, did not at all please others.
  Rutland Barrington once approached Gilbert with the suggestion

that, as the audience always demanded an encore to one of his numbers, it might be a good idea to write an additional 'encore' verse. Gilbert dismissed the suggestion with a brusque, 'Encore means sing it again.'

Isidore Godfrey recalls: 'It was around 1930 that Rupert D'Oyly Carte decided that something really must be done about the encores. The performances were tending to go on for ever—a couple of hand-claps and the artists would be away again. One of the first cuts made in the encores was in the song of the Duke and Duchess in *Gondoliers*—Henry Lytton and Bertha Lewis. They were both very upset and seemed to think that it was some reflection on them. I remember that Lytton came back to the stage, threw up his arms, and stalked off. Of course, while some people agreed that the restriction of the encores was to be welcomed, others were highly annoyed about it. It is difficult to please all the people all the time.'

'His series of judgments in F sharp minor, given *andante* in six-eight time, are among the most remarkable effects ever produced in a Court of Chancery. He is, perhaps, the only living instance of a judge whose decrees have received the honour of a double *encore*.'
—Lord Mountararat in praise of the Lord Chancellor (I).

Engaged, or Cheviot's Choice Gilbert's farcical play of this name was presented at the Haymarket Theatre in 1877, shortly before *The Sorcerer* was produced at the Opera Comique. In 1962, two lecturers at Bristol University, George Rowell and Kenneth Mobbs, wedded it to Sullivan music other than that of the famous operas. The resulting comic opera was very well received when presented by Bristol Opera School, followed by productions at the Theatre Royal, Windsor, and in London by the Grosvenor Light Opera Company and at the Guildhall School of Music and Drama.

The plot concerns a young man who discovers on his wedding day that he may already be married by Scottish law and there are complications brought about by people whose incomes depend upon his marital status. Sullivan's overture 'Di Ballo' is used to introduce the work and also to provide an effective finale to the second act. The original play has been cut to allow twenty-two musical numbers to be introduced.

Epithalamia 'Let furtive epithalamia resound through these ancient halls.'—Baroness von Krakenfeldt (D). An epithalamium was a song of blessing on a newly married couple.

Equality Thinking of his own situation, Sir Joseph Porter (HMS) comes out with a firm pronouncement in favour of equality, so far as marriage is concerned, at any rate. It is his official view that there is no reason why a man like himself should not marry a woman of lower social status. But he forgets that the argument can be taken further. Encouraged by his judgment, Josephine on her part sees no reason why she, a captain's daughter, should not marry a mere sailor.

Alexis (S), in the full flush of his own happiness is all for the breaking down of artificial barriers for everyone, but he finds that the cause has so far progressed slowly.

Alexis: 'Still, I have made some converts to the principle that men and women should be coupled in matrimony without distinction of rank. I have lectured on the subject at Mechanics' Institutes and the mechanics were unanimous in favour of my views. I have preached in workhouses, beershops and Lunatic Asylums and I have been received with enthusiasm. I have addressed navvies on the advantages that would accrue to them if they married wealthy ladies of rank, and not a navvy dissented!'

Aline: 'Noble fellows! And yet there are those who hold that the uneducated classes are not open to argument! And what do the countesses say?'

Alexis: 'Why, at present, it can't be denied, the aristocracy hold aloof.'

Aline: 'Ah, the working man is the true Intelligence after all!'

Alexis: 'He is a noble creature when he is sober.'

Equality is, of course, the great idea of Marco and Giuseppe Palmieri when they reign jointly as King. 'When every one is somebodee, then no one's anybody!' as Don Alhambra sings. (G).

Estates The principal figures in the Gilbert and Sullivan story left estates as follows:

1900	Sir Arthur Sullivan	£54,527
1901	Richard D'Oyly Carte	£240,817
1911	Sir W. S. Gilbert	£111,971
1913	Mrs Richard D'Oyly Carte (Helen Lenoir)	£117,670
1948	Rupert D'Oyly Carte	£288,436

Sullivan, it might be mentioned, was a great lover of the tables at Monte Carlo and also, at an early stage, lost nearly all his savings through the bankruptcy of a firm of brokers.

Etiquette 'The man who bites his bread, or eats peas with a knife, I look upon as a lost creature, and he who has not acquired the proper way of entering or leaving a room is the object of my pitying horror. There are those in this village who bite their nails, dear aunt, and nearly all are wont to use their pocket combs in public places.'—Rose Maybud (R).

Evans, Eleanor Stage director of the D'Oyly Carte Company in 1949 and later Director of Productions, Eleanor Evans sang in the chorus from 1921 until 1937, also playing Plaintiff (J) and Ada and Lady Psyche (PI), and returned to the chorus from 1941 until 1944. She was married to Darrell Fancourt.

Everard, Henriette She created the roles of Mrs Partlet (S) and Little Buttercup (HMS) and came in for particular commendation for the way in which she carried on with the latter part during the 'battle' of the Opera Comique when the directors of the Comedy Opera Company tried to seize the scenery and properties. She was chosen to create the role of Ruth (PP) but met with an accident before the first night and the part was taken over by Emily Cross. She did, however, play the part in some later performances. She died in 1881.

'Every day, as the days roll on' Solo for Zorah, the bridesmaid, at the opening of the opera (R).

Evett, Robert Principal tenor with D'Oyly Carte at the beginning of the century, Robert Evett made his first stage appearance with the company on tour and his first London appearance at the Savoy Theatre in *The Gondoliers* in 1898. He was born in Warwickshire in 1874.

'Expressive glances shall be our lances' Trio for Hilarion, Cyril and Florian (PI).

Eyre, Marjorie After training in Derby, her home-town, Marjorie Eyre studied at the Royal College of Music and joined D'Oyly Carte in 1924, singing principal soprano roles the following year. Later she turned to the soubrette parts, in which she continued until she left the company in 1946. Her roles included Constance (S), Hebe (HMS), Edith (PP), Patience, Angela, Saphir and Ella (P), Iolanthe, Phyllis and Celia (I), Melissa (PI), Yum-Yum and Pitti-Sing (M), Rose Maybud and Mad Margaret (R), Phoebe (Y), Tessa and Giulia (G). In 1926 Marjorie Eyre married baritone Leslie Rands and they were together throughout their D'Oyly Carte careers in Britain, Canada and America and with the Australia and New Zealand Gilbert and Sullivan Company in 1949, 1950 and 1951.

Fairfax, Colonel (Y) *Tenor* Colonel Fairfax, condemned to die on the block but saved by a clever trick, was first played by Courtice Pounds. The first verse of his lovely tenor aria, 'Is Life a Boon?' was chosen by Gilbert to be inscribed on the memorial to Sullivan on the Victoria Embankment.

'Fair is Rose as the bright May-day' Chorus of professional bridesmaids at the opening of the opera (R).

'Fair moon, to thee I sing' Captain Corcoran's song, to mandolin accompaniment, which opens the second act (HMS).

Fancourt, Darrell Though audiences probably associated him most closely with the role of the Mikado, which he played more than 3,000 times, Darrell Fancourt used to say that his favourite parts were Dick Deadeye (HMS) and Sir Roderick Murgatroyd (R). He had an immensely impressive presence and by his style and manner appeared on the stage to be bigger than in fact he was. He was born in London in 1888, educated at Bedford School and in Germany, and his singing teachers included Lilli Lehmann, Signor Randegger and Sir Henry Wood. He had wide concert experience in this country and on the Continent but, before joining D'Oyly Carte in 1920, had appeared only once on the stage—singing Prince

'Fare thee well, attractive stranger' Ensemble for the Queen and the fairies after their first meeting with Strephon (I).

'Farewell, my own' Octet as Ralph Rackstraw is led away in custody (HMS).

'Farewell! Thou hadst my heart' Rose Maybud's solo (R).

Galitzky in Borodin's opera *Prince Igor*, conducted by Albert Coates in the 1919 Beecham season at Covent Garden. His roles included Sir Marmaduke Pointdextre (S), Dick Deadeye (HMS), Pirate King (PP), Colonel Calverley (P), Earl of Mountararat (I), Arac (PI), Mikado, Sir Roderick Murgatroyd (R) and Sergeant Meryll (Y), to which he added Bouncer (C) during an American season. Awarded the O.B.E. in the Coronation Honours, Darrell Fancourt continued his association with D'Oyly Carte until 1953. In that season at Sadler's Wells Theatre he was to have made his farewell appearance as the Mikado but fell ill before the performance and died a few weeks later at the age of sixty-five.

Though he was renowned for his security and reliability as an artist, one of the stories told of him concerns a rare moment of absent-mindedness. During an interval of the *Yeomen* he became engrossed in a book and suddenly heard his name being called. He rushed on to the stage just in time for his entrance—but forgetting that he had taken off his wig and was still wearing his specs! The unexpected apparition moved those on the stage to laughter but the show went on.

Ferguson, Catherine In her first season in 1917, Catherine Ferguson sang nine of the mezzo-soprano roles, among them Constance (S), Hebe (HMS), Iolanthe, Pitti-Sing (M), Phoebe (Y) and Tessa (G). She later added Mad Margaret (R) and remained with D'Oyly Carte until 1922.

Fiametta (G) *Soprano* A contadina (Italian peasant), originally played by Nellie Lawrence.

Fielding 'The humour of Fielding'—Colonel Calverley (P). The reference is to Henry Fielding, the London magistrate and writer (1707–54), whose most famous novel is *Tom Jones*.

Fildes 'Lord Fildes and Viscount Millais (when they come) we'll welcome sweetly.'—King Paramount (U). Sir Luke Fildes, English artist (1844–1927), painted several Royal portraits. His well-known painting, 'The Doctor', is in the Tate Gallery, London.

Findlay, Josephine The first artist to play the role of Zorah, one of the professional bridesmaids (R).

First Nights It was usually Gilbert's practice to spend his time during a première pacing restlessly about the Thames Embankment near the Savoy Theatre. In his earliest days, however, he seems to have been much less apprehensive. Of the performance of his first burlesque, *Dulcamara, or The Little Duck and the Great Quack*, he recalled later: 'It never entered my head that the piece would fail and I even had the audacity to pre-invite a dozen people to supper after the performance. The piece succeeded, as it happened, and the supper-party finished the evening appropriately enough. But I have since learned something about the risks inseparable from every first night and I would as soon invite friends to supper after a forthcoming amputation at the hip-joint.'

He did, at any rate, manage to keep up an appearance of equanimity, as on the first night of *Princess Ida*. A voluble and excited Frenchman, who had been responsible for the armour in the production, rushed up to him and enthused: 'Monsieur, savez-vous que vous avez là un succès solide?' 'Oh, I think it's going very well,' allowed Gilbert. 'Mais, vous êtes si calme!' exclaimed the Frenchman in amazement. ('I think he wanted me to kiss all the carpenters,' commented Gilbert.)

'First you're born—and I'll be bound you find a dozen strangers round you' King Paramount's song (U).

Fishe, Scott The original Mr Goldbury (U) and Prince of Monte Carlo (D), Scott Fishe sang also Florian (PI) and the Mikado.

Fisher, Walter H. The original player of the role of the Defendant (J). He also played Grosvenor (P) in a tour some years later.

Fitzaltamont, Mr Originator of the role of Tom Tucker, the midshipmite (HMS). It seems, however, that this was no more than a stage name, given to whichever youngster played the part. As *Pinafore* was first performed in 1878 and 'Mr. Fitzaltamont' was still playing the part on tour up to 1888, he could hardly remain the same diminutive figure for ten years!

Fitzbattleaxe, Captain (U) *Tenor* Charles Kenningham was the first artist to play Captain Fitzbattleaxe of the 1st Life Guards.

'Five years have flown since I took wing' Princess Zara's solo on her return to Utopia from England, with chorus of her escort of the 1st Life Guards (U).

Flattery 'Are you a courtier? Come, then, ply your trade. Tell me some lies.'—King Gama (PI).

The Duke of Dunstable (P) uses the word 'toffee' and explains: 'For 'toffee' read flattery, adulation and abject deference, carried to such a pitch that I began, at last, to think that man was born bent at an angle of forty-five degrees!'

Fleta (I) *Soprano* One of the leading fairies, Fleta was first played by Sybil Grey.

Flirting A new law in Titipu makes the crime of flirting punishable by death.

Yum-Yum: 'To flirt is capital.'
Nanki-Poo: 'It *is* capital.' (M).

Florian (PI) *Baritone* Charles Ryley was the first artist to play the role of Florian, one of Hilarion's friends.

Flowers of Progress, The Alternative title of *Utopia, Limited*.

'Flowers that bloom in the spring, The' Nanki-Poo and Ko-Ko, with Yum-Yum, Pitti-Sing and Pooh-Bah (M).

Flynn, Radley In his first season with D'Oyly Carte in 1928, Radley Flynn sang Giorgio (G) and during his 23 years with the company his roles included Foreman and Usher (J), Bob Beckett and Dick Deadeye (HMS), Pirate King (PP), Private Willis (I), Scynthius (PI), Mikado and Go-To (M), Old Adam (R) and Sergeant Meryll (Y). He is married to contralto Ella Halman.

'For a month to dwell in a dungeon cell' Trio for Arac, Guron and Scynthius (PI).

Foreman of the Jury (J) *Bass* The original player was C. Kelleher.

'For every one who feels inclined' Marco and Giuseppe's pronouncement of their policy as joint King—'And all shall equal be.' (G).

Forgery 'If a man can't forge his own will, whose will can he forge?'—Robin Oakapple (R).

'For he's gone and married Yum-Yum' Finale to the opera (M).

'For riches and rank I do not long' Phyllis's ballad in the finale to the first act (I).

'For some ridiculous reason' Chant by the Pirate King, in which he contends that, because of his leap-year birthday, Frederic is 'only five and a little bit over' (PP).

Fortescue, Miss A noted beauty of the day, Miss Fortescue was the first artist to play Lady Ella (P) and Celia (I). She had had earlier association with Gilbert when she played Galatea in his straight play, *Pygmalion and Galatea*. In 1884 she figured, as Emily May Finney, in a much-publicised breach-of-promise action, in which she was awarded £10,000 damages against the Hon Arthur William Carrier.

'For the merriest fellows are we, tra la' Antonio's song with the chorus at the start of the opera (G).

Fra Angelican 'How Fra Angelican!'—Lady Saphir (P). Fra Angelico (c. 1387–1455), famed Italian painter of religious subjects.

Francesca di Rimini More usually Francesca *da* Rimini, Bunthorne's reference (P) is to the young married woman who guiltily loved her husband's younger brother Paolo, as a result of which both were put to death. Her story is told in Dante's *Inferno*.

Frederic (PP) *Tenor* In the London production George Power was the first artist to play Frederic, who is mistakenly apprenticed to a pirate instead of to a pilot.

'Free from his fetters grim' Colonel Fairfax's ballad (Y).

'From the sunny Spanish shore' Entrance of the Duke and Duchess of Plaza-Toro, with their daughter Casilda and their attendant Luiz (G).

Fryatt, John Later a leading character tenor with Sadler's Wells Opera, John Fryatt was formerly with D'Oyly Carte. Joining the chorus in 1952, he soon moved into principal roles which included Defendant (J), Hilarion (PI), Leonard Meryll (Y) and Luiz (G).

Gama, King (PI) *Baritone* George Grossmith was the first artist to play the role of King Gama, whom everybody says is 'such a disagreeable man.'

Gardiner, Evelyn Joining D'Oyly Carte in 1921, Evelyn Gardiner was in the chorus for three years, also playing Inez (G) and occasionally the Duchess of Plaza-Toro (G). She was away from the company until 1936, returning to take over the long list of leading contralto roles from Dorothy Gill. She left the company in 1939 and went out to Australia.

Garnet, Sir 'Skill of Sir Garnet in thrashing a cannibal.'—Colonel Calverley (P). Sir Garnet Wolseley, later Viscount Wolseley (1833–1913) was a distinguished British soldier, who led campaigns in many parts of the world, his last active service being the Nile Expedition for the relief of General Gordon.

Garry, Herbert Between 1922 and 1924, Herbert Garry sang the Defendant (J), Earl Tolloller (I), Box (C) and Leonard Meryll (Y). He returned to D'Oyly Carte in the war years, singing the Duke of Dunstable (P), Nanki-Poo (M), Fairfax (Y) and Marco (G) between 1939 and 1946.

Gask 'Let Gask (secede) from Gask.'—Princess Ida. Gasks were well-known textile merchants in Oxford Street, London.

'Gently, gently' Trio for Hilarion, Cyril and Florian (PI).

Gerolstein 'It's a very good part in Gerolstein.'—Julia Jellicoe (D). The operettas of Jacques Offenbach (1819–80) had a great vogue in London in the sixties and seventies of the last century—

until, that is, Gilbert and Sullivan came on the scene. *The Grand Duchess of Gerolstein* was, however, revived at the Savoy Theatre in 1897, the year after *The Grand Duke*.

Getting on in the World The operas provide numerous hints on the art of getting on. The Learned Judge (J), for instance, took the early precaution of falling in love with 'a rich attorney's elderly, ugly daughter.' Sir Joseph Porter (HMS) began as an office boy, polishing up the handle of the big front door, but, by carefully avoiding ever going to sea, eventually became 'Ruler of the Queen's Navee.' The Duke of Plaza-Toro (G) makes the fullest use of the publicity value of his title in order to keep his head above water. Robin Oakapple (R), however, knows to his cost that modesty is a fatal handicap:

> If you wish in the world to advance,
> Your merits you're bound to enhance,
> You must stir it and stump it,
> And blow your own trumpet,
> Or, trust me, you haven't a chance!

And of course, there must always be jobs for the boys—Marco,' on taking on the joint Kingship of Barataria: 'And we may take our friends with us, and give them places about the Court?' Don Alhambra: 'Undoubtedly. That's always done!' (G).

Gianetta (G) *Soprano* Geraldine Ulmar was the original Gianetta, a contadina (Italian peasant). But Cyril Rollins and R. John Witts in *The D'Oyly Carte Opera Company in Gilbert and Sullivan Operas*, list no fewer than fourteen other artists who played the role during the run of the original production: Carrie Donald, Alice Baldwin, Mina Cleary, Nita Carritte, Maude Holland, Nellie Lawrence, Esther Palliser, Louise Pemberton, Norah Phyllis, Emily Squire, Cissie Saumarez, Amy Sherwin, Annie Schuberth and Leonore Snyder.

Gideon Crawle The splendidly melodramatic name, Gideon Crawle, reeking of Dickensian devilment, long remained a puzzle in the libretto of *Ruddigore*. When the second act opens, Robin Oakapple has assumed his evil burden as Sir Ruthven Murgatroyd. His faithful servant, Old Adam Goodheart, has become his wicked henchman. Suddenly Sir Ruthven was made to address Adam as 'Gideon Crawle', a name that had not been previously mentioned. What happened was that, in the initial performance, there were six verses in the opening duet for Sir Ruthven and Adam ('I once was as meek as a new-born lamb.') But immediately afterwards, Gilbert decided to cut out three of the verses:

ROBIN:
My face is the index of my mind,
All venom and spleen and gall—ha! ha!
Or, properly speaking,
It soon will be reeking
With venom and spleen and gall—ha! ha!

ADAM:
My name from Adam Goodheart you'll find
I've changed to Gideon Crawle—ha! ha!
For a bad Bart's steward
Whose heart is much *too* hard,
Is always Gideon Crawle—ha! ha!

BOTH:
How providential when you find
The face an index to the mind,
And evil men compelled to call
Themselves by names like Gideon Crawle!

Gilbert had decided that Adam should retain his name throughout the opera and *not* change it to Gideon Crawle. The libretto was altered accordingly—but one reference was overlooked and persisted through many editions.

Gilbert and Sullivan for All Formed in 1963 with the idea of presenting songs and scenes from the operas, informally in modern dress, Gilbert and Sullivan for All has as its directors Donald Adams, former principal bass, Norman Meadmore, former stage director, and Thomas Round, former principal tenor of the D'Oyly Carte Company. Many of the artists who appear with them are past and present stars of D'Oyly Carte. In addition to their hundreds of performances in Britain, they have also visited the United States. They have widened their scope with full-scale productions of *The Mikado*, *The Pirates of Penzance* and, with the ancient walls of Newark Castle as a background, *The Yeomen of the Guard*.

Gilbert and Sullivan, The A combination of pub and fascinating exhibition in John Adam Street, in the Adelphi, London, this was formerly the St Martin's Tavern but was reconstructed and reopened in its present form as one of the Whitbread 'theme' houses in 1962. It is appropriately placed close to the Savoy Theatre and to the site in the Adelphi where Richard D'Oyly Carte lived during the planning and presentation of many of the operas. High over the bar are placed miniature stages, with settings and characters painted on glass for *Trial by Jury, HMS Pinafore, The Pirates of Penzance, Patience, Iolanthe, Princess Ida, The Mikado, Ruddigore, The Yeomen of the Guard* and *The Gondoliers*. In a corner stands Pooh-Bah in the costume designed by Charles Ricketts in 1926 and worn in turn by Leo Sheffield, Sydney Granville, Hilton Layland, Richard Watson, Fisher Morgan and Kenneth Sandford. The fan Pooh-Bah holds is autographed by members of the D'Oyly Carte Company. More than a hundred items, some of them the property of Whitbread's and others on loan from Miss Bridget D'Oyly Carte, are on display. They include photographs, caricatures, historic programmes, autograph letters, facsimiles of some of Gilbert's original prompt-books with his notes about details of production, costume designs and collections of cigarette cards of characters from the operas. A facsimile of Sullivan's manuscript of 'Free from his fetters grim' (Y) has attached to it a note from Courtice Pounds, the original Colonel Fairfax, saying 'He particularly requested me—after running it through with him at the piano on the rostrum—to stand on the stage and sing it as well as I could to impress Gilbert.' Many Americans are among those who call at the Gilbert and Sullivan and look round the exhibits.

Gilbert and Sullivan Society, The The Secretary is Miss Clare Lambert, 273 Northfield Avenue, Ealing, London W.5.

Gill, Dorothy Though she had been with D'Oyly Carte for an earlier period, Dorothy Gill succeeded to the principal contralto roles after the tragic death of Bertha Lewis in a car accident in 1931. In these roles—Katisha, Dame Carruthers and the rest of them—she established herself as an artist in the true tradition, with a fine voice, impeccable diction, stage presence and sense of character. In her younger days she entertained the troops in France during World War I and, in the 1920's, appeared in Nigel Playfair's famed production of *The Beggar's Opera* at the Lyric Theatre, Hammersmith. She was with D'Oyly Carte for a year before going out to Australia and New Zealand, rejoining the company on her return to England and remaining with them until 1936. She died in 1969.

Gilliland, Helen Born in Dublin in 1897, Helen Gilliland made her first stage appearance with the D'Oyly Carte Company on tour when she was twenty. She first appeared in London as Casilda (G) two years later and also sang Aline (S), Mabel (PP), Phyllis (I) and Yum-Yum (M). She added Patience in 1921 and, after leaving the company, starred in many musicals in the West End of London in the 20's and 30's. She was drowned at sea in a torpedoed ship in December 1942.

Gillingham, Joan Many of the leading mezzo-soprano roles were sung by Joan Gillingham, who was with D'Oyly Carte from 1946 until 1951. She sang Hebe (HMS), Kate (PP), Saphir (P), Leila (I), Peep-Bo (M) and Vittoria (G) in her first season, moving on later to Angela (P), Edith (PP), Iolanthe, Pitti-Sing (M), Phoebe (Y), Tessa (G) and Mad Margaret (R). Miss Gillingham, who appeared in the film, *The Story of Gilbert and Sullivan*, presented in London in 1953, died in September 1958.

Gillow's 'And everything that isn't old, from Gillow's.'— Josephine (HMS). The reference is to Waring and Gillow, the London firm of house furnishers.

Girton Girton College for the higher education of women was comparatively new when *Utopia, Limited* was first performed in 1893. Founded in a house in Hitchin in 1869, the College was moved to Cambridge in 1873. There are several references in the opera:

'Oh, maiden, rich in Girton lore.'—Chorus.
'Princess Zara . . . has taken a high degree at Girton.'—Calynx.
'At Girton all is wheat, and idle chaff is never heard within its walls.'—Princess Zara.

Giulia (G) *Soprano* Giulia, a contadina (Italian peasant), was first played by Norah Phyllis.

Giuseppe Palmieri (G) *Baritone* The baritone brother of the two gondoliers was originally played by Rutland Barrington.

'Go, breaking heart' Lady Ella's song after the opening chorus. (P).

Godfrey, Isidore It was with an understandable flourish that Isidore Godfrey, a non-smoker, lit my cigarette for me. The lighter he used was a gift to him from his friends when he celebrated 40 years with the D'Oyly Carte Opera Company. At the time of his retirement in 1968—though he has continued to act as adviser—he had in fact been with the company for 42 years, 39 of them as musical director. The once fiery red head, familiar to countless audiences both in Britain and abroad, has turned white in the service of Gilbert and Sullivan and its owner has established himself as an outstanding authority on the scores of the operas.

Perhaps Fate would in any case have drawn Isidore Godfrey to the operas but certainly it was a happy accident that took him to D'Oyly Carte. Born in London, he went to the Haberdashers School and then on to the Guildhall School of Music and Drama, where he won the Gold Medal for piano. At that time it was his intention to make his career as a concert pianist.

'But,' he told me, 'they had started a conductors' class at the school and we were each allowed to have a go at conducting the school orchestra. It just happened that when I was conducting, Sir Landon Ronald, the principal, walked in. A week or two later he called me in, told me that Rupert D'Oyly Carte was looking for a chorus master and assistant musical director and arranged an interview for me.

'I got the job and joined what was then called the "New" company in Manchester. By the way, Manchester has played quite an important part in my life—I joined D'Oyly Carte there, celebrated my fortieth anniversary there, and had my farewell party there—though I had fallen ill and was not able to attend the party, at which I was represented by my wife!

'The first complete opera I conducted was *The Mikado* at Croydon. Rupert D'Oyly Carte and all of them had come down from London and it was quite an occasion for me. I was transferred to the first company in 1926 and three years later became musical director in succession to Harry Norris.'

He has conducted all the operas with the exception of *The Grand Duke* and *Utopia, Limited*, though he has recorded excerpts from the latter. He has a high regard for *The Sorcerer*, which he conducted before the war.

'Of course all sorts of amusing things have happened through the years,' he told me. 'I remember one night when Donald Adams, as the Pirate King, drew his sword and accidentally let it slip out of his hand, narrowly missing me in the pit. I solemnly handed it back to him—but thought afterwards that I should have given him my baton!

'In the old days, when we went to America, we would pick up perhaps eight orchestral players in the first town, take them with us on the tour and make up the orchestra with local players from each of the towns we visited. It was jolly hard work, rehearsing all the time. On one occasion, I was rehearsing the *Mikado* overture when I noticed that one of the double-basses was plucking the strings in the opening bars. I pointed out that it was not to be played *pizzicato* but *arco*, with the bow. 'Yeah,' he said. 'But I haven't got a bow.' That's how it was sometimes!'

Isidore Godfrey, who was awarded the O.B.E. in the 1965 Birthday Honours, was married to the late Ann Drummond-Grant, the distinguished D'Oyly Carte contralto. In 1967, he succeeded the late Sir Malcolm Sargent as President of the Associate Members of the D'Oyly Carte Opera Trust.

Gods Grown Old, The Alternative title of *Thespis*.

Gold 'All that glitters is not gold.'—Little Buttercup (HMS). Shakespeare's line in *The Merchant of Venice* is: 'All that *glisters* is not gold.'

Goldbury, Mr (U) *Bass-baritone* The company promoter and later Comptroller of the Utopian Household was first played by Scott Fische.

GONDOLIERS, THE; or The King of Barataria First performed at the Savoy Theatre, London, on December 7, 1889, conducted by Sullivan. Initial run of 554 performances.

The cast for the original production was:

THE DUKE OF PLAZA-TORO (*Grandee of Spain*)	Mr Frank Wyatt
LUIZ (*his attendant*)	Mr Wallace Brownlow
DON ALHAMBRA DEL BOLERO (*the Grand Inquisitor*)	Mr W. H. Denny
MARCO PALMIERI	Mr Courtice Pounds
GIUSEPPE PALMIERI	Mr Rutland Barrington
ANTONIO	Mr A. Medcalf
FRANCESCO (*Venetian gondoliers*)	Mr Charles Rose
GIORGIO	Mr George De Pledge
ANNIBALE	Mr J. Wilbraham
OTTAVIO	Mr Charles Gilbert
THE DUCHESS OF PLAZA-TORO	Miss Rosina Brandram
CASILDA (*her daughter*)	Miss Decima Moore

GIANETTA		Miss Geraldine Ulmar
TESSA		Miss Jessie Bond
FIAMETTA	*(contadine)*	Miss Nellie Lawrence
VITTORIA		Miss Annie Cole
GIULIA		Miss Norah Phyllis
INEZ *(the King's foster-mother)*		Miss Annie Bernard

The first act opens on the Piazetta in Venice, with the contadine (Italian peasants) preparing bouquets for the gondoliers of their choice:

> List and learn, ye dainty roses,
> Roses white and roses red,
> Why we bind you into posies
> Ere your morning bloom has fled.
> By a law of maiden's making,
> Accents of a heart that's aching,
> Even though that heart be breaking,
> Should by maiden be unsaid:
> Though they love with love exceeding,
> They must seem to be unheeding—
> Go ye then and do their pleading,
> Roses white and roses red!

> FIAMETTA:
> Two there are for whom, in duty,
> Every maid in Venice sighs—
> Two so peerless in their beauty
> That they shame the summer skies.
> We have hearts for them, in plenty,
> They have hearts, but all too few.
> We, alas, are four and twenty!
> They, alas, are only two!

The gondoliers begin to arrive but the girls make it clear that the two to whom they have all given their hearts are the brothers Marco and Giuseppe Palmieri, who will soon be coming to choose their brides. Nevertheless, Antonio and the others sing a jolly chorus:

> For the merriest fellows are we, tra la,
> That ply on the emerald sea, tra la;
> With loving and laughing,
> And quipping and quaffing,
> We're happy as happy can be, tra la.

With sorrow we've nothing to do, tra la,
And care is a thing to pooh-pooh, tra la;
And Jealousy yellow,
Unfortunate fellow,
We drown in the shimmering blue, tra la.

Marco and Giuseppe come ashore and there are mutual exchanges
of greeting:

MARCO AND GIUSEPPE:
Buon' giorno, signorine!

GIRLS:
Gondolieri carissimi!
Siamo contadine!

MARCO AND GIUSEPPE:
Servitori umilissimi!
Per chi questi fiori—
Questi fiori, bellissimi?

GIRLS:
Per voi, bei signori,
O eccellentissimi!

The two gondoliers, almost buried under the bouquets pressed
upon them by the girls, sing together:

We're called gondolieri,
But that's a vagary,
It's quite honorary
The trade that we ply.

For gallantry noted
Since we were short-coated,
To beauty devoted,
$\begin{cases} \text{Giuseppe} \\ \text{Are Marco} \end{cases}$ and I.

When morning is breaking,
Our couches forsaking,
To greet their awaking
With carols we come.

At summer day's nooning,
When weary lagooning,
Our mandolins tuning,
We lazily thrum.

When vespers are ringing,
To hope ever clinging,
With songs of our singing
A vigil we keep.

When daylight is fading,
Enwrapt in night's shading,
With soft serenading
We sing them to sleep.

But it is time for Marco and Giuseppe to choose their brides.
They are blindfolded and undertake to marry any two they catch
but, even though there is a great to-do to prevent them cheating,
they somehow manage to catch Gianetta and Tessa.

GIANETTA:
Thank you, gallant gondolieri!
In a set and formal measure
It is scarcely necessary
To express our pleasure.
Each of us to prove a treasure,
Conjugal and monetary,
Gladly will devote our leisure,
Gay and gallant gondolieri.
Tra, la, la, la, la, la . . .

TESSA:
Gay and gallant gondolieri!
Take us both and hold us tightly.
You have luck extraordinary;
We might both have been unsightly!
If we judge your conduct rightly,
'Twas a choice involuntary;
Still we thank you most politely,
Gay and gallant gondolieri!
Tra, la, la, la, la, la. . . .

They dance off together, as a gondola arrives, bearing the
Duke and Duchess of Plaza-Toro, their daughter Casilda and—for
they are a hard-up lot—their solitary attendant, Luiz, carrying a
drum.

DUKE:
From the sunny Spanish shore,
The Duke of Plaza-Tor'—

DUCHESS:
And His Grace's Duchess true—

CASILDA:
And His Grace's daughter, too—

LUIZ:
And His Grace's private drum
To Venetia's shores have come:

ALL:
And if ever, ever, ever
They get back to Spain,
They will never, never, never
Cross the sea again—

DUKE:
Neither that Grandee from the Spanish shore,
The noble Duke of Plaza-Tor'—

DUCHESS:
Nor His Grace's Duchess, staunch and true—

CASILDA:
You may add, His Grace's daughter, too—

LUIZ:
Nor his Grace's own particular drum
To Venetia's shores will come.

ALL:
And if ever, ever, ever
They get back to Spain,
They will never, never, never
Cross the sea again!

The Duke and his party are depressed at the absence of pomp and ceremony on their arrival but, as Luiz departs to announce that they are there, the Duke lets his daughter into a secret. When she was six months old she was married by proxy to the infant son and heir of the wealthy King of Barataria! He explains further:

'Shortly after the ceremony that misguided monarch abandoned the creed of his forefathers and became a Wesleyan Methodist of the most bigoted and persecuting type. The Grand Inquisitor, determined that the innovation should not be perpetuated in Barataria, caused your smiling and unconscious husband to be stolen and conveyed to Venice. A fortnight since the Methodist Monarch and all his Wesleyan Court were killed in an insurrection, and we are here to ascertain the whereabouts of your husband, and to hail you, our daughter, as Her Majesty, the reigning Queen of Barataria!'

Womanlike, Casilda points out that she has nothing to wear, for they are penniless, and she is not altogether satisfied when he reveals that he is turning himself into a limited company. Degrading? The Duke of Plaza-Toro does not follow fashions—he leads them:

> In enterprise of martial kind,
> When there was any fighting,
> He led his regiment from behind—
> He found it less exciting.
> But when away his regiment ran,
> His place was at the fore, O—
> That celebrated,
> Cultivated,
> Underrated
> Nobleman,
> The Duke of Plaza-Toro!
>
> ALL:
> In the first and foremost flight, ha, ha!
> You always found that knight, ha, ha!
> That celebrated. . . .
>
> DUKE:
> When, to evade Destruction's hand,
> To hide they all proceeded,
> No soldier in that gallant band
> Hid half as well as he did.
> He lay concealed throughout the war,
> And so preserved his gore, O!
> That unaffected,
> Undetected,
> Well-connected
> Warrior,
> The Duke of Plaza-Toro!
>
> ALL:
> In every doughty deed, ha, ha!
> He always took the lead, ha, ha!
> That unaffected. . . .
>
> DUKE:
> When told that they would all be shot
> Unless they left the service,
> That hero hesitated not,
> So marvellous his nerve is.
> He sent his resignation in,
> The first of all his corps, O!

That very knowing,
Overflowing,
Easy-going
Paladin,
The Duke of Plaza-Toro!

ALL:
To men of grosser clay, ha, ha!
He always showed the way, ha, ha!
That very knowing. . . .

A fresh complication arises when the Duke and Duchess have left—and Casilda and Luiz rush into each other's arms. She tells him that she had been married to the baby King of Barataria and Luiz, on his part, reveals that his mother was the nurse to whom the Royal baby was entrusted. They sing of their lost happiness:

LUIZ:
There was a time—
A time for ever gone—ah, woe is me!
It was no crime
To love but thee alone—ah, woe is me!
One heart, one life, one soul,
One aim, one goal—
Each in the other's thrall,
Each all in all, ah, woe is me!

BOTH:
Oh, bury, bury—let the grave close o'er
The days that were—that never will be more!
Oh, bury, bury love that all condemn,
And let the whirlwind mourn its requiem!

CASILDA:
Dead as the last year's leaves—
As gathered flowers—ah, woe is me!
Dead as the garnered sheaves,
That love of ours—ah, woe is me!
Born but to fade and die
When hope was high,
Dead and as far away
As yesterday! ah, woe is me!

The Duke and Duchess return with Don Alhambra del Bolero, Grand Inquisitor of Spain, who tells them that the King is in Venice, working as a gondolier:

I stole the Prince, and I brought him here,
And left him gaily prattling,
With a highly respectable gondolier,
Who promised the Royal babe to rear,
And teach him the trade of a timoneer
With his own beloved bratling.
Both of the babes were strong and stout,
And, considering all things, clever.
Of that there is no manner of doubt—
No probable, possible shadow of doubt—
No possible doubt whatever.

But owing, I'm much disposed to fear,
To his terrible taste for tippling,
That highly respectable gondolier
Could never declare with a mind sincere
Which of the two was his offspring dear,
And which the Royal stripling!
Which was which he could never make out
Despite his best endeavour.
Of *that* there is no manner of doubt—
No probable, possible shadow of doubt—
No possible doubt whatever.

Time sped, and when at the end of a year
I sought that infant cherished,
That highly respectable gondolier
Was lying a corpse on his humble bier—
I dropped a Grand Inquisitor's tear—
That gondolier had perished.
A taste for drink, combined with gout,
Had doubled him up for ever.
Of *that* there is no manner of doubt—
No probable, possible shadow of doubt—
No possible doubt whatever.

The children followed his old career—
(This statement can't be parried)
Of a highly respectable gondolier:
Well, one of the two (who will soon be here)—
But *which* of the two is not quite clear—
Is the Royal Prince you married!
Search in and out and round about,
And you'll discover never

A tale so free from every doubt—
All probable, possible shadow of doubt—
All possible doubt whatever!

It is a tangle, indeed, but Don Alhambra assures them that
Luiz's mother, now the wife of 'a highly respectable and old-
fashioned brigand', will be brought and will no doubt say which
of the two brothers is Casilda's husband.

DUKE, DUCHESS, CASILDA, LUIZ and GRAND INQUISITOR:
Try we life-long, we can never
Straighten out life's tangled skein,
Why should we, in vain endeavour,
Guess and guess and guess again?

LUIZ:
Life's a pudding full of plums,

DUCHESS:
Care's a canker that benumbs.

ALL:
Life's a pudding full of plums,
Care's a canker that benumbs.
Wherefore waste our elocution
On impossible solution?
Life's a pleasant institution,
Let us take it as it comes!

Set aside the dull enigma,
We shall guess it all too soon;
Failure brings no kind of stigma—
Dance we to another tune!

String the lyre and fill the cup,
Lest on sorrow we should sup.
Hop and skip to Fancy's fiddle,
Hands across and down the middle—
Life's perhaps the only riddle
That we shrink from giving up!

They go off and the gondoliers and girls arrive.

TESSA:
When a merry maiden marries,
Sorrow goes and pleasure tarries;
Every sound becomes a song,
All is right, and nothing's wrong!

From to-day and ever after
Let our tears be tears of laughter.
Every sigh that finds a vent
Be a sigh of sweet content!
When you marry merry maiden,
Then the air with love is laden;
Every flower is a rose,
Every goose becomes a swan,
Every kind of trouble goes
Where the last year's snows have gone!

CHORUS:
Sunlight takes the place of shade
When you marry merry maid!

TESSA:
When a merry maiden marries,
Sorrow goes and pleasure tarries;
Every sound becomes a song,
All is right, and nothing's wrong!
Gnawing Care and aching Sorrow,
Get ye gone until to-morrow;
Jealousies in grim array,
Ye are things of yesterday!
When you marry merry maiden,
Then the air with joy is laden;
All the corners of the earth
Ring with music sweetly played;
Worry is melodious mirth,
Grief is joy in masquerade;

CHORUS:
Sullen night is laughing day—
All the year is merry May!

The entry of Don Alhambra casts a damper on their high spirits and he, in turn, finds it 'extremely awkward' when he learns that the two couples are married. He tells them that *one* of the gondoliers is King of Barataria and that, until it is ascertained which one it is, both shall reign jointly. Overcoming their Republican scruples Marco and Giuseppe agree, though the girls are distressed at being told that for the time being they will not be allowed to accompany them to Barataria.

GIANETTA:
Kind sir, you cannot have the heart
Our lives to part

From those to whom an hour ago
We were united!
Before our flowing hopes you stem,
Ah, look at them,
And pause before you deal this blow,
All uninvited!
You men can never understand,
That heart and hand
Cannot be separated when
We go a-yearning;
You see, you've only women's eyes
To idolize,
And only women's hearts, poor men,
To set *you* burning!
Ah me, you men will never understand
That woman's heart is one with woman's hand!

Some kind of charm you seem to find
In womankind—
Some source of unexplained delight
(Unless you're jesting),
But what attracts you, I confess,
I cannot guess,
To me a woman's face is quite
Uninteresting!
If from my sister I were torn,
It could be borne—
I should, no doubt, be horrified,
But I could bear it;—
But Marco's quite another thing—
He is my King,
He has my heart and none beside
Shall ever share it!
Ah me, you men will never understand
That woman's heart is one with woman's hand!

They brighten up when Don Alhambra assures them that in
due course they will be reunited.

GIANETTA:
Then one of us will be a Queen,
And sit on a golden throne,
With a crown instead
Of a hat on her head,

And diamonds all her own!
With a beautiful robe of gold and green,
I've always understood;
I wonder whether
She'd wear a feather?
I rather think she should!

ALL:
Oh, 'tis a glorious thing, I ween,
To be a regular Royal Queen!
No half-and-half affair, I mean,
But a right-down regular Royal Queen!

MARCO:
She'll drive about in a carriage and pair,
With the king on her left-hand side,
And a milk-white horse,
As a matter of course,
Whenever she wants to ride!
With beautiful silver shoes to wear
Upon her dainty feet;
With endless stocks
Of beautiful frocks,
And as much as she wants to eat!

TESSA:
Whenever she condescends to walk,
Be sure she'll shine at that,
With her haughty stare,
And her nose in the air,
Like a well-born aristocrat!
At elegant high society talk
She'll bear away the bell,
With her 'How de do?'
And her 'How are you?'
And 'I trust I see you well!'

GIUSEPPE:
And noble lords will scrape and bow,
And double themselves in two,
And open their eyes
In blank surprise
At whatever she likes to do.
And everybody will roundly vow

She's fair as flowers in May,
And say, 'How clever!'
At whatsoever
She condescends to say!

The gondoliers and contadine arrive and Marco and Giuseppe assure them that, though they are to be Kings, they will respect everyone's 'Republican fallacies.'

MARCO:
For every one who feels inclined,
Some post we undertake to find
Congenial with his frame of mind—
And all shall equal be.

GIUSEPPE:
The Chancellor in his peruke—
The Earl, the Marquis, and the Dook,
The Groom, the Butler, and the Cook—
They all shall equal be.

MARCO:
The Aristocrat who banks with Coutts—
The Aristocrat who hunts and shoots—
The Aristocrat who cleans our boots—
They all shall equal be.

GIUSEPPE:
The Noble Lord who rules the State—
The Noble Lord who cleans the plate—

MARCO:
The Noble Lord who scrubs the grate—
They all shall equal be.

GIUSEPPE:
The Lord High Bishop orthodox—
The Lord High Coachman on the box—

MARCO:
The Lord High Vagabond in the stocks—
They all shall equal be.

ALL:
Sing high, sing low,
Wherever they go,
They all shall equal be.
The Earl, the Marquis, and the Dook,
The Groom, the Butler, and the Cook,

The Aristocrat who banks with Coutts,
The Aristocrat who cleans the boots,
The Noble Lord who rules the State,
The Noble Lord who scrubs the grate,
The Lord High Bishop orthodox,
The Lord High Vagabond in the stocks. . . .

Marco and Giuseppe say good-bye to their wives, each of whom
has a request to make:

GIANETTA:
Now, Marco dear,
My wishes hear;
While you're away
It's understood
You will be good,
And not too gay.
To every trace
Of maiden grace
You will be blind,
And will not glance
By any chance
On womankind!

If you are wise,
You'll shut your eyes
Till we arrive,
And not address
A lady less
Than forty-five.
You'll please to frown
On every gown
That you may see;
And, O my pet,
You won't forget
You've married me!
And O my darling, O my pet,
Whatever else you may forget,
In yonder isle beyond the sea,
Do not forget you've married me!

TESSA:
You'll lay your head
Upon your bed

At set of sun.
You will not sing
Of anything
To any one.
You'll sit and mope
All day, I hope,
And shed a tear
Upon the life
Your little wife
Is passing here.

And if so be
You think of me,
Please tell the moon:
I'll read it all
In rays that fall
On the lagoon:
You'll be so kind
As tell the wind
How you may be,
And send me words
By little birds
To comfort me!
And O my darling, O my pet,
Whatever else you may forget,
In yonder isle beyond the sea,
Do not forget you've married me!

Amid the general excitement of departure, Marco sings:

Away we go
To a balmy isle,
Where the roses blow
All the winter while.

ALL:
Then away we/they go to an island fair
That lies in a Southern sea:
Then away we/they go to an island fair,
Then away, then away, then away!

The men board a xebeque—a little craft once familiar in the
Mediterranean—and the girls wave farewell as the curtain falls.

The second act opens at the court of Barataria, with Marco and
Giuseppe seated on two thrones and busily cleaning the crown and

sceptre while their attendants are very much at ease in various occupations. After the opening chorus, they state their position:

> Two kings, of undue pride bereft,
> Who act in perfect unity,
> Whom you can order right and left
> With absolute impunity.
> Who put their subjects at their ease
> By doing all they can to please!
> And thus, to earn their bread-and-cheese,
> Seize every opportunity.

Giuseppe reviews their democratic approach in detail:

> Rising early in the morning
> We proceed to light the fire,
> Then our Majesty adorning
> In its work-a-day attire,
> We embark without delay
> On the duties of the day.
>
> First, we polish off some batches
> Of political despatches,
> And foreign politicians circumvent;
> Then, if business isn't heavy,
> We may hold a Royal *levée*,
> Or ratify some Acts of Parliament.
> Then we probably review the household troops—
> With the usual 'Shalloo humps!' and 'Shalloo hoops!'
> Or receive with ceremonial and state
> An interesting Eastern potentate.
> After that we generally
> Go and dress our private valet—
> (It's a rather nervous duty—he's a touchy little man)—
>
> Write some letters literary
> For our private secretary—
> He is shaky in his spelling, so we help him if we can.
> Then, in view of cravings inner,
> We go down and order dinner;
> Then we polish the Regalia and the Coronation Plate—
> Spend an hour in titivating
> All our Gentlemen-in-Waiting;
> Or we run on little errands for the Ministers of State.

Oh, philosophers may sing
Of the troubles of a King;
Yet the duties are delightful, and the privileges great;
But the privilege and pleasure
That we treasure beyond measure
Is to run on little errands for the Ministers of State.

After luncheon (making merry
On a bun and glass of sherry),
If we've nothing in particular to do,
We may make a Proclamation,
Or receive a Deputation—
Then we possibly create a Peer or two.
Then we help a fellow-creature on his path—
With the Garter or the Thistle or the Bath.
Or we dress and toddle off in semi-State
To a festival, a function, or a *fête*.
Then we go and stand as sentry
At the Palace (private entry),
Marching hither, marching thither, up and down and to
    and fro,
While the warrior on duty
Goes in search of beer and beauty
(And it generally happens that he hasn't far to go).
He relieves us, if he's able,
Just in time to lay the table,
Then we dine and serve the coffee, and at half-past twelve
    or one,
With a pleasure that's emphatic,
We retire to our attic
With the gratifying feeling that our duty has been done!

Oh, philosophers may sing
Of the troubles of a King,
But of pleasures there are many and of worries there are
    none;
And the culminating pleasure
That we treasure beyond measure
Is the gratifying feeling that our duty has been done!

Everything is most amiable, but they do miss the wives they left
behind three months ago. There is only one recipe for perfect
happiness, Marco points out:

Take a pair of sparkling eyes,
Hidden, ever and anon,
In a merciful eclipse—
Do not heed their mild surprise—
Having passed the Rubicon,
Take a pair of rosy lips;
Take a figure trimly planned—
Such as admiration whets—
(Be particular in this);
Take a tender little hand,
Fringed with dainty fingerettes,
Press it—in parenthesis;—
Ah! Take all these, you lucky man—
Take and keep them, if you can!

Take a pretty little cot—
Quite a miniature affair—
Hung about with trellised vine,
Furnish it upon the spot
With the treasures rich and rare
I've endeavoured to define.
Live to love and love to live—
You will ripen at your ease,
Growing on the sunny side—
Fate has nothing more to give.
You're a dainty man to please
If you're not satisfied.
Ah! Take my counsel, happy man;
Act upon it, if you can!

They do not have to wait long for feminine society, for the chorus
of contadine come rushing in:

Here we are, at the risk of our lives,
From ever so far, and we've brought your wives—
And to that end we've crossed the main,
And we don't intend to return again!

FIAMETTA:
Though obedience is strong,
Curiosity's stronger—
We waited for long,
Till we couldn't wait longer.

VITTORIA:
It's imprudent, we know,
But without your society
Existence was slow,
And we wanted variety—

GIRLS:
So here we are, at the risk of our lives,
And we've brought your wives—
And to that end we've crossed the main,
And we don't intend to return again!

Gianetta and Tessa rush into the arms of Marco and Giuseppe and breathlessly ply them with questions about the state of affairs. The question of who *is* king cannot yet be answered, but they all settle for a lively dance:

Dance a cachucha, fandango, bolero,
Xeres we'll drink—Manzanilla, Montero—
Wine, when it runs in abundance, enhances
The reckless delight of that wildest of dances!
To the pretty pitter-pitter-patter,
And the clitter-clitter-clitter-clatter—
Clitter—clitter—clatter,
Pitter—pitter—patter,
Patter, patter, patter, patter, we'll dance.
Old Xeres we'll drink—Manzanilla, Montero;
For wine, when it runs in abundance, enhances
The reckless delight of that wildest of dances!

Don Alhambra arrives on the scene and, considerably shaken by the sight of the servants taking equal part in the festivities, is informed by Giuseppe that, the Monarchy having been re-modelled on republican principles, all departments rank equally. Don Alhambra describes a similar experiment:

There lived a King, as I've been told,
In the wonder-working days of old,
When hearts were twice as good as gold,
And twenty times as mellow.
Good-temper triumphed in his face,
And in his heart he found a place
For all the erring human race
And every wretched fellow.

When he had Rhenish wine to drink
It made him very sad to think
That some, at junket or at jink,
Must be content with toddy.
He wished all men as rich as he
(And he was rich as rich could be),
So to the top of every tree
Promoted everybody.

Lord Chancellors were cheap as sprats,
And Bishops in their shovel hats
Were plentiful as tabby cats—
In point of fact, too many.
Ambassadors cropped up like hay,
Prime Ministers and such as they
Grew like asparagus in May,
And Dukes were three a penny.
On every side Field Marshals gleamed,
Small beer were Lords Lieutenant deemed,
With Admirals the ocean teemed
All round his wide dominions.
And Party Leaders you might meet
In twos and threes in every street,
Maintaining, with no little heat,
Their various opinions.

That King, although no one denies
His heart was of abnormal size,
Yet he'd have acted otherwise
If he had been acuter.
The end is easily foretold,
When every blessed thing you hold
Is made of silver, or of gold,
You long for simple pewter.
When you have nothing else to wear
But cloth of gold and satins rare,
For cloth of gold you cease to care—
Up goes the price of shoddy.
In short, whoever you may be,
To this conclusion you'll agree,
When everyone is somebodee,
Then no one's anybody!

Gianetta and Tessa enter unobserved and are listening while Don
Alhambra communicates important news to Marco and Giuseppe,

who are unimpressed to hear that the Duke and Duchess of Plaza-
Toro and their beautiful daughter Casilda have arrived at Barataria.
But they take notice when Don Alhambra tells them: 'Many years
ago when you (whichever you are) were a baby, you (whichever
you are) were married to a little girl who has grown up to be the
most beautiful young lady in Spain. That beautiful young lady will
be here to claim you (whichever you are) in half an hour, and I
congratulate that one (whichever it is) with all my heart.'

The girls come forward and are understandably distressed that
the husband of one of them had already been married as a baby.
Departing, Don Alhambra tells them that the old lady who nursed
the Royal child is at the moment in the torture chamber, waiting
to be interviewed. The two couples try to disentangle the situation
in a quartet which begins calmly but becomes more and more
agitated:

> In a contemplative fashion,
> And a tranquil frame of mind,
> Free from every kind of passion,
> Some solution let us find.
> Let us grasp the situation,
> Solve the complicated plot—
> Quiet, calm deliberation
> Disentangles every knot.

Each of them has something to say while the others maintain
the 'contemplative' mood and they depart with their problem far
from being solved.

With choral ceremony, the Duke and Duchess enter with their
daughter Casilda and the Duchess outlines the progress of her own
married life:

> On the day when I was wedded
> To your admirable sire,
> I acknowledge that I dreaded
> An explosion of his ire.
> I was overcome with panic—
> For his temper was volcanic,
> And I didn't dare revolt,
> For I feared a thunderbolt!
> I was always very wary,
> For his fury was ecstatic—
> His refined vocabulary
> Most unpleasantly emphatic.

To the thunder
Of this Tartar
I knocked under
Like a martyr;
When intently
He was fuming,
I was gently
Unassuming—
When reviling
Me completely,
I was smiling
Very sweetly:
Giving him the very best, and getting back the
　　very worst—
That is how I tried to tame your great progenitor
　　—at first!
But I found that a reliance
On my threatening appearance,
And a resolute defiance
Of marital interference,
And a gentle intimation
Of my firm determination
To see what I could do
To be wife and husband too
Was the only thing required
For to make his temper supple,
And you couldn't have desired
A more reciprocating couple.
Ever willing
To be wooing,
We were billing—
We were cooing;
When I merely
From him parted
We were nearly
Broken-hearted—
When in sequel
Reunited,
We were equal-
Ly delighted
So with double-shotted guns and colours nailed
　　unto the mast,
I tamed your insignificant progenitor—at last!

So much for the Duchess's method of establishing marital ascendancy. The Duke—with the Duchess, of course, determined not to be ignored—outlines some of the advantages to be derived from imaginative use of a position such as his.

DUKE:
Small titles and orders
For Mayors and Recorders
I get—and they're highly delighted—

DUCHESS:
They're highly delighted!

DUKE:
MP's baronetted,
Sham Colonels gazetted,
And second-rate Aldermen knighted—

DUCHESS:
Yes, Aldermen knighted.

DUKE:
Foundation-stone laying
I find very paying;
It adds a large sum to my makings—

DUCHESS:
Large sum to his makings.

DUKE:
At charity dinners
The best of speech-spinners,
I get ten per cent on the takings—

DUCHESS:
One-tenth of the takings.
I present any lady
Whose conduct is shady
Or smacking of doubtful propriety—

DUKE:
Doubtful propriety.

DUCHESS:
When Virtue would quash her,
I take and whitewash her,
And launch her in first-rate society—

DUKE:
First-rate society!

DUCHESS:
I recommend acres
Of clumsy dressmakers—
Their fit and their finishing touches—

DUKE:
Their finishing touches.

DUCHESS:
A sum in addition
They pay for permission
To say that they make for the Duchess—

DUKE:
They make for the Duchess!
Those pressing prevailers,
The ready-made tailors,
Quote me as their great double-barrel—

DUCHESS:
Their great double-barrel.

DUKE:
I allow them to do so,
Though Robinson Crusoe
Would jib at their wearing apparel!

DUCHESS:
Such wearing apparel!

DUKE:
I sit, by selection,
Upon the direction
Of several Companies bubble—

DUCHESS:
All Companies bubble!

DUKE:
As soon as they're floated
I'm freely bank-noted—
I'm pretty well paid for my trouble—

DUCHESS:
He's paid for his trouble!
At middle-class party
I play at *écarté*—
And I'm by no means a beginner—

DUKE:
She's not a beginner.

DUCHESS:
To one of my station
The remuneration—
Five guineas a night and my dinner—

DUKE:
And wine with her dinner.

DUCHESS:
I write letters blatant
On medicines patent—
And use any other you mustn't—

DUKE:
Believe me, you mustn't—

DUCHESS:
And vow my complexion
Derives its perfection
From somebody's soap—which it doesn't—

DUKE:
It certainly doesn't!
We're ready as witness
To any one's fitness
To fill any place or preferment—

DUCHESS:
A place or preferment.
We're often in waiting
At junket or *fêting*,
And sometimes attend an interment—

DUKE:
We enjoy an interment.

BOTH:
In short, if you'd kindle
The spark of a swindle,
Lure simpletons into your clutches—
Yes; into your clutches.
Or hoodwink a debtor,
You cannot do better

DUCHESS:
Than trot out a Duke or a Duchess—

DUKE:
A Duke or a Duchess!

On the arrival of Marco and Giuseppe, the Duke suggests to them that, as one of them is King, they ought to be rather more dignified in the presence of the Court. He offers a lesson in deportment:

> I am a courtier grave and serious
> Who is about to kiss your hand:
> Try to combine a pose imperious
> With a demeanour nobly bland. . . .

The others join him in the familiar gavotte, Marco and Giuseppe earning his praise for their efforts in following his instructions. The Duke and Duchess leave the young people alone and they are joined by Gianetta and Tessa. Casilda tells them that she was married as a baby—and is in love with someone else. The other couples, on their part, confide that they too are married. They express their bewilderment in a quintet:

> Here is a case unprecedented!
> Here are a King and Queen ill-starred!
> Ever since marriage was invented
> Never was known a case so hard!
>
> MARCO and GIUSEPPE:
> I may be said to have been bisected,
> By a profound catastrophe!
>
> CASILDA, GIANETTA and TESSA:
> Through a calamity unexpected
> I am divisible into three!
>
> ALL:
> O moralists all,
> How can you call
> Marriage a state of unitee,
> When excellent husbands are bisected,
> And wives divisible into three?
> Moralists all,
> How can you call
> Marriage a state of union true?
>
> CASILDA, GIANETTA and TESSA:
> One-third of myself is married to half of ye or you.
>
> MARCO and GIUSEPPE:
> When half of myself has married one-third of ye or you!

Their quandary is soon resolved. The stage fills up as Don Alhambra brings forward Inez, the foster-mother, who gives them the truth and solves all their problems:

The Royal Prince was by the King entrusted
To my fond care, ere I grew old and crusted;
When traitors came to steal his son reputed,
My own small boy I deftly substituted!
The villains fell into the trap completely—
I hid the Prince away—still sleeping sweetly;
I called him 'son' with pardonable slyness—
His name, Luiz! Behold his Royal Highness!

Luiz places a crown on Casilda's head and they all join in the final chorus:

Once more gondolieri,
Both skilful and wary,
Free from this quandary
Contented are we. Ah!
From Royalty flying,
Our gondolas plying,
And merrily crying
Our 'premé,' 'stalì!' Ah!—
So good-bye cachucha, fandango, bolero—
We'll dance a farewell to that measure—
Old Xeres, adieu—Manzanilla—Montero—
We leave you with feelings of pleasure!

Gondoliers (G)   With Marco and Giuseppe Palmieri, the other gondoliers are Antonio, Francesco, Giorgio, Annibale and Ottavio, played in the original production by Messrs A. Medcalf, Charles Rose, George De Pledge, J. Wilbraham and Charles Gilbert respectively.

'Good Grand Duke of Pfennig-Halbpfennig, The'   Chorus of chamberlains (D).

'Good morrow, good lover!'   Phyllis's greeting to her sweetheart Strephon, the Arcadian shepherd (I).

'Good morrow, good mother!'   Song by the Arcadian shepherd, Strephon, on meeting Iolanthe (I).

Gordon, J. M.   Some forty years ago, the present writer encountered the Man with the Notebook, one of the famed characters in the story of Gilbert and Sullivan opera. He was standing at the back of the dress circle in the Theatre Royal, Newcastle-upon-Tyne, peering through his gold-rimmed spectacles, carefully following

I

every movement and intonation of the players on the stage, and busily writing in his notebook. That was John McRobbie Gordon, who had worked on the stage with Gilbert and whose memory had preserved every detail of the productions as they were when Gilbert was alive. Gilbert's views constituted his Bible and any deviation by the players was promptly pointed out after the performance. Born in Aberdeen, Gordon had a musical training and at one time sang with the Dan Godfrey Quartet in Bournemouth. He was stage director of the D'Oyly Carte Opera Company from 1907 until 1939 but was with the company much earlier. Isidore Godfrey, musical director of the company for thirty-nine years, recalled J. M. Gordon to me: 'He was entirely wrapped up in the operas. He used to live on an apple and a glass of whisky! He was always around, standing under one of the lights, busily writing in his notebook. I remember that, once when we were in America, we bought him a special pencil with a light on it—but he never used it. His knowledge of the operas was tremendous and he never missed the smallest detail in a performance. Even in his later years he was very nimble on his feet and could show the artists exactly how the dances should be done.' Charles Reid describes Gordon in *Malcolm Sargent: A Biography*: 'He trod the wings as one treads a chancel. Once during a rehearsal at the Princes, he accidentally brushed against a set of tubular bells backstage. At their faint jingle he whipped round and shushed them, finger on lips.'

Gordon, Marjorie Born in Southsea, she made her first stage appearance in the chorus of the *Yeomen* with the D'Oyly Carte Company in Liverpool in 1915 when she was twenty-two. She later played leading parts including Yum-Yum and Patience before going into a number of other musical shows.

Goss, Julia After understudying leading soprano parts with the D'Oyly Carte Company, Julia Goss succeeded Valerie Masterson in these roles in January 1969. Though born in Scotland, she was brought up in London, where she studied music and singing at Trinity College of Music. While still at college she did a great deal of concert and operatic work, as well as amateur dramatics with a local society and singing in a church choir. She joined the D'Oyly Carte chorus in 1967, immediately on leaving Trinity College. But she thought she had failed her audition, as she was stopped halfway through her test-piece. The reason, however, was simply that the management had heard enough to know that here was their next principal soprano! Julia Goss's leading roles are

Aline (S), Mabel (PP), Lady Ella (P), Lady Psyche (PI), Yum-Yum (M), Rose Maybud (R) and Casilda (G).

Go-To (M) *Bass* This character is not to be found in the original cast of *The Mikado*. Indeed, he is not really a character at all; he is a voice. He was introduced, not for dramatic reasons, but entirely for musical ones. The madrigal, 'Brightly dawns our wedding day,' early in the second act, was allotted to Yum-Yum, Pitti-Sing, Nanki-Poo and Pish-Tush, but the voice of the artist singing the last-named is not always suited to the music for the baritone in the madrigal. After about a month of the original run at the Savoy Theatre, the part of Go-To was introduced simply to sing in the madrigal.

Goulding, Charles A member of the D'Oyly Carte Company for eighteen years, Charles Goulding was singing leading tenor roles for seventeen of them. He went into the chorus in 1918 and the following year was singing Earl Tolloller (I), Nanki-Poo (M), Marco (G) and, unusually for a tenor, Strephon. Through the years he sang the leading tenor role in all the operas in the repertoire, including Box in the Sullivan–Burnand *Cox and Box*.

GRAND DUKE, THE; or The Statutory Duel First performed at the Savoy Theatre, London, on March 7, 1896, conducted by Sullivan. It ran for 123 performances.

The cast for the 'New and Original Comic Opera' was:

RUDOLPH (*Grand Duke of Pfennig-Halbpfennig*)	Mr Walter Passmore
ERNEST DUMMKOPF (*a Theatrical Manager*)	Mr Charles Kenningham
LUDWIG (*his Leading Comedian*)	Mr Rutland Barrington
DR TANNHÄUSER (*a Notary*)	Mr Scott Russell
THE PRINCE OF MONTE CARLO	Mr R. Scott Fishe
VISCOUNT MENTONE	Mr E. Carleton
BEN HASHBAZ (*a Costumier*)	Mr C. Herbert Workman
HERALD	Mr Jones Hewson
THE PRINCESS OF MONTE CARLO (*Betrothed to Rudolph*)	Miss Emmie Owen
THE BARONESS VON KRAKENFELDT (*Betrothed to Rudolph*)	Miss Rosina Brandram
JULIA JELLICOE (*an English Comedienne*)	Mme Ilka von Palmay
LISA (*a Soubrette*)	Miss Florence Perry

OLGA		Miss Mildred Baker
GRETCHEN		Miss Ruth Vincent
BERTHA	*(Members of Ernest Dummkopf's Theatrical Company)*	Miss Jessie Rose
ELSA		Miss Ethel Wilson
MARTHA		Miss Beatrice Perry

As the curtain rises we are in the market-place of Speisesaal, in the Grand Duchy of Pfennig-Halbpfennig. The members of a theatrical company, of which Ernest Dummkopf is the manager, are enjoying a repast in celebration of the forthcoming marriage of Lisa, the soubrette, to Ludwig, the principal comedian. 'Won't it be a pretty wedding?' sing the chorus, while other women members of the company make some comments about the bride's ill-fitting dress and unbecoming hair-do.

Several complications at once come to light. There is a conspiracy afoot to depose the Grand Duke and put Ernest Dummkopf in his place. Meanwhile, no parson will be available to marry Lisa and Ludwig until six o'clock because the Grand Duke Rudolph has summoned a convocation of all the clergy to settle the details of his own marriage to the wealthy Baroness von Krakenfeldt. And as the theatrical company is to present *Troilus and Cressida* at seven o'clock there is nothing for it but to have the wedding breakfast for Lisa and Ludwig in advance.

There is a great deal of play with the eating of sausage-rolls, the secret sign of those who are involved in the conspiracy.

> LUDWIG:
> By the mystic regulation
> Of our dark Association,
> Ere you open conversation
> With another kindred soul,
> You must eat a sausage-roll!

Ernest arrives, confident not only that he will succeed Rudolph as Grand Duke but also that, having managed a theatrical company, he is fully equipped for the job:

> Were I a king in very truth,
> And had a son—a guileless youth—
> In probable succession;
> To teach him patience, teach him tact,
> How promptly in a fix to act,
> He should adopt, in point of fact,
> A manager's profession.

To that condition he should stoop
(Despite a too fond mother),
With eight or ten 'stars' in his troupe,
All jealous of each other!
Oh, the man who can rule a theatrical crew,
Each member a genius (and some of them two),
And manage to humour them, early and late,
Can govern this tuppeny State!

Both A and B rehearsal slight—
They say they'll be 'all right at night'
(They've both to go to school yet);
C in each act *must* change her dress,
D *will* attempt to 'square the Press';
E won't play Romeo unless
His grandmother plays Juliet;
F claims all hoydens as her rights
(She's played them thirty seasons);
And G must show herself in tights
For two convincing reasons—
Two very well-shaped reasons!
Oh, the man who can drive a theatrical team,
With wheelers and leaders in order supreme,
Can govern and rule, with a wave of his fin,
All Europe—with Ireland thrown in!

It is generally agreed that, when Ernest becomes Grand Duke,
all the members of the company will be given official positions in
keeping with their standing in the theatrical profession. The
beautiful English actress Julia Jellicoe points out—to Ernest's
delight—that, as leading lady, she will obviously have to become
Grand Duchess. 'How would I play this part—the Grand Duke's
bride?' she sings.

But all is not plain sailing. Ludwig arrives in a state of agitation
and reveals ('Ten minutes since I met a chap') that he has given
away the plot to the Duke's detective, mistaking him for a con-
spirator.

The Notary, however, has an idea. He points out that there is
an old law ('About a century since') involving a procedure known
as the Statutory Duel whereby to avoid bloodshed the drawing of
cards decides an issue, the loser being pronounced officially dead
and the winner taking over all his assets and responsibilities. They
will be able to lull the Grand Duke's suspicions by letting it be
known that they, the actors, have discovered the plot. Ludwig and

Ernest, each accusing the other of being the guilty party, can 'fight' a Statutory Duel—and, as the Act is due to expire the following day, the loser will soon be able to become officially alive again! The duel takes place and Ludwig wins.

The Grand Duke makes his appearance, though there is nothing very grand about him. Indeed, he is a feeble little creature, dressed in old and patched clothes. Economy is his watchword:

> A pattern to professors of monarchical autonomy,
> I don't indulge in levity or compromising *bonhomie*,
> But dignified formality, consistent with economy,
> Above all other virtues I particularly prize.
> I never join in merriment—I don't see joke or jape any—
> I never tolerate familiarity in shape any—
> This, joined with an extravagant respect for tuppence-ha'penny,
> A keynote to my character sufficiently supplies.
>
> I weigh out tea and sugar with precision mathematical—
> Instead of beer, a penny each—my orders are emphatical—
> (Extravagance unpardonable, any more than that I call),
> But, on the other hand, my Ducal dignity to keep—
> All Courtly ceremonial—to put it comprehensively—
> I rigidly insist upon (but not, I hope, offensively)
> Whenever ceremonial can be practised inexpensively—
> And, when you come to think of it, it's really very cheap!

Rudolph is congratulating himself on the fact that the Baroness's income is considerable while her ideas of economy are on a par with his own, when the lady herself appears with the disturbing information that she has discovered that Rudolph was betrothed in infancy to the Princess of Monte Carlo. Rudolph, however, brushes this aside by pointing out that he did not take up the contract because the Prince was persistently poor. Anyway, he says, the contract becomes void if she has not married by the time she becomes of age—as she will to-morrow. The Baroness and Rudolph indulge in a duet about the joys of (economical) married life, 'As o'er our penny roll we sing.'

Left alone, Rudolph reads the report of his private detective and is plunged into despair at the news of the plot to depose him:

> When you find you're a broken-down critter,
> Who is all in a trimmle and twitter,
> With your palate unpleasantly bitter,
> As if you'd just eaten a pill—

When your legs are as thin as dividers,
And you're plagued with unruly 'insiders,'
And your spine is all creepy with spiders,
And you're highly gamboge in the gill—
Creepy! Creepy!
When you've got a beehive in your head,
And a sewing machine in each ear,
And you feel that you've eaten your bed,
And you've got a bad headache *down here*—
When such facts are about,
And these symptoms you find
In your body or crown—
It's a shady look out,
You may make up your mind
That you'd better lie down!

When your lips are all smeary—like tallow,
And your tongue is decidedly yellow,
With a pint of warm oil in your *swallow*,
And a pound of tin-tacks in your chest—
When you're down in the mouth with the vapours,
And all over your Morris wall-papers
Black-beetles are cutting their capers,
And crawly things never at rest—
Crawly things! Crawly things!
When you doubt if your head is your own,
And you jump when an open door slams—
Then you've got to a state which is known
To the medical world as 'jim-jams.'
If such symptoms you find
In your body or head,
They're not easy to quell—
You make may up your mind
You are better in bed,
For you're not at all well!

Ludwig comes along, intending to break to Rudolph the news
of the plot and the 'killing' of the plotter in a Statutory Duel
but, seeing that Rudolph is in such a state of distress, he has another
idea. Why should not the two of them fight a Statutory Duel—a
duel with cards—and, by cheating, arrange that Rudolph shall be
'killed?' Thus Ludwig, taking his place, will be the one to be
deposed and, as the law becomes void on the following day,
Rudolph can then 'come to life' again. In the presence of all the

135

public they stage a violent quarrel ('Big bombs, small bombs, great guns and little ones!'), Rudolph is 'killed' and Ludwig hailed as the Grand Duke in his place.

> LUDWIG:
> Oh, a Monarch who boasts intellectual graces
> Can do, if he likes, a good deal in a day—
> Can put all his friends in conspicuous places,
> With plenty to eat and with nothing to pay!

Julia Jellicoe points out ('Ah, pity me, my comrades true') that, as leading lady, she and not Lisa must now marry Ludwig. Lisa and Julia sing a duet ('Oh, listen to me, dear') in which the latter insists that, as a soubrette, Lisa could not possibly play the leading role of Grand Duchess. 'The die is cast, my hope has perished!' sings Lisa, and goes off weeping.

The second act opens on the following morning, when all the members of the new court, wearing the *Troilus and Cressida* costumes, greet the newly-married Ludwig and Julia. Ludwig announces that he intends to revive the manners of ancient Greece but adds a qualification that some of the classical customs would hardly be suitable for the present day:

Yes, on reconsideration, there are customs of that nation
Which are not in strict accordance with the habits of our day,
And when I come to codify, their rules I mean to modify,
Or Mrs Grundy, p'r'aps, may have a word or two to say.
For they hadn't macintoshes or umbrellas or galoshes—
And a shower with their dresses must have played the very deuce,
And it must have been unpleasing when they caught a fit of sneezing,
For, it seems, of pocket handkerchiefs they didn't know the use.
They wore little underclothing—scarcely anything—or nothing—
And their dress of Coan silk was quite transparent in design—
Well, in fact, in summer weather, something like the 'altogether',
And it's *there*, I rather fancy, I shall have to draw the line!

Lisa, still distressed at losing Ludwig, begs Julia to look after him dutifully:

> Take care of him—he's much too good to live,
> With him you must be very gentle:
> Poor fellow, he's so highly sensitive,
> And O, so sentimental!
> Be sure you never let him sit up late
> In chilly open air conversing—
> Poor darling, he's extremely delicate,
> And wants a deal of nursing!

When Lisa has gone, Ludwig and Julia have a long discourse about the way in which the role of the Grand Duchess should be played ('Now, Julia, come, consider it from this dainty point of view'). He urges that she should be submissive and affectionate, while she favours a much more passionate and dominating performance.

The Baroness von Krakenfeldt bursts in upon them in a rage ('With fury indescribable I burn') and is told by Ludwig that, far from the law about the Statutory Duel having expired, he has revived it for another hundred years—so that those who have been "killed" remain dead! To his surprise, the Baroness is delighted, pointing out that, as he has now resumed all Rudolph's responsibilities, he is now bound to marry *her*. 'Now away to the wedding we go,' sings the Baroness, with the chorus. It is now Julia who is left weeping: 'Broken every promise plighted—all is darksome—all is dreary.'

Things are no brighter for Ernest Dummkopf who, coming forward to claim Julia, is informed by her that as the law has been revived for another hundred years he will remain legally 'dead'. In a duet with Julia, Ernest sings:

> If the light of love's lingering ember
> Has faded in gloom,
> You cannot neglect, O remember,
> A voice from the tomb!

They go off in opposite directions and the wedding party re-appears, to be regaled by the Baroness with a song:

> I once gave an evening party
> (A sandwich and cut-orange ball),
> But my guests had such appetites hearty
> That I couldn't enjoy it, enjoy it at all!
> I made a heroic endeavour
> To look unconcerned, but in vain,
> And I vowed that I never—oh never—
> Would ask anybody again!
> But there's a distinction decided—
> A difference truly immense—
> When the drink that you drink is provided, provided,
> At somebody else's expense.
> So bumpers—aye, ever so many—
> The cost we may safely ignore!
> For the wine doesn't cost us a penny,
> Tho' it's Pommery seventy-four!

But there are further complications. The Prince of Monte Carlo arrives with his daughter and, far from being in his former impecunious state, he has invented a game called roulette and has made himself a fortune! Now he has brought his daughter who, still being under twenty-one, claims the Grand Duke in marriage. In the midst of the general consternation, the Notary appears and points out that there has been a 'little mistake' regarding Ludwig's card-duel with Rudolph. He has found that the law specifically states that an ace is to count as the lowest card—and Ludwig won the duel by producing an ace. So, not having succeeded to the Dukedom, he had no power to revive the law. There is a general pairing-off of the various couples as they all sing the closing chorus:

> Happy couples, lightly treading,
> Castle chapel will be quite full!
> Each shall have a pretty wedding
> As, of course, is only rightful,
> Though the brides be fair or frightful.
> Contradiction little dreading,
> This will be a day delightful—
> Such a pretty, pretty wedding!
> Such a pretty wedding!
> Such a charming wedding!
> Happy couples, each shall have,
> Shall have, a wedding!

Granville, Sydney Famed in the 'Pooh-Bah' roles, Sydney Granville played a long list of parts in the course of a distinguished D'Oyly Carte career extending over thirty-five years: Cox (C), Usher and Judge (J), Bill Bobstay (HMS), Samuel and Sergeant of Police (PP), Grosvenor (P), Strephon and Private Willis (I), Florian and King Hildebrand (PI), Pish-Tush and Pooh-Bah (M), Sir Despard Murgatroyd (R), Sir Richard Cholmondeley and Wilfred Shadbolt (Y), Luiz, Giuseppe and Don Alhambra (G). Born in Bolton, he started his career in grand opera with the Moody-Manners Company and first appeared with D'Oyly Carte in 1907. In his last season in 1942 he played Pooh-Bah, Wilfred Shadbolt and Don Alhambra when in his mid-sixties. He was in the film of *The Mikado* made in 1938. Sydney Granville, who was married to Anna Bethell, died in 1959, aged eighty-one.

Gray, Warwick The first artist to play Guron (PI).

Great Minds 'Yet his must be a mind of no common order, or he would not dare to teach my dear father to dance a hornpipe on the cabin table.'—Josephine, of Sir Joseph Porter (HMS).

Green, Martyn After wide experience with the D'Oyly Carte Company, Martyn Green officially succeeded to all the 'Lytton parts'—Ko-Ko, Jack Point, Lord Chancellor, etc.—in 1934. Born in 1899, he studied singing with his father, William Green, a well-known tenor of his day, and with Gustav Garcia at the Royal College of Music. Early in World War I he got himself into the Army at the age of fifteen and after a few months was discharged for being under age. But a clerical error listed him as eighteen and he joined up again later the same year. He was wounded in action. Green made his first stage appearance in the chorus of *A Southern Maid*, in which Jose Collins starred, at the Theatre Royal, Nottingham, in 1919, and was in various shows before joining the D'Oyly Carte chorus. His first part was Luiz in *The Gondoliers*. In 1938 he added John Wellington Wells (S) to his long list of roles and he played Ko-Ko in the film of *The Mikado* made just before World War II, during which he served in the R.A.F. He rejoined the D'Oyly Carte Company in 1946 and remained with them for a further five years, eventually going to America. In 1959 he faced with great courage the ordeal of having his left leg amputated when it was crushed in a New York lift. But he made a good recovery and has continued to play an active part in show business in America. He published a book of reminiscences, *Here's a How-De-Do* (Max Reinhardt), in 1952.

Gretchen (D) *Mezzo-soprano* Ruth Vincent was the first artist to play Gretchen, member of Dummkopf's theatrical company.

Grey, Sybil The first artist to sing the roles of Fleta (I), Sacharissa (PI) and Peep-Bo (M).

Gridley, Lawrence After creating the role of Captain Sir Edward Corcoran (U), Lawrence Gridley went on to sing many other parts with the D'Oyly Carte Company—Pooh-Bah (M), Dick Deadeye (HMS), Sergeant of Police (PP), Wilfred Shadbolt (Y), Don Alhambra (G), Mikado, Private Willis (I), Scaphio (U), King Hildebrand (PI), Ludwig (D), Learned Judge (J), Dr Daly (S) and Grosvenor (P).

Griffin, Elsie Like many D'Oyly Carte artists, Elsie Griffin had never been on the professional stage until she joined the company. She was born in Bristol and had just started singing in oratorio and concerts when she went into the company in 1919 and within a year was singing Aline (S), Josephine (HMS), Mabel (PP), Ella (P), Phyllis (I), Kate (Y) and Gianetta (G). Later she added Yum-Yum (M), Rose Maybud (R) and Casilda (G). She has special memories of seasons at the Princes Theatre where members of the Royal Family frequently attended—and there was one performance of *Iolanthe* which she will not readily forget. To the surprise of all the cast, stage manager J. M. Gordon told them that they were going to be twenty minutes late in starting the performance, a highly unusual thing. The reason was that members of the real House of Lords were coming along in a body to see the show! Miss Griffin, who left the company in 1927, is married to baritone Ivan Menzies, Both she and her husband have been for some years closely associated with the Moral Re-Armament Movement.

Griffin, Joseph He was with D'Oyly Carte from 1923 until 1931, his roles including Bouncer (C), Usher (J), Notary (S), Samuel (PP), King Hildebrand (PI), Pish-Tush (M), Old Adam (R) and the Lieutenant (Y). It is recalled of him that on one memorable occasion his top denture flew out while he was in full song—but was deftly caught by him and replaced without interruption to the flow.

Griffiths, Neville Later a member of Sadler's Wells Opera, Neville Griffiths joined the D'Oyly Carte chorus in 1948 and during his ten years with the company sang Ralph Rackstraw (HMS), Frederic (PP), Nanki-Poo (M) and Marco (G).

Grig 'From morn to night our lives shall be as merry as a grig.'— Ludwig (D). A grig is a cricket but Brewer's *Dictionary of Phrase and Fable* points out that this may not be the origin of the ancient phrase, 'grig' possibly being a corruption of 'Greek'.

Grossmith, George One of the most famous names in the Gilbert and Sullivan story, George Grossmith was the original player of the roles of John Wellington Wells (S), making his first professional appearance on the dramatic stage in that part, Sir Joseph Porter (HMS), Major-General Stanley in the London production (PP), Reginald Bunthorne (P), Lord Chancellor (I), King Gama (PI),

Ko-Ko (M), Robin Oakapple (R) and Jack Point (Y). Born in December 1847, he came, so to speak, in the middle of a 'George Grossmith sandwich'. His father, also George, was a reporter in Bow Street police court and an entertainer and lecturer in concert halls, drawing-rooms and institutes. His son (George III, that is) became a well-known West End actor and manager associated with a long series of musicals. Grossmith himself was originally billed in the Gilbert and Sullivan operas as 'George Grossmith, Jnr', for his father was still alive. It was during a performance of *Pirates* that Grossmith, Snr had a seizure while presiding at a Savage Club dinner. His son made a dash from the Opera Comique, where he was playing Major-General Stanley, and arrived just before his father died. From *Patience* onwards the billing was simply 'George Grossmith'.

In his early days, George Grossmith, who was educated at North London Collegiate School, assisted his father in reporting Bow Street police court for *The Times* although by his early twenties he was also doing vocal sketches at the piano in order to augment his income. In this capacity he appeared in the concert entertainment toured by Mrs Howard Paul, who was later engaged to create the role of Lady Sangazure in *The Sorcerer* at the Opera Comique. Meanwhile George had been seen by both Sullivan and Gilbert in charity performances of *Trial by Jury* and it was Sullivan who thought of him as the artist to play John Wellington Wells in *The Sorcerer*. As Grossmith recalled in *A Society Clown* (Arrowsmith, 1888), Sullivan sang over to him the patter song 'My name is John Wellington Wells' and said, 'You can do that?' Grossmith thought he could. 'Very well,' said Sullivan, 'if you can do that you can do the rest.' While feeling that it was a rewarding part which would suit him, Grossmith wondered, on meeting Gilbert, whether it ought not to be played by 'a fine man with a fine voice.' Gilbert dismissed the suggestion. 'That,' he said, 'is exactly what we don't want.'

The nimble Grossmith was a 'nervy' and temperamental artist, not lacking in confidence in his own abilities but tending to worry about audience reaction and the general success of the performance.

Gilbert continuously guided him in matters of characterisation and the stressing, or more often the *under*stressing, of various points. There was, for instance, the occasion when Gilbert pulled him up about putting in an extra bit of 'business'. 'I get an enormous laugh by it,' argued Grossmith. 'So you would if you sat on a pork pie,' snapped Gilbert. He had his clashes with Sullivan, too. During rehearsal of *Princess Ida* he inquired, with apparent innocence, about the significance of lines which included, 'This seems unnecessarily severe.' Sullivan explained that this was because King Gama was about to be thrown into prison. 'Oh,' said Grossmith, 'I thought they referred to my having been detained here three hours a day for the past fortnight singing them.' Sullivan conceded that he might attend rehearsals only when his presence was actually required. It is interesting to note that Grossmith, who had to be held on a tight rein by Gilbert, was the joint author, with his brother Weedon Grossmith, of that masterpiece of *under*statement, *The Diary of a Nobody*, in which are recorded the experiences of the egregious Mr Pooter. The admirably apt title of that book, by the way, was suggested to the Grossmiths by F. C. Burnand, the librettist of Sullivan's *Cox and Box*.

In his playing of Jack Point, Grossmith—presumably with Gilbert's agreement—avoided the suggestion of tragedy and, after his final collapse, would give a little wriggle to indicate that he was still very much alive. Yet when, in later years, Lytton gave his performance a tragic ending, Gilbert expressed his approval of this view. Grossmith left D'Oyly Carte in 1889 during the run of the *Yeomen* and the later part of his career was mainly as a successful entertainer at the piano both in Britain and America. He died at Folkestone in 1912.

Grosvenor, Archibald (P) *Baritone* The role of the 'idyllic poet' was originally played by Rutland Barrington. Gilbert at first named the character Algernon but, when it was pointed out to him that a member of the Duke of Westminster's family was called Algernon Grosvenor, he changed the name to Archibald.

Grosvenor Gallery 'A greenery-yallery, Grosvenor Gallery, foot-in-the-grave young man!'—Reginald Bunthorne (P). Grosvenor Gallery was opened in London in 1877 with the original object of holding an annual exhibition of pictures by artists who were supposed not to enjoy the favour of the Royal Academy. Some of the pictures exhibited incurred ridicule, in which Gilbert joins.

Guizot, Mr Colonel Calverley is referring (P) to Francois Pierre Guillaume Guizot (1787–1874), the French politician who, as Prime Minister, was largely responsible for bringing about the revolution of 1848, through his refusal to yield to various popular demands.

Gurneys 'At length I became as rich as the Gurneys.'—Learned Judge (J). The reference here may be to the Norwich banking house of Gurney & Co., one member of which, Joseph John Gurney (1788–1847), was noted for his philanthropy.

Guron (PI) *Baritone* Guron, one of King Gama's three sons, was first played by Warwick Gray.

Guthrie, Tyrone *HMS Pinafore* was produced by Tyrone Guthrie at Stratford, Ontario, in 1960 and *The Pirates of Penzance* the following year. Both productions were brought to Her Majesty's Theatre, London, in 1962. Several of the artists were Canadian and others were already well known in London as members of Sadler's Wells Opera. The cast for *Pinafore* included Donald Young (Boatswain), Irene Byatt (Buttercup), Howell Glynne (Dick Deadeye), Andrew Downie (Ralph Rackstraw), Harry Mossfield (Captain Corcoran), Marion Studholme (Josephine), Eric House (Sir Joseph Porter), Joan Ryan (Hebe) and Emyr Green (Carpenter's Mate). That for *Pirates* included Irene Byatt (Ruth), Donald Young (Samuel), Andrew Downie (Frederic), Harry Mossfield (Pirate King), Annabelle Adams (Edith), Genevieve Gordon (Kate), Marion Studholme (Mabel), Eric House (Major-General Stanley) and Howell Glynne (Sergeant of Police). Tyrone Guthrie, born in Tunbridge Wells in 1900, already had a long list of theatrical productions to his credit. Without making any drastic breaks with tradition, his Gilbert and Sullivan productions moved along easily and brightly. In *Pinafore* an amusingly incongruous touch was provided by having Dick Deadeye busy at *petit point*—rather reminiscent of the pirate Smee and his sewing-machine in *Peter Pan*. Guthrie, who was knighted in 1961 for his services to the theatre, died in May, 1971.

Gwynne, Julia The original Edith (PP), Lady Saphir (P) and Leila (I), Julia Gwynne married George Edwardes, who became business manager for D'Oyly Carte at the Opera Comique in 1875 and went with him to the Savoy. In 1885 he became joint manager with John Hollingshead of the Gaiety Theatre and the following year became manager of the theatre, which he directed for nearly thirty years, during which he produced a long series of successful musical plays.

Hadfield, Abby Mezzo-soprano Abby Hadfield studied at the Royal Manchester College of Music and worked in television and as a professional model before joining the D'Oyly Carte Company in 1963. She is married to Peter Riley, stage manager of the company.

Hall, Shirley Plaintiff (J), Phyllis (I), Yum-Yum (M), Rose Maybud (R) and Casilda (G) were sung by Shirley Hall with D'Oyly Carte between 1951 and 1954.

Halman, Ella Principal contralto with D'Oyly Carte for eleven years, Ella Halman joined the chorus of the company in 1937 and the following year sang the small role of Inez (G). In 1940 she took over the principal contralto roles from Evelyn Gardiner, singing Ruth (PP), Lady Jane (P), Fairy Queen (I), Katisha (M), Dame Hannah (R), Dame Carruthers (Y), and the Duchess of Plaza-Toro (G) during 1940–41. Miss Halman, who left the company in August, 1951, is married to Radley Flynn.

Hamlet 'Flavour of Hamlet.' Shakespeare's Hamlet is one of the decidedly mixed assembly of personages, real and fictional, rattled off by Colonel Calverley in his patter song (P).

Hancock, Thomas After singing the roles of the Defendant (J) and Leonard Meryll (Y) with D'Oyly Carte in 1937, Thomas Hancock returned to the company from 1945 until 1950, singing the Duke of Dunstable (P), Earl Tolloller (I), Fairfax (Y), Marco (G) and Box (C).

Hannah, Dame (R) *Contralto* Rosina Brandram was the first artist to play the role.

Hannibal The great Carthaginian soldier (c. 247–183 BC) is mentioned by Colonel Calverley (P): 'The genius strategic of Caesar or Hannibal.'

'Happily coupled are we' Duet for Richard Dauntless and Rose Maybud (R).

'Happy couples, lightly treading' Finale to the opera (D).

Harding, Muriel Muriel Harding joined the D'Oyly Carte chorus in 1945 and in the next few years sang Lady Ella (P), Kate (Y), Plaintiff (J) and Zorah (R). In the years before she left the company in 1954, she was singing Josephine (HMS), Mabel (PP), Elsie Maynard (Y), Gianetta (G), Patience, Lady Psyche (PI) and Princess Ida. She is married to Donald Adams.

'Hark, the hour of ten is sounding' Opening chorus of *Trial by Jury*.

Haswell, Bowden The first artist to play Calynx (U).

'Having been a wicked baronet a week' Robin Oakapple's opening to the finale of the opera (R).

Headsman (Y) Though he neither sings nor speaks, the Headsman, first played by H. Richards, cuts an impressive figure at the end of the first act, standing centre-stage as Elsie Maynard faints in Fairfax's arms. The Headsman was the subject of one of the most famous D'Oyly Carte posters, designed by Dudley Hardy for the 1897 revival of the *Yeomen* and used for many years. The block and axe from the original production were acquired by Gilbert and kept at his home, Grim's Dyke, Harrow Weald.

Heart Richard Dauntless: 'Does your honour know what it is to have a heart?
   Sir Despard Murgatroyd: 'My honour knows what it is to have a complete apparatus for conducting the circulation of the blood through the veins and arteries of the human body.' (R).

'Hearts do not break!' Katisha's song in the second act (M).

Hebe (HMS) *Mezzo-soprano* The role of Sir Joseph Porter's first cousin, who eventually marries him, was first played by Jessie Bond, thus beginning her long association with the Savoy operas.

Helen of Troy 'Aline is rich, and she comes of a sufficiently old family, for she is the seven thousand and thirty-seventh in direct descent from Helen of Troy. True, there was a blot on the escutcheon of that lady—that affair with Paris—but where is the family, other than my own, in which there is no flaw?'—Sir Marmaduke Pointdextre (S).

Helicon 'If you'd climb the Helicon.'—Lady Psyche (PI). To climb the Helicon is to be gifted with poetic inspiration, the Helicon in mythology being the mountain range in Greece in which the Muses had their home.

Heliogabalus 'I quote in elegiacs all the crimes of Heliogabalus.'—Major-General Stanley (PP). Fortunately, the General does not enter into detail about the most perverted of Roman Emperors. His reign (218–22 AD) is described in Gibbon's *Decline and Fall of the Roman Empire*. There is a further reference to him in *Utopia, Limited*: 'If this high-class journal is to be believed, His Majesty is one of the most Heliogabalian profligates that ever disgraced an autocratic throne!'—Tarara.

'He loves! If in the bygone years' Iolanthe's ballad (I).

Henri, Louie (Lady Lytton) She joined the D'Oyly Carte chorus for the first provincial tour of *Princess Ida* in 1884, shortly after she had married (later Sir) Henry A. Lytton, who joined the chorus at the same time under the name of H. A. Henri, understudying the role of King Gama but not playing it at that time. Louie Henri went on to sing several of the principal mezzo-soprano roles—Ada (PI), Josephine (HMS), Edith (PP), Phoebe (Y), Pitti-Sing (M), Iolanthe, Nekaya (U) and Melissa (PI). She sang Tessa in the first revival of *The Gondoliers* at the Savoy in 1898. She died in 1947.

'Here is a case unprecedented!' Quintet for Marco, Giuseppe, Casilda, Gianetta and Tessa (G).

'Here's a how-de-do!' Trio for Yum-Yum, Nanki-Poo and Ko-Ko (M).

'Here's a man of jollity' Chorus as Jack Point and Elsie Maynard make their first entrance (Y).

'Hereupon we're both agreed' Duet for Jack Point and Wilfred Shadbolt—'Tell a tale of cock and bull.' (Y).

'Here we are, at the risk of our lives' Chorus, with soloists, when the girls arrive in Barataria (G).

Herold (D) *Baritone* The role was first played by Jones Hewson.

Hervey, Rose The original Kate (Y), Rose Hervey also sang Celia and Phyllis (I), Rose maybud (R), Yum-Yum (M), Elsie Maynard (Y) and Gianetta (G).

Hessians 'A lover's professions, when uttered in Hessians, are eloquent everywhere.'—Colonel Calverley (P). The top-boots known as Hessians were first worn by German soldiers and were adopted in England in the 19th century.

Hewson, Jones The original Herald (D), Jones Hewson also played Mikado, Pish-Tush and Pooh Bah (M), Pirate King (PP), Bouncer (C), Arac (PI) and Corcoran (U).

Heyland, Michael After studying the horn, drama and singing at the Guildhall School of Music and Drama, London, Michael Heyland enjoyed miscellaneous experience—including playing in pantomime with Cyril Fletcher—before being appointed in 1970 as production director of D'Oyly Carte in succession to Herbert Newby.

Highlows 'Highlows pass as patent leathers.'—Little Buttercup (HMS). Highlows are high shoes reaching over the ankles.

Hilarion (PI) *Tenor* Henry Bracy was the first artist to play the role.

Hildebrand, King (PI) *Bass–baritone* Rutland Barrington was the first artist to play the role.

Hills, Trevor Joining the D'Oyly Carte chorus in 1951, Trevor Hills went on to sing the Judge (J), Samuel and Sergeant of Police (PP), PrivateWillis (I), Scynthius (PI), Pooh-Bah (M), Sir Despard (R),Wilfred Shadbolt (Y), Don Alhambra (G) and Bouncer (C). He left the company in 1956.

Hindmarsh, Jean Born in Leeds, Jean Hindmarsh was runner-up in the Kathleen Ferrier Memorial Award contest in 1955 and was at once invited to audition for the D'Oyly Cote Company, which she joined as a principal the following year and went on to sing many of the leading soprano roles. She left the company in 1960 but returned as a guest artist in 1961–2, when she went with them on their American tour.

Hipparchus 'Hipparchus 'twas—BC one sixty-three.'—Hilarion (PI). The Greek astronomer who invented trigonometry and also the system of fixing positions by circles of latitude and longitude.

H.M.S. PINAFORE; or The Lass That Loved a Sailor First performed at the Opera Comique, London, on May 25, 1878, conducted by Sullivan. Initial run of 571 performances.

The cast of the first production of *Pinafore*—'An Entirely Original Nautical Comic Opera'—was:

THE RT HON. SIR JOSEPH PORTER, KCB (*First Lord of the Admiralty*)	Mr Geo. Grossmith, Jnr
CAPT. CORCORAN (*Commanding HMS Pinafore*)	Mr Rutland Barrington
RALPH RACKSTRAW (*Able Seaman*)	Mr George Power
DICK DEADEYE (*Able Seaman*)	Mr Richard Temple
BILL BOBSTAY (*Boatswain*)	Mr Fred Clifton
BOB BECKET (*Carpenter*)	Mr Dymott
TOM TUCKER (*Midshipmite*)	Mr Fitzaltamont
SERJEANT OF MARINES	Mr Talbot
JOSEPHINE (*the Captain's Daughter*)	Miss Emma Howson
HEBE (*Sir Joseph's First Cousin*)	Miss Jessie Bond
LITTLE BUTTERCUP (*a Portsmouth Bumboat Woman*)	Miss Henriette Everard

After the overture, the curtain rises to reveal the quarter-deck of *HMS Pinafore*. It is a busy scene, with sailors splicing ropes, polishing the brasswork and doing other tasks, which they do not appear by any means to resent:

> We sail the ocean blue,
> And our saucy ship's a beauty;
> We're sober men and true,
> And attentive to our duty.
> When the balls whistle free
> O'er the bright blue sea,
> We stand to our guns all day;

When at anchor we ride
On the Portsmouth tide,
We have plenty of time to play.
Ahoy! Ahoy! Ahoy!

On to the scene comes Little Buttercup, a buxom woman of uncertain age, who is to play an important part in the plot of the opera. She has a large basket on her arm and as, she points out, the sailors have just been paid, now is their chance to spend all they can afford on her wares:

I'm called Little Buttercup—dear Little Buttercup,
Though I could never tell why,
But still I'm called Buttercup—poor Little Buttercup,
Sweet Little Buttercup I!

I've snuff and tobaccy, and excellent jacky,
I've scissors, and watches, and knives;
I've ribbons and laces to set off the faces
Of pretty young sweethearts and wives.

I've treacle and toffee, I've tea and I've coffee,
Soft tommy and succulent chops;
I've chickens and conies, and pretty polonies,
And excellent peppermint drops.

Then buy of your Buttercup—dear Little Buttercup,
Sailors should never be shy;
So, buy of your Buttercup—poor little Buttercup,
Come, of your Buttercup buy!

Not all the sailors are gay and handsome. The exception shuffles into view through the crowd—the misshapen, dark-visaged Dick Deadeye, who frankly declares his ugliness. 'I'm three-cornered too, aint I?' he snarls. 'You are rather triangular,' agrees Buttercup. But none of them has much time for Deadeye. Anyhow, a much more attractive figure emerges through the hatchway, 'the smartest lad in all the fleet, Ralph Rackstraw', a name which at once brings forth murmurs of 'Remorse! Remorse!' from Buttercup.

He is in pensive mood and sings a madrigal, with the chorus of sailors echoing his words:

The Nightingale
Sighed for the moon's bright ray,
And told his tale
In his own melodious way!
He sang 'Ah, well-a-day!'

The lowly vale
For the mountain vainly sighed,
To his humble wail
The echoing hills replied.
They sang, 'Ah well-a-day!'

I know the value of a kindly chorus,
But choruses yield little consolation,
When we have pain and sorrow too before us!
I love—and love, alas, above my station.

He goes on to explain his situation in an attractive ballad:

A maiden fair to see,
The pearl of minstrelsy,
A bud of blushing beauty;
For whom proud nobles sigh,
And with each other vie
To do her menial's duty.

A suitor, lowly born,
With hopeless passion torn,
And poor beyond denying,
Has dared for her to pine,
At whose exalted shrine
A world of wealth is sighing.

Unlearned he in aught
Save that which love has taught,
(For love had been his tutor);
Oh, pity, pity me—
Our captain's daughter she,
And I that lowly suitor!

With the appearance of the commanding officer, Captain
Corcoran, we soon realise why this is in the main a happy ship.
Excessive politeness rather than tough discipline is clearly the order
of things. After inquiring after the health of his crew and exchanging
courtesies with them, the captain explains himself:

CAPTAIN:
I am the Captain of the *Pinafore*!

ALL:
And a right good captain, too!

CAPTAIN:
You're very, very good,
And be it understood,
I command a right good crew.

ALL:
We're very, very good,
And be it understood,
He commands a right good crew.

CAPTAIN:
Though related to a peer,
I can hand, reef and steer,
And ship a selvagee;
I am never known to quail
At the fury of a gale,
And I'm never, never sick at sea!

ALL:
What, never?

CAPTAIN:
No, never!

ALL:
What, *never*?

CAPTAIN:
Hardly ever!

ALL:
He's hardly ever sick at sea!
Then give three cheers, and one cheer more,
For the hardy Captain of the *Pinafore*!

CAPTAIN:
I do my best to satisfy you all—

ALL:
And with you we're quite content.

CAPTAIN:
You're exceedingly polite,
And I think it only right
To return the compliment.

ALL:
We're exceedingly polite,
And he thinks it only right
To return the compliment.

CAPTAIN:
Bad language or abuse
I never, never use,
Whatever the emergency;
Though 'Bother it' I may
Occasionally say,
I never use a big, big D—

ALL:
What, never?

CAPTAIN:
No, never!

ALL
What, *never*?

CAPTAIN:
Hardly ever!

ALL:
Hardly ever swears a big, big D—
Then give three cheers, and one cheer more,
For the well-bred Captain of the *Pinafore*!

But, as he confesses in a sudden burst of confidence to Little Buttercup when they are left alone, he is sad about the attitude of his daughter Josephine, who is sought in marriage by none less than Sir Joseph Porter, the First Lord of the Admiralty, and 'she does not seem to tackle kindly to it.' They go off and Josephine herself appears, singing a sad little ballad:

Sorry her lot who loves too well,
Heavy the heart that hopes but vainly,
Sad are the sighs that own the spell,
Uttered by eyes that speak too plainly;
Heavy the heart that bows the head
When love is alive and hope is dead!

Sad is the hour when sets the sun—
Dark is the night to earth's poor daughters,
When to the ark the wearied one
Flies from the empty waste of waters!
Heavy the sorrow that bows the head
When love is alive and hope is dead!

The captain's worst fears are realised when he re-enters and hears from Josephine that her heart is already given to a humble sailor on board his own ship. But he cheers up somewhat when she assures him: 'I have a heart, and therefore I love; but I am your daughter and therefore I am proud. Though I carry my love with me to the tomb, he shall never, never know it.' She retires to her cabin, taking with her a photograph of Sir Joseph Porter, pressed into her hands by her father, with the words: 'It may help to bring you to a more reasonable frame of mind.'

From offstage, women's voices are heard in a barcarolle:

> Over the bright blue sea
> Comes Sir Joseph, KCB,
> Wherever he may go
> Bang-bang the loud nine-pounders go!
> Shout o'er the bright blue sea
> For Sir Joseph Porter, KCB

But before we see Sir Joseph there is a flurry of attractive young women—his sisters and his cousins and his aunts—for wherever he goes he takes them with him, a curious procedure perhaps, but one which provides Gilbert with an unusual way of bringing his female chorus to the stage.

To loud cheers and the accompaniment of a drum roll, the dapper figure of Sir Joseph appears, with his cousin Hebe. With interruptions from his lively relatives, he expounds:

> I am the monarch of the sea,
> The ruler of the Queen's Navee,
> Whose praise Great Britain loudly chants.
> (And we are his sisters and his cousins and his aunts!)
> When at anchor here I ride,
> My bosom swells with pride,
> And I snap my fingers at a foeman's taunts;
> (And so do his sisters and his cousins and his aunts!)
> But when the breezes blow,
> I generally go below,
> And seek the seclusion that a cabin grants!
> (And so do his sisters and his cousins and his aunts!
> His sisters and his cousins,
> Whom he reckons up by dozens,
> And his aunts!)

Sir Joseph then obliges with an account of the unusual manner in which he reached the high office in which he finds himself:

> When I was a lad I served a term
> As office boy to an Attorney's firm.

I cleaned the windows and swept the floor,
And I polished up the handle of the big front door.
I polished up that handle so carefullee
That now I am the Ruler of the Queen's Navee!

As office boy I made such a mark
That they gave me the post of a junior clerk.
I served the writs with a smile so bland,
And I copied all the letters in a big round hand—
I copied all the letters in a hand so free,
That now I am the Ruler of the Queen's Navee!

In serving writs I made such a name
That an articled clerk I soon became;
I wore clean collars and a brand-new suit
For the pass examinations of the Institute.
That pass examination did so well for me,
That now I am the Ruler of the Queen's Navee!

Of legal knowledge I acquired such a grip
That they took me into the partnership.
And that junior partnership I ween
Was the only ship that I ever had seen.
That kind of ship so suited me,
That now I am the Ruler of the Queen's Navee!

I grew so rich that I was sent
By a pocket borough into Parliament.
I always voted at my party's call,
And I never thought of thinking for myself at all.
I thought so little, they rewarded me
By making me the Ruler of the Queen's Navee!

Now landsmen all, whoever you may be,
If you want to rise to the top of the tree,
If your soul isn't fettered to an office stool,
Be careful to be guided by the golden rule—
Stick close to your desks and never go to sea,
And you all may be Rulers of the Queen's Navee!

Sir Joseph treats Captain Corcoran to a brief homily on the proper attitude to his crew. 'That you are their Captain is an accident of birth,' he says. 'I cannot permit these noble fellows to be patronized because an accident of birth has placed you above them and them below you.' And he insists that any request to these noble fellows must be accompanied by an 'if you please.' He hands to Ralph a copy of a song he has composed for the use of the Royal Navy. 'It is,' he explains, 'designed to encourage independence of thought and action in the lower branches of the service, and to teach the principle that a British sailor is any man's equal, excepting mine.'

After his departure they try out his song:

> A British tar is a soaring soul,
> As free as a mountain bird,
> His energetic fist should be ready to resist
> A dictatorial word.
> His nose should pant and his lip should curl,
> His cheeks should flame and his brow should furl,
> His bosom should heave and his heart should glow,
> And his fist be ever ready for a knock-down blow.
>
> His eyes should flash with an inborn fire,
> His brow with scorn be wrung;
> He never should bow down to a domineering frown,
> Or the tang of a tyrant tongue.
> His foot should stamp and his throat should growl,
> His hair should twirl and his face should scowl;
> His eyes should flash and his breast protrude,
> And this should be his customary attitude!

They dance off, leaving Ralph alone—to be met by Josephine. He pours out his problem in the words of a simple sailor: 'In me there meet a combination of antithetical elements which are at eternal war with one another. Driven hither by objective influences —thither by subjective emotions—wafted one moment into blazing day, by mocking hope—plunged the next into the Cimmerian darkness of tangible despair, I am but a living ganglion of irreconcilable emotions. . . . I hope I make myself clear, lady?' 'His simple eloquence goes to my heart,' murmurs Josephine.

Ralph takes the plunge: 'Even though Jove's armoury were launched at the head of the audacious mortal whose lips, unhallowed by relationship, dared to breathe that precious word, yet would I breathe it once, and then perchance be silent evermore. Josephine, in one brief breath I will concentrate the hopes, the doubts, the anxious fears of six weary months. Josephine, I am a British sailor, and I love you!' Quite a good effort even for the smartest lad in all the fleet, but Josephine is true to the dictates of class distinction. They sing a duet, revealing their true feelings in asides:

JOSEPHINE:
Refrain, audacious tar,
Your suit from pressing;
Remember what you are,
And whom addressing!

(*Aside*)
I'd laugh my rank to scorn
In union holy,
Were he more highly born
Or I more lowly!

RALPH:
Proud lady, have your way,
Unfeeling beauty!
You speak and I obey,
It is my duty!
I am the lowliest tar
That sails the water,
And you, proud maiden, are
My captain's daughter!

(*Aside*)
My heart with anguish torn
Bows down before her;
She laughs my love to scorn,
Yet I adore her!

The finale to the first act opens with the despairing Ralph
announcing that the only thing left for him to do is to blow his
brains out. There are sympathetic sounds from the chorus, interrupted by the 'I told you so, I told you so' of Dick Deadeye, but
nobody does anything to avert the tragedy. Indeed, the boatswain
loads a pistol and hands it to Ralph, who puts it to his head while
his messmates stop their ears.

But instead of a loud report there is the hurried entry of Josephine,
crying 'Ah! Stay your hand! I love you!' followed by a rapturous
ensemble from all except Dick Deadeye:

He thinks he's won his Josephine,
But though the sky is now serene,
A frowning thunderbolt above
May end their ill-assorted love
Which now is all ablaze.

> Our Captain, ere the day is gone,
> Will be extremely down upon
> The wicked men who art employ
> To make his Josephine less coy
> In many various ways.

But Dick Deadeye is brushed aside amid the general jollification and the planning for Josephine and Ralph to steal ashore that night to be married.

The tune of Little Buttercup's opening song provides an entr'acte and, when the curtain rises on the second act, *HMS Pinafore* is bathed in moonlight. This is fortunate for the chastened Captain Corcoran, as it enables him to sing, to his own mandolin accompaniment:

> Fair moon, to thee I sing,
> Bright regent of the heavens,
> Say, why is everything
> Either at sixes or at sevens?
> I have lived hitherto
> Free from breath of slander,
> Beloved by all my crew—
> A really popular commander.
> But now my kindly crew rebel,
> My daughter to a tar is partial,
> Sir Joseph storms, and, sad to tell,
> He threatens a court martial!
> Fair moon, to thee I sing,
> Bright regent of the heavens,
> Say, why is everything
> Either at sixes or at sevens?

Little Buttercup, who has a way of turning up when the Captain is around, tells him that she has gipsy blood in her veins and can read destinies. She embarks on a series of mixed-up proverbs with such lines as:

> Black sheep dwell in every fold;
> All that glitters is not gold;
> Storks turn out to be just logs;
> Bulls are but inflated frogs.

The Captain joins her in a duet but, understandably bewildered, sums up with the comment: 'Incomprehensible as her utterances are, I nevertheless feel that they are dictated by a sincere regard for me.'

Meanwhile, Sir Joseph is becoming more and more irritated at Josephine's lack of response to his eloquent pleadings and Captain Corcoran points out to him that it is probable that his exalted rank has dazzled her. Perhaps Sir Joseph could reason with her and assure her that it is a standing rule at the Admiralty that love levels all ranks?

Josephine, on her part, is pondering upon the choice that lies before her:

> The hours creep on apace,
> My guilty heart is quaking!
> Oh, that I might retrace
> The step that I am taking!
> Its folly it were easy to be showing,
> What I am giving up and whither going.
> On the one hand, papa's luxurious home,
> Hung with ancestral armour and old brasses,
> Carved oak and tapestry from distant Rome,
> Rare 'blue and white' Venetian glasses,
> Rich oriental rugs, luxurious sofa pillows,
> And everything that isn't old, from Gillow's.
> And on the other a dark and dingy room,
> In some back street with stuffy children crying,
> Where organs yell, and clacking housewives fume,
> And clothes are hanging out all day a-drying.
> With one cracked looking-glass to see your face in,
> And dinner served up in a pudding basin!
>
> A simple sailor, lowly born,
> Unlettered and unknown,
> Who toils for bread from early morn
> Till half the night has flown!
> No golden rank can he impart—
> No wealth of house or land—
> No fortune save his trusty heart,
> And honest brown right hand!
> And yet he is so wondrous fair
> That love for one so passing rare,
> So peerless in his manly beauty,
> Were little else than solemn duty!
> Oh, god of love, and god of reason, say,
> Which of you twain shall my poor heart obey!

Sir Joseph arrives with the Captain and proceeds to assure Josephine 'officially' that love is a platform upon which all ranks

meet, little realising that he is effectively pleading the case for Ralph
and Josephine. Sir Joseph, the Captain and Josephine—all delighted,
but for different reasons—then embark on the liveliest ensemble in
the opera, with Sir Joseph having a high old time ringing every
kind of bell he can lay his hands on:

CAPTAIN:
Never mind the why and wherefore,
Love can level ranks, and therefore,
Though his lordship's station's mighty,
Though stupendous be his brain,
Though your tastes are mean and flighty
And your fortune poor and plain,

CAPTAIN and SIR JOSEPH:
Ring the merry bells on board-ship,
Rend the air with warbling wild,
For the union of his/my lordship
With a humble captain's child!

CAPTAIN:
For a humble captain's daughter—

JOSEPHINE:
For a gallant captain's daughter—

SIR JOSEPH:
And a lord who rules the water—

JOSEPHINE (aside)
And a *tar* who ploughs the water!

ALL:
Let the air with joy be laden,
Rend with songs the air above,
For the union of a maiden
With the man who owns her love!

SIR JOSEPH:
Never mind the why and wherefore,
Love can level ranks, and therefore,
Though your nautical relation
In my set could hardly pass—
Though you occupy a station
In the lower middle class—

CAPTAIN AND SIR JOSEPH:
Ring the merry bells etc.

JOSEPHINE:
Never mind the why and wherefore,
Love can level ranks, and therefore
I admit the jurisdiction:
Ably have you played your part;
You have carried firm conviction
To my hesitating heart.

CAPTAIN and SIR JOSEPH:
Ring the merry bells, etc.

It is now that Dick Deadeye plays his hand. Shuffling up to the Captain he reveals the plan for the elopement of Ralph and Josephine that night:

DICK DEADEYE:
Kind Captain, I've important information,
Sing hey, the kind commander that you are,
About a certain intimate relation,
Sing hey, the merry maiden and the tar.

CAPTAIN:
Good fellow, in conundrums you are speaking,
Sing hey, the mystic sailor that you are;
The answer to them vainly I am seeking;
Sing hey, the merry maiden and the tar.

DICK DEADEYE:
Kind Captain, your young lady is a-sighing,
Sing hey, the simple captain that you are,
This very night with Rackstraw to be flying;
Sing hey, the merry maiden and the tar.

CAPTAIN:
Good fellow, you have given timely warning,
Sing hey, the thoughtful sailor that you are;
I'll talk to Master Rackstraw in the morning,
Sing hey, the cat-o'-nine tails and the tar.

Captain Corcoran wraps himself in a heavy cloak and lurks in the shadows as the crew tiptoe in, while Ralph and Josephine prepare to depart. Throwing off his cloak, the Captain suddenly reveals himself:

Pretty daughter of mine,
I insist upon knowing
Where you may be going
With these sons of the brine.

For my excellent crew,
Though foes they could thump any,
Are scarcely fit company,
My daughter, for you.

To the Captain's horror, Ralph declares his love for Josephine,
completely justifying his actions by the simple fact that he is an
Englishman, while the boatswain clinches the argument with the
splendidly mock-Jingo pronouncement:

For he might have been a Roosian,
A French or Turk or Proosian,
Or perhaps Ital-ian!
But in spite of all temptations
To belong to other nations,
He remains an Englishman!

Not perhaps surprisingly, the Captain bursts out with 'Damme,
it's too bad!', as Sir Joseph emerges, hears this terrible language and,
without waiting for an explanation, banishes Corcoran to his cabin.
But when, immediately afterwards, he learns the truth, he has Ralph
handcuffed and thrown into the dungeon.

Little Buttercup, however, throws dramatic light on the situation with her confession:

BUTTERCUP:
A many years ago,
When I was young and charming,
As some of you may know,
I practised baby-farming.

ALL:
Now this is most alarming!
When she was young and charming,
She practised baby-farming,
A many years ago.

BUTTERCUP:
Two tender babes I nussed,
One was of low condition,
The other, upper crust,
A regular patrician.

ALL:
Now, this is the position,
One was of low condition,
The other a patrician,
A many years ago.

BUTTERCUP:

Oh, bitter is my cup!
However could I do it?
I mixed those children up,
And not a creature knew it!

ALL:

However could you do it?
Some day, no doubt, you'll rue it,
Although no creature knew it,
So many years ago.

BUTTERCUP:

In time each little waif
Forsook his foster-mother,
The well-born babe was Ralph—
Your Captain was the other!

ALL:

They left their foster-mother.
The one was Ralph, our brother,
Our Captain was the other,
A many years ago.

At Sir Joseph's summons, Ralph conveniently appears dressed as
a Captain and Corcoran as an ordinary seaman. Even Dick Deadeye
joins Josephine, Hebe and Ralph in a quartet:

Oh joy, oh rapture unforeseen,
The clouded sky is now serene,
The god of day—the orb of love,
Has hung his ensign high above,
The sky is all ablaze.

With wooing words and loving song,
We'll chase the lagging hours along,
And if he finds (I find) the maiden coy,
We'll murmur forth decorous joy
In dreamy roundelay.

Everybody suddenly makes up his mind. Ralph embraces his
Josephine, Corcoran turns to little Buttercup, and Sir Joseph settles
for the first cousin, Hebe.

Hobbs, Frederick Business manager of the D'Oyly Carte Company for sixteen years until his death in 1942, Frederick Hobbs had
earlier sung a number of the leading bass and baritone roles. He

joined the company in 1913 and in his first season sang Colonel Calverley (P), Lord Mountararat (I), Arac (PI), Pish-Tush (M), Lieutenant of the Tower (Y) and Luiz (G). His later roles included Samuel (PP), Sir Marmaduke (S), Dick Deadeye (HMS), Pirate King (PP), Sergeant Meryll (Y) and Giuseppe (G).

Holland, Lyndsie Lyndsie Holland took over the leading contralto roles with the D'Oyly Carte Company in May, 1971—Lady Sangazure (S), Little Buttercup (HMS), Ruth (PP), Lady Jane (P), Fairy Queen (I), Lady Blanche (PI), Katisha (M), Dame Hannah (R), Dame Carruthers (Y) and Duchess of Plaza-Toro (G). Born in Stourbridge, she studied at Birmingham School of Music, worked as a telephonist and spent three years with the Midland Music Makers Grand Opera Society before joining the chorus of Sadler's Wells Opera. She joined D'Oyly Carte in December, 1970, and was immediately given the role of Lady Sangazure in the new production of *The Sorcerer*.

Hollingsworth, J The original Counsel for the Plaintiff (J).

Hood, Ann Though she originally intended to be a doctor, Ann Hood turned to music and studied with Dame Eva Turner at the Royal Academy, and while still there made her stage debut as one of the Three Boys in *The Magic Flute* at the Royal Opera House, Covent Garden. Joining D'Oyly Carte as a principal, she sang Josephine (HMS), Patience, Princess Ida, Rose Maybud (R), Elsie Maynard (Y) and Gianetta (G). She left the company in 1966, for further study.

Hood, Marion The original Mabel (PP) in the London production.

Horace 'From Ovid and Horace.'—Robin Oakapple (R). Horace, the Roman lyric poet, lived from 65 BC to 8 AD.

'Hour of gladness is dead and gone, The' Katisha's solo in the finale to the first act (M).

'Hours creep on apace, The' Josephine's scena, in which she weighs up the differences between living in luxury and marrying a poor sailor (HMS).

'How beautifully blue the sky' Chattering chorus for the girls (PP).

Howell and James 'A Howell and James young man.'—Archibald Grosvenor (P). Drapery and fancy goods establishment in Regent Street, London.

'How say you maiden, will you wed' Trio for Elsie Maynard, Jack Point and Lieutenant of the Tower (Y).

Howson, Emma The first artist to sing Josephine (HMS), Emma Howson also sang Patience in New York.

'How would I play this part—the Grand Duke's bride?' Julia Jellicoe's ballad (D).

Hunting In a discussion about fox-hunting, someone put forward the view that the fox enjoyed the chase. 'I should like to hear the fox on that point,' said Gilbert, a devoted lover of animals.
And again: 'Deer-stalking would be a very fine sport if only the deer had guns.'

Hutchison, Linda Anne She sings the principal roles of Plaintiff (J), Constance (S), Josephine (HMS), Patience (P), Phyllis (I), Elsie Maynard (Y) and Gianetta (G). Born in Scotland, she studied elocution there before going to the Guildhall School of Music and Drama, London. While still at the Guildhall, she auditioned for D'Oyly Carte and was at once offered a position in the chorus, moving on to leading soprano roles after only a year as a chorister. In 1971 she married a professor at the Royal Academy of Music. As well as a singer, Miss Hutchison is an accomplished ballet dancer.

'I am a courtier grave and serious' The Duke of Plaza-Toro—with the Duchess, Casilda, Marco and Giuseppe—gives a lesson in deportment (G).

'I am a maiden, cold and stately' Trio for Hilarion, Cyril and Florian after they have dressed up as girl graduates (PI).

'I am so proud' Pooh-Bah's part in the first-act trio with Ko-Ko and Pish-Tush (M).

'I am the Captain of the Pinafore' Captain Corcoran's song in which he vows that he never uses 'a big, big D—.' (HMS).

'I am the monarch of the sea' Sir Joseph Porter's song on arrival aboard the *Pinafore*—with his sisters and his cousins and his aunts.

'I am the very model of a modern Major-General' Major-General Stanley's patter-song in which he reveals that he knows about almost everything except military matters (PP).

'I built upon a rock' Princess Ida's song (PI).

I cannot tell what this love may be' Patience's song after her first entrance.

'Ida was a twelve month old' Hilarion's ballad (PI).

'If Saphir I choose to marry' Quintet for the Duke, Colonel, Major, Angela and Saphir (P).

'If somebody there chanced to be' Rose Maybud's ballad about the book of etiquette which governs her life (R).

'If the light of love's lingering ember' Duet for Ernest Dummkopf and Julia Jellicoe (D).

'If there be pardon in your breast' Patience's plea to Reginald Bunthorne (P).

'If we're weak enough to tarry' Duet for Strephon and Phyllis (I).

'If you ask us how we live' Leila's solo after the fairies have entered at the start of the opera (I).

'If you give me your attention I will tell you what I am' King Gama's song—'And I can't think why' (PI).

'If you go in, you're sure to win' Lively trio for Lord Chancellor, Earl of Mountararat and Earl Tolloller—'Faint heart never won fair lady!' (I).

'If you're anxious for to shine in the high aesthetic line' Reginald Bunthorne's song, in which one of the recommendations is to 'walk down Piccadilly with a poppy or a lily in your mediaeval hand.' (P).

'If you think that, when banded in unity' Trio for Scaphio, Phantis and the King (U).

'If you want a receipt for that popular mystery' Colonel Calverley's song about the varied qualities that go to the making of a Heavy Dragoon (P).

'If you want to know who we are' Opening chorus of the 'gentlemen of Japan.' (M).

'I have a song to sing, O!' Duet for Elsie Maynard and Jack Point, sung on their first appearance and repeated as the finale to the opera (Y). This lyric of Gilbert's gave Sullivan a good deal of trouble in the setting but, fortunately, the two of them seem to have been on reasonably amiable terms at this stage. Though Gilbert always insisted that he had little musical knowledge, it was he who came up with a suggestion which met the present case. Asked by Sullivan if he had any likely idea in his mind, he hummed a snatch of a song that he had heard sailors singing. 'That will do,' enthused

Sullivan, 'I've got it.' Later Gilbert joked about the incident:'I have sometimes thought that he exclaimed, "That will do—I've got it" because my humming was more than he could bear. But he always assured me that it had given him the necessary clue.'

'I heard one day a gentleman say' Pish-Tush's part in the first-act trio with Ko-Ko and Pooh-Bah (M).

'I hear the soft note of the echoing voice' Ensemble for Ella, Saphir, Angela, Duke, Major, Colonel and chorus in the finale to the first act (P).

'I know a youth who loves a little maid' Duet for Robin Oakapple and Rose Maybud (R).

'I love him, I love him, with fervour unceasing' Duet for Plaintiff and Defendant. (J).

'I'm called Little Buttercup' Opening song of Mrs Cripps, better known as Little Buttercup, the Portsmouth bumboat woman (HMS).

'I'm Captain Corcoran, KCB' The Captain's solo on his first appearance (U), when he harks back to the 'Hardly ever!' gag from *Pinafore*.

'I'm telling a terrible story' Ensemble for Major-General Stanley, pirates and girls (PP).

'I'm very much pained to refuse' Phyllis's solo when she first rejects the joint advances of the Earl of Mountararat and Earl Tolloller (I).

'In a contemplative fashion' Quartet for Marco, Giuseppe, Gianetta and Tessa (G).

'In babyhood upon her lap I lay' Strephon's ballad in the finale to the first act (I).

'In bygone days I had thy love' Rose Maybud's ballad (R).

Income Tax King Gama (PI) gives as one of the reasons for his unpopularity: 'I know everybody's income and what everybody earns; and I carefully compare it with the income-tax returns.'

And Sir Ruthven Murgatroyd (R), listing his 'crimes' before the ghosts of his ancestors, confesses: 'On Tuesday I made a false income-tax return.' 'Ha! ha!' retort the ghosts. 'That's nothing. Nothing at all. Everybody does that. It's expected of you.'

When *Princess Ida* was produced in 1884, the standard rate of British income-tax stood at fivepence in the pound. No doubt there was a heartfelt reaction from the audience to the reference in *Ruddigore* three years later. They were then smarting under the impact of a rise to sevenpence in the pound!

'In enterprise of martial kind' The Duke of Plaza-Toro's song, outlining the advantages of leading one's troops from behind (G).

'In every mental lore' Duet for the wise men, Scaphio and Phantis, on their first entrance (U).

Inez (G) *Contralto* The foster-mother to the King of Barataria was originally played by Annie Bernard.

Infallibility 'I am the Apostle of Simplicity. I am called 'Archibald the All-Right'—for I am infallible.'—Archibald Grosvenor (P).

Injustice 'It's an unjust world, and virtue is triumphant only in theatrical performances.

> See how the fates their gifts allot,
> For A is happy—B is not.
> Yet B is worthy, I dare say,
> Of more prosperity than A.' (M).

'In lazy languor, motionless' Opening chorus of the maidens (U).

'In sailing o'er life's ocean wide' Ensemble for Richard Dauntless, Robin Oakapple and Rose Maybud (R).

'In vain to us you plead—Don't go!' Duet for Leila and Celia, teasing Their Lordships (I).

IOLANTHE; or The Peer and the Peri First performed at the Savoy Theatre, London, on November 25, 1882, conducted by Sullivan. Initial run of 398 performances.

The original cast for the 'Fairy Opera' was:

THE LORD CHANCELLOR	Mr George Grossmith
THE EARL OF MOUNTARARAT	Mr Rutland Barrington
THE EARL TOLLOLLER	Mr Durward Lely
PRIVATE WILLIS (*of the Grenadier Guards*)	Mr Charles Manners
STREPHON (*an Arcadian Shepherd*)	Mr Richard Temple
QUEEN OF THE FAIRIES	Miss Alice Barnett
IOLANTHE (*a Fairy, Strephon's Mother*)	Miss Jessie Bond
CELIA ⎫	Miss Fortescue
LEILA ⎬ (*Fairies*)	Miss Julia Gwynne
FLETA ⎭	Miss Sybil Grey
PHYLLIS (*an Arcadian Shepherdess and Ward in Chancery*)	Miss Leonora Braham

The curtain rises on an Arcadian scene, with a river crossed by a rustic bridge. Leila, Celia and Fleta lead on the fairies, who sing as they dance round:

> Tripping hither, tripping thither,
> Nobody knows why or whither;
> We must dance and we must sing,
> Round about our fairy ring!

> CELIA:
> We are dainty little fairies,
> Ever singing, ever dancing;
> We indulge in our vagaries
> In a fashion most entrancing.
> If you ask the special function
> Of our never-ceasing motion,
> We reply, without compunction,
> That we haven't any notion!

> LEILA:
> If you ask us how we live,
> Lovers all essentials give—
> We can ride on lovers' sighs,
> Warm ourselves in lovers' eyes,
> Bathe ourselves in lovers' tears,
> Clothe ourselves with lovers' fears,
> Arm ourselves with lovers' darts,
> Hide ourselves in lovers' hearts.
> When you know us you'll discover
> That we almost live on lover!

Celia, Leila and Fleta recall that it is twenty-five years since Iolanthe, 'the life and soul of Fairyland,' was banished by the Fairy

Queen for having committed the sin of marrying a mortal. She is working out her sentence of penal servitude at the bottom of the stream! But the Fairy Queen enters and, yielding to the pleading of the others, agrees to bring Iolanthe back. They call out and Iolanthe, clad in weeds, rises from the water.

Iolanthe is pardoned by the Queen and, her water-weeds falling away, she is revealed clothed as a fairy once more. The Queen places a diamond coronet on her head and the fairies express their joy:

> Welcome to our hearts again,
> Iolanthe! Iolanthe!
> We have shared thy bitter pain,
> Iolanthe! Iolanthe!
> Every heart and every hand
> In our loving little band
> Welcomes thee to Fairyland,
> Iolanthe!

She reveals that she has a son called Strephon, an Arcadian shepherd ('He's a fairy down to the waist but his legs are mortal'), who is in love with Phyllis, a Ward in Chancery. A moment later Strephon dances in, playing upon a flageolet. He greets his mother:

> Good morrow, good mother!
> Good mother, good morrow!
> By some means or other,
> Pray banish your sorrow!
> With joy beyond telling
> My bosom is swelling,
> So join in a measure
> Expressive of pleasure,
> For I'm to be married to-day—to-day—
> Yes, I'm to be married to-day!

Strephon tells his mother that although the Lord Chancellor has turned down his plea to marry Phyllis, a Ward in Chancery, they intend to go ahead with their marriage. He is a little taken aback when the other fairies are introduced to him as his aunts and he speaks of the problems of being half a fairy. ('My brain is a fairy brain but from the waist downwards I'm a gibbering idiot.') The Queen suggests that she might make him a Member of Parliament.

They all bid him farewell, with their good wishes:

QUEEN:
Fare thee well, attractive stranger.

FAIRIES:
Fare thee well, attractive stranger.

QUEEN:
Shouldst thou be in doubt or danger,
Peril or perplexitee,
Call us and we'll come to thee!

FAIRIES:
Aye! Call us, and we'll come to thee!
Tripping hither, tripping thither,
Nobody knows why or whither;
We must now be taking wing
To another fairy ring!

Strephon is greeted by Phyllis, singing and dancing and playing upon a flageolet:

Good morrow, good lover!
Good lover, good morrow!
I prithee discover,
Steal, purchase or borrow
Some means of concealing
The care you are feeling,
And join in a measure
Expressive of pleasure,
For we're to be married to-day—to-day—
Yes, we're to be married to-day!

Strephon chides her with the fact that half the House of Lords are sighing at her feet. They agree that they must get married without delay:

PHYLLIS:
None shall part us from each other,
One in life and death are we;
All in all to one another—
I to thee and thou to me!

BOTH:
Thou the tree and I the flower—
Thou the idol; I the throng—
Thou the day and I the hour—
Thou the singer; I the song!

STREPHON:
All in all since that fond meeting,
When, in joy, I woke to find
Mine the heart within thee beating,
Mine the love that heart enshrined!

BOTH:
Thou the stream and I the willow—
Thou the sculptor; I the clay—
Thou the ocean; I the billow—
Thou the sunrise; I the day!

They go off together, and the Peers arrive, in all the splendour of their ceremonial robes and accompanied by a band of the Brigade of Guards:

Loudly let the trumpet bray!
Tantantara!
Proudly bang the sounding brasses!
Tzing! Boom!
As upon its lordly way
This unique procession passes,
Tantantara! Tzing! Boom!
Bow, bow, ye lower middle classes!
Bow, bow, ye tradesmen, bow, ye masses!
Blow the trumpets, bang the brasses!
Tantantara! Tzing! Boom!
We are peers of highest station,
Paragons of legislation,
Pillars of the British nation!
Tantantara! Tzing! Boom!

The Lord Chancellor comes in, attended by his train-bearer, and explains some of the difficulties of being responsible for attractive Wards in Chancery:

The Law is the true embodiment
Of everything that's excellent.
It has no kind of fault or flaw,
And I, my Lords, embody the Law.
The constitutional guardian I
Of pretty young Wards in Chancery,
All very agreeable girls—and none
Are over the age of twenty-one.
A pleasant occupation for
A rather susceptible Chancellor!

But though the compliment implied
Inflates me with legitimate pride,
It nevertheless can't be denied
That it has its inconvenient side.
For I'm not so old, and not so plain,
And I'm quite prepared to marry again,
But there'd be the deuce to pay in the Lords
If I fell in love with one of my Wards!
Which rather tries my temper, for
I'm *such* a susceptible Chancellor!

And every one who'd marry a Ward
Must come to me for my accord,
And in my court I sit all day,
Giving agreeable girls away,
With one for him—and one for he—
And one for you—and one for ye—
And one for thou—and one for thee—
But never, oh, never a one for me!
Which is exasperating for
A highly susceptible Chancellor!

They get down to the business of the day. The Peers have asked
the Lord Chancellor to decide which of them shall be permitted
to marry Phyllis but he confesses that he himself is 'singularly
attracted' by her, though there are many difficulties in the way of
him giving her to himself. ('Ah, my Lords, it is indeed painful to
have to sit upon a woolsack which is stuffed with such thorns as
these!'). Phyllis is called before them.

LORD TOLLOLLER:
Of all the young ladies I know
This pretty young lady's the fairest;
Her lips have the rosiest show,
Her eyes are the richest and rarest.
Her origin's lowly, it's true,
But of birth and position I've plenty;
I've grammer and spelling for two,
And blood and behaviour for twenty!

LORD MOUNTARARAT:
Though the views of the House have diverged
On every conceivable motion,
All questions of Party are merged
In a frenzy of love and devotion;

If you ask us distinctly to say
What Party we claim to belong to,
We reply, without doubt or delay,
The Party we're singing this song to!

PHYLLIS:
I'm very much pained to refuse,
But I'll stick to my pipes and my tabors;
I can spell all the words that I use,
And my grammar's as good as my neighbours'.
As for birth—I was born like the rest,
My behaviour is rustic but hearty,
And I know where to turn for the best,
When I want a particular Party!

To her assertion that 'in lowly cot alone is virtue found,' Lord
Tolloller sings up on behalf of the aristocracy:

Spurn not the nobly born
With love affected,
Nor treat with virtuous scorn
The well-connected.
High rank involves no shame—
We boast an equal claim
With him of humble name
To be respected!
Blue blood! blue blood!
When virtuous love is sought
Thy power is naught,
Though dating from the Flood,
Blue blood!
Spare us the bitter pain
Of stern denials,
Nor with low-born disdain
Augment our trials.
Hearts just as pure and fair
May beat in Belgrave Square
As in the lowly air
Of Seven Dials!
Blue blood! blue blood!
Of what avail art thou
To serve us now?
Though dating from the Flood,
Blue blood!

But to their horror, Phyllis confesses that she is betrothed to Strephon, who rushes in and claims her. Lords Mountararat and Tolloller sum up the feelings of the Peers:

> 'Neath this blow
> Worse than stab of dagger—
> Though we mo—
> Mentarily stagger,
> In each heart
> Proud are we innately—
> Let's depart,
> Dignified and stately!
>
> ALL:
> Though our hearts she's badly bruising,
> In another suitor choosing,
> Let's pretend it's most amusing.
> Ha! ha! ha! Tan-ta-ra!

Left alone with the Lord Chancellor, Strephon insists that the whole of Nature has impelled him to love Phyllis. Unimpressed, the Lord Chancellor points out that he has always kept his duty strictly before his eyes:

> When I went to the Bar as a very young man,
> (Said I to myself—said I),
> I'll work on a new and original plan,
> (Said I to myself—said I),
> I'll never assume that a rogue or a thief
> Is a gentleman worthy implicit belief,
> Because his attorney has sent me a brief,
> (Said I to myself—said I!).
>
> Ere I go into court I will read my brief through,
> (Said I to myself—said I),
> And I'll never take work I'm unable to do,
> (Said I to myself—said I),
> My learned profession I'll never disgrace
> By taking a fee with a grin on my face,
> When I haven't been there to attend to the case,
> (Said I to myself—said I!).
>
> I'll never throw dust in a juryman's eyes,
> (Said I to myself—said I),
> Or hoodwink a judge who is not over-wise,
> (Said I to myself—said I),

Or assume that the witnesses summoned in force
In Exchequer, Queen's Bench, Common Pleas or
   Divorce,
Have perjured themselves as a matter of course,
(Said I to myself—said I!).

In other professions in which men engage,
(Said I to myself—said I),
The Army, the Navy, the Church, and the Stage,
(Said I to myself—said I),
Professional licence, if carried too far,
Your chance of promotion will certainly mar—
And I fancy the rule might apply to the Bar,
(Said I to myself—said I!).

On the Lord Chancellor's departure Iolanthe enters and Strephon bemoans to her the fact that the law has interposed and he and Phyllis are separated for ever. Iolanthe comforts him with the assurance that she will lay his case before the Fairy Queen. Meanwhile, the Peers, with Phyllis, have crept in unseen and proceed to mishear what follows—to Phyllis's horror at what she believes to be Strephon's unfaithfulness.

STREPHON (*to* IOLANTHE):
When darkly looms the day,
And all is dull and grey,
To chase the gloom away,
On thee I'll call!

LORD MOUNTARARAT (*aside to* PHYLLIS):
I think I heard him say,
That on a rainy day,
To while the time away,
On her he'd call!

IOLANTHE (*to* STREPHON):
When tempests wreck thy bark,
And all is drear and dark,
If thou shouldst need an Ark,
I'll give thee one!

LORD TOLLOLLER:
I heard the minx remark,
She'd meet him after dark,
Inside St. James's Park,
And give him one!

PHYLLIS:
The prospect's very bad,
My heart so sore and sad
Will never more be glad
As summer's sun!

They all merge in an ensemble in which each expresses his or her own point of view. Then Phyllis steps forward and confronts Strephon:

Oh, shameless one, tremble!
Nay, do not endeavour
Thy fault to dissemble,
We part—and for ever!
I worshipped him blindly,
He worships another—

STREPHON:
Attend to me kindly,
This lady's my mother!

There is general confusion and the Peers are laughing derisively as the Lord Chancellor enters and Iolanthe throws a veil over her face. Lord Mountararat explains to the Lord Chancellor:

This gentle man is seen,
With a maid of seventeen,
A-taking of his *dolce far niente*;
And wonders he'd achieve,
For he asks us to believe
She's his mother—and he's nearly five-and-twenty!

LORD CHANCELLOR:
Recollect yourself, I pray,
And be careful what you say—
As the ancient Romans said, *festina lente*.
For I really do not see
How so young a girl could be
The mother of a man of five-and-twenty!

STREPHON:
In babyhood
Upon her lap I lay,
With infant food
She moistenèd my clay;
Had she withheld
The succour she supplied,
By hunger quelled,
Your Strephon might have died!

M

They are all deeply moved by this but Lord Mountararat rallies them:

But as she's not
His mother, it appears,
Why weep these hot
Unnecessary tears?
And by what laws
Should we so joyously
Rejoice, because
Our Strephon did not die?
Oh, rather let us pipe our eye
Because our Strephon did not die!

They all weep, and Iolanthe, who has kept her face hidden from the Lord Chancellor, slips away unnoticed. Phyllis dismisses Strephon and vows that she will marry one of the Peers:

PHYLLIS:
For riches and rank I do not long—
Their pleasures are false and vain;
I gave up the love of a lordly throng
For the love of a simple swain.
But now that simple swain's untrue,
With sorrowful heart I turn to you—
A heart that's aching,
Quaking, breaking,
As sorrowful hearts are wont to do!

The riches and rank that you befall
Are the only baits you use,
So the richest and rankiest of you all
My sorrowful heart shall choose.
As none are so noble—none so rich
As this couple of lords, I'll find a niche
In my heart that's aching,
Quaking, breaking,
For one of you two—and I don't care which!

Phyllis addresses both Lords Mountararat and Tolloller, to the puzzlement of everybody:

To you I give my heart so rich!
(ALL: 'To which?')
I do not care!
To you I yield—it is my doom!

(To whom?)
I'm not aware!
I'm yours for life if you but choose.
(She's whose?)
That's your affair!
I'll be a countess, shall I not?
(Of what?)
I do not care!

ALL:
Lucky little lady!
Strephon's lot is shady;
Rank, it seems, is vital,
'Countess' is the title,
But of what I'm not aware!

Strephon appears and calls the fairies to his aid. They trip on, followed by the Queen, who assures the Peers that Iolanthe really *is* his mother. They persist in their disbelief:

LORD TOLLOLLER:
I have often had a use
For a thorough-bred excuse
Of a sudden (which is English for *repente*),
But of all I ever heard
This is much the most absurd,
For she's seventeen, and he is five-and-twenty!

ALL:
Though she is seventeen, and he's only five-and-
    twenty!
Oh, fie! our Strephon is a rogue!

LORD MOUNTARARAT:
Now, listen, pray, to me,
For this paradox will be
Carried, nobody at all *contradicente*.
Her age, upon the date
Of his birth was *minus* eight,
If she's seventeen, and he is five-and-twenty!

ALL:
To say she is his mother is an utter bit of folly!
Oh, fie! our Strephon is a rogue!
Perhaps his brain is addled, and it's very melancholy!
Taradiddle, taradiddle, tol lol lay!

I wouldn't say a word that could be reckoned as
  injurious,
But to find a mother younger than her son is very
  curious,
And that's a kind of mother that is usually spurious.
Taradiddle, taradiddle, tol lol lay!

LORD CHANCELLOR:
Go away, madam;
I should say, madam,
You display, madam,
Shocking taste.
It is rude, madam,
To intrude, madam,
With your brood, madam,
Brazen-faced!
You come here, madam,
Interfere, madam,
With a peer, madam.
(I am one.)
You're aware madam,
What you dare, madam,
So take care, madam,
And begone!

The Queen gives them a piece of her mind and the Peers are
considerably shaken to realise that they are faced by 'an influential
fairy'. She makes her pronouncement:

Henceforth, Strephon, cast away
Crooks and pipes and ribbons so gay—
Flocks and herds that bleat and low;
Into Parliament you shall go!

ALL:
Into Parliament he shall go!
Backed by our/their supreme authority,
He'll command a large majority;
Into Parliament he shall go!

QUEEN:
In the Parliamentary hive,
Liberal or Conservative—
Whig or Tory—I don't know—
But into Parliament you shall go!

The Peers exclaim in alarm and plead for mercy as the Queen addresses them:

> Every Bill and every measure
> That may gratify his pleasure,
> Though your fury it arouses,
> Shall be passed by both your Houses!
> You shall sit if he sees reason,
> Through the grouse and salmon season;
> He shall end the cherished rights
> You enjoy on Friday nights:
> He shall prick that annual blister,
> Marriage with deceased wife's sister:
> Titles shall enoble, then,
> All the Common Councilmen:
> Peers shall teem in Christendom,
> And a Duke's exalted station
> Be attained by Com-
> Petitive Examination!

There is general uproar and the act ends with the Peers on their knees, begging for mercy, while the fairies threaten them with their wands.

The setting for the second act is Palace Yard, Westminster. On sentry duty, Private Willis of the Grenadier Guards is thinking aloud:

> When all night long a chap remains
> On sentry-go, to chase monotony
> He exercises of his brains,
> That is, assuming that he's got any.
> Though never nurtured in the lap
> Of luxury, yet I admonish you,
> I am an intellectual chap,
> And think of things that would astonish you.
> I often think it is comical—Fal, lal, la!
> How nature always does contrive—Fal, lal, la! la!
> That every boy and every gal
> That's born into the world alive
> Is either a little Liberal
> Or else a little Conservative!
> Fal, lal, la!

When in that House MP's divide,
If they've a brain and cerebellum, too,
They've got to leave that brain outside,
And vote just as their leaders tell 'em to.
But then the prospect of a lot
Of dull MP's in close proximity,
All thinking for themselves, is what
No man can face with equanimity.
Then let's rejoice with loud Fal, lal,—Fal, lal, la!
That nature always does contrive—Fal, lal, la! la!
That every boy and every gal
That's born into the world alive,
Is either a little Liberal
Or else a little Conservative!
Fal, lal, la!

Celia, Leila, Fleta and the other fairies enter and trip round the stage singing:

Strephon's a Member of Parliament!
Carries every Bill he chooses.
To his measures all assent—
Showing that fairies have their uses.
Whigs and Tories
Dim their glories,
Giving an ear to all his stories—
Lords and Commons are both in the blues:
Strephon makes them shake in their shoes!
Shake in their shoes!
Shake in their shoes!
Strephon makes them shake in their shoes!

From Westminster Hall enter the Peers, highly discomfited by Strephon's Parliamentary activities:

Strephon's a Member of Parliament!
Running a-muck of all abuses.
His unqualified assent
Somehow nobody now refuses.
Whigs and Tories
Dim their glories,
Giving an ear to all his stories—
Carrying every Bill he may wish:
Here's a pretty kettle of fish!

Kettle of fish!
Kettle of fish!
Here's a pretty kettle of fish!

Lord Mountararat expresses his annoyance at Strephon's introduction of a Bill to throw the Peerage open to competitive examination. He insists that the House of Peers does quite nicely as it is:

When Britain really ruled the waves—
(In good Queen Bess's time)
The House of Peers made no pretence
To intellectual eminence,
Or scholarship sublime;
Yet Britain won her proudest bays
In good Queen Bess's glorious days!

When Wellington thrashed Bonaparte,
As every child can tell,
The House of Peers, throughout the war,
Did nothing in particular,
And did it very well:
Yet Britain set the world ablaze
In good King George's glorious days!

And while the House of Peers withholds
Its legislative hand,
And noble statesmen do not itch
To interfere with matters which
They do not understand,
As bright will shine Great Britain's rays
As in King George's glorious days!

Leila and Celia are rather attracted by the splendidly robed Peers
but point out that they are powerless to influence Strephon:

LEILA:
In vain to us you plead—
Don't go!
Your prayers we do not heed—
Don't go!
It's true we sigh,
But don't suppose
A tearful eye
Forgiveness shows.
Oh, no!
We're very cross indeed—
Don't go!

CELIA:
Your disrespectful sneers—
Don't go!
Call forth indignant tears—
Don't go!
You break our laws—
You are our foe:
We cry, because
We hate you so!
You know!
You very wicked Peers!
Don't go!

LORDS MOUNTARARAT and TOLLOLLER:
Our disrespectful sneers,
Ha, ha!
Call forth indignant tears,
Ha, ha!
If that's the case, my dears—
We'll go!

The Peers having departed, the Fairy Queen arrives and upbraids the fairies for their weakness in admiring their lordships. At the same time she confesses to being decidedly impressed by Private Willis—though she has firmly suppressed her feelings:

Oh, foolish fay,
Think you, because
His brave array
My bosom thaws,
I'd disobey
Our fairy laws?
Because I fly
In realms above,
In tendency
To fall in love,
Resemble I
The amorous dove?
Oh, amorous dove!
Type of Ovidius Naso!
This heart of mine
Is soft as thine,
Although I dare not say so!

On fire that glows
With heat intense
I turn the hose
Of common sense,
And out it goes
At small expense!
We must maintain
Our fairy law;
That is the main
On which to draw—
In that we gain
A Captain Shaw!
Oh, Captain Shaw!
Type of true love kept under!
Could thy Brigade
With cold cascade
Quench my great love, I wonder!

After the departure of the Fairy Queen and her attendants, a
distressed Phyllis enters, insisting that she hates Strephon—'a man
who goes about with a mother considerably younger than himself!'
—and wondering why, being engaged to two noblemen at the
same time, she is not in better spirits. Lords Mountararat and
Tolloller arrive and engage in a vigorous discussion on their respective merits as a husband for Phyllis. But when it comes to the
suggestion of fighting a duel, they decide that the sacred ties of
friendship are paramount. Private Willis, still on sentry duty, joins
the three of them in a quartet:

LORD TOLLOLLER:
Though p'r'aps I may incur your blame,
The things are few
I would not do
In Friendship's name!

LORD MOUNTARARAT:
And I may say I think the same;
Not even love
Should rank above
True Friendship's name!

PHYLLIS:
Then free me, pray; be mine the blame;
Forget your craze
And go your ways
In Friendship's name!

ALL:

Oh, many a man, in Friendship's name,
Has yielded fortune, rank and fame!
But no one yet, in the world so wide,
Has yielded up a promised bride!

WILLIS:

Accept, O Friendship, all the same,

ALL:

This sacrifice to thy dear name!

They go off and, in a miserable frame of mind, the Lord Chancellor enters:

Love, unrequited, robs me of my rest:
Love, hopeless love, my ardent soul encumbers:
Love, nightmare-like, lies heavy on my chest,
And weaves itself into my midnight slumbers!

In one of the most brilliant of all the patter-songs, he proceeds to
describe the nightmare to end all nightmares:

LORD CHANCELLOR:

When you're lying awake with a dismal headache, and repose is
    taboo'd by anxiety,
I conceive you may use any language you choose to indulge in,
    without impropriety;
For your brain is on fire—the bedclothes conspire of usual slumber
    to plunder you:
First your counterpane goes, and uncovers your toes, and your sheet
    slips demurely from under you;
Then the blanketing tickles—you feel like mixed pickles—so
    terribly sharp is the pricking,
And you're hot, and you're cross, and you tumble and toss till
    there's nothing 'twixt you and the ticking.
Then the bedclothes all creep to the ground in a heap, and you pick
    'em all up in a tangle;
Next your pillow resigns and politely declines to remain at its usual
    angle!
Well, you get some repose in the form of a doze, with hot eye-balls
    and head ever aching,
But your slumbering teems with such horrible dreams that you'd
    very much better be waking;
For you dream you are crossing the Channel, and tossing about in a
    steamer from Harwich—

Which is something between a large bathing machine and a very
small second-class carriage—
And you're giving a treat (penny ice and cold meat) to a party of
friends and relations—
They're a ravenous horde—and they all came aboard at Sloane
Square and South Kensington Stations.
And bound on that journey you find your attorney (who started
that morning from Devon);
He's a bit undersized, and you don't feel surprised when he tells you
he's only eleven.
Well, you're driving like mad with this singular lad (by-the-by the
ship's now a four-wheeler),
And you're playing round games, and he calls you bad names when
you tell him that 'ties pay the dealer';
But this you can't stand, so you throw up your hand, and you find
you're as cold as an icicle,
In your shirt and your socks (the black silk with gold clocks),
crossing Salisbury Plain on a bicycle:
And he and his crew are on bicycles, too—which they've somehow
or other invested in—
And he's telling the tars all the particulars of a company he's
interested in—
It's a scheme of devices to get at low prices all goods from cough
mixtures to cables
(Which tickled the sailors), by treating retailers as though they were
all vegetables—
You get a good spadesman to plant a small tradesman (first take off
his boots with a boot-tree),
And his legs will take root, and his fingers will shoot, and they'll
blossom and bud like a fruit-tree—
From the greengrocer tree you get grapes and green pea, cauliflower,
pineapple and cranberries,
While the pastrycook plant, cherry brandy will grant, apple puffs,
and three-corners and Banburys—
The shares are a penny, and ever so many are taken by Rothschild
and Baring,
And just as a few are allotted to you, you awake with a shudder
despairing—
You're a regular wreck, with a crick in your neck, and no wonder
you snore, for your head's on the floor, and you've needles and pins
from your soles to your shins, and your flesh is a-creep, for your
left leg's asleep, and you've cramp in your toes, and a fly on your
nose, and some fluff in your lung, and a feverish tongue, and a

thirst that's intense, and a general sense that you haven't been sleeping in clover;
But the darkness has passed, and it's daylight at last, and the night has been long—ditto-ditto my song—and thank goodness they're both of them over!

Understandably, Gilbert's stage direction says that the Lord Chancellor must then fall exhausted on a seat! Lords Mountararat and Tolloller return and the Lord Chancellor explains that he had applied to himself, in his official capacity, for permission to marry his Ward—'I deeply grieve to say that in declining to entertain my last application to myself, I presumed to address myself in terms which render it impossible for me ever to apply to myself again.' Their Lordships cheer him with the assurance that he might well make further application, and they all enter into a trio with a splendid swing to it:

LORD MOUNTARARAT:
If you go in
You're sure to win—
Yours will be the charming maidie:
Be your law
The ancient saw,
'Faint heart never won fair lady!'

ALL:
Faint heart never won fair lady!
Every journey has an end—
When at the worst affairs will mend—
Dark the day when dawn is nigh—
Hustle your horse and don't say die!

LORD TOLLOLLER:
He who shies
At such a prize
Is not worth a maravedi,
Be so kind
To bear in mind—
Faint heart never won fair lady!

ALL:
Faint heart never won fair lady!
While the sun shines make your hay—
Where a will is, there's a way—
Beard the lion in his lair—
None but the brave deserve the fair!

LORD CHANCELLOR:
I'll take heart
And make a start—
Though I fear the prospect's shady—
Much I'd spend
To gain my end—
Faint heart never won fair lady!

ALL:
Faint heart never won fair lady!
Nothing venture, nothing win—
Blood is thick, but water's thin—
In for a penny, in for a pound—
It's Love that makes the world go round!

They dance off, arm in arm. Strephon enters in low spirits, encounters Phyllis, and the situation is strained between them—until he explains that the reason for his mother's youth is that she is a fairy and that he is himself a fairy down to the waist! 'I quite understand,' says Phyllis. 'Whenever I see you kissing a very young lady, I shall know it's an elderly relative.' They decide that they must marry without delay:

STREPHON:
If we're weak enough to tarry
Ere we marry
You and I,
Of the feelings I inspire,
You may tire
By and by.
For peers with flowing coffers
Press their offers—
That is why
I am sure we should not tarry
Ere we marry,
You and I!

PHYLLIS:
If we're weak enough to tarry
Ere we marry,
You and I,
With a more attractive maiden,
Jewel-laden,
You may fly.
If by chance we should be parted,
Broken-hearted

I should die—
So I think we will not tarry
Ere we marry,
You and I.

Phyllis's next line could never fail to bring a laugh from the
audience in the old days—'But does your mother know you're—
I mean, is she aware of our engagement?' A popular song of the
time had the opening line, 'Does your mother know you're out?'
Iolanthe comes in and gives them both her blessing—and reveals
that the Lord Chamberlain is her husband and Strephon's father!
Phyllis and Strephon go off as the Lord Chamberlain enters and
Iolanthe steps aside, drawing a veil over her face. His Lordship is in
high spirits and informs the audience that, after having made a
further and successful application to himself in his official capacity,
he now considers himself engaged to Phyllis. But Iolanthe steps
forward and pleads for Strephon:

He loves! If in the bygone years
Thine eyes have ever shed
Tears—bitter, unavailing tears,
For one untimely dead—
If, in the eventide of life,
Sad thoughts of her arise,
Then let the memory of thy wife
Plead for my boy—he dies!

He dies! If fondly laid aside
In some old cabinet,
Memorials of thy long-dead bride
Lie, dearly treasured yet,
Then let her hallowed bridal dress—
Her little dainty gloves—
Her withered flowers—her faded tress—
Plead for my boy—he loves!

The Lord Chancellor, though touched by the appeal, insists that
he is engaged to Phyllis—until Iolanthe reveals that *she* is his wife.
The Fairy Queen enters and rules that Iolanthe must die for having
broken their laws. The fairies point out, however, that if this is so
they must *all* die: 'We are all fairy duchesses, marchionesses,
countesses, viscountesses and baronesses.' But the Lord Chancellor
intervenes and, as 'an old Equity draftsman', suggests that by the
addition of a single word the law becomes: 'Every fairy shall die

who *doesn't* marry a mortal.' The Fairy Queen solves her own problem by taking Private Willis, who promptly sprouts wings.

Lords Mountararat and Tolloller take the view that, as the Peerage is to be recruited in future from persons of intelligence, they on their part may as well go off to Fairyland. Wings spring from the shoulders of all the Peers and the opera whirls to an end to the tune of the earlier 'Love that makes the world go round' trio:

> Soon as we may,
> Off and away!
> We'll commence our journey airy—
> Happy are we—
> As you can see,
> Every one is now a fairy!
>
> Though as a general rule we know
> Two strings go to every bow,
> Make up your minds that grief 'twill bring
> If you've two beaux to every string.
>
> Up in the sky,
> Ever so high,
> Pleasures come in endless series;
> We will arrange
> Happy exchange—
> House of Peers for House of Peris!
>
> Up in the air, sky-high, sky-high,
> Free from Wards in Chancery,
> I/he will be surely happier, for
> I'm/he's such a susceptible Chancellor.

Iolanthe (I) *Mezzo-soprano* Jessie Bond was the first artist to play Iolanthe.

'I once gave an evening party' Baroness von Krakenfeldt's song (D).

'I once was as meek as a new-born lamb' Duet for Robin Oakapple and Old Adam at the opening of the second act (R).

'I once was a very abandoned person' Duet for the reformed Sir Despard Murgatroyd and Mad Margaret (R). ('We only cut respectable capers').

'I rejoice that it's decided' Quintet for Alexis, Aline, Sir Marmaduke, Zorah and Dr Daly (R).

Ireland 'Great Britain is that monarchy sublime,
To which some add (but others do not) Ireland.'
—King Paramount (U).

Isabel (PP) *Mezzo-soprano* The role was first played in the London production by Neva Bond.

'I shipped, d'ye see, in a Revenue sloop' Richard Dauntless's ballad when he makes his first ebullient appearance (R). Surprising though it may seem to us, there were sections in France which took strong exception to this song about the 'darned Mounseer', failing to understand that Gilbert's shafts were directed not at French cowardice but at British boastfulness. Gilbert even received challenges to duels and one incensed critic wrote: 'It is well to remember that Messrs Gilbert and Sullivan have long tried—in vain—to foist one of their operettas on Paris; this may be their revenge out of spite.'

'Is life a boon?' Colonel Fairfax's lovely ballad (Y), the first words of which are inscribed on the memorial to Sullivan on the Thames Embankment. While it is well known that a work which falls easily on the ear of the listener has not necessarily come easily to its creator, it does seem difficult to believe to-day that Sullivan's brilliant and fluent score for the *Yeomen* caused him considerable trouble. This ballad, for instance, did not please Gilbert in its original version—nor, probably, Sullivan himself—and the composer had two more shots at it before it emerged in what now seems its inevitable form.

'I stole the Prince, and I brought him here' Don Alhambra's song—'No possible doubt whatever.' (G).

Italian Terms Naturally, it is in *The Gondoliers* that most Italian words and phrases are introduced by Gilbert. They are mostly familiar terms that are in common everyday usage:
Buon' giorno, signorine! . . . Good morning, young ladies!
Gondolieri carissimi! . . . Dearest gondoliers!
Siamo contadine! . . . We are peasant girls!
Servitori umilissimi! . . . Your humble servants!
Per chi questi fiori—questi fiori bellissimi? . . . For whom are these flowers—these lovely flowers?
Per voi, bei signori, O eccellentissimi! . . . For you, handsome sirs, O most excellent!

O ciel'! . . . O Heavens!
Cavalieri . . . Gentlemen.
Signorina, io t' amo! . . . I love you, young lady!
Poveri gondolieri! . . . Poor gondoliers!

'It's clear that mediaeval art alone retains its zest' Trio for
the Duke, Colonel and Major (P).

'It's understood, I think, all round' Quartet for Captain
Fitzbattleaxe, Princess Zara, Scaphio and Phantis (U).

'I've jibe and joke and quip and crank' Jack Point's recitative
and song—'I've wisdom from the East and from the West.' (Y).

Jackson, Susan Joining D'Oyly Carte in 1967, she was born in Cheshire of a musical family and studied at the Royal Manchester College of Music where, in addition to her singing studies, she gained a teacher's degree in piano. Later at the London Opera Centre for three years, she won the Leverhulme Trust Award and went on to appear with the New Opera Company at the Cheltenham Festival, at Glyndebourne Festival, on radio and in Carl Ebert's production of *The Marriage of Figaro* on television. Her principal roles with D'Oyly Carte include Josephine (HMS), Patience, Phyllis (I), Rose Maybud (R) and Gianetta (G). She left the company in August 1969.

Jacky The 'excellent jacky', which Little Buttercup (HMS) carries among the wares in her basket, is strong plug tobacco.

James (PP) This member of the pirate band, played by John Le Hay, was named in the cast of the single 'copyright' performance at Paignton in 1879. His only function, however, was to provide a suitor for the third principal sister of Mabel and Isabel, a role since allotted to a member of the chorus.

Jane, The Lady (P) *Contralto* Alice Barnett was the original player of this formidable 'rapturous maiden'.

Japanese In addition to the fact that there was a Japanese exhibition in progress in Knightsbridge at the time of the production of *The Mikado*, Britain was in the midst of a general Japanese cult. It was the 'done thing' to have Japanese bric-à-brac and the like around the place. With his sense of topicality, Gilbert makes several references in the operas, such as:

'I do *not* long for all one sees that's Japanese.'—Reginald Bunthorne (P).

'Something Japanese—it matters not what.'—Lady Jane (P).

Jay, Isabel Principal soprano with D'Oyly Carte at the turn of the century, Isabel Jay was born in London in 1879 and studied at the Royal Academy of Music, where she won a gold medal for operatic singing. She made her first stage appearance at the Savoy Theatre as Elsie Maynard (Y) and her later roles included the Plaintiff (J), Josephine (HMS), Mabel (PP), Patience, Phyllis (I) and Tessa (G). She retired from the stage in 1911.

Jellicoe, Julia (D) *Soprano* Ilka von Palmay was the first artist to play the role of the English comedienne.

Johnston, Edith The original player of the role of Salata (U).

Jones, Peggy Ann Principal mezzo-soprano with D'Oyly Carte, Peggy Ann Jones comes from Newark, where she studied the piano from an early age, also taking diplomas in interior design, architecture and dress design. She worked in a bank for a while but studied music in her spare time and when only sixteen scored a big success in the title role of *Rose Marie* with a local amateur operatic society and went on to win prizes at the Nottingham Festival. She joined the D'Oyly Carte Company in 1958 and her leading roles now include Mrs Partlet (S), Edith (PP), Lady Angela (P), Iolanthe, Pitti-Sing (M), Mad Margaret (R) and Phoebe (Y). Miss Jones's main hobby is ciné photography and she has made several films with members of the company playing parts far removed from their usual roles.

Jorum 'None so knowing as he/At brewing a jorum of tea.' A jorum is a large drinking-vessel, used particularly for strong punch. Here, however (S), the reference is to a rather milder tipple—a jorum of *tea*, brewed by the vicar.

Josephine (HMS) *Soprano* The role of Captain Corcoran's daughter was first played by Emma Howson.

Judge (J) *Baritone* The original player of the Learned Judge was Frederic Sullivan, the composer's brother, whose fatal illness brought the first run of *Trial* to a close.

Jullien 'The science of Jullien, the eminent musico.'—Colonel Calverley (P). Louis Antoine Jullien (1812–60) was a French musician who spent some years in London where he presented Promenade Concerts before the days of Henry Wood and Queen's Hall.

Jupiter (T) An aged Olympian, played by John Maclean.

Juvenal 'And the works of Juvenal.'—Lady Psyche (PI). Roman satirical writer (AD 60–140), whose works include a vicious satire on women.

Kalyba, Princess (U) *Mezzo-soprano* Florence Perry was the first artist to play King Paramount's daughter.

Kate (PP) *Mezzo-soprano* Lilian La Rue was the first to play the role in the London production.

Kate (Y) *Soprano* Rose Hervey was the first artist to play the role of Kate, niece of Dame Carruthers, housekeeper of the Tower of London.

Katisha (M) *Contralto* She may be 'an Elderly Lady' but Katisha' the Mikado's Daughter-in-law Elect, does not readily give up the hunt. She is at pains to point out that beauty lies not in the face alone and is frank in her catalogue of her own particular attractions: 'My face is unattractive!... But I have a left shoulder-blade that is a miracle of loveliness. People come miles to see it. My right elbow has a fascination that few can resist.... It is on view Tuesdays and Fridays, on presentation of visiting card. As for my circulation, it is the largest in the world.' The role was first played by Rosina Brandram.

Kavanagh, Albert Associated with D'Oyly Carte for thirty-one years, Albert Kavanagh sang almost every leading baritone and bass-baritone role, including Scaphio (U). He joined the chorus in 1890, singing Colonel Calverley (P) three years later. He left the company in 1921.

Kelleher, C The original player of the Foreman of the Jury (J).

Kenningham, Charles The original Captain Fitzbattleaxe (U) and Ernest Dummkopf (D), Charles Kenningham sang also Nanki-Poo (M), Colonel Fairfax (Y), Marco (G) and Cyril (PI).

'Kind captain, I've important information' Duet for Captain and Dick Deadeye, in which the latter reveals that Josephine plans to run away with Ralph Rackstraw and marry in secret (HMS).

'Kind sir, you cannot have the heart' Gianetta's song at the start of the finale to the first act (G).

'King of autocratic power we, A' King Paramount's song on his first entrance (U).

King of Barataria, The Alternative title of *The Gondoliers*.

King Paramount (U) *Bass-Baritone* The King of Utopia was first played by Rutland Barrington.

Kirtle 'I'll swallow my kirtle!'—Dame Carruthers (Y). In Elizabethan times a full kirtle was a petticoat and jacket.

Kissing The Lieutenant of the Tower (Y), testing Jack Point's skill as a jester: 'We will suppose that I caught you kissing the kitchen wench under my very nose.'
Point: 'Under *her* very nose, good sir—not under yours! *That* is where *I* would kiss her.'
When C. H. Workman was rehearsing the part of Jack Point, Gilbert pulled him up for being rather too enthusiastic in his kissing of Elsie Maynard and Phoebe. 'Ah, I see,' said Workman, obediently, 'you would not kiss them more than once.' 'Oh, *I* would,' rejoined Gilbert with enthusiasm, 'But I must ask *you* not to.'

Knight, Gillian Later one of the principals of Sadler's Wells Opera, she joined D'Oyly Carte in 1959—in quite a strenuous way. She was born in Redditch, sang in the church choir and, after singing lessons locally, won a scholarship to the Royal Academy of Music. After doing a good deal of concert work while still at the Academy, she ended her student days by learning eight Gilbert and Sullivan roles in eight weeks and going straight on tour with the D'Oyly Carte Company as a principal. Her roles with the company were Little Buttercup (HMS), Ruth (PP), Lady Jane (P), Fairy Queen (I), Lady Blanche (PI), Katisha (M), Dame Hannah (R), Dame Carruthers (Y) and the Duchess of Plaza-Toro (G). She left the company in 1965 and soon afterwards joined Sadler's Wells Opera, with whom her roles have included Suzuki (*Madam Butterfly*), Ragonde (*Count Ory*), Maddalena (*Rigoletto*), Berta (*The*

Barber of Seville), Isabella (*The Italian Girl in Algiers*), Dryade (*Ariadne on Naxos*) and, as a change from the Fairy Queen, the title role in *Iolanthe*.

Knightsbridge When asked by the Mikado for the present address of Nanki-Poo, Ko-Ko replied: 'Knightsbridge', a topical allusion to the fact that there was a Japanese exhibition in progress in Knightsbridge at the time of the first production of the opera. Later, however, with Gilbert's authority, some other local place-name has been substituted. In *Utopia, Limited*, on the appearance of the Life Guards, the chorus sing of 'Knightsbridge nursemaids' ('At stern duty's call you leave them,/Though you know how that must grieve them!')—a reference to the propinquity of the Guards' barracks.

Kodak 'To diagnose our modest pose the Kodaks do their best.'— Kalyba (U). George Eastman, the American inventor, perfected his first Kodak camera in 1888, only five years before *Utopia, Limited* was produced.

Ko-Ko (M) *Baritone* George Grossmith was the first to play the cheap little tailor who is taken from the county jail and made Lord High Executioner of Titipu, the reasonable argument being that, as he had been condemned to death, he 'cannot cut off another's head until he's cut his own off.' Ko-Ko's 'toe gag', in which his big toe suddenly stands upright and is pressed down by his fan, came into existence through an accident. Henry A. Lytton dislocated his toe while playing Jack Point and later, when dancing around as Ko-Ko, he stepped on a tack, pulled back his foot suddenly, saw that his big toe was standing up—and pressed it back with his fan. It was a double-jointed toe and Lytton kept the gag in from then onwards.

TWO LOVE-SICK MAIDENS

'Lady fair, of lineage high, A' Lady Psyche's song about Darwinian Man (PI).

Language To suit his purpose and the jingle of his lines, Gilbert sometimes went in for inventing words. For instance: 'I've come here to be matrimonially matrimonified.'—Baroness von Krakenfeldt (D). In the course of conversation, Gilbert was once pulled up for saying that someone was 'coyful'—how could anybody be full of coy? 'For that matter,' he retorted, 'how could anyone be full of bash?'

La Rue, Lilian The first artist to sing Kate (PP) in the London production, Lilian La Rue also made some appearances as Hebe (HMS).

Lass That Loved a Sailor, The Alternative title of *HMS Pinafore*.

Last Nights The end of the first repertory season at the Savoy Theatre in 1907 was celebrated in formidable style. Starting at 4 pm, the performance consisted of the first act of *The Yeomen of the Guard* and the second act of *The Gondoliers*, then an interval of seventy-five minutes, followed by the second act of *Patience*, the first act of *Iolanthe* and, to top things off, the scene between Ko-Ko and Katisha from the second act of *The Mikado*. The idea of a 'surprise' evening for the last night of a D'Oyly Carte season in London has long been established—perhaps the 'wrong' overture or acts from two different operas or, in one instance, a mock *Trial by Jury*. The plan is always kept secret until the night and everyone in the audience is given a souvenir of the occasion. On the Last Night of the 1961 season at the Savoy the audience had a particular surprise—a new production of the first act of *The Gondoliers* by George A. Foa, prior to the full production being toured and later taken to America. In 1968, an excerpt from *Patience* was given in 'hippy' style.

Law Though his own early experiences in the legal profession were far from rewarding, Gilbert had a passionate interest in the law throughout his life. His first success in collaboration with Sullivan, *Trial by Jury*, was set in a court of law and one of his most effective comic characters was the Lord Chancellor himself (I). It would seem that lawyers generally found *Trial* great fun but there was one exception in the person of Mr Justice Kakewich whose judgments were from time to time quashed in the Appeal Court. Gilbert wrote of him: 'He says he likes all my plays except *Trial by Jury*. He seems to think that in holding the proceedings up to ridicule I was trenching on his prerogative.'

On the slightest provocation Gilbert would bring an action in the courts. Early in his career he sued the *Pall Mall Gazette* for having described his play *The Wicked World* as 'coarse and indecent.' He lost the action but was in no way deterred from bringing proceedings against anyone by whom he felt aggrieved. There was a notable clash with Sir Edward Carson in a case in which Gilbert sued the theatrical paper *The Era*. But in the long list of his legal actions surely the saddest was that in which he sued his colleagues, Sullivan and D'Oyly Carte, after the notorious 'carpet quarrel'.

In Ko-Ko's 'little list' of those who 'never would be missed' (M), Gilbert had a dig at judges who go in for making comic remarks from the height of the Bench:

'And that *Nisi Prius* nuisance, who just now is rather rife,
The judicial humorist—I've got *him* on the list!'

Yet, when in later life he sat on the Bench at Edgware Petty Sessions, he was himself guilty on at least one occasion. An old man and woman had appeared before the magistrates, asking for a separation order, and the woman, after describing her husband's cruel behaviour, had added that he had an abscess in his back. 'Not,' murmured Gilbert, 'a case of abscess makes the heart grow fonder.'

'Whether you're an honest man or whether you're a thief
Depends on whose solicitor has given me my brief.'—
Sir Bailey Barre, QC, MP (U).

'The Law is the true embodiment
Of everything that's excellent.
It has no kind of fault or flaw,
And I, my Lords, embody the Law.'—
Lord Chancellor (I).

'Law is the true embodiment, The' Lord Chancellor's song on his first entrance (I).

Lawlor, Thomas His principal baritone roles include Counsel (J), Captain Corcoran (HMS), Strephon (I), Pish-Tush (M), Guron (PI) and Giuseppe (G). Born in Dublin, he graduated at the National University of Ireland with a degree in philosophy and for some time taught English, geography and Gaelic. But he carried on with singing studies at the Municipal School of Music, Dublin, and was awarded the Sam Heilbut Major Scholarship to the Guildhall School of Music and Drama, where he studied for three years. While in Dublin he had appeared in many amateur performances and after turning professional he appeared in such musicals as *Brigadoon*, as well as doing concert and oratorio work. He joined D'Oyly Carte in 1965.

Lawrence, Nellie The original Fiametta (G), Nellie Lawrence also sang Isabel (PP).

Lawson, Winifred This attractive soprano, who was born in London in 1894, had an early career on the concert platform and then sang the Countess in *The Marriage of Figaro* at the Old Vic and also Marguerite in *Faust*. She made her first appearance with the D'Oyly Carte Company in the title role of *Princess Ida* at the Princes Theatre in 1922 and went on to sing Phyllis (I), Casilda (G), Patience, Yum-Yum (M) and Elsie Maynard (G). She toured for a time as Lili in *Lilac Time* before rejoining the company at the Savoy in the 1929–30 season and touring in this country and in Australia. Miss Lawson, who wrote an autobiography, *A Song To Sing-O!* (Michael Joseph, 1955), died in 1961.

Layland, Hilton In his first year with D'Oyly Carte Hilton Layland sang Private Willis (I), Pooh-Bah (M), Wilfred Shadbolt (Y) and Don Alhambra (G), adding the Usher (J), Bill Bobstay (HMS), Sergeant of Police (PP) and Sir Despard (R) before leaving the company in 1925. He returned from 1944 until 1947, singing Samuel (PP).

Le Hay, John The original Phantis (U), John Le Hay sang also John Wellington Wells (S), Sir Joseph Porter (HMS) and Major-General Stanley (PP). In the single 'copyright' performance of *Pirates* at Paignton in 1879, he played James, a pirate character not named in later casts.

Leila (I) *Mezzo-soprano* One of the leading fairies, Leila was first played by Julia Gwynne.

Lely, Durward A Scottish tenor whose real name was Lyall, he created the roles of the Duke of Dunstable (P), Earl Tolloller (I), Cyril (PI), Nanki-Poo (M) and Richard Dauntless (R). He also sang Frederic (PP). In later years he returned to Scotland, where he lived to a great age.

Leman 'The lily-white laughing leman.'—Julia Jellicoe (D). A leman is a sweetheart or paramour.

'Let all your doubts take wing' Duet for Scaphio and Phantis (U).

'Let's give three cheers for the sailor's bride' Chorus which closes the first act of *Pinafore*.

'Let's seal this mercantile pact' Ensemble at the close of the first act (U).

'Let the merry cymbals sound' Chorus at the opening of the finale to the first act (P).

Lewis and Allenby 'Let Lewis (secede) from Allenby!'—Princess Ida. Lewis and Allenby were well-known drapers and milliners in Regent Street, London.

Lewis, Bertha Leading contralto with the D'Oyly Carte Company for twenty years, Bertha Lewis had the security of voice and dignity of manner which made her a worthy successor to Rosina Brandram, the originator of many of the parts. A Londoner, Bertha Lewis studied at the Royal Academy of Music and sang on the concert platform and in grand opera. She first appeared at the Savoy Theatre when she was twenty-one, not in Gilbert and Sullivan but in a piece called *A Welsh Sunset*. She joined the chorus of the D'Oyly Carte Company at the Princes Theatre in 1919. Her first leading role was Katisha, which she took over when another artist had fallen ill. Her roles included Lady Sangazure (S), Little Buttercup (HMS), Ruth (PP), Lady Jane (P), Fairy Queen (I), Lady Blanche (PI), Katisha (M), Dame Hannah (R), Dame Carruthers (Y) and Duchess of Plaza-Toro (G). Bertha Lewis died after a car crash in 1931, shortly before her 44th birthday. The car, driven by Sir Henry Lytton from Manchester, went into a skid on the wet road and overturned near their destination in Cambridge. Lytton received only minor injuries but Miss Lewis died soon afterwards in a Cambridge nursing home. The company, playing *Iolanthe* that night, were not told of her death until after the performance.

Lewis, Rudolph The original Old Adam Goodheart (R) and Fourth Yeoman (Y).

Life and Death 'Keep a stout heart, good fellow—we are soldiers, and we know how to die, thou and I. Take my word for it, it is easier to die well than to live well—for, in sooth, I have tried both.' —Colonel Fairfax (Y).

'Like a ghost his vigil keeping' Duet for Wilfred Shadbolt and Jack Point, in which they give a highly coloured account of the 'death' of Colonel Fairfax (Y).

Lisa (D) *Soprano* Florence Perry was the first artist to play the role of Lisa, the soubrette.

'List and learn, ye dainty roses' Chorus of the peasant girls at the opening of the opera (G).

'Little maid of Arcadee' Apart from the chorus 'Climbing over rocky mountain', this song, sung by Sparkeion, is the only surviving number from *Thespis*, the first Gilbert and Sullivan piece.

Lloyd-Jones, Beti Contralto Beti Lloyd-Jones was an early starter in the musical world. She was born in Crosby, Liverpool, of musical parents of Welsh origin and made her first public appearance singing in Welsh at an Eisteddfod at the tender age of four. She sang contralto roles with several amateur societies before joining D'Oyly Carte in 1957. She is a keen golfer, motorist and ciné-photography enthusiast.

'Long years ago—fourteen, maybe' Duet for Patience and Lady Angela (P).

Lord Chancellor (I) *Baritone* The 'highly susceptible Chancellor', who sits in court all day 'giving agreeable girls away', was first played by George Grossmith.

Lothario 'A regular out-and-out Lothario.' Robin Oakapple, of his foster-brother Richard Dauntless (R). The character of the gay libertine appears in two early plays, Sir William Davenant's *The Cruel Brother* (1630) and Nicholas Rowe's *The Fair Penitent* (1703).

'Loudly let the trumpets bray! Tantantara!' Entrance of the procession of Peers (I).

'Love feeds on hope, they say, or love will die' Lady Angela's song after the opening chorus (P).

'Love feeds on many kinds of food, I know' Alexis's aria (S).

'Love is a plaintive song' Patience's ballad in the second act.

Lozenge Plot The idea of a magic lozenge which entirely changed the character of anyone who took it was a sort of 'King Charles' Head' with Gilbert throughout his career. Over and over again when a new opera was required, he would suggest some variation on the Magic Lozenge theme—to be rejected by Sullivan who desperately wanted to escape from this harking-back to topsy-turvydom. Gilbert's first straight play, *Dulcamara*, had a love-philtre as its central idea—though in this case the magic potion was in fact good rich Burgundy. Another play of his, *The Wicked World*, had the same sort of magic-potion theme. In *The Sorcerer* he was still in the world of love-philtres. But try as Gilbert did through the years, there had been quite enough of magic potions for Sullivan's taste.

Lucius Junius Brutus 'My father, the Lucius Junius Brutus of his race.'—Nanki-Poo (M). First consul of ancient Rome.

Ludwig (D) *Bass-baritone* Rutland Barrington was the first artist to play Ludwig, leading comedian of Dummkopf's theatrical company.

Lugg, William The original player of Scynthius (PI).

Luiz (G) *Tenor* The Duke of Plaza-Toro's attendant, the real King of Barataria and in love with Casilda, was first played by Wallace Brownlow.

Lying Pooh-Bah (M) manages to make the more imaginative flights of fancy sound almost respectable: 'Merely corroborative detail, intended to give artistic verisimilitude to an otherwise bald and unconvincing narrative.'

Lytton, (Sir) Henry A. It was by a set of curious chances that Henry A. Lytton, one of the famed names in the Gilbert and Sullivan story, found himself in the world of Savoy opera. It was, in fact, all for the love of a lady. Though he did not 'create' any of the roles, he became one of the most distinguished players of the 'little men' parts and in the course of his long career he also played a great number of others. The list is formidable: Judge, Counsel and Usher (J), John Wellington Wells, Dr Daly and Sir Marmaduke Pointdextre (S), Sir Joseph Porter, Dick Deadeye and Captain Corcoran (HMS); Major-General Stanley, Samuel and Pirate King (PP); Grosvenor and Bunthorne (P); Lord Chancellor, Strephon and Lord Mountararat (I); King Gama and Florian (PI); Ko-Ko and Mikado (M); Robin Oakapple (R); Jack Point, Sir Richard Cholmondeley and Wilfred Shadbolt (Y); Duke of Plaza-Toro and Giuseppe (G); King Paramount (U); and Rudolph (D).

Lytton, who was born in London in 1867, had never appeared in anything more ambitious than school plays at St Mark's College, Chelsea, until he sang in the D'Oyly Carte chorus. It came about in strange fashion. When still at school he fell in love with a young actress called Louie Henri and, taking time off from school, promptly married her at the age of seventeen. On his return to school the headmaster was about to beat him as a punishment for his absence but, with a full sense of the drama of the situation, young Lytton said, 'No! You would be thrashing a married man!' He was thrashed all the more. Louie had joined the D'Oyly Carte chorus and, about to set out on tour, was determined to have her young husband with her. But, thinking that the management frowned upon the younger members of the company marrying, asked if her 'brother' might have an audition. Lytton was accepted, joined the chorus at £2 a week and went on tour with *Princess Ida*, understudying King Gama but not playing the role on that occasion. His chance to play a principal part came in London three years later. For some years an actor called Eric Lewis had been George Grossmith's understudy—but Grossmith was never ill! So Lewis resigned and Lytton became understudy. A week later Grossmith *did* fall ill and Lytton was called in from touring to play Robin Oakapple in *Ruddigore* at the Savoy.

In those early days he still appeared under the stage name of 'H. A. Henri'. Lytton left D'Oyly Carte for a few years in order to go briefly into management and also to appear in a number of other productions, among them Edward German's *Merrie England*. He returned in 1908 and steadily established himself as one of the key members of the company. When he retired in 1934 after celebrating his stage jubilee, he received a national testimonial in the form of an album containing the signatures of subscribers to a presentation fund, among them the Prime Minister, Ramsay MacDonald, and his two predecessors, Stanley Baldwin and Lloyd George. Lytton retained his extraordinary command of the audience right up to the end of his career. He could not read music but he had a keen ear and feeling for rhythm and an unfailing sense of character and the timing of a line. The present writer interviewed him during his farewell tour and remembers him as an ebullient off-stage personality and highly entertaining raconteur. He died in 1936, at the age of 69. Lady (Louie) Lytton—Lytton had been knighted in 1930—died in 1947.

Mabel (PP) *Soprano* Major-General Stanley's daughter was first played in the London production by Marion Hood, making her stage debut.

Macaulay 'Wit of Macaulay, who wrote of Queen Anne.'— Colonel Calverley (P). Thomas Babington Macaulay, later Lord Macaulay, the historian and poet, was born in Leicestershire in 1800 and died in London in 1859. He was buried in Westminster Abbey.

McIntosh, Nancy The original Princess Zara (U), Nancy McIntosh was a beautiful young American soprano who came to London to complete her studies. Shortly after she had made her debut at a concert in London, she was invited to sing at a dinner-party at which Gilbert was present. As she related years afterwards to Leslie Baily (*The Gilbert & Sullivan Book*) Gilbert asked someone who she was, then came over and told her he was looking for a soprano for his next opera. After she had been to the Savoy to sing to Sullivan, she was given the part, in which she made her first stage appearance. Later Gilbert and Lady Gilbert, who had no children of their own, adopted Nancy McIntosh as their daughter. In Gilbert's will she inherited many of his papers and personal effects. She died in 1954 at the age of eighty.

Mackenzie, Gordon After making his professional debut with D'Oyly Carte in 1954, Gordon Mackenzie, who was born in Greenock, left the company two years later to concentrate on solo work in Britain, the U.S. and Canada. He returned to the company in 1962.

Madame Louise 'We're Madame Louise young girls.' (P). Madame Louise's was a fashionable London millinery establishment.

Mad Margaret (R) *Mezzo-soprano* Jessie Bond was the first artist to play Mad Margaret, whose craziness is soothed by the magic word 'Basingstoke'. It was her favourite among many roles.

'Magnet hung in a hardware shop, A' Archibald Grosvenor's song, in which he relates the fable of the Magnet and the Churn (P).

'Maiden fair to see, A' Ralph Rackstraw's ballad (HMS).

Major-General Stanley (PP) *Baritone* In the London production, George Grossmith was the original player of the Major-General, with his brilliant patter-song in which he reveals that he knows about almost everything except military matters.

Make-up 'Art and nature, thus allied,
      Go to make a pretty bride.' (M).

Mamelon 'When I know what is meant by "mamelon" and "ravelin".'—Major-General Stanley (PP). Mamelon is a word for a mound used in fortifications.

Man 'Man is Nature's sole mistake!'—Lady Psyche (PI).

Manfred 'Little of Manfred (but not very much of him).'— Colonel Calverley (P). Lord Byron's poem, published in 1817, has as its hero Count Manfred, who sells himself to the Devil and lives in solitude in the Alps.

Manners, Charles His real name was Southcote Mansergh. He possessed a fine bass voice, and was only twenty-six when he created the role of Private Willis, the Grenadier Guards sentry (I). Born in London of Irish descent, he studied in Dublin, at the Royal Academy of Music in London, and in Italy, and had been a member of the D'Oyly Carte chorus for a year when he was given the role of Willis. He sang also Dick Deadeye (HMS) and Samuel (PP) on tour. In 1890 he married the distinguished soprano Fanny Moody and they appeared together in Meyerbeer's opera *Robert le Diable* at Covent Garden in the same year. Two years later they sang the the roles of Tatiana and Gremin when Tchaikovsky's *Eugene Onegin* had its first London performance, conducted by the young Henry Wood at the Olympic Theatre. In 1897 Manners and his wife formed the Moody-Manners Opera Company, which embarked on busy touring activities and gave seasons at Covent Garden in 1902 and 1903 and at Drury Lane in 1904. The company was in operation

O

until 1916. Charles Manners died in Dublin in 1955 at the age of ninety-seven.

Manuscripts As might have been expected in view of his close association, Sullivan left the manuscript of the most popular opera, *The Mikado*, to the Royal Academy of Music, but, as though anxious to be fair to the other establishment, he left to the Royal College of Music the manuscript of that other masterpiece, *The Yeomen of the Guard*. That of *Iolanthe* he left to his friend Richard D'Oyly Carte and it is now owned by Miss Bridget D'Oyly Carte. The *Ruddigore* manuscript, formerly owned by Lady Gilbert's family, is now in the possession of the Savoy Theatre.

In 1966 a sale of some of Sullivan's original manuscripts took place at Sothebys, arranged by Charles Russell & Co., trustees and solicitors acting on behalf of Mrs. Grandcourt, daughter of Mrs Bashford, who was formely the wife of Herbert Sullivan (nephew and heir of Sir Arthur Sullivan). So that some, at any rate, of these scores might be retained in this country, an appeal fund was organised, with considerable success.

The results of the auction were: *Trial by Jury*, £9,000, America; *The Sorcerer*, £2,000, bought privately; *H.M.S. Pinafore*, £6,000, America; *The Pirates of Penzance*, £5,000, America; *Patience*, £5,500, bought through the fund and lodged in the British Museum; *Princess Ida*, £4,500, bought through the fund and lodged in the Bodleian Library, Oxford; *The Gondoliers*, £5,500, bought through the fund and lodged in the British Museum. Sullivan's diaries went for £11,000 to America.

'Man who would woo a fair maid, A' Trio for Elsie Maynard, Phoebe and Fairfax—'It is purely a matter of skill.' (Y).

'Man will swear and man will storm' Lady Psyche's solo about the undesirable qualities of Man (PI).

'Many years ago, A' Little Buttercup's song in which she confesses that she had mixed up Captain Corcoran and Ralph Rackstraw when they were babies (HMS).

Marathon 'I quote the fights historical, from Marathon to Waterloo, in order categorical.'—Major-General Stanley (PP). The Battle of Marathon, in which the Greeks inflicted a severe defeat upon the Persians, was fought on the plain twenty-two miles from Athens. The courier who carried the news of victory to Athens dropped dead after delivering his message. The Marathon Race of to-day takes its name from the episode.

Maravedi 'Not worth a maravedi.' (I). Small-value Spanish coin of the 11th–12th centuries.

Marco Palmieri (G) *Tenor* The tenor brother of the two gondoliers was originally played by Courtice Pounds.

Marriage and Divorce Strephon: 'I think we shall be very happy.' Phyllis: 'We won't wait long.'—'No. We might change our minds. We'll get married first.'—'And change our minds afterwards?'—'That's the usual course.' (I).
   Lieutenant of the Tower: 'You two, eh? Are ye man and wife?' Jack Point: 'No, sir: for though I am a fool, there is a limit to my folly.' (Y).
   'Divorce is nearly obsolete in England.' (U).

Mars (T) An aged Olympian, originally played by Frank Wood.

Martha (D) *Soprano* Beatrice Perry was the first artist to play Martha, a member of Dummkopf's theatrical company.

Martin, Marian After playing leading roles in an amateur Gilbert and Sullivan society, Liverpool-born Marian Martin joined the D'Oyly Carte Company at the age of nineteen. Her roles include Kate (PP), Lady Angela (P), Leila (I) and Peep-Bo (M). She is married to baritone George Cook and left the company in 1969 to start a family.

Mason, Ralph His principal roles include Box (C), Defendant (J), Alexis (S), Ralph Rackstraw (HMS), Duke of Dunstable (P), Earl Tolloller (I), Cyril (PI), Dick Dauntless (R), Leonard Meryll (Y) and Marco (G). He was born in Brighton, sang as a boy soprano in church choirs and appeared in various Gilbert and Sullivan productions at Brighton Grammar School. He originally joined the D'Oyly Carte Company in 1959 but left in 1963 to go into the *My Fair Lady* company at Drury Lane, appearing many times as Freddy Eynsford-Hill in that successful musical. However, the call of Gilbert and Sullivan was strong and he rejoined D'Oyly Carte in 1965. Ralph Manson is married to Anne Sessions, whom he met as a fellow-member of the company.

Masterson, Valerie Born in Cheshire, Valerie Masterson studied for some time at the Matthay School of Music, Liverpool, and for four years at the Royal College of Music. Before joining the D'Oyly Carte Company, she had also studied in Milan and had spent a year in Salzburg with the Landestheater Opera Company. With D'Oyly Carte she soon distinguished herself in a number of leading soprano roles such as Josephine (HMS), Mabel (PP), Princess Ida, Yum-Yum (M), Elsie Maynard (Y) and Casilda (G). She left the company in 1969, and appears frequently with the Gilbert and Sullivan for All organisation.

Maxim gun 'With Maxim gun and Nordenfelt.'—Captain Corcoran (U). The Maxim gun was a machine-gun devised by the Anglo-American inventor Sir Hiram Maxim and introduced into the British Army in 1889, four years before *Utopia, Limited* was produced.

May, Alice The first artist to play the role of Aline (S).

Maybud, Rose (R) *Soprano* The village maiden whose life is governed by her little book of etiquette was first played by Leonora Braham.

Maynard, Elsie (Y) *Soprano* Geraldine Ulmar was the original player of Elsie Maynard, the strolling singer, companion of Jack Point and the lady for whose love he sighs.

Medcalf, A. The original Second Yeoman (Y) and Antonio (G).

Melene (U) *Soprano* May Bell was the first artist to play the Utopian maiden.

Melissa (PI) *Mezzo-soprano* Jessie Bond was the original Melissa, Lady Blanche's daughter.

Melville, Winnie Winnie Melville joined D'Oyly Carte in 1929, when her husband, Derek Oldham, returned to the company. Her roles included Josephine (HMS), Mabel (PP), Yum-Yum (M), Rose Maybud (R). Elsie Maynard (Y) and Gianetta (G). Her first West End appearance was in a revue, *See-Saw*, at the Comedy Theatre, and two years later she was with the Folies Bergères in Paris, followed by musicals and operettas in London. She died in 1937, in her early forties.

Memorials The most familiar memorials to Gilbert and Sullivan—setting aside, of course, their greatest memorials, the operas they left for posterity—are appropriately placed not far from each other on the Victoria Embankment and only a short walk from the scene of their triumphs, the Savoy Theatre.

That to Sullivan, who died on November 22, 1900, is by Sir William Goscombe John and shows a female figure weeping beneath a bust of the composer. The inscription was suggested by Gilbert, who was asked if he could choose something appropriate from the libretti of the operas. In a letter to Sullivan's nephew he wrote: 'It is difficult to find anything quite fitted to so sad an occasion, but I think this might do.' His choice came from *The Yeomen of the Guard*:

> Is life a boon?
> If so, it must befall
> That Death, whene'er he call
> Must call too soon!

The Embankment memorial to Gilbert, unveiled four years after his death on May 29, 1911, is by Sir George Frampton, R.A., whose later works include the memorial to Nurse Cavell near Trafalgar Square, and the Peter Pan statue in Kensington Gardens. The figures of Tragedy and Comedy flank the Gilbert memorial, Comedy holding small figures of Mikado and other characters from the operas. The inscription reads: 'His Foe Was Folly & His Weapon Wit.' It was suggested by Anthony Hope (Sir Anthony Hope Hawkins, author of many romantic novels, including *The Prisoner of Zenda*), whose first idea was 'Folly was his foe, and wit his weapon.' But a friend pointed out that if the words were interchanged they would make a more effective line, to which Hope at once agreed.

There are other memorials. Sullivan had expressed in writing, a wish to be buried in Brompton Cemetery beside his father, mother and brother—brother Fred, who had first played the role of the Learned Judge in 'Trial by Jury'—but it was decided at the last moment that he should be buried in St Paul's Cathedral, where there is in the crypt a memorial, also by Sir William Goscombe John, showing a full-length figure playing a lyre and beneath it a medallion bearing a head of Sullivan.

Gilbert was cremated at Golder's Green and Lady Gilbert had a memorial tablet, bearing a bas-relief portrait of her husband, placed in Harrow Weald Church.

At the time when Sullivan's funeral procession was passing along the Embankment on the way to St. Paul's Cathedral, Richard D'Oyly Carte was lying desperately ill at his home in the Adelphi, close by. He died a few months later, and in 1902 a memorial window, designed by E. J. Priest, was unveiled by Sir Henry Irving in the Savoy Chapel.

Mentone, Viscount (D) The role was first played by E. Carleton.

Menzies, Ivan He joined the D'Oyly Carte chorus in 1920, later played most of the 'little men' roles and was for some time under-study to Henry Lytton. He spent a considerable time touring in Gilbert and Sullivan operas in Australia and elsewhere. 'The first time I played the Duke of Plaza-Toro, I started by catching my spurs and falling into the canal,' he told me. 'It was decidedly not traditional—I damn nearly broke my neck.' Ivan Menzies is married to Elsie Griffin. Both have been closely associated with the Moral Re-Armament Movement for some years.

Mercury (T) An aged Olympian, played by Nelly Farren. A great favourite at the old Gaiety, she had been in Gilbert's burlesque, *Robert the Devil*, one of three pieces with which the theatre had opened. It would seem that Nelly had no great singing voice but a vivid personality and a comely pair of legs. She was married to Robert Soutar, the Gaiety's stage manager, who also had a part in *Thespis*. Some years afterwards, when Nelly was ill, a benefit performance was given for her at Drury Lane, the bill including *Trial by Jury*, with Gilbert himself appearing in the small role of the Associate. Nelly Farren died at the age of fifty-eight in 1904.

Merovingian 'Of the early Merovingian period.'—The Prince of Monte Carlo's unflattering description of the Baroness von Kraken-feldt (D). The Merovingians ruled over France from about AD 500 to 750.

'Merrily ring the luncheon bell' Chorus with solos by Blanche and Cyril (PI).

Merryman and his Maid, The Alternative title of *The Yeomen of the Guard*.

Meryll, Leonard (Y) *Tenor* W. R. Shirley was the original player of Sergeant Meryll's son, who is impersonated by the condemned Colonel Fairfax.

Meryll, Phoebe (Y) *Mezzo-soprano* Sergeant Meryll's daughter was originally played by Jessie Bond.

Meryll, Sergeant (Y) *Bass-baritone* Sergeant Meryll, of the Yeomen of the Guard, one of whose trials is to be persistently pursued by the ageing Dame Carruthers, was first played by Richard Temple.

Mezzo-sopranos Principal mezzo-soprano roles in the operas are: Hebe (HMS); Kate (PP); Lady Angela (P); Iolanthe and Leila (I); Melissa (PI); Pitti-Sing (M); Mad Margaret (R); Phoebe (Y); Tessa and Vittoria (G); Gretchen, Bertha and Elsa (D).

Micawber, Mr Colonel Calverley brings the famous character from Dickens's *David Copperfield* into his patter song (P).

'Mighty maiden with a mission' Chorus of girl graduates greeting Princess Ida, the head of their university (PI).

Mikado, The; or The Town of Titipu First performed at the Savoy Theatre, London, on March 14, 1885, conducted by Sullivan. Initial run of 672 performances.

The cast for the original production was:

THE MIKADO OF JAPAN	Mr Richard Temple
NANKI-POO (*his son, disguised as a wandering minstrel and in love with Yum-Yum*)	Mr Durward Lely
KO-KO (*Lord High Executioner of Titipu*)	Mr George Grossmith
POOH-BAH (*Lord High Everything Else*)	Mr Rutland Barrington
PISH-TUSH (*a Noble Lord*)	Mr Frederick Bovill
YUM-YUM	Miss Leonora Braham
PITTI-SING (*Three sisters,*	Miss Jessie Bond
PEEP-BO *wards of Ko-Ko*)	Miss Sybil Grey
KATISHA (*an elderly lady, in love with Nanki-Poo*)	Miss Rosina Brandram

As the curtain rises on the first act, set in the courtyard of Ko-Ko's palace in Titipu, the male chorus at once put the audience in the picture:

> If you want to know who we are,
> We are gentlemen of Japan;
> On many a vase and jar—
> On many a screen and fan,
> We figure in lively paint:
> Our attitude's queer and quaint—
> You're wrong if you think it ain't, oh!

If you think we are worked by strings,
Like a Japanese marionette,
You don't understand these things:
It is simply Court etiquette.
Perhaps you suppose this throng
Can't keep it up all day long?
If that's your idea, you're wrong, oh!

Nanki-Poo, guitar on his back and carrying a sheaf of ballads, arrives and asks if anyone can tell him where he can find Ko-Ko's ward, Yum-Yum. He is in a state of some agitation but nevertheless gives an account of himself before further pressing his inquiry:

A wandering minstrel I—
A thing of shreds and patches,
Of ballads, songs and snatches,
And dreamy lullaby!
My catalogue is long,
Through every passion ranging,
And to your humours changing
I tune my supple song!
Are you in sentimental mood?
I'll sigh with you,
Oh, sorrow, sorrow!
On maiden's coldness do you brood?
I'll do so, too—
Oh, sorrow!
I'll charm your willing ears
With songs of lovers' fears,
While sympathetic tears
My cheeks bedew—
Oh, sorrow!
But if patriotic sentiment is wanted,
I've patriotic ballads cut and dried;
For where'er our country's banner may be planted,
All other local banners are defied!
Our warriors, in serried ranks assembled,
Never quail—or they conceal it if they do—
And I shouldn't be surprised if nations trembled
Before the mighty troops of Titipu!

And if you call for a song of the sea,
We'll heave the capstan round,
With a yeo heave ho, for the wind is free,

Her anchor's a-trip and her helm's a-lee,
Hurrah for the homeward bound!
To lay aloft in a howling breeze
May tickle a landsman's taste,
But the happiest hour a sailor sees
Is when he's down
At an inland town,
With his Nancy on his knees, yeo-ho!
And his arm around her waist!

Without telling them the whole truth about himself, Nanki-Poo, the disguised son of the Mikado, explains that, when he was a member of the Titipu Town Band and was taking the hat round, he saw Yum-Yum. They fell in love at once but she was betrothed to Ko-Ko, a cheap tailor, 'and I saw that my suit was hopeless'. But after quitting the town in despair, he learned that Ko-Ko had been condemned to death for flirting. Now it is a question of finding Yum-Yum.

Nanki-Poo's high hopes are dashed once more when Pish-Tush, a noble lord, informs him that Ko-Ko was reprieved and raised to the rank of Lord High Executioner under the following 'remarkable circumstances';

Our great Mikado, virtuous man,
When he to rule our land began,
Resolved to try
A plan whereby
Young men might best be steadied.
So he decreed, in words succinct,
That all who flirted, leered or winked,
(Unless connubially linked),
Should forthwith be beheaded.
And I expect you'll all agree
That he was right to so decree.
And I am right,
And you are right,
And all is right as right be!

This stern decree, you'll understand,
Caused great dismay throughout the land;
For young and old
And shy and bold
Were equally affected.
The youth who winked a roving eye,
Or breathed a non-connubial sigh,

Was thereupon condemned to die—
He usually objected.
And you'll allow, as I expect,
That he was right to so object.
And I am right,
And you are right,
And everything is quite correct!

And so we straight let out on bail
A convict from the county jail,
Whose head was next
On some pretext
Condemnèd to be mown off,
And made *him* Headsman, for we said,
'Who's next to be decapited
Cannot cut off another's head
Until he's cut his own off.'
And we are right, I think you'll say,
To argue in this kind of way:
And I am right,
And you are right,
And all is right—too-looral-lay!

Nanki-Poo is properly impressed when there appears on the
scene a 'haughty and exclusive person', Pooh-Bah, who after giving
a brief run-down of his ancestry, announces that he is First Lord of
the Treasury, Lord Chief Justice, Commander-in-Chief, Lord High
Admiral, Master of the Buckhounds, Groom of the Back Stairs,
Archbishop of Titipu and Lord Mayor, both acting and elect, all
rolled into one. He holds out little hope for Nanki-Poo:

Young man, despair,
Likewise go to,
Yum-Yum the fair
You must not woo.
It will not do:
I'm sorry for you,
You very imperfect ablutioner!
This very day
From school Yum-Yum
Will wend her way,
And homeward come,
With beat of drum
And a rum-tum-tum,
To wed the Lord High Executioner!

And the brass will crash,
And the trumpets bray,
And they'll cut a dash
On their wedding day.
She'll toddle away, as all aver,
With the Lord High Executioner!

It's a hopeless case,
As you may see,
And in your place
Away I'd flee;
But don't blame me—
I'm sorry to be
Of your pleasure a diminutioner.
They'll vow their pact
Extremely soon,
In point of fact
This afternoon.
Her honeymoon.
With that buffoon
At seven commences, so *you* shun her!

The chorus of nobles hails the arrival of Ko-Ko himself:

Behold the Lord High Executioner!
A personage of noble rank and title—
A dignified and potent officer,
Whose attentions are particularly vital!
Defer, defer
To the Lord High Executioner!

Ko-Ko outlines his progress to high office and, after pointing out
that 'there will be no difficulty in finding plenty of people whose
loss will be a distinct gain to society at large,' goes into some detail
on the subject:

Taken from the county jail
By a set of curious chances;
Liberated then on bail
On my own recognizances;
Wafted by a favouring gale
As one sometimes is in trances,
To a height that few can scale,
Save by long and weary dances;

Surely, never had a male
Under such-like circumstances
So adventurous a tale,
Which may rank with most romances.

As some day it may happen that a victim must be found,
I've got a little list—I've got a little list
Of society offenders who might well be underground,
And who never would be missed—who never would be missed!
There's the pestilential nuisances who write for autographs—
All people who have flabby hands and irritating laughs—
All children who are up in dates and floor you with 'em flat—
All persons who in shaking hands, shake hands with you like *that*—
And all third persons who on spoiling *tête-à-têtes* insist—
They'd none of 'em be missed—they'd none of 'em be missed!

There's the banjo serenader, and the others of his race,
And the piano organist—I've got him on the list!
And the people who eat peppermint and puff it in your face,
They never would be missed—they never would be missed!
Then the idiot who praises, with enthusiastic tone,
All centuries but this, and every country but his own;
And the lady from the provinces, who dresses like a guy,
And 'who doesn't think she dances but would rather like to try';
And that singular anomaly, the lady novelist—
I don't think she'd be missed—I'm *sure* she'd not be missed!

And that *Nisi Prius* nuisance, who just now is rather rife,
The Judicial humorist—I've got *him* on the list!
All funny fellows, comic men, and clowns of private life—
They'd none of 'em be missed—they'd none of 'em be missed.
And apologetic statesmen of a compromising kind,
Such as—what d'ye call him—Thing'em-bob, and likewise—
                                        Never-mind,
And 'St—'st—'st— and What's-his-name, and also You-know-who
The task of filling up the blanks I'd rather leave to *you*.
But it really doesn't matter whom you put upon the list,
For they'd none of 'em be missed—they'd none of 'em be missed!

(In Ko-Ko's song, Gilbert used various alternatives to such characters as the piano-organist and lady novelist—critic, dramatist, motorist, bicyclist, for example. Other alternatives, sometimes suggested by the artist playing Ko-Ko, have been used since.)

Ko-Ko and Pooh-Bah depart, discussing the matter of the expense of a slap-up wedding, expense which will have to pass the scrutiny of Pooh-Bah in his various capacities ('I don't say that all these distinguished people couldn't be squared') and the hitherto exclusively male scene is brightened by a flutter of femininity with the arrival of Yum-Yum, Pitti-Sing, Peep-Bo and their schoolfellows:

Comes a train of little ladies
From scholastic trammels free,
Each a little bit afraid is,
Wondering what the world can be!

Is it but a world of trouble—
Sadness set to song?
Is its beauty but a bubble
Bound to break ere long?

Are its palaces and pleasures
Fantasies that fade?
And the glory of its treasures
Shadow of a shade?

Schoolgirls we, eighteen and under,
From scholastic trammels free,
And we wonder—how we wonder!—
What on earth the world can be!

YUM-YUM, PEEP-BO and PITTI-SING:
Three little maids from school are we,
Pert as a schoolgirl well can be,
Filled to the brim with girlish glee,
Three little maids from school!

YUM-YUM:
Everything is a source of fun. (*Chuckle*)

PEEP-BO:
Nobody's safe, for we care for none! (*Chuckle*)

PITTI-SING:
Life is a joke that's just begun! (*Chuckle*)

THE THREE:
Three little maids from school!
(*Dancing*)
Three little maids who, all unwary,
Come from a ladies' seminary,
Freed from its genius tutelary—
Three little maids from school!

YUM-YUM:
One little maid is a bride, Yum-Yum—

PEEP-BO:
Two little maids in attendance come—

PITTI-SING:
Three little maids is the total sum.

THE THREE:
Three little maids from school!

YUM-YUM:
From three little maids take one away.

PEEP-BO:
Two little maids remain, and they—

PITTI-SING:
Won't have to wait very long, they say—

THE THREE:
Three little maids from school!
(*Dancing*)
Three little maids who, all unwary,
Come from a ladies' seminary,
Freed from its genius tutelary—
Three little maids from school!

With no great show of enthusiasm, Yum-Yum allows Ko-Ko to kiss her—but, catching sight of Nanki-Poo, rushes over to him with the other two girls, chattering merrily around him. Ko-Ko suggests that he might be introduced and Nanki-Poo, expecting an angry reaction, blurts out that he loves Yum-Yum. 'Anger!' says Ko-Ko. 'Not a bit, my boy. Why, I love her myself. Charming little girl, isn't she? Very glad to hear my opinion backed by a competent authority. Thank you very much. Good-bye . . . Take him away.'

At much pain to his dignity, Pooh-Bah is persuaded by Ko-Ko to say 'how-de-do' to the girls, who join him in a quartet:

YUM-YUM, PEEP-BO, PITTI-SING:
So please you, Sir, we much regret
If we have failed in etiquette
Towards a man of rank so high—
We shall know better by and by.

YUM-YUM:
But youth, of course, must have its fling,
So pardon us,
So pardon us,

222

PITTI-SING:
And don't, in girlhood's happy spring,
Be hard on us,
Be hard on us,
If we're inclined to dance and sing.
Tra la la. . . .

POOH-BAH:
I think you ought to recollect
You cannot show too much respect
Towards the highly titled few;
But nobody does, and why should you?
That youth at us should have its fling,
Is hard on us,
Is hard on us;
To our prerogative we cling—
So pardon us,
So pardon us,
If we decline to dance and sing.
Tra la la. . . .

The crowd departs and Yum-Yum and Nanki-Poo find themselves together. He confides to her that he is really the son of the Mikado but that, ordered by his father to marry Katisha, an elderly lady of the court, he had fled and joined the town band as second trombone. The young lovers point out to each other that under the new law it is an offence to flirt and that in addition Yum-Yum is engaged to Ko-Ko. But:

NANKI-POO:
Were you not to Ko-Ko plighted,
I would say in tender tone,
'Loved one, let us be united—
Let us be each other's own!'
I would merge all rank and station,
Worldly sneers are nought to us,
And, to mark my admiration,
I would kiss you fondly thus—(*Kisses her*)

BOTH:
I/he would kiss you/me fondly thus—(*Kiss*).

YUM-YUM:
But as I'm engaged to Ko-Ko,
To embrace you thus, *con fuoco*,
Would distinctly be no *gioco*,
And for yam I should get toco—

223

BOTH:
Toco, toco, toco, toco—

NANKI-POO:
So, in spite of all temptation,
Such a theme I'll not discuss,
And on no consideration
Will I kiss you fondly thus—(*Kisses her*)
Let me make it clear to you,
This is what I'll never do!
This, oh this, oh this, oh this—(*Kisses her*)
(Both) This, oh this . . .

They depart in opposite directions on seeing the approach of Ko-Ko, who is joined by Pooh-Bah and Pish-Tush, bearing a letter from the Mikado, which points out that no executions have taken place in Titipu for a year and that unless somebody is beheaded within the month the post of Lord High Executioner will be abolished and Titipu reduced to the rank of a village. It is suggested to Ko-Ko that, as he is under sentence of death anyway, he is the obvious victim. To his protest that a man can't cut off his own head, Pooh-Bah dryly observes: 'A man might try.' Ko-Ko has a bright idea—he will appoint Pooh-Bah as Lord High Substitute, an honour which Pooh-Bah declines with dignity: 'I must set bounds to my insatiable ambition!' They join in an ingenious trio, each of them having his own words and his own tune;

KO-KO:
My brain it teems
With endless schemes
Both good and new
For Titipu;
But if I flit,
The benefit
That I'd diffuse
The town would lose!
Now every man
To aid his clan
Should plot and plan
As best he can,
And so,
Although
I'm ready to go,
Yet recollect
'Twere disrespect

Did I neglect
To thus effect
This aim direct,
So I object—

POOH-BAH:
I am so proud
If I allowed
My family pride
To be my guide,
I'd volunteer
To quit this sphere
Instead of you
In a minute or two.
But family pride
Must be denied,
And set aside,
And mortified.
And so,
Although
I wish to go,
And greatly pine
To brightly shine,
And take the line
Of a hero fine,
With grief condign
I must decline—

PISH-TUSH:
I heard one day
A gentleman say
That criminals who
Are cut in two
Can hardly feel
The fatal steel,
And so are slain
Without much pain.
If this is true
It's jolly for you;
Your courage screw
To bid us adieu
And go
And show
Both friends and foe

How much you dare.
I'm quite aware
It's your affair,
Yet I declare
I'd take your share,
But I don't much care—

ALL:

To sit in solemn silence in a dull, dark dock,
In a pestilential prison, with a life-long lock,
Awaiting the sensation of a short, sharp shock
From a cheap and chippy chopper on a big, black block!

Ko-Ko is brooding about his dilemma when he spots Nanki-Poo, carrying a rope. As Yum-Yum is going to marry Ko-Ko, the only thing left for him to do is to commit suicide. Light dawns upon Ko-Ko—'Substitute!'—and he persuades the young man to be beheaded. 'You'll have a month to live, and you'll live like a fighting cock at my expense. When the day comes there'll be a grand public ceremonial—you'll be the central figure—no one will attempt to deprive you of that distinction.' To clinch the deal, Ko-Ko even agrees to Nanki-Poo marrying Yum-Yum, providing he dies in a month's time.

The stage fills, and when Ko-Ko announces that he has found a volunteer, the crowd greets the news: 'The Japanese equivalent for Hear, Hear, Hear!'

KO-KO:

He yields his life if I'll Yum-Yum surrender.
Now I adore that girl with passion tender,
And could not yield her with a ready will,
Or her allot,
If I did not
Adore myself with passion tenderer still!

The young lovers join with the others in a joyous ensemble:

The threatened cloud has passed away,
And brightly shines the dawning day;
What though the night may come too soon,
There's yet a month of afternoon!
Then let the throng
Our joy advance,
With laughing song
And merry dance,

With joyous shout and ringing cheer,
Inaugurate our/their brief career!
A day, a week, a month, a year—
Or far or near, or far or near,
Life's eventime comes much too soon,
You'll live at least a honeymoon!

Pooh-Bah adds his somewhat qualified congratulations to Nanki-Poo:

As in a month you've got to die,
If Ko-Ko tells us true,
'Twere empty compliment to cry
'Long life to Nanki-Poo!'
But as one month you have to live
As fellow-citizen,
This toast with three times three we'll give—
'Long life to you—till then!'

Suddenly Katisha enters dramatically to dominate the finale to the act in grand operatic manner:

Oh fool, that fleest
My hallowed joys!
Oh blind, that seest
No equipoise!
Oh rash, that judgest
From half, the whole!
Oh base, that grudgest
Love's lightest dole!
Thy heart unbind,
Oh fool, oh blind!
Give me my place,
Oh rash, oh base!
Pink cheek that rulest,
Where wisdom serves!
Bright eye that foolest
Heroic nerves!
Rose lip, that scornest
Lore-laden years!
Smooth tongue, that warnest
Who rightly hears!
Thy doom is nigh,
Pink cheek, bright eye!
Thy knell is rung,
Rose lip, smooth tongue!

Pitti-Sing and the others try to maintain the festive mood:

> Away, nor prosecute your quest—
> From our intention, well expressed,
> You cannot turn us!
> The state of your connubial views
> Towards the person you accuse
> Does not concern us!
> For he's going to marry Yum-Yum—
>
> CHORUS:
> Yum-Yum!
>
> PITTI-SING:
> Your anger pray bury,
> For all will be merry,
> I think you had better succumb—
>
> CHORUS:
> Cumb-cumb!
>
> PITTI-SING:
> And join our expressions of glee.
> On this subject I pray you be dumb—
>
> CHORUS:
> Dumb-dumb!
>
> PITTI-SING:
> You'll find there are many
> Who'll wed for a penny—
> The word for your guidance is 'Mum'—
>
> CHORUS:
> Mum-mum!
>
> PITTI-SING:
> There's lots of good fish in the sea!

But Katisha persists:

> The hour of gladness
> Is dead and gone;
> In silent sadness
> I live alone!
> The hope I cherished
> All lifeless lies,
> And all has perished
> Save love, which never dies!

Oh, faithless one, this insult you shall rue!
In vain for mercy on your knees you'll sue.
I'll tear the mask from your disguising!
Prepare yourselves for news surprising!

She tries desperately to reveal Nanki-Poo's identity but every time she gets as far as 'He is the son of your ...' her voice is drowned by the chorus shouting in Japanese, 'Oh ni! bikkuri shakkuri to!', and the word 'Mikado' is never heard.

The act ends with a big ensemble, the chorus maintaining their joyous mood and Katisha vowing vengeance:

Ye torrents roar!
Ye tempests howl!
Your wrath outpour
With angry growl!
Do ye your worst, my vengeance call
Shall rise triumphant over all!
Prepare for woe,
Ye haughty lords,
At once I go
Mikado-wards.
My wrongs with vengeance shall be crowned!
My wrongs with vengeance shall be crowned!

She sweeps off in a fury, forcing her way through the crowd.

The second act is set in Ko-Ko's garden, with Yum-Yum busy at her bridal toilet, the girls helping her in dressing her hair and making up her face:

Braid the raven hair—
Weave the supple tress—
Deck the maiden fair
In her loveliness—
Paint the pretty face—
Dye the coral lip—
Emphasize the grace
Of her ladyship!
Art and Nature, thus allied,
Go to make a pretty bride.

PITTI-SING:
Sit with downcast eye—
Let it brim with dew—
Try if you can cry—
We will do so, too.

When you're summoned, start
Like a frightened roe—
Flutter, little heart,
Colour, come and go!
Modesty at marriage-tide
Well becomes a pretty bride!

Modesty is not, in fact, the charming Yum-Yum's most noticeable characteristic. Looking in the mirror, she ponders: 'Sometimes I sit and wonder, in my artless Japanese way, why it is that I am so much more attractive than anybody else in the whole world.' Left alone by the others, she develops the theme in the lovely song with Sullivan's gracefully-turned melody:

The sun, whose rays
Are all ablaze
With ever-living glory,
Does not deny
His majesty—
He scorns to tell a story!
He don't exclaim
'I blush for shame,
So kindly be indulgent.'
But, fierce and bold,
In fiery gold,
He glories all effulgent!
I mean to rule the earth,
As he the sky—
We really know our worth,
The sun and I!

Observe his flame,
That placid dame,
The moon's Celestial Highness;
There's not a trace
Upon her face
Of diffidence or shyness:
She borrows light
That, through the night,
Mankind may all acclaim her!
And, truth to tell,
She lights up well,
So I, for one, don't blame her!
Ah, pray make no mistake,

> We are not shy;
> We're very wide awake,
> The moon and I!

Her friends, Pitti-Sing and Peep-Bo, return and somewhat tact-lessly remind her that her lover is to die in a month's time and Nanki-Poo, on arriving with Pish-Tush, finds them in tears. He is not altogether successful in his effort to cheer them up with the suggestion: 'We'll call each second a minute—each minute an hour—each hour a day—and each day a year. At that rate we've about thirty years of married happiness before us!' But the tears are never far away as they sing the madrigal:

> Brightly dawns our wedding day;
> Joyous hour we give thee greeting!
> Whither, whither art thou fleeting?
> Fickle moment, prithee stay!
> What though mortal joys be hollow?
> Pleasures come, if sorrows follow:
> Though the tocsin sound, ere long
> Ding Dong! Ding Dong!
> Yet until the shadows fall
> Over one and over all,
> Sing a merry madrigal—
> Fal-la-fal-la.! (*They burst into tears.*)

> Let us dry the ready tear,
> Though the hours are surely creeping
> Little need for woeful weeping,
> Till the sad sundown is near.
> All must sip the cup of sorrow—
> I to-day and thou to-morrow;
> This the close of every song—
> Ding dong! Ding dong!
> What, though solemn shadows fall,
> Sooner, later, over all?
> Sing a merry madrigal—
> Fal-la—Fal-la.! (*Tears.*)

There is worse to follow. Ko-Ko brings them the distinctly disturb-ing news that he has just had authoritatively from Pooh-Bah—in all his capacities—that the law says that, when a married man is beheaded, his wife is buried alive. Yum-Yum, while not wishing to appear selfish, points out that this revelation does throw a somewhat different light on the matter. But, grim though the situation is, it calls forth the liveliest passage in the whole opera, providing ample opportunity for comic variations of 'business' on the part of Ko-Ko:

YUM-YUM:
Here's a how-de-do!
If I marry you,
When your time has come to perish,
Then the maiden whom you cherish
Must be slaughtered, too!
Here's a how-de-do!

NANKI-POO:
Here's a pretty mess!
In a month, or less,
I must die without a wedding!
Let the bitter tears I'm shedding
Witness my distress,
Here's a pretty mess!

KO-KO:
Here's a state of things!
To her life she clings!
Matrimonial devotion
Doesn't seem to suit her notion—
Burial it brings!
Here's a state of things!

ALL
With a passion that's intense
I/you worship and adore,
But the laws of common sense
We/you oughtn't to ignore.
If what he says/I say is true,
'Tis death to marry you!
Here's a pretty state of things!
Here's a pretty how-de-do!

In despair Nanki-Poo, protesting that he cannot live without Yum-Yum, pulls out a dagger and threatens to do away with himself at once. As this does not suit Ko-Ko, who insists upon a decapitation, Nanki-Poo says, 'Very well, then—behead me—at once.' But Ko-Ko is not ready yet ('Why, I never even killed a bluebottle!') and anyhow, bursting into tears, he would never have taken the job if he had not thought that the duties were purely nominal.

A solution is found just before the arrival of the Mikado. Nanki-Poo and Yum-Yum will be married by the Archbishop of Titipu (one of Pooh-Bah's numerous functions) and will go into hiding, while the others *pretend* to the Mikado that the execution has taken place.

The Mikado enters with Katisha in procession, with the chorus singing:

> Miya sama, miya sama,
> On n'm-ma no mayé ni
> Pira-Pira suru no wa
> Nan gia na
> Toko tonyaré tonyaré na?

MIKADO:
> From every kind of man
> Obedience I expect;
> I'm the Emperor of Japan—

KATISHA:
> And I'm his daughter-in-law elect!
> He'll marry his son
> (He's only got one)
> To his daughter-in-law elect.

MIKADO:
> My morals have been declared
> Particularly correct;

KATISHA:
> But they're nothing at all, compared
> With those of his daughter-in-law elect!
> Bow—Bow—
> To his daughter-in-law elect!

MIKADO:
> In a fatherly kind of way
> I govern each tribe and sect,
> All cheerfully own my sway—

KATISHA:
> Except his daughter-in-law elect!
> As tough as a bone,
> With a will of her own,
> Is his daughter-in-law elect!

MIKADO:
> My nature is love and light.
> My freedom from all defect—

Is insignificant quite,
Compared with his daughter-in-law elect!
Bow—Bow—
To his daughter in-in-law elect!

The Mikado treats them to a summary of the appropriate punishments he has devised:

A more humane Mikado never
Did in Japan exist.
To nobody second,
I'm certainly reckoned
A true philanthropist.
It is my very humane endeavour
To make, to some extent,
Each evil liver
A running river
Of harmless merriment.
My object all sublime
I shall achieve in time—
To let the punishment fit the crime,
The punishment fit the crime;
And make each prisoner pent
Unwillingly represent
A source of innocent merriment,
Of innocent merriment!
All prosy dull society sinners,
Who chatter and bleat and bore,
Are sent to hear sermons
From mystical Germans
Who preach from ten till four.
The amateur tenor, whose vocal villainies
All desire to shirk,
Shall, during off-hours,
Exhibit his powers
To Madame Tussaud's waxwork.
The lady who dyes a chemical yellow,
Or stains her grey hair puce,
Or pinches her figger,
Is painted with vigour
And permanent walnut juice.
The idiot who, in railway carriages,

Scribbles on window-panes,
We only suffer
To ride on a buffer
In Parliamentary trains.
The advertising quack who wearies
With tales of countless cures,
His teeth, I've enacted,
Shall all be extracted
By terrified amateurs.
The music-hall singer attends a series
Of masses and fugues and 'ops'
By Bach, interwoven
With Spohr and Beethoven,
At classical Monday Pops.
The billiard sharp whom anyone catches,
His doom's extremely hard—
He's made to dwell
In a dungeon cell
On a spot that's always barred.
And there he plays extravagant matches
In fitless finger-stalls
On a cloth untrue,
With a twisted cue
And elliptical billiard balls!

The Mikado is gratified to learn that an execution *has* taken place and asks for a description of the remarkable scene. Ko-Ko, Pitti-Sing and Pooh-Bah bring their imaginations to bear with colourful effect:

KO-KO:
The criminal cried as he dropped him down,
In a state of wild alarm—
With a frightful, frantic, fearful frown,
I bared my big right arm.
I seized him by his little pig-tail,
And on his knees fell he,
As he squirmed and struggled,
And gurgled and guggled,
I drew my snickersnee!
Oh, never shall I
Forget the cry,

Or the shriek that shriekèd he,
As I gnashed my teeth
When from its sheath
I drew my snickersnee!

CHORUS:
We know him well.
He cannot tell
Untrue or groundless tales—
He always tries
To utter lies,
And every time he fails.

PITTI-SING:
He shivered and shook as he gave the sign
For the stroke he didn't deserve;
When all of a sudden his eye met mine,
And it seemed to brace his nerve;
For he nodded his head and kissed his hand,
    And he whistled an air, did he,
As the sabre true
Cut cleanly through
His cervical vertebrae!
When a man's afraid
A beautiful maid
Is a cheering sight to see;
And it's oh, I'm glad
That moment sad
Was soothed by the sight of me!

CHORUS:
Her terrible tale
You can't assail,
With truth it quite agrees!
Her taste exact
For faultless tact
Amounts to a disease.

POOH-BAH:
Now though you'd have said that head was dead
(For its owner dead was he),
It stood on its neck, with a smile well-bred,
And bowed three times to me!
It was none of your impudent off-hand nods,
But as humble as could be;

For it clearly knew
The deference due
To a man of pedigree!
And it's oh, I vow
This deathly bow
Was a touching sight to see;
Though trunkless, yet
It couldn't forget
The deference due to me!

CHORUS:
This haughty youth,
He speaks the truth
Whenever he finds it pays;
And in this case
It all took place
Exactly as he says!

The Mikado is duly impressed but points out that he had come on quite a different matter, the disappearance of his son, whom he now believes to be in the town, disguised as a Second Trombone. And Katisha, reading the death certificate, sees the name—Nanki-Poo! Amid the frantic apologies of the three miscreants, the Mikado, while agreeing that it is all very unfortunate, fixes an after-lunch appointment for their executions for 'compassing the death of the Heir Apparent'. 'I don't want any lunch,' says Pooh-Bah.

With the Mikado expressing his sympathy with them in their predicament, they all join in a glee about the injustice of the world:

MIKADO:
See how the Fates their gifts allot,
For A is happy—B is not.
Yet B is worthy, I dare say,
Of more prosperity than A!

KO-KO, POOH-BAH and PITTI-SING:
Is B more worthy?

KATISHA:
I should say
He's worth a great deal more than A.

TOGETHER:
Yet A is happy!
Oh, so happy!
Laughing, Ha! ha!
Chaffing, Ha! ha!
Nectar quaffing, Ha! ha! ha!

Ever joyous, ever gay,
Happy, undeserving A!

KO-KO, POOH-BAH and PITTI-SING:
If I were Fortune—which I'm not—
B should enjoy A's happy lot,
And A should die in miserie—
That is, assuming I am B.

MIKADO and KATISHA:
But *should* A perish?

KO-KO, POOH-BAH and PITTI-SING:
That should he
(Of course, assuming I am B).
B should be happy!
Oh, so happy!
Laughing, Ha! ha!
Chaffing, Ha! ha!
Nectar quaffing, Ha! ha! ha!
But condemned to die is he,
Wretched, meritorious B!

After the oddly assorted party has broken up, Ko-Ko encounters
Nanki-Poo, who suggests that the only solution to the problem is
for Ko-Ko to marry Katisha. 'In that case I could come to life
without any fear of being put to death,' he says. 'When Katisha is
married, existence will be as welcome as the flowers in spring.'

NANKI-POO:
The flowers that bloom in spring, Tra, la,
Breathe promise of merry sunshine—
As we merrily dance and we sing, Tra la,
We welcome the hope that they bring, Tra la,
Of a summer of roses and wine.
And that's what we mean when we say that a thing
Is welcome as flowers that bloom in the spring.
Tra la la . . .

KO-KO:
The flowers that bloom in the spring, Tra la,
Have nothing to do with the case.
I've got to take under my wing, Tra la,
A most unattractive old thing, Tra la,
With a caricature of a face.
And that's what I mean when I say, or I sing,
'Oh, bother the flowers that bloom in the spring.'
Tra la la . . . .

Katisha then has a big dramatic scene to herself. Though she is subjected throughout the opera to jibes about her age and plainness of looks, she does have the compensation of being given some splendidly dramatic music to sing:

> Alone, and yet alive! Oh, sepulchre!
> My soul is still my body's prisoner!
> Remote the peace that Death alone can give—
> My doom, to wait! my punishment, to live!
> Hearts do not break!
> They sting and ache
> For old love's sake,
> But do not die,
> Though with each breath
> They long for death,
> As witnesseth
> The living I!
> Oh, living I!
> Come, tell me why,
> When hope is gone,
> Dost thou stay on?
> Why linger here,
> Where all is drear?
> Oh, living I!
> Come, tell me why,
> When hope is gone,
> Dost thou stay on?
> May not a cheated maiden die?

To Katisha's amazement, Ko-Ko appears and begs her to marry him, protesting that he cannot live without her love. She refuses to believe him. 'Who knows so well as I that no one ever died of a broken heart!' she says—but softens when Ko-Ko tells her a touching little tale:

> On a tree by a river a little tom-tit
> Sang 'Willow, titwillow, titwillow!'
> And I said to him, 'Dicky-bird, why do you sit
> Singing 'Willow, titwillow, titwillow?'
> 'Is it weakness of intellect, birdie?' I cried,
> 'Or a rather tough worm in your little inside?'
> With a shake of his poor little head, he replied,
> 'Oh, willow, titwillow, titwillow!'

He slapped at his chest, as he sat on that bough,
Singing, 'Willow, titwillow, titwillow!'
And a cold perspiration bespangled his brow,
Oh, willow, titwillow, titwillow!
He sobbed and he sighed, and a gurgle he gave,
Then he threw himself into the billowy wave,
And an echo arose from the suicide's grave—
'Oh, willow, titwillow, titwillow!'

Now I feel just as sure as I'm sure that my name
Isn't Willow, titwillow, titwillow,
That 'twas blighted affection that made him exclaim,
'Oh, willow, titwillow, titwillow!'
And if you remain callous and obdurate, I
Shall perish as he did, and you will know why,
Though I probably shall not exclaim as I die,
'Oh, willow, titwillow, titwillow!'

Katisha yields to his entreaties and they go into a lively duet, in
which they insist that there are many beauties other than the
obvious ones:

KATISHA:
There is beauty in the bellow of the blast,
There is grandeur in the growling of the gale,
There is eloquent outpouring
When the lion is a-roaring,
And the tiger is a-lashing of his tail!

KO-KO:
Yes, I like to see a tiger
From the Congo or the Niger,
And especially when lashing of his tail!
Volcanoes have a splendour that is grim,
And earthquakes only terrify the dolts,
But to him who's scientific
There is nothing that's terrific
In the falling of a flight of thunderbolts!

KO-KO:
Yes, in spite of all my meekness,
If I have a little weakness,
It's a passion for a flight of thunderbolts!

BOTH:
If that is so,
Sing derry down derry!
It's evident, very,
Our tastes are one.
Away we'll go and merrily marry,
Nor tardily tarry
Till day is done!

KO-KO:
There is beauty in extreme old age—
Do you fancy you are elderly enough?
Information I'm requesting
On a subject interesting:
Is a maiden all the better when she's tough?

KATISHA:
Throughout this wide dominion
It's the general opinion
That she'll last a good deal longer when she's tough.

KO-KO:
Are you old enough to marry, do you think?
Won't you wait until you're eighty in the shade?
There's a fascination frantic
In a ruin that's romantic;
Do you think you are sufficiently decayed?

KATISHA
To the matter that you mention
I have given some attention,
And I think I am sufficiently decayed.

BOTH:
If that is so,
Sing derry down derry! . . .

After a capital lunch the Mikado arrives to witness the executions
of Ko-Ko, Pitti-Sing and Pooh-Bah, but Nanki-Poo bursts in
with the words, 'The Heir Apparent is *not* slain!' Katisha flies into
a rage at Ko-Ko, and the Mikado points out that there is still the
little matter of the elaborate lying about the execution of Nanki-Poo.
But Ko-Ko comes up with a 'logical' explanation: 'When your
Majesty says, "Let a thing be done," it's as good as done—practically,
it *is* done—because your Majesty's will is law. Your Majesty says,
"Kill a gentleman," and a gentleman is told off to be killed. Consequently that gentleman is as good as dead—practically, he *is* dead—
and if he is dead, why not say so?'

'Nothing could possibly be more satisfactory!' agrees the Mikado, and they all let loose their high spirits: 'For he's gone and married Yum-Yum (Yum-Yum!) . . .'

YUM-YUM and NANKI-POO:
The threatened cloud has passed away,
And fairly shines the dawning day;
What though the night may come too soon,
We've years and years of afternoon!

SIX PRINCIPALS;
Then let the throng
Our joy advance,
With laughing song
And merry dance.

ALL:
With joyous shout and ringing cheer,
Inaugurate our/their new career!

Mikado *Bass-baritone* Though he reels off with relish the punishments which fit the crime, it cannot be said that the Mikado is not the soul of amiability about it.: 'I forget the punishment for compassing the death of the Heir Apparent. . . Something lingering, with boiling oil in it, I fancy. Something of that sort. I think boiling oil occurs in it, but I'm not sure. I know it's something humorous, but lingering, with either boiling oil or melted lead. Come, come, don't fret—I'm not a bit angry.' Richard Temple was the first to play the Mikado.

Millais 'Lord Fildes and Viscount Millais (when they come) we'll welcome sweetly.'—King Paramount (U). Sir John Everett Millais (1829–96), the English painter, was one of the founders of the group known as the Pre-Raphaelite Brotherhood and later became president of the Royal Academy.

Minerva 'Minerva, oh, hear me!'—Princess Ida. Minerva was the Roman goddess of wisdom and the patroness of the arts.

Mistaken Identity It was not by any means only Gilbert who made use of mistaken identity and disguises in working out his plots. These had been favourite devices of dramatists for years; Shakespeare was certainly not above employing them. In the operas,

Captain Corcoran and Ralph Rackstraw have been mixed up as babies (HMS); the real King of Barataria is neither Marco nor Giuseppe, the gondoliers, but Luiz, the Duke of Plaza-Toro's attendant (G); Robin Oakapple is really Sir Ruthven Murgatroyd (a 'barrowknight', as his seafaring foster-brother calls him) (R); Strephon, the Arcadian shepherd, is a fairy, or at any rate half a fairy, from the waist upwards (I); Colonel Fairfax masquerades as Leonard Meryll (Y); and Nanki-Poo, son of the Mikado, shows a nice touch of imagination by disguising himself as second trombone in the Titipu Town Band.

Gilbert had his own quip about a case of mistaken identity on a private occasion. He was sitting beside a young woman when she suddenly exclaimed, 'Oh, Sir William, there's a wasp on your sleeve. You'll be stung!' 'I have no great opinion of the intellect of the insect,' replied Gilbert. 'But it is not such a fool as to take me for a flower.'

And there was an episode at the Garrick Club. As Gilbert wrote in happier circumstances:

'I've just been elected to the Garrick Club, for which I was blackballed thirty-seven years ago—through a case of mistaken identity, for I was quite unknown then and the Committee thought they were pilling another man. When they discovered their mistake, they asked me to put myself up again, but it occurred to me that, as the mistake was theirs, it was theirs to rectify it. Moreover, I am not one of those who turn the second cheek to the smiter. So matters have remained until the other day, when the Committee did me the honour of selecting me for immediate election "on account of my public distinction" (!). As Heaven has signified its displeasure at the action of the Committee of thirty-seven years ago by sweeping them off the face of the earth, and as I had no quarrel with the present Committee, who are all my very good friends, I accepted the honour they had proposed to confer on me.'

Mitchell, Margaret Joining the D'Oyly Carte chorus in 1943, Margaret Mitchell played her first principal part, Fleta (I), in the following season. Her later roles included Edith (PP), Ella (P), Yum-Yum (M), Kate (Y), Casilda (G), Patience, Phyllis (I) and Rose Maybud (R). She was with the company until 1951.

'Miya sama, miya sama' On the entrance of the Mikado in the second act of the opera, the chorus sing the first verse of a marching-song—the equivalent of, say, 'Tipperary'—sung by Japanese royalist troops in about 1870 during a revolt led by General Saige against the Mikado. To quell the rising, the Emperor dispatched a force under the command of Prince Arisugawa, to whom he gave as a mascot a small pennant which he wore suspended from his horse's bridle. The verse means: 'O! Prince, what is that fluttering in front of your horse?' The second verse of the song, not used in the opera, goes:

'Are wa!
Cheketi Seibatsu Seyo Tono
Nishikino Mihata O
Shira Baika
Toko Tonyaré Tonyaré Na!'

Answering the question asked in the first verse, this means: 'Don't you see—this is the Royal banner—entrusted to me that I may defeat the enemies of the Crown. Don't you see!'

Monday Pops 'At classical Monday Pops.'—The Mikado.
'More fun than Monday Pops'—Archibald Grosvenor (P).
The Monday Pops were popular concerts of classical music held in St James's Hall, opened in 1858 on part of the site of what is now the Piccadilly Hotel.

Moore, Decima When she was only eighteen, Decima Moore made her first stage appearance—creating the role of Casilda (G) at the Savoy Theatre in 1889. She was born at Brighton and studied at Blackheath Conservatoire of Music. Her first experience with Gilbert, recalled by her in Leslie Baily's *The Gilbert and Sullivan Book*, was typical of his approach. Asked whether she had ever acted, she replied, 'No.' To which Gilbert retorted: 'So much the better for you. You've nothing to unlearn.' In 1905 she married Brigadier-General Sir Gordon Guggisberg, who was for many years a colonial governor in West Africa. She originated the Women's Emergency Corps in 1914 and founded the British Navy, Army and Air Force Club, which she ran in Paris in World Wars I and II. She received the honour of CBE. Apart from Gilbert and Sullivan, Decima Moore appeared in a great number of other musical shows. She died in February 1964.

'More humane Mikado never did in Japan exist, A' The Mikado's song in which he lists the various punishments designed to 'fit the crime'. The 'billiard sharp' is one of the types he selects for special mention and it might be noted that Gilbert himself was keen on the game. When Sullivan was abroad, Gilbert wrote to him: 'I send you Cook on Billiards—the study of that work has made me what I am in Billiards, and if you devote six or eight hours a day to it regularly, you may hope to play up to my form when you return.'

Morey, Cynthia Later a member of Sadler's Wells Opera, Cynthia Morey joined the D'Oyly Carte chorus in 1950 and during her seven years with the company sang many leading roles, including Plaintiff (J), Mabel (PP), Patience, Celia and Phyllis (I), Psyche and Sacharissa (PI), Yum-Yum (M), Rose Maybud (R) and Gianetta (G).

Morgan, Fisher A member of the D'Oyly Carte Company from 1950 until 1956, Fisher Morgan sang a number of leading roles, including Bouncer (C), Learned Judge (J), Sergeant of Police (PP), Private Willis (I), King Hildebrand (PI), Pooh-Bah (M), Sir Despard (R), Wilfred Shadbolt (Y) and Don Alhambra (G). He died in January 1959.

Morris 'To Swinburne and Morris.'—Robin Oakapple (R). William Morris (1834–96), the English poet and artist, was a prominent member of the group known as the Pre-Raphaelite Brotherhood.

Mountararat, Earl of (I) *Baritone* Rutland Barrington was the first artist to play Lord Mountararat, who sings of the days 'when Britain really ruled the waves'.

Murgatroyd, Major (P) *Baritone* Frank Thornton was the original player of this officer of the Dragoon Guards.

Murgatroyd, Sir Despard (R) *Baritone* Rutland Barrington was the original player of Sir Despard who, in the belief that his brother is dead, temporarily inherits the Witch's Curse.

Murgatroyd, Sir Roderic (R) *Bass* Richard Temple was the first artist to play Sir Roderic, the twenty-first baronet and central figure in the Ghosts' High Noon scene in the picture-gallery.

Murton, Mr The original Third Yeoman (Y).

Music 'I know only two tunes. One is "God Save the Queen"—the other isn't.'—W. S. Gilbert.

Hesketh Pearson in *Gilbert and Sullivan* tells of a composer who wrote from Australia, suggesting a collaboration with Gilbert, adding, 'Though by profession a chemist, I am a born musician.' To which Gilbert replied, 'I should prefer to collaborate with a born chemist who is a musician by profession.'

A gushing American woman was enthusing to Gilbert about Sullivan's music and comparing it with that of 'dear Baytch', as she pronounced 'Bach'. Was Baytch still composing? 'On the contrary, madam,' replied Gilbert. 'Dear Baytch is by way of *de*composing.'

'My boy, you may take it from me' Robin Oakapple's song about the handicaps suffered by a man of diffident nature (R).

'My brain it teems with endless schemes' Ko-Ko's part in the first act trio with Pooh-Bah and Pish-Tush (M).

'My eyes are fully open to my awful situation' Trio for Robin Oakapple, Sir Despard Murgatroyd and Mad Margaret (R).

'My goodness me! What shall we do ? Chorus (D).

'My name is John Wellington Wells' The song in which the Sorcerer, the 'dealer in magic and spells,' introduces himself (S).

Mystical Germans 'Sent to hear sermons from mystical Germans who preach from ten till four.'—(M). A group of Lutheran evangelists had recently visited England from Germany.

Nanki-Poo (M) *Tenor* The Mikado's son, disguised as a wandering minstrel and formerly the second trombone in the Titipu Town Band, was first played by Durward Lely.

Narcissus 'Ah, I am a very Narcissus!'—Archibald Grosvenor (P), looking at himself in a hand-mirror. The description is apt. Psychoanalysts of to-day use the term 'narcissism' to describe abnormal admiration for oneself. In Greek mythology Narcissus brushed aside the affection of Echo, who wilted and died. His fate was to fall in love with his own image, as seen reflected in a fountain. Plunging in, he died, and those who came to retrieve his body found only the flower that bears his name.

Nash, Royston In March 1970, Royston Nash—then Captain Nash—led and conducted a section of the Royal Marines Band, Deal, on the stage in the first act of the D'Oyly Carte production of *HMS Pinafore* at Sadler's Wells Theatre, London. In the following year he was appointed musical director of D'Oyly Carte. A Bournemouth man, he studied at the Royal Marines School of Music and took his L.R.A.M. in conducting. After studies on the trumpet and in conducting at the Royal Academy of Music, London, he was awarded a certificate of merit for orchestral conducting and the Musicians' Company bronze medal for harmony. He was for three years director of music to the Commander-in-Chief, Mediterranean, also conducting the Malta Choral Society; then director of music to the Commander-in-Chief, Portsmouth, and eventually going back in that capacity to the Royal Marines School of Music, Deal.

National Operatic and Dramatic Association The Gilbert and Sullivan operas retain their enormous popularity with amateur societies, whose central organisation is the National Operatic and Dramatic Association. Founded in 1899 for the express purpose of bringing together members of the various societies, the Association's membership has steadily increased and now embraces 1,400 affiliated societies and nearly 1,300 individual members. It was registered as a charity under the Charities Act 1960. Headquarters: 1 Crestfield Street, London W.C.1.

Naylor, Kathleen Isabel (PP), Lady Saphir (P), Fleta (I), Ada and Sacharissa (PI), Peep-Bo (M), Ruth (R) and Vittoria (G) were sung by Kathleen Naylor, who joined the D'Oyly Carte chorus in 1933 and left the company in 1938.

''Neath this blow, worse than stab of dagger' Duet for Earl of Mountararat and Earl Tolloller (I).

Nekaya, Princess (U) *Soprano* Emmie Owen was the first artist to play King Paramount's daughter.

Nelson, Lord 'The pluck of Lord Nelson aboard of the *Victory*.'—Colonel Calverley (P).

'Never mind the why and wherefore' Lively trio for Sir Joseph, Captain Corcoran and Josephine, with Sir Joseph's comic bell-ringing antics (HMS).

Newby, Herbert Though the audience do not now see him on the stage, Herbert Newby—appointed company manager of D'Oyly Carte in 1970—has as complete a Gilbert and Sullivan background as one could wish. He was born in Oldham, began singing as a boy soprano and, warmly encouraged by his father, took part in local Gilbert and Sullivan activities. After service in the RAF, he was a professional soloist in Manchester Cathedral Choir before joining the D'Oyly Carte chorus in 1947, moving on to understudy and then singing principal tenor roles including Ralph Rackstraw (HMS), Duke of Dunstable (P), Earl Tolloller (I) and Nanki-Poo (M). He became deeply interested in the technical side of the company and was stage director from 1956 until 1961 and director of productions from then until 1970. He is married to Ceinwen Jones, for many years a mezzo-soprano with the company.

Nicemis (T) Member of a travelling theatrical company, played by Constance Loseby, one of the Gaiety company and formerly on the music-halls.

Nickell-Lean, Elizabeth In her first season with D'Oyly Carte in 1931, Elizabeth Nickell-Lean sang Isabel (PP), Peep-Bo (M), Ruth (R) and Giulia (G). Roles she sang during her six years with the company included Saphir (P), Melissa, Ada and Sacharissa (PI), Pitti-Sing (M), Margaret (R), Phoebe (Y) and Tessa (G).

'Night has spread her pall once more' Opening chorus to the second act (Y).

'Nightingale sighed for the moon's bright ray, The' Madrigal sung by Ralph Rackstraw and chorus (HMS).

Nightmare In its juxtaposition of incongruous things and ideas, the Lord Chancellor's song (I)—'When you're lying awake with a dismal headache'—is as brilliant an impression of a nightmare as one could wish for.

'None shall part us from each other' Duet for Strephon and his sweetheart, Phyllis (I).

Nordenfelt 'With Maxim gun and Nordenfelt.'—Captain Corcoran (U). The Nordenfelt was an early form of machine-gun.

Nosology In the song in which he introduces himself, John Wellington Wells (S), refers to 'mystic nosology', the scientific classification of diseases.

Notary (S) *Bass* Fred Clifton was the first artist to play the part.

'Now away to the wedding we go' Song for Baroness von Krakenfeldt and chorus (D).

'Now is not this ridiculous' Chorus of dragoons, bewildered at being ignored by the girls (P).

'Now, Julia, come' Duet for Ludwig and Julia (D).

'Now to the banquet we press' Opening of the finale to the first act, with the duet, 'Oh love, true love!' for Aline and Alexis (S).

'Now wouldn't you like to rule the roast' Duet for Melissa and Lady Blanche (PI).

In the Orchestra.

Oakapple, Robin (R) *Baritone* The village youth, who is really Sir Ruthven Murgatroyd, inheritor of the Witch's Curse, was originally played by George Grossmith. It was during the run of this piece that Grossmith fell ill and there stepped into the part his young understudy, Henry Lytton, later to become one of the most famed of Savoyards.

'O'er the season vernal' Solo by the Plaintiff (J).

'Of all the young ladies I know' Earl Tolloller's solo (I).

Official Pronouncements 'It is one of the happiest characteristics of this glorious country that official utterances are invariably regarded as unanswerable.'—Sir Joseph Porter (HMS).

'Of happiness the very pith' Opening chorus to the second act (G).

'Oh, admirable art! Oh, neatly-planned invention!' Duet for Princess Zara and Captain Fitzbattleaxe (U).

'Oh, a monarch who boasts intellectual graces' Ludwig's song in the finale to the first act (D).

'Oh! a private buffoon is a light-hearted loon' Jack Point's song about the problems and hazards of a professional jester (Y).

'Oh, better far to live and die under the brave black flag I fly' The Pirate King's declaration of the splendours of his profession (PP).

'Oh, dry the glistening tear' Chorus of Major-General Stanley's daughters with which the second act opens (PP).

'Oh, foolish fay' Fairy Queen's song—'Oh, Captain Shaw!' (I).

'Oh fool, that fleest my hallowed joys!' Katisha's song in the finale to the first act (M).

'Oh, gentlemen, listen, I pray' Song by the Defendant, explaining the reasons for his change of heart (J).

'Oh, goddess wise, that lovest light' Princess Ida's aria (PI).

'Oh, happy the blossom that blooms on the lea' Trio for Dame Hannah, Adam and Zorah (R).

'Oh, happy the flowers that blossom in June' Duet for Sir Despard Murgatroyd and Mad Margaret (R).

'Oh, happy the lily when kissed by the bee' Duet for Rose Maybud and Richard Dauntless (R).

'Oh, happy young heart' Aline's waltz-time aria (S).

'Oh, I have wrought much evil with my spells!' Scene between Lady Sangazure and Mr Wells, with the duet 'Hate me! I drop my H's.' (S).

'Oh, is there not one maiden breast' Frederic's song (PP).

'Oh joy, oh rapture unforeseen' Quartet for Josephine, Hebe, Ralph Rackstraw and Dick Deadeye, leading to the close of the opera. It had been heard earlier as an ensemble for sailors, relatives and Josephine, at a time when expressions of rapture were premature (HMS).

'Oh, joyous boon! oh, mad delight!' Ensemble for Aline, Alexis, Dr Daly and Chorus, leading towards the finale (S).

'Oh, listen to me, dear' Duet for Lisa and Julia in the finale to the first act (D).

'Oh, may we copy all her maxims wise' King Paramount' solo in the finale to the opera (U).

'Oh, my voice is sad and low' Dr Daly's song (S), with its wistful comment that every girl is 'engaged to So-and-so'.

'Oh, the rapture unrestrained' Duet for Lady Sophy and King Paramount (U).

'Oh, why am I moody and sad?' Sir Despard Murgatroyd's song, with interpolations by the chorus (R).

'Oh, wretched the debtor who's signing a deed!' Robin Oakapple's solo at the end of the first act (R).

Old Adam Goodheart (R) *Bass* Rudolph Lewis was the original player of the role.

Oldham, Derek Principal tenor in many D'Oyly Carte productions, including *The Sorcerer*, *HMS Pinafore*, *Iolanthe*, *The Mikado*, *The Yeomen of the Guard* and *The Gondoliers*, Derek Oldham was born in Accrington and was a bank clerk in his early days. He made his first stage appearance in an operetta, *The Daring of Diane* at the London Pavilion when he was twenty-two and was later in *The Chocolate Soldier*. After serving in World War I, during which he won the Military Cross, he joined D'Oyly Carte in 1919 and was with them for three years before going into a number of West End musicals. He returned to the company in 1929 and remained for some years. Derek Oldham, who married Winnie Melville in 1923, died in March 1968, at the age of seventy-five.

Olga (D) *Soprano* Mildred Baker was the first artist to play Olga, member of Dummkopf's theatrical company.

'O make way for the wise men!' The chorus's greeting for the first entrance of Scaphio and Phantis (U).

'On a tree by a river a little tom-tit' Ko-Ko's pathetic little song—'Oh, willow, titwillow, titwillow.' (M).

One Tree Hill 'I often roll down One Tree Hill.'—John Wellington Wells (S). The reference is to a small public park at Honor Oak commanding a splendid view of London.

'O ni! bikkuri shakkuri to!' When Katisha (M) attempts to reveal Nanki-Poo's identity, the crowd interrupts with this Japanese expression. It has no strict English interpretation but the sense is: 'O! he was frightened to death!'

'On the day when I was wedded' Duchess of Plaza-Toro's song (G).

'O rapture, when alone together' Duet for Casilda and Luiz, the first indication to the audience that they are lovers (G).

Orchestras Luiz: 'Your Grace, the band are sordid persons who required to be paid in advance.'
   Duchess of Plaza-Toro: 'That's so like a band!'

Osborn, Leonard A Londoner, Leonard Osborn was appearing in amateur shows while he was a chemist in a silk-printing mills at £3 10s a week. Somebody mentioned to him that Rupert D'Oyly Carte was paying £4 a week for choristers and so, he says, 'I found myself earning £4 a week for doing what I enjoyed instead of £3 10s for what I didn't.' His first part was that of First Yeoman in 1937 and by the time World War II started he had played Defendant (J), Francesco (G) and Leonard Meryll (Y). After service as a Flight-Lieutenant in the RAF, he returned to D'Oyly Carte to sing a long list of principal tenor roles—Tolloller (I), Nanki-Poo (M), Duke of Dunstable (P), Fairfax (Y), Marco (G), Box (C), Richard Dauntless (R) and Cyril (PI). He left the company in 1959 but, while running a business in Croydon, has continued to produce the operettas for amateur companies.
   Leonard Osborn recalls a slight contretemps while he was playing Marco in *The Gondoliers* in Liverpool. 'I knew by experience that, after the arrival of the ducal party in the second act, I was off the stage for just as long as it took to smoke one cigarette,' he says. 'But this was at the time when Dalton, as Chancellor of the Exchequer, had put up the price and I had given up smoking. Without a cigarette, I misjudged the time. Martyn Green (Duke of Plaza-Toro) frantically ad-libbed as the call-boy went in search of me and I came down the flights of steps from my dressing-room. You can imagine that, as I went on to the stage with Giuseppe, Martyn made much of his line, "Ah! Their Majesties!" as though to say, "And about time, too!"'
   In *Ruddigore* he used to make his entrance as Richard Dauntless by leaping over the railings—but one night at Stratford-upon-Avon

the leap was much too spectacular to be pleasant. 'We used to have the railings draped with fish-netting and I arranged for the props man to leave a gap through which I could grasp the rail,' he recalls. 'This night, however, my hand slipped and I really came a cropper, cracking my elbow and a couple of ribs. But I managed to get through, hornpipe and all, and by the time I got off the stage and collapsed, my understudy, Fred Sinden, was waiting to go on. Despite the fall, Dick Dauntless remains my favourite part. But they are all, in their way, wonderful parts.'

Otto 'Breathing concentrated otto.'—Counsel for the Plaintiff (J). Otto is an alternative form of attar, the fragrant oil obtained from rose petals.

'Our great Mikado, virtuous man' Pish-Tush's song about the laws against flirting (M).

'Over the bright blue sea' Barcarolle sung off-stage, heralding the arrival of Sir Joseph Porter (HMS).

Overtures The composition of the overtures to the operas has long been a matter for discussion. Some of them were undoubtedly written by Sullivan, while others were probably sketched out by him and the details written in by another hand. From notes kindly supplied to me by the D'Oyly Carte Opera Company, the following picture emerges:

Cox and Box The overture is by Sullivan, in his own handwriting.

Trial by Jury There is no overture but the whole of the score is in Sullivan's handwriting.

The Sorcerer The overture is in Hamilton Clarke's writing, while the rest of the score is in Sullivan's.

HMS Pinafore The overture was sketched out by Sullivan, whose handwriting appears at intervals, while details were arranged by Alfred Cellier. The Entr'acte is in Cellier's writing.

The Pirates of Penzance The same procedure was followed as in the case of the *Pinafore* overture. In 1919 a re-arranged overture was prepared by Geoffrey Toye.

Patience Overture sketched out by Sullivan and filled in by someone unknown.

Iolanthe Overture by Sullivan and in his writing, except for some copying details from later parts of the opera.

Princess Ida The same procedure as in *Iolanthe*.

The Mikado The overture probably prepared by Hamilton Clarke.

Ruddigore As some numbers to which reference was made in the original overture were no longer included in the performance of the opera, Geoffrey Toye prepared a more suitable overture in 1920.

The Yeomen of the Guard Overture by Sullivan.

The Gondoliers Overture by Sullivan, in his own handwriting.

Utopia, Limited There is no overture.

The Grand Duke Overture by Sullivan, in his own handwriting.

Ovidius Naso 'Oh, amorous dove! Type of Ovidius Naso!' sings the Fairy Queen (I). She is referring to the Roman poet, better known as Ovid, whose works include *The Art of Love*, with instructions for gaining and retaining the affections of a lover. Robin Oakapple (R) also refers to the poet: 'From Ovid and Horace.'

Owen, Emmie Creator of the roles of Princess Nekaya (U) and Princess of Monte Carlo (D), Emmie Owen played also Peep-Bo (M), Gianetta (G), Elsie Maynard (Y), Hebe (HMS), Saphir (P) and Patience.

Paddington Pollaky Colonel Calverley (P) is referring to Ignatius Paul Pollaky, a famed Austrian-born private detective, who lived on Paddington Green in the 1860's.

Paget 'Coolness of Paget about to trepan.'—Colonel Calverley (P). Sir James Paget (1814–99) was an eminent British surgeon. Trepanning is a medical term used in connection with brain surgery.

'Painted emblems of our race' Chorus of family portraits when they have stepped out of their frames in the picture-gallery (R).

   This scene has special significance for the distinguished bass, Owen Brannigan, who, though he has never appeared in them on the stage, has recorded most of the leading bass roles in the operas. While the young Brannigan was working as a joiner in London, he was paying for singing lessons at the Guildhall School of Music and was given the part of one of the ancestors in the picture gallery in a students' performance of *Ruddigore*. Sir Landon Ronald, principal of the School, had been ill and was brought into a rehearsal in a wheel-chair. 'Arrange a special audition for the third portrait from the right,' he said to one of his staff. The 'third portrait from the right' was Owen Brannigan—and the audition won him a scholarship.

Palmer, Christene Principal contralto with the D'Oyly Carte Company, Christene Palmer was born in Geelong, Australia, and began her musical studies there. Moving to Melbourne, she joined the National School of Opera and the Oriana Madrigal Choir. During 1958 and 1960 she sang leading parts with the Elizabethan Opera Trust and was a soloist at the annual Bach Festivals in Melbourne. She came to London in 1961 to continue her studies and for two seasons sang at Glyndebourne. She joined D'Oyly Carte in 1965 and sings the leading contralto roles—Little Buttercup (HMS), Ruth (PP), Lady Jane (P), Fairy Queen (I), Lady Blanche (PI), Katisha (M), Dame Hannah (R), Dame Carruthers (Y) and Duchess of Plaza-Toro (G).

Pandaean 'Gaily pipe Pandaean pleasure.' (P). The reed-pipes of Pan, god of flocks and herds and the personification of wild nature.

Parker, Alison Born in York, she went to school in Berkshire, where she became prominent in various amateur productions. After four years study at the Royal College of Music, London, she joined D'Oyly Carte in 1965. She is married to Brian Peach, a chorister with the company.

Parkes, Clifford Immediately after appearing on a television programme, Clifford Parkes was invited to audition for D'Oyly Carte and joined the company as a bass in 1965. Born in Staffordshire, he studied for four years at the Guildhall School of Music and Drama, London. He left D'Oyly Carte to go to Covent Garden in August 1969.

Parliamentary Pickford 'He's a Parliamentary Pickford—he carries everything!' declares Lord Mountararat (I), referring to the well-known firm of commercial carriers.

Parliamentary Trains Faced with to-day's so-called football supporters who do much more than 'scribble on window-panes', the Mikado would no doubt find a punishment considerably more drastic than riding on a buffer in Parliamentary trains. The term is a reference to the Railway Regulation Act passed by Parliament in 1844.

Party Politics 'Government by Party! Introduce that great and glorious element—at once the bulwark and foundation of England's greatness—and all will be well! No political measures will endure because one Party will assuredly undo all that the other Party has done; and while grouse is to be shot, and foxes worried to death, the legislative action of the country will be at a standstill. Then there will be sickness in plenty, endless lawsuits, crowded jails, interminable confusion in the Army and Navy, and, in short, general and unexampled prosperity!'—Princess Zara (U).

Partlet, Mrs (S) *Contralto* A pew-opener in the village of Ploverleigh, originally played by Henriette Everard.

R   257

Passmore, Walter The original Tarara (U) and Rudolph (D), Walter Passmore later followed George Grossmith in the "little men' roles in the operas. He was born in London in 1867 and, a talented musician, he toured as pianist with concert parties and in musicals before making his first London stage appearance at the Savoy in a show called *Jane Annie* in 1893, creating the part of Tarara later the same year. It was Walter Passmore who, rehearsing the role of Sir Joseph Porter for a revival of *Pinafore*, suggested to Gilbert that he might walk around with his nose in the air, 'as though raising it above an unpleasant smell.' 'Unpleasant smell?' said Gilbert. 'Well, you're the best judge of that, Passmore.' After leaving D'Oyly Carte, Passmore played in a great number of musical shows. He died in 1946, aged seventy-nine.

PATIENCE; or Bunthorne's Bride First performed at the Opera Comique, London, on April 23, 1881, conducted by Sullivan, and transferred to the newly-built Savoy Theatre on October 10. Initial run of 578 performances.

The cast for the first performance of the 'New and Original Aesthetic Opera' was:

REGINALD BUNTHORNE (*a Fleshly Poet*)		Mr George Grossmith
ARCHIBALD GROSVENOR (*an Idyllic Poet*)		Mr Rutland Barrington
MR BUNTHORNE'S SOLICITOR		Mr G. Bowley
COLONEL CALVERLEY	*Officers of*	Mr Richard Temple
MAJOR MURGATROYD	*Dragoon*	Mr Frank Thornton
LIEUT. THE DUKE OF DUNSTABLE	*Guards*	Mr Durward Lely
THE LADY ANGELA		Miss Jessie Bond
THE LADY SAPHIR	(*Rapturous Maidens*)	Miss Julia Gwynne
THE LADY ELLA		Miss Fortescue
THE LADY JANE		Miss Alice Barnett
PATIENCE (*a Village Milkmaid*)		Miss Leonora Braham

When the curtain rises on the first act we are outside Castle Bunthorne. Groups of young women, wearing aesthetic draperies, are playing on various stringed instruments. They are the Rapturous Maidens but at the moment there is nothing very rapturous about them. They are, in fact, in the depths of misery:

> Twenty love-sick maidens we,
> Love-sick all against our will.
> Twenty years hence we shall be
> Twenty love-sick maidens still.
> Twenty love-sick maidens we,
> And we die for love of thee.

ANGELA:

Love feeds on hope, they say, or love will die—
(Ah, miserie!)
Yet my love lives, although no hope have I!
(Ah, miserie!)
Alas, poor heart, go hide thyself away—
To weeping concords tune thy roundelay!
(Ah, miserie!)

CHORUS:

All our love is all for one,
Yet that love he heedeth not,
He is coy and cares for none,
Sad and sorry is our lot!
Ah, miserie!

ELLA:

Go, breaking heart,
Go, dream of love requited;
Go, foolish heart,
Go, dream of lovers plighted;
Go, madcap heart,
Go, dream of never waking;
And in thy dream
Forget that thou art breaking!
(Ah, miserie!)

They reveal that the reason for their plight is that they are all in love with the poet Reginald Bunthorne, who remains insensible. The elderly Lady Jane enters and tells them that Reginald, on his part, has fallen in love with the village milkmaid, Patience, to whom love is up to now a sealed book. But, while chiding the others, Lady Jane confides to the audience in an aside: 'Oh, Reginald, if you but knew what a wealth of golden love is waiting for you, stored up in this rugged old bosom of mine, the milkmaid's triumph would be short indeed!'

Patience herself appears and, questioned by the others, confesses that it is true that she has never loved:

PATIENCE:

I cannot tell what this love may be
That cometh to all, but not to me.
It cannot be kind as they'd imply,
Or why do these ladies sigh?
It cannot be joy and rapture deep,
Or why do these gentle ladies weep?

It cannot be blissful as 'tis said,
Or why are their eyes so wondrous red?
Though everywhere true love I see
A-coming to all, but not to me,
I cannot tell what this love may be!
For I am blithe and I am gay,
While they sit sighing night and day.
Think of the gulf 'twixt them and me,
'Fa la la la!'—and 'Miserie!'

CHORUS:
Yes, she is blithe. . . .

If love is a thorn, they show no wit
Who foolishly hug and foster it.
If love is a weed, how simple they
Who gather it, day by day!
If love is a nettle that makes you smart,
Then why do you wear it next your heart?
And if it be none of these, say I,
Ah, why do you sit and sob and sigh?

CHORUS:
For she is blithe. . . .

Patience has news for the others that the 35th Dragoon Guards
have arrived in the village, but it is her turn to be surprised when
the maidens, all of whom were engaged to Dragoon Guards only
a year ago, now express indifference. Since then, Angela points
out, 'our tastes have been etherealized.' They go off, singing.
Patience, too, leaves—and the Dragoon Guards arrive:

The soldiers of our Queen
Are linked in friendly tether;
Upon the battle scene
They fight the foe together.
There every mother's son
Prepared to fight and fall is;
The enemy of one
The enemy of all is!

Colonel Calverley enters and throws off an elaborate patter-song
in which Gilbert has introduced all sorts of varied allusions, mainly
for their sound effect rather than their bearing on the matter:

If you want a receipt for that popular mystery,
Known to the world as a Heavy Dragoon,
Take all the remarkable people in history,
Rattle them off to a popular tune.
The pluck of Lord Nelson on board of the *Victory*—
Genius of Bismarck devising a plan—
The humour of Fielding (which sounds contradictory)—
Coolness of Paget about to trepan—
The science of Jullien, the eminent musico—
Wit of Macaulay, who wrote of Queen Anne—
The pathos of Paddy, as rendered by Boucicault—
Style of the Bishop of Sodor and Man—
The dash of a D'Orsay, divested of quackery—
Narrative powers of Dickens and Thackeray—
Victor Emmanuel—peak-haunting Peveril—
Thomas Aquinas, and Doctor Sacheverell—
Tupper and Tennyson—Daniel Defoe—
Anthony Trollope and Mr Guizot! ah!
Take of these elements all that is fusible,
Melt 'em all down in a pipkin or crucible,
Set 'em to simmer and take off the scum,
And a Heavy Dragoon is the residuum!

If you want a receipt for this soldier-like paragon,
Get at the wealth of the Czar (if you can)—
The family pride of a Spaniard from Aragon—
Force of Mephisto pronouncing a ban—
A smack of Lord Waterford, reckless and rollicky—
Swagger of Roderick, heading his clan—
The keen penetration of Paddington Pollaky—
Grace of an Odelisque on a divan—
The genius strategic of Caesar or Hannibal—
Skill of Sir Garnet in thrashing a cannibal—
Flavour of Hamlet—the Stranger, a touch of him—
Little of Manfred (but not very much of him)—
Beadle of Burlington—Richardson's show—
Mr Micawber and Madame Tussaud! ah!
Take of these elements all that is fusible,
Melt 'em all down in a pipkin or crucible,
Set 'em to simmer and take off the scum,
And a Heavy Dragoon is the residuum!

They are naturally interested when Reginald Bunthorne enters, ostentatiously composing a poem and followed by the maidens, walking two-and-two and singing:

> In a doleful train
> Two and two we walk all day—
> For we love in vain!
> None so sorrowful as they
> Who can only sigh and say,
> Woe is me, alackaday!

This of course infuriates the gallant Dragoons:

> Now is not this ridiculous—and is not this preposterous?
> A thorough-paced absurdity—explain it if you can.
> Instead of rushing eagerly to cherish us and foster us,
> They all prefer this melancholy literary man.
> Instead of slyly peering at us,
> Casting looks endearing at us,
> Blushing at us, flushing at us—flirting with a fan;
> They're actually sneering at us, fleering at us, jeering at us!
> Pretty sort of treatment for a military man!

ANGELA:
> Mystic poet, hear our prayer,
> Twenty love-sick maidens we—
> Young and wealthy, dark and fair—
> All of country family.
> And we die for love of thee—
> Twenty love-sick maidens we!

But Bunthorne, in an aside, lets the audience into a secret:

> Though my book I seem to scan
> In a rapt ecstatic way,
> Like a literary man
> Who despises female clay,
> I hear plainly all they say,
> Twenty love-sick maidens they!

SAPHIR:
> Though so excellently wise,
> For a moment mortal be,
> Deign to raise thy purple eyes
> From thy heart-drawn poesy.
> Twenty love-sick maidens see—
> Each is kneeling on her knee!

BUNTHORNE (*aside*):
Though, as I remarked before,
Any one convinced would be
That some transcendental lore
Is monopolising me,
Round the corner I can see
Each is kneeling on her knee!

With a great show of mental effort, Bunthorne finishes composing his poem and, despite a loud 'No!' from the Dragoons, insists upon reading it. 'It is,' he explains, 'the wail of the poet's heart on discovering that everything is commonplace. To understand it, cling passionately to one another and think of faint lilies.' It is called 'Oh, Hollow! Hollow! Hollow!':

What time the poet hath hymned
The writhing maid, lithe-limbed,
Quivering on amaranthine asphodel,
How can he paint her woes,
Knowing, as well he knows,
That all can be set right with calomel?

When from the poet's plinth
The amorous calocynth
Yearns for the aloe, faint with rapturous thrills,
How can he hymn their throes
Knowing, as well he knows,
That they are only uncompounded pills?

Is it, and can it be,
Nature hath this decree,
Nothing poetic in the world shall dwell?
Or that in all her works
Something poetic lurks,
Even in calocynth and calomel?
I cannot tell.

This pretentious rubbish draws sighs of rapture from the ladies, though Patience reasonably describes it as nonsense. Colonel Calverley's reminder that the ladies are engaged to the officers of Dragoons draws from Saphir the pronouncement: 'It can never be. You are not Empyrean. You are not Della Cruscan. You are not even Early English. Oh, be Early English ere it is too late!' Lady Jane is critical of the officers uniforms: 'Red and Yellow! Primary colours! Oh, South Kensington!' On the Duke of Dunstable pointing out that they don't see how the uniforms could be improved, Lady Jane retorts: 'No, you wouldn't. Still, there *is* a cobwebby grey velvet, with a tender bloom like cold gravy, which, made Florentine fourteenth-century, trimmed with Venetian leather and Spanish altar lace, and surmounted with something Japanese—it matters not what—would at least be early English!'

As the ladies withdraw, Colonel Calverley reflects upon the insult to the British uniform:

When I first put this uniform on,
I said, as I looked in the glass,
'It's one to a million
That any civilian
My figure and form will surpass.
Gold lace has a charm for the fair,
And I've plenty of that, and to spare.
While a lover's professions,
When uttered in Hessians,
Are eloquent everywhere!'
A fact that I counted upon,
When I first put this uniform on!

DRAGOONS:
By a simple coincidence, few
Could ever have counted upon,
The same thing occurred to me,
When I first put this uniform on!

COLONEL:
I said, when I first put it on,
'It is plain to the veriest dunce
That every beauty
Will feel it her duty
To yield to its glamour at once.
They will see that I'm freely gold-laced
In a uniform handsome and chaste'—
But the peripatetics
Of long-haired aesthetics
Are very much more to their taste—
Which I never counted upon,
When I first put this uniform on!

DRAGOONS:
By a simple coincidence, few
Could ever have counted upon,
I didn't anticipate that,
When I first put this uniform on!

The Dragoons storm off, and Bunthorne appears—to let us a little further into his secret:

> Am I alone,
> And unobserved? I am!
> Then let me own
> I'm an aesthetic sham!
> This air severe
> Is but a mere
> Veneer!
> This cynic smile
> Is but a wile
> Of guile!
> This costume chaste
> Is but good taste
> Misplaced!
> Let me confess!
> A languid love for lilies does *not* blight me!
> Lank limbs and haggard cheeks do *not* delight me!
> I do *not* care for dirty greens
> By any means.
> I do *not* long for all one sees
> That's Japanese.
> I am *not* fond of uttering platitudes
> In stained-glass attitudes.
> In short, my mediaevalism's affectation,
> Born of a morbid love of admiration!
>
> If you're anxious for to shine in the high aesthetic
>   line as a man of culture rare,
> You must get up all the germs of the transcendental
>   terms, and plant them everywhere.
> You must lie upon the daisies and discourse in novel
>   phrases of your complicated state of mind.
> The meaning doesn't matter if it's only idle chatter
>   of a transcendental kind.
> And every one will say,
> As you walk your mystic way,
> 'If this young man expresses himself in terms too
>   deep for *me*,
> Why, what a very singularly deep young man this
>   deep young man must be!'
> Be eloquent in praise of the very dull old days which
>   have long since passed away,

And convince 'em, if you can, that the reign of
   good Queen Anne was Culture's palmiest day.
Of course you will pooh-pooh whatever's fresh and
   new, and declare it's crude and mean,
For Art stopped short in the cultivated court of the
   Empress Josephine.
And every one will say,
As you walk your mystic way,
'If that's not good enough for him which is good
   enough for *me*,
Why, what a very cultivated kind of youth this kind
   of youth must be!'
Then a sentimental passion of a vegetable fashion
   must excite your languid spleen,
An attachment *à la Plato* for a bashful young potato,
   or a not-too-French French bean!
Though the Philistines may jostle, you will rank as
   an apostle in the high aesthetic band,
If you walk down Piccadilly with a poppy or a lily
   in your mediaeval hand.
And every one will say
As you walk your flowery way,
'If he's content with a vegetable love which would
   certainly not suit *me*,
Why, what a most particularly pure young man this
   pure young man must be!'

At the end of his song Patience enters and he professes his love,
even going so far as to confide to her that he does not really *like*
poetry. But it is all to no purpose and he goes off reciting:

      Oh, to be wafted away
      From this black Aceldama of sorrow,
      Where the dust of an earthy to-day
      Is the earth of a dusty to-morrow!

Lady Angela enters and gives Patience a brief lecture on the purity
and unselfishness of love but the milkmaid points out, in some
distress, that apart from a great-aunt she has never loved anyone
since she was a baby:

      Long years ago, fourteen, maybe,
      When but a tiny babe of four,
      Another baby played with me,
      My elder by a year or more.

A little child of beauty rare,
With marvellous eyes and wondrous hair,
Who, in my child-eyes, seemed to me
All that a little child should be!
Ah, how we loved, that child and I!
How pure our baby joy!
How true our love—and, by the by,
He was a little boy!

ANGELA:
Ah, old, old tale of Cupid's touch!
I thought as much—I thought as much!
He *was* a little boy!

PATIENCE:
Pray don't misconstrue what I say—
Remember, pray—remember, pray,
He was a *little* boy!

ANGELA:
No doubt! Yet, spite of all your pains,
The interesting fact remains—
He was a little *boy*!

The bewildered Patience, convinced that falling in love must be a duty, decides that she must do something about it at once. Archibald Grosvenor appears on the scene:

Prithee, pretty maiden—prithee, tell me true,
(Hey, but I'm doleful, willow willow waly!)
Have you e'er a lover a-dangling after you?
Hey willow waly O!
I would fain discover
If you have a lover?
Hey willow waly O!

PATIENCE:
Gentle sir, my heart is frolicsome and free—
(Hey, but he's doleful, willow willow waly!)
Nobody I care for comes a-courting me—
Hey willow waly O!
Nobody I care for
Comes a-courting—therefore
Hey willow waly O!

GROSVENOR:
Prithee, pretty maiden, will you marry me?
(Hey, but I'm hopeful, willow willow waly!)
I may say, at once, I'm a man of propertee—
Hey willow waly O!
Money, I despise it;
Many people prize it.
Hey willow waly O!

PATIENCE:
Gentle sir, although to marry I design—
(Hey, but he's hopeful, willow willow waly!)
As yet I do not know you, and so I must decline.
Hey willow waly O!
To other maidens go you—
As yet I do not know you,
Hey willow waly O!

Grosvenor is shocked that Patience does not recognise him as the childhood friend of fifteen years earlier. ('Oh, Chronos, Chronos, this is too bad of you!') But he points out that, though his childhood love for Patience has never faded, he has the misfortune to be so beautiful that every woman falls in love with him on sight. He is a poet, too: 'I am the Apostle of Simplicity. I am called "Archibald the All-Right"—for I am infallible!'

The way seems clear for them until Patience realises that, as love must be unselfish—so she has been told—she cannot truly love anyone so perfect as Grosvenor, a sentiment with which he entirely agrees. They part, appreciating that, though she cannot love him, there is nothing to prevent him loving *her*.

PATIENCE:
Though to marry you would very selfish be—

GROSVENOR:
Hey, but I'm doleful—willow willow waly!

PATIENCE:
You may, all the same, continue loving me—

GROSVENOR:
Hey willow waly O!

BOTH:
All the world ignoring,
You'll/I'll go on adoring—
Hey willow waly O!

They go off despairingly in opposite directions, and the stage fills as Bunthorne, garlanded but looking miserable, is led on by Angela and Saphir, followed by a procession of maidens, dancing classically and playing upon archaic instruments. The chorus give forth:

> Let the merry cymbals sound,
> Gaily pipe Pandaean pleasure,
> With a Daphnephoric bound
> Tread a gay but classic measure.
> Every heart with hope is beating,
> For at this exciting meeting
> Fickle Fortune will decide
> Who shall be our Bunthorne's bride!

The Dragoons arrive and are understandably astonished at the spectacle:

> Now tell us, we pray you,
> Why thus they array you—
> Oh, poet, how say you—
> What is it you've done?

DUKE OF DUNSTABLE:
> Of rite sacrificial,
> By sentence judicial,
> This seems the initial,
> Then why don't you run.

COLONEL CALVERLEY:
> They cannot have led you
> To hang or behead you,
> Nor may they *all* wed you,
> Unfortunate one!

DRAGOONS:
> Then tell us, we pray you,
> Why thus they array you—
> Oh, poet, how say you—
> What is it you've done?

BUNTHORNE:
> Heart-broken at my Patience's barbarity,
> By the advice of my solicitor,
> In aid—in aid of a deserving charity,
> I've put myself up to be raffled for!

Amid the general excitement and consternation, the Dragoons plead with the girls to remain faithful to them.

269

DUKE OF DUNSTABLE:
Your maiden hearts, ah, do not steel
To pity's eloquent appeal,
Such conduct British soldiers feel.
Sigh, sigh, all sigh!

To foeman's steel we rarely see
A British soldier bend the knee,
Yet, one and all, they kneel to ye—
Kneel, kneel, all kneel!

Our soldiers very seldom cry,
And yet—I need not tell you why—
A tear-drop dews each martial eye!
Weep, weep, all weep!

Bunthorne, who has been impatient during the Dragoons' sighing, kneeling and weeping, becomes all businesslike:

Come, walk up, and purchase with avidity,
Overcome your diffidence and natural timidity,
Tickets for the raffle should be purchased with rapidity,
Put in half a guinea and a husband you may gain—
Such a judge of blue-and-white and other kinds of pottery—
From early Oriental down to modern terra-cotta-ry—
Put in half a guinea—you may draw him in a lottery—
Such an opportunity may not occur again.

DRAGOONS:
We've been thrown over, we're aware,
But we don't care—but we don't care!
There's fish in the sea, no doubt of it,
As good as ever came out of it,
And some day we shall get our share,
So we don't care—so we don't care!

Lady Jane comes on the scene as the maidens blindfold themselves and sing:

Oh, Fortune, to my aching heart be kind!
Like us, thou art blindfolded, but not blind!
    (*Uncovering an eye*)
Just raise your bandage, thus, that you may see,
And give the prize, and give the prize to me!
    (*Covering eyes again*)

BUNTHORNE:
Come, Lady Jane, I pray you draw the first!

JANE (*joyfully*):
He loves me best!

BUNTHORNE (*aside*):
I want to know the worst!

Lady Jane is just about to draw the first ticket from the bag when
Patience comes in and stays her hand. Patience kneels to Bunthorne
and sings:

> If there be pardon in your breast
> For this poor penitent,
> Who with remorseful thought opprest
> Sincerely doth repent;
> If you, with one so lowly, still
> Desire to be allied,
> Then you may take me, if you will,
> For I will be your bride!

ALL:
Oh, shameless one!
Oh, bold-faced thing!
Away you run—
Go, take your wing,
You shameless one!
You bold-faced thing!

BUNTHORNE:
How strong is love! For many and many a week
She's loved me fondly and has feared to speak,
But Nature, for restraint too mighty far,
Has burst the bonds of Art—and here we are!

But Patience, pointing out that he is wrong, proceeds to explain
with interpolations by the others:

> True love must single-hearted be—
> (*Bunthorne*: Exactly so!)
> From every selfish fancy free—
> (*Bunthorne*: Exactly so!)
> No idle thought of gain or joy
> A maiden's fancy should employ—
> True love must be without alloy.
> (*All*: Exactly so!)
> Imposture to contempt must lead—
> (*Colonel*: Exactly so!)
> Blind vanity's dissension's seed—
> (*Major*: Exactly so!)

> It follows, then, a maiden who
> Devotes herself to loving *you* (*to Bunthorne*)
> Is prompted by no selfish view—
> (*All*: Exactly so!)

Bunthorne, declaring that there is now no chance for any other, embraces Patience and they go off together. Angela, Saphir and Ella join the Colonel, Duke and Major in a sestette:

> I hear the soft note of the echoing voice
> Of an old, old love, long dead—
> It whispers my sorrowing heart 'rejoice'—
> For the last sad tear is shed—
> The pain that is all but a pleasure will change
> For the pleasure that's all but pain,
> And never, oh never, our hearts will range
> From that old, old love again!

As the girls embrace the officers, Patience and Bunthorne return, followed by Grosvenor, walking slowly and engrossed in a book.

> ANGELA:
> But who is this, whose god-like grace
> Proclaims he comes of noble race?
> And who is this, whose manly face
> Bears sorrow's interesting trace?
>
> GROSVENOR:
> I am a broken-hearted troubadour,
> Whose mind's aesthetic and whose tastes are pure!
>
> ANGELA:
> Aesthetic! He is aesthetic!
>
> GROSVENOR:
> Yes, yes—I am aesthetic
> And poetic!
>
> ALL THE LADIES:
> Then, we love you!

With Bunthorne, Patience and the Dragoons exclaiming, 'They love him! Horror!' and Grosvenor echoing, 'They love me! Horror! Horror! Horror!', they all plunge into the whirling ensemble that closes the first act:

> GIRLS:
> Oh, list while we a love confess
> That words imperfectly express.

Those shell-like ears, ah, do not close
To blighted love's distracting woes!

PATIENCE:
List, Reginald, while I confess
A love that's all unselfishness;
That it's unselfish, goodness knows,
You won't dispute it, I suppose?

GROSVENOR:
Again my cursed comeliness
Spreads hopeless anguish and distress!
Thine ears, oh Fortune, do not close
To my intolerable woes.

BUNTHORNE:
My jealousy I can't express,
Their love they openly confess;
His shell-like ears he does not close
To their recital of their woes.

The second act is set in a glade. Leaning pensively on a 'cello, Lady Jane muses on the fickle way in which the maidens have deserted Bunthorne because of his affection for Patience. 'Fools!' she bursts out. 'Of that fancy he will soon weary—and then I, who alone am faithful to him, shall reap my reward. But do not dally too long, Reginald, for my charms are ripe, Reginald, and already they are decaying. Better secure me ere I have gone too far!' She develops the theme:

Sad is that woman's lot who, year by year,
Sees, one by one, her beauties disappear,
When Time, grown weary of her heart-drawn sighs,
Impatiently begins to 'dim her eyes'!
Compelled, at last, in life's uncertain gloamings,
To wreathe her wrinkled brow with self-saved
    'combings',
Reduced, with rouge, lip-salve, and pearly grey,
To 'make up' for lost time as best she may!

Silvered is the raven hair,
Spreading is the parting straight,
Mottled the complexion fair,
Halting is the youthful gait,
Hollow is the laughter free,
Spectacled the limpid eye—
Little will be left of me
In the coming by and by!

Fading is the taper waist,
Shapeless grows the shapely limb,
And although severely laced,
Spreading is the figure trim!
Stouter than I used to be,
Still more corpulent grow I—
There will be too much of me
In the coming by and by!

As she leaves, Grosvenor comes in, reading abstractedly and followed by the maidens, playing on archaic instruments. They plead with him:

Turn, oh, turn in this direction.
Shed, oh, shed a gentle smile,
With a glance of sad perfection
Our poor fainting hearts beguile!
On such eyes as maidens cherish
Let thy fond adorers gaze,
Or incontinently perish
In their all-consuming rays!

With the girls grouped adoringly around him, Grosvenor condescends to read two of his poems:

Gentle Jane was as good as gold,
She always did as she was told;
She never spoke when her mouth was full,
Or caught bluebottles their legs to pull,
Or spilt plum jam on her nice new frock,
Or put white mice in the eight-day clock,
Or vivisected her last new doll,
Or fostered a passion for alcohol.
And when she grew up she was given in marriage
To a first-class earl who keeps his carriage!

Teasing Tom was a very bad boy,
A great big squirt was his favourite toy;
He put live shrimps in his father's boots,
And sewed up the sleeves of his Sunday suits;
He punched his poor little sisters' heads,
And cayenne-peppered their four-post beds;
He plastered their hair with cobbler's wax,
And dropped hot halfpennies down their backs.
The consequence was he was lost totally,
And married a girl in the *corps de bally*!

Grosvenor finds the swooning reception of his work beginning to cloy: 'Ladies, I am sorry to appear ungallant, but this is Saturday, and you have been following me about ever since Monday. I should like the usual half-holiday. I shall take it as a personal favour if you will allow me to close early to-day. . . . It is best to speak plainly. I know that I am loved by you, but I never can love you in return, for my heart is fixed elsewhere! Remember the fable of the Magnet and the Churn.' He sings it for them:

> A magnet hung in a hardware shop,
> And all around was a loving crop
> Of scissors and needles, nails and knives,
> Offering love for all their lives;
> But for iron the magnet felt no whim,
> Though he charmed iron, it charmed not him;
> From needles and nails and knives he'd turn,
> For he'd set his love on a Silver Churn!
> His most aesthetic,
> Very magnetic
> Fancy took this turn—
> 'If I can wheedle
> A knife or a needle,
> Why not a Silver Churn?'
>
> And Iron and Steel expressed surprise,
> The needles opened their well-drilled eyes,
> The penknives felt 'shut up,' no doubt,
> The scissors declared themselves 'cut out',
> The kettles they boiled with rage, 'tis said,
> While every nail went off its head,
> And hither and thither began to roam,
> Till a hammer came up—and drove them home.
> While this magnetic,
> Peripatetic
> Lover he lived to learn,
> By no endeavour
> Can magnet ever
> Attract a Silver Churn!

The girls go off despondently and Patience, coming upon Grosvenor, is at pains to draw from him assurances that he loves her, while she on her part insists that she must love Bunthorne from a sense of duty, even though it makes her miserable. After Grosvenor's departure, Bunthorne, hotly followed by Lady Jane, finds Patience in tears. She tells Bunthorne that she considers Grosvenor to be 'the noblest, purest and most perfect being' she has ever met but that it is her duty *not* to love him. Bunthorne irritably suggests that she doesn't know what love is. 'Yes, I do,' insists Patience. 'There was a happy time when I didn't, but a bitter experience has taught me.' When left alone, she sings:

> Love is a plaintive song,
> Sung by a suffering maid,
> Telling a tale of wrong,
> Telling of hope betrayed;
> Tuned to each changing note,
> Sorry when *he* is sad,
> Blind to his every mote,
> Merry when he is glad!
> Love that no wrong can cure,
> Love that is always new,
> That is the love that's pure,
> That is the love that's true!
>
> Rendering good for ill,
> Smiling at every frown,
> Yielding your own self-will,
> Laughing your tear-drops down;
> Never a selfish whim,
> Trouble, or pain to stir;
> Everything for him,
> Nothing at all for her!
> Love that will aye endure,
> Though the rewards be few,
> That is the love that's pure,
> That is the love that's true!

Patience goes off, weeping. A thoroughly irritated Bunthorne arrives with Lady Jane and protests that, until the appearance of Grosvenor on the scene, it was he who was generally admired. 'But,' he says, 'I will show the world I can be as mild as he. If they want insipidity, they shall have it. I'll meet this fellow on his own ground and beat him on it.' Lady Jane promises to help him:

JANE:
So go to him and say to him, with compliment ironical—

BUNTHORNE:
Sing 'Hey to you—
Good day to you'—
And that's what I shall say!

JANE:
'Your style is much too sanctified—your cut is too
    canonical'—

BUNTHORNE:
Sing 'Bah to you—
Ha! Ha! to you'—
And that's what I shall say!

JANE:
'I was the beau ideal of the morbid young aesthetical—
To doubt my inspiration was regarded as heretical—
Until you cut me out with your placidity emetical.'—

BUNTHORNE:
Sing 'Booh to you—
Pooh, pooh to you'—
And that's what I shall say!

BOTH:
Sing 'Hey to you—good day to you'—
Sing 'Bah to you—ha! ha! to you'—
Sing 'Booh to you—pooh, pooh to you'—
And that's what you/I shall say!

BUNTHORNE:
I'll tell him that unless he will consent to be more jocular—

JANE:
Sing 'Booh to you—
Pooh, pooh to you'—
And that's what you should say!

BUNTHORNE:
To cut his curly hair, and stick an eyeglass in his ocular—

JANE:
Sing 'Bah to you—
Ha! ha! to you'—
And that's what you should say!

BUNTHORNE:
To stuff his conversation full of quibble and of quiddity—
To dine on chops and roly-poly pudding with avidity—
He'd better clear away with all convenient rapidity.

JANE:
Sing 'Hey to you—
Good day to you'—
And that's what you should say!

BOTH:

Sing 'Booh to you—pooh, pooh to you'—
Sing 'Bah to you—ha! ha! to you'—
Sing 'Hey to you—good day to you'—
And that's what I/you shall/should say!

After Lady Jane and Bunthorne have departed, the three officers appear, but they are much changed men. They have abandoned their uniforms and, not to be outdone by their aesthetic rivals, are wearing long hair and other marks of aestheticism. They move stiffly, striking 'classical' attitudes. They explain their behaviour in a trio:

It's clear that mediaeval art alone retains its zest,
To charm and please its devotees we've done our little best.
We're not quite sure if all we do has the Early English ring;
But, as far as we can judge, it's something like the thing:
You hold yourself like this (*attitude*),
You hold yourself like that (*attitude*),
By hook and crook you try to look both angular and flat
   (*attitude*)
We venture to expect
That what we recollect,
Though but a part of true High Art, will have its due effect.

If this is not exactly right, we hope you won't upbraid;
You can't get high Aesthetic tastes, like trousers, ready made.
True views on Mediaevalism Time alone will bring,
But, as far as we can judge, it's something like this sort of thing:
You hold yourself like this (*attitude*),
You hold yourself like that (*attitude*),
By hook and crook you try to look both angular and flat
   (*attitude*),
To cultivate the trim
Rigidity of limb,
You ought to get a Marionette, and form your style on him
   (*attitude*).

They are far from sure of themselves but they take heart when Angela and Saphir appear and are duly impressed. The ladies are not yet prepared to commit themselves but the three officers do go so far as to discuss who shall take whom, if all goes well. It is impressed upon the Duke that, as the person of superior lineage, he would take first choice. All five indulge in a dance, changing their partners as they sing:

278

DUKE (*taking Saphir*):
If Saphir I choose to marry,
I shall be fixed up for life;
Then the Colonel need not tarry,
Angela can be his wife.

MAJOR (*dancing alone*):
In that case unprecedented,
Single I shall live and die—
I shall have to be contented
With their heartfelt sympathy!

ALL:
He will have to be contented
With our heartfelt sympathy!

DUKE (*taking Angela*):
If on Angy I determine,
At my wedding she'll appear,
Decked in diamond and ermine,
Major then can take Saphir!

COLONEL (*dancing alone*):
In that case unprecedented,
Single I shall live and die—
I shall have to be contented
With their heartfelt sympathy!

DUKE (*taking both Angela and Saphir*):
After some debate internal,
If on neither I decide,
Saphir then can take the Colonel,
Angy be the Major's bride!
(*dancing alone*)
In that case unprecedented,
Single I must live and die—
I shall have to be contented
With their heartfelt sympathy!

ALL:
He will have to be contented
With our heartfelt sympathy.

The five of them dance off arm-in-arm. Grosvenor strolls in, admiring his features in a hand-mirror ('Ah, I am a very Narcissus!') and is met by the moody and frustrated Bunthorne, who protests at the way in which the girls have transferred their adoration. Grosvenor insists that his beauty and the attentions of the girls are a positive embarrassment to him and Bunthorne, at first by threatening to visit a curse upon him, persuades him to promise to bring about a complete change in his looks and manner. 'I have long wished for a reasonable pretext for such a change as you suggest,' confesses Grosvenor. 'It has come at last. I do it on compulsion!' They join in a duet:

BUNTHORNE:
When I go out of door,
Of damozels a score
(All sighing and burning,
And clinging and yearning)
Will follow me as before.
I shall, with cultured taste,
Distinguish gems from paste,
And 'High diddle diddle'
Will rank as an idyll,
If I pronounce it chaste!

BOTH:
A most intense young man,
A soulful-eyed young man,
An ultra-poetical, super-aesthetical,
Out-of-the-way young man!

GROSVENOR:
Conceive me, if you can,
An every-day young man:
A commonplace type,
With a stick and a pipe,
And a half-bred black-and-tan;
Who thinks suburban 'hops'
More fun than 'Monday Pops',
Who's fond of his dinner,
And doesn't get thinner
On bottled beer and chops.

BOTH:
A commonplace young man,
A matter-of-fact young man,
A steady and stolid-y, jolly Bank-holiday
Every-day young man!

BUNTHORNE:
A Japanese young man,
A blue-and-white young man,

Francesca di Rimini, miminy, piminy,
Je-ne-sais-quoi young man!

GROSVENOR:
A Chancery Lane young man,
A Somerset House young man,
A very delectable, highly respectable,
Threepenny-bus young man!

BUNTHORNE:
A pallid and thin young man,
A haggard and lank young man,
A greenery-yallery, Grosvenor Gallery,
Foot-in-the-grave young man!

GROSVENOR:
A Sewell & Cross young man,
A Howell & James young man,
A pushing young particle—'What's the next
   article?'—
Waterloo House young man!

BUNTHORNE:
Conceive me, if you can,
A crotchety, cracked young man,
An ultra-poetical, super-aesthetical,
Out-of-the-way young man!

GROSVENOR:
Conceive me, if you can,
A matter-of-fact young man,
An alphabetical, arithmetical,
Every-day young man!

Bunthorne is left alone and Patience encounters him, dancing about in quiet satisfaction. When he assures her that he has completely changed and has modelled himself on Grosvenor, Patience is at first delighted—but then points out that she can never be his: 'Love, to be pure, must be absolutely unselfish, and there can be nothing unselfish in loving so perfect a being as you have now become!'

More surprises are in store. Grosvenor enters, followed by the ladies and the Dragoons, all dancing merrily. He is a very different Grosvenor—he has had his hair cut and he is wearing an ordinary suit and hat.

GROSVENOR:
I'm a Waterloo House young man,
A Sewell & Cross young man,
A steady and stolid-y, jolly Bank-holiday,
Every-day young man!

GIRLS:
We're Swears & Wells young girls,
We're Madame Louise young girls,
We're prettily pattering, cheerily chattering,
Every-day young girls!

Patience is at first shocked by the change in Grosvenor but, when he assures her that he has sworn always to be a commonplace young man, she exclaims: 'Why, then, there's nothing to prevent my loving you with all the fervour at my command!' 'Crushed again!' murmurs the defeated Bunthorne. But Lady Jane, still a model of aestheticism, claims him and they embrace.

The three officers arrive and the Duke announces his choice of a bride: 'In common fairness, I think I ought to choose the only one among you who has the misfortune to be distinctly plain. . . . Jane!' (Bunthorne: 'Crushed again!')

DUKE:
After much debate internal,
I on Lady Jane decide,
Saphir now may take the Colonel,
Angy be the Major's bride!

BUNTHORNE:
In that case unprecedented,
Single I must live and die—
I shall have to be contented
With a tulip or li*ly*!

ALL:
He will have to be contented
With a tulip or li*ly*!
Greatly pleased with one another,
To get married we decide.
Each of us will wed the other,
Nobody be Bunthorne's Bride!

And so, despite the opera's sub-title, there is no bride for Bunthorne.

Patience (P) *Soprano* The village milkmaid was originally played by Leonora Braham.

'Pattern to professors of monarchical autonomy, A' Rudolph's song (D).

Paul, Mrs Howard The original Lady Sangazure (S), Mrs Howard Paul, a woman of commanding presence, had a decidedly varied career. Before she was chosen by Gilbert, she had sung Lucy Lockit in *The Beggar's Opera*—and later Macheath! She had played Lady Macbeth, doubling the part of Hecate, with Phelps at Drury Lane, and she had toured her own entertainment, with the young George Grossmith singing songs at the piano and Rutland Barrington also in the company. One of her more unusual gifts was that she had a freak voice and, as well as her natural contralto, could sing tenor or baritone. One of the features of her touring entertainment was her impersonation of the celebrated tenor Sims Reeves. When Gilbert was casting *HMS Pinafore*, he originally considered Mrs Howard Paul for the role of Hebe but the part eventually went to Jessie Bond, starting her on her long series of leading roles. Mrs Howard Paul—Isabella Featherstone was her maiden name—died in 1879, two years after the premiere of *Pinafore*.

Paynim 'As an old Crusader struck his Paynim foe.' (PI). Paynim or heathen was the Crusaders' term for a Moslem.

Peckham 'Peckham an Arcadian Vale.'—Counsel for the Plaintiff (J). District of south-east London.

Peep-Bo (M) *Soprano* One of the Three Little Maids, wards of Ko-Ko, originally played by Sybil Grey.

Peer and the Peri, The Alternative title of *Iolanthe*.

Peers 'The House of Peers, throughout the war, did nothing in particular, and did it very well.'—Earl of Mountararat (I).
'For self-contained dignity, combined with airy condescension, give me a British Representative Peer!'—Celia (I).
'It so happens that if there is an institution in Great Britain which is not susceptible of any improvement at all, it is the House of Peers!'—Earl of Mountararat (I).

Penley, W. S. Though he did not originate the parts, W. S. Penley played the Judge, Foreman of the Jury and Usher (J). But it was in the field of farce that he later achieved fame, notably in *Charley's Aunt*, which had a run of nearly 1,500 performances at the Royalty Theatre, and also in *The Private Secretary*. Son of a schoolmaster, Penley was born at St Peter's, Thanet, in 1851 and, after being a chorister at the Chapel Royal and at Westminster Abbey, made his first stage appearance in 1870. He died in 1912.

Pepper, B. R. The first artist to play the Usher, with his stentorian 'Silence in Court!' (J).

'Perhaps if you address the lady' Duet for King Gama and King Hildebrand (PI).

Perry, Beatrice The original Martha (D), Beatrice Perry also played Fleta (I) and Peep-Bo (M).

Perry, Florence Creator of the roles of Princess Kalyba (U) and Lisa (D), Florence Perry played also Yum-Yum (M), Phoebe (Y), Gianetta (G), Phyllis (I) and Josephine (HMS).

Peveril 'Peak-haunting Peveril'—Colonel Calverley (P). *Peveril of the Peak* is the title of one of the novels of Sir Walter Scott (1771–1832).

Phantis (U) *Baritone* Phantis, one of the judges of the Utopian Supreme Court, was originally played by John Le Hay.

Philomel 'Soft the song of Philomel.'—Princess Zara (U). The Poetic name for a nightingale, derived from Philomela who in Greek mythology was changed into a bird.

Phylla (U) *Soprano* Florence Easton was the first artist to play the Utopian maiden.

Phyllis 'Come, Chloe and Phyllis.' (R). The name of Phyllis is often used in poetic and romantic writings for a rustic sweetheart.

Phyllis (I) *Soprano* Leonora Braham was the first artist to play Phyllis, an Arcadian shepherdess and ward in chancery.

Phyllis, Norah The original Giulia (G), Norah Phyllis sang Gianetta in some performances of the first production. Her other roles were Elsie Maynard (Y) and Casilda (G).

Pineapple Poll As the copyright in Sullivan's music expired at the end of 1950, it was permissible to present this ballet the following year. In three scenes, it has Sullivan music arranged by Charles Mackerras and was first given by Sadler's Wells Theatre Ballet at Sadler's Wells Theatre in March 1951, with décor and costumes by Osbert Lancaster and choreography by John Cranko. It was later revived by the Royal Ballet at Covent Garden.

The plot is freely adapted from one of Gilbert's Bab Ballads, 'The Bumboat Woman's Story', from which Gilbert had taken ideas for *Pinafore*. In the ballad Poll is seventy years of age ('Ah! I've been young in my time, and I've played the deuce with men! I'm speaking of ten years past—I was barely sixty then!'). For the purposes of the ballet she is much younger but, as in the ballad, she is in love with the commander of *HMS Hot Cross Bun*, and disguises herself as a man in order to go to sea—only to discover that all the crew are girls disguised as men!

Mackerras's score consists entirely of Sullivan tunes, ingeniously interwoven and freshly orchestrated. All the operas from *Trial by Jury* to *The Gondoliers* are drawn upon, together with *Cox and Box* and the overture 'Di Ballo'.

Though born in the United States in 1925, Charles Mackerras was brought up in Australia from the age of two and came to Britain in 1947. Originally a woodwind player, he soon concentrated on conducting, directing many notable performances at Sadler's Wells and Covent Garden, particularly of operas by Mozart and Janáček. In 1965 he was appointed 'first conductor' of Hamburg State Opera and in 1969 he also became musical director of Sadler's Wells Opera.

PIRATES OF PENZANCE, THE; or The Slave of Duty

First presented in London at the Opera Comique on April 3, 1880. Initial run of 363 performances. It had opened in New York on December 31, 1879, and there had been a single 'copyright' performance at the Royal Bijou Theatre, Paignton, Devon, on December 30.

The cast of the London premiere at the Opera Comique on April 3, 1880, was:

MAJOR-GENERAL STANLEY	Mr George Grossmith, Jnr
THE PIRATE KING	Mr Richard Temple

SAMUEL (*his Lieutenant*)	Mr George Temple
FREDERIC (*the Pirate Apprentice*)	Mr George Power
SERGEANT OF POLICE	Mr Rutland Barrington
MABEL (*General Stanley's Daughter*)	Miss Marion Hood
EDITH	Miss Julia Gwynne
KATE	Miss Lilian La Rue
ISABEL	Miss Neva Bond
RUTH (*a Pirate Maid of Work*)	Miss Emily Cross

The curtain rises on a gay scene on the rocky coast of Cornwall.
Though Frederic, one of their number, is looking somewhat gloomy
and thoughtful, the pirates are celebrating the fact that he has
completed his apprenticeship to their trade:

> Pour, oh, pour the pirate sherry;
> Fill, oh fill the pirate glass;
> And, to make us more than merry,
> Let the pirate bumper pass.

> SAMUEL:
> For to-day our pirate 'prentice
> Rises from indenture freed;
> Strong his arm and keen his scent is;
> He's a pirate now indeed!

> ALL:
> Here's good luck to Frederic's ventures;
> Frederic's out of his indentures.

> SAMUEL:
> Two-and-twenty now he's rising,
> And alone he's fit to fly,
> Which we're bent on signalizing
> With unusual revelry.

> ALL:
> Here's good luck to Frederic's ventures, etc.

Frederic surprises them all by announcing to the Pirate King that,
as the slave of duty, he did his best for them while under his indentures, but that now that he is free he proposes to leave them that
night. His presence with them was, in any case due to an error.
Ruth, the pirate maid-of-work, explains how it arose:

> When Frederic was a little lad he proved so brave and daring,
> His father thought he'd 'prentice him to some career sea-faring.
> I was, alas, his nurserymaid, and so it fell to *my* lot
> To take and bind the promising boy apprentice to a *pilot*.

A life not bad for a hardy lad, though surely not a high lot,
Though I'm a nurse, you might do worse than make your
    boy a pilot.

I was a stupid nurserymaid, on breakers always steering,
And I did not catch the word aright, through being hard of
    hearing;
Mistaking my instructions, which within my brain did gyrate,
I took and bound this promising boy apprentice to a *pirate*.
A sad mistake it was to make and doom him to a vile lot:
I bound him to a pirate—you—instead of to a pilot.

I soon found out, beyond all doubt, the scope of this disaster,
But I hadn't the face to return to my place, and break it to my
    master.
A nurserymaid is not afraid of what you people *call* work,
So I made up my mind to go as a kind of piratical maid-of-
    all-work.
And that is how you find me now, a member of your shy lot,
Which you wouldn't have found, had he been bound appren-
    tice to a pilot.

The Pirate King comments that they are not very successful in
making piracy pay, and Frederic, his sense of duty permitting him
to help them until his indentures are completed at midnight, points
out that they are much too tender-hearted and also that, being
orphans themselves, they never molest an orphan. 'Everyone we
capture says he's an orphan,' declares Frederic. 'The last three
ships we took proved to be manned entirely by orphans, and so
we had to let them go. One would think that Britain's mercantile
navy was recruited solely from her orphan asylums—which we
know is not the case.'

There is also a problem about Ruth, the only woman Frederic
has seen since he went to sea at the age of eight. He has had no
chance of comparing her with another and, despite Samuel's
'There are the remains of a fine woman about Ruth,' neither
Frederic nor the pirates are eager to have her on their hands. Faced
with the prospect of having to exterminate the pirates out of a
sense of duty after midnight, Frederic suggests that the Pirate King
should instead return with him to civilisation. But the King will
have none of it:

> Oh, better far to live and die
> Under the brave black flag I fly,
> Than play a sanctimonious part,
> With a pirate head and a pirate heart.

Away to the cheating world go you,
Where pirates all are well-to-do;
But I'll be true to the song I sing,
And live and die a pirate king.
For I am a Pirate King.

ALL:
You are!

KING:
And it is, it is a glorious thing
To be a Pirate King.

ALL:
Hurrah!
Hurrah for our Pirate King!

KING:
When I sally forth to seek my prey
I help myself in a royal way:
I sink a few more ships, it's true,
Than a well-bred monarch ought to do;
But many a king on a first-class throne,
If he wants to call his crown his own,
Must manage somehow to get through
More dirty work than ever *I* do,
For I am a Pirate King.

ALL:
You are!
Hurrah for the Pirate King!

KING:
And it is, it is a glorious thing
To be a Pirate King!

ALL:
It is!
Hurrah for our Pirate King!

Ruth pleads with Frederic to take her with him, but her case is lost when he sees a bevy of very attractive young women in the distance:

FREDERIC:
You told me you were fair as gold!

RUTH:
And, master, am I not so?

FREDERIC:
And now I see you're plain and old.

RUTH:
I'm sure I'm not a jot so.

FREDERIC:
Upon my innocence you play.

RUTH:
I'm not the one to plot so.

FREDERIC:
Your face is lined, your hair is grey.

RUTH:
It's gradually got so.

FREDERIC:
Faithless woman, to deceive me,
I who trusted so!

RUTH:
Master, master, do not leave me!
Hear me, ere you go!
My love without reflecting,
Oh, do not be rejecting.
Take a maiden tender—her affection raw and green,
At very highest rating,
Has been accumulating
Summers seventeen—summers seventeen.
Don't, beloved master,
Crush me with disaster.
What is such a dower to the dower I have here?
My love unabating
Has been accumulating
Forty-seven year—forty-seven year!

After Ruth has departed in despair, Frederic hides in a cave as the girls, all daughters of Major-General Stanley, arrive, clambering over the rocks:

> Climbing over rocky mountain,
> Skipping rivulet and fountain,
> Passing where the willows quiver
> By the ever-rolling river,
> Swollen with the summer rain;
> Threading long and leafy mazes
> Dotted with unnumbered daisies;

Scaling rough and rugged passes,
Climb the hardy little lasses,
Till the bright sea-shore they gain!

EDITH:
Let us gaily tread the measure,
Make the most of fleeting leisure;
Hail it as a true ally,
Though it perish by and by.

Every moment brings a treasure
Of its own especial pleasure,
Though the moments quickly die,
Greet them gaily as they fly.

KATE:
Far away from toil and care,
Revelling in fresh sea air,
Here we live and reign alone
In a world that's all our own.
Here in this our rocky den,
Far away from mortal men,
We'll be queens, and make decrees—
They may honour them who please.

The girls are understandably frightened by Frederic's 'effective
but alarming costume' and by his news that he is a pirate, though
he assures them that he renounces his profession that evening. He
appeals to them:

Oh, is there not one maiden breast
Which does not feel the moral beauty
Of making worldly interest
Subordinate to sense of duty?
Who would not give up willingly
All matrimonial ambition,
To rescue such an one as I
From this unfortunate position?

Oh, is there not one maiden here
Whose homely face and bad complexion
Have caused all hopes to disappear
Of ever winning man's affection?
To such an one, if such there be,
I swear by Heaven's arch above you,
If you will cast your eyes on me—
However plain you be—I'll love you!

There is no response from the girls until Mabel enters and sings the florid song which, like much else in the work, is a deliberate skit on the conventions of Italian opera:

> Poor wandering one!
> Though thou hast surely strayed,
> Take heart of grace,
> Thy steps retrace,
> Poor wandering one!
> Poor wandering one!
> If such poor love as mine
> Can help thee find
> True peace of mind—
> Why, take it, it is thine!
> Take heart, fair days will shine;
> Take any heart—take mine!
>
> ALL:
> Take heart, no danger lowers;
> Take any heart—but ours!

It is clear that Mabel and Frederic are mutually attracted. Edith gathers her sisters round her:

> What ought we to do,
> Gentle sisters, say?
> Propriety, we know,
> Says we ought to stay;
> While sympathy exclaims,
> 'Free them from your tether—
> Play at other games—
> Leave them here together.'
>
> KATE:
> Her case may, any day,
> Be yours, my dear, or mine.
> Let her make her hay
> While the sun doth shine.
> Let us compromise,
> (Our hearts are not of leather):
> Let us shut our eyes,
> And talk about the weather.

They all take up a chattering chorus about the weather—while keeping their ears open for what Mabel and Frederic have to say to each other:

How beautifully blue the sky,
The glass is rising very high,
Continue fine I hope it may,
And yet it rained but yesterday.
To-morrow it may pour again,
(I hear the country wants some rain),
Yet people say, I know not why,
That we shall have a warm July.

MABEL:
Did ever maiden wake
From dream of homely duty,
To find her daylight break
With such exceeding beauty?
Did ever maiden close
Her eyes on waking sadness,
To dream of such exceeding gladness?

FREDERIC:
Did ever pirate roll
His soul in guilty dreaming,
And wake to find that soul
With peace and virtue beaming?

This is all very idyllic, but Frederic, going off with Mabel, warns that the pirates will be arriving at any time. The girls are taking the hint—but too late! The pirates have crept in stealthily and each seizes a girl—'Here's a first-rate opportunity to get married with impunity. . . .' But they are checked when Mabel steps forward:

Hold, monsters! Ere your private caravanserai
Proceed, against our will, to wed us all,
Just bear in mind that we are Wards in Chancery,
And father is a Major-General!

And Major-General Stanley himself appears and delivers one of the most brilliant of the patter songs:

I am the very model of a modern Major-Gineral,
I've information vegetable, animal and mineral;
I know the kings of England, and I quote the fights historical,
From Marathon to Waterloo, in order categorical;
I'm very well acquainted too with matters mathematical,
I understand equations, both the simple and quadratical,
About binomial theorem I'm teeming with a lot o'news—
With many cheerful facts about the square of the hypotenuse.

I'm very good at integral and differential calculus,
I know the scientific names of beings animalculous;
In short, in matters vegetable, animal, and mineral,
I am the very model of a modern Major-Gineral.

I know our mythic history, King Arthur's and Sir Caradoc's,
I answer hard acrostics, I've a pretty taste for paradox,
I quote in elegiacs all the crimes of Heliogabalus,
In conics I can floor peculiarities parabolous.
I can tell undoubted Raphaels from Gerard Dows and Zoffanies,
I know the croaking chorus from the *Frogs* of Aristophanes,
Then I can hum a fugue of which I've heard the music's din afore,
And whistle all the airs from that infernal nonsense *Pinafore*.

Then I can write a washing bill in Babylonic cuneiform,
And tell you every detail of Caractacus's uniform;
In short, in matters vegetable, animal, and mineral,
I am the very model of a modern Major-Gineral.

In fact, when I know what is meant by 'mamelon' and 'ravelin',
When I can tell at sight a Mauser rifle from a javelin,
When such affairs as sorties and surprises I'm more wary at,
And when I know precisely what is meant by 'commissariat',
When I have learnt what progress has been made in modern
    gunnery,
When I know more of tactics than a novice in a nunnery;
In short, when I've a smattering of elemental strategy,
You'll say a better Major-Gener*al* has never *sat* a gee—

For my military knowledge, though I'm plucky and adventury,
Has only been brought down to the beginning of the century;
But still in matters vegetable, animal, and mineral,
I am the very model of a modern Major-Gineral.

The pirates are determined to hold on to their captures but the
Major-General has a sudden inspiration. 'Tell me,' he asks, 'have
you ever known what it is to be an orphan?' With interpolations
of 'Poor fellow!' from the pirates, he pleads:

> These children whom you see
> Are all that I can call my own!
> Take them away from me
> And I shall be indeed alone.

If pity you can feel,
Leave me my sole remaining joy—
See, at your feet they kneel;
Your hearts you cannot steel
Against the sad, sad tale of the lonely orphan boy!

But in the ensemble that follows, he admits, aside, that he is 'telling a terrible story.' The Pirate King is, however, convinced:

Although our dark career
Sometimes involves the crime of stealing,
We rather think that we're
Not altogether void of feeling.
Although we live by strife,
We're always sorry to begin it,
For what, we ask, is life
Without a touch of Poetry in it?

They all kneel and sing the somewhat banal chorus:

Hail, Poetry, thou heaven-born maid!
Thou gildest e'en the pirate's trade:
Hail, flowing fount of sentiment!
All hail, Divine Emollient!

There are hurrahs for the 'orphan boy', Ruth makes a final unsuccessful appeal to Frederic, the Major-General waves a Union Jack and the Pirate King the skull-and-cross-bones, and the curtain falls.

The second act opens on a ruined chapel by moonlight, with a pensive Major-General surrounded by his daughters. The girls sing:

Oh, dry the glistening tear
That dews that martial cheek;
Thy loving children hear,
In them thy comfort seek.
With sympathetic care
Their arms around thee creep,
For oh, they cannot bear
To see their father weep!

MABEL:
Dear father, why leave your bed
At this untimely hour,
When happy daylight is dead,
And darksome dangers lower?

See, Heaven has lit her lamp,
The twilight hour is past,
The chilly night air is damp,
And the dews are falling fast!
Dear father, why leave your bed
When happy daylight is dead?

The Major-General is plunged into despair at the thought that his
false description of himself as an orphan has brought shame on his
ancestors, and he is not comforted when Frederic arrives and
points out that he bought the property only a year ago. 'I don't
know whose ancestors they *were*, but I know whose ancestors they
are,' groans the Major-General. But the time for the attack on the
pirates has arrived and he calls upon Frederic to summon his forces.
   The Police, in single file, march in and form up.

SERGEANT:
When the foeman bares his steel,
Tarantara! tarantara!
We uncomfortable feel,
Tarantara!
And we find the wisest thing,
Tarantara! tarantara!
Is to slap our chests and sing
Tarantara!
For when threatened with émeutes,
Tarantara! tarantara!
And your heart is in your boots,
Tarantara!
There is nothing brings it round,
Like the trumpet's martial sound,
Tarantara! tarantara!
Tarantara-ra-ra-ra-ra!

MABEL:
Go, ye heroes, go to glory,
Though you die in combat gory,
Ye shall live in song and story.
Go to immortality!
Go to death, and go to slaughter;
Die, and every Cornish daughter
With her tears your grave shall water.
Go, ye heroes, go and die!

POLICE:
Though to us it's evident,
Tarantara! tarantara!
These attentions are well meant,
Tarantara!
Such expressions don't appear,
Tarantara! tarantara!
Calculated men to cheer,
Tarantara!
Who are going to meet their fate
In a highly nervous state,
Tarantara, tarantara, tarantara!
Still to us it's evident
These attentions are well meant.
Tarantara, tarantara, tarantara!

There is much more in this vein, with the Police singing 'Away, away . . . Forward on the foe!' but, in true operatic manner, taking an unconscionable time in making a move, while the Major-General breaks in with, 'Yes, but you *don't* go!' Left alone for a moment, Frederic is expressing satisfaction at having at last the opportunity of atoning for his piratical past, when the Pirate King and Ruth appear and present a pistol at each of his ears. There is a new twist in the story.

RUTH:
When you had left our pirate fold,
We tried to raise our spirits faint,
According to our custom old,
With quip and quibble quaint.
But all in vain the quips we heard,
We lay and sobbed upon the rocks,
Until to somebody occurred
A startling paradox.

FREDERIC:
A paradox?

RUTH:
A paradox!
A most ingenious paradox!
We've quips and quibbles heard in flocks,
But none to beat this paradox!
Ha! ha! ha! ha! Ho! ho! ho! ho!

KING:

We knew your taste for curious quips,
For cranks and contradictions queer,
And with the laughter on our lips,
We wished you there to hear.
We said, 'If we could tell it him,
How Frederic would the joke enjoy!'
And so we've risked both life and limb
To tell it to our boy.

The King then solemnly chants:

For some ridiculous reason, to which, however, I've no desire to
be disloyal,
Some person in authority, I don't know who, very likely the
Astronomer Royal,
Has decided that, although for such a beastly month as February,
twenty-eight days as a general rule are plenty,
One year in every four his days shall be reckoned as nine-and-
twenty.
Through some singular coincidence—I shouldn't be surprised if it
were owing to the agency of an ill-natured fairy—
You are the victim of this clumsy arrangement, having been born
in leap-year, on the twenty-ninth of February,
And so, by a simple arithmetical process, you'll easily discover
That though you've lived twenty-one years, yet, if we go by
birthdays, you're only five and a little bit over!

To Frederic's dismay, the King produces a document showing that
he is apprenticed until his twenty-first *birthday* and, when it is
pointed out to him that it is his duty to remain, he can no longer
resist. Further, his duty now impels him to reveal to the King that
the Major-General is *not* an orphan. 'He is doomed!' declares the
King. After Ruth and the King have gone, Mabel comes to say
goodbye to Frederic before he sets out against the Pirates. But he
tells her the truth about his age—and their dilemma leads into one
of the most charming and graceful passages in the opera.

MABEL:
Stay, Frederic, stay!
They have no legal claim,
No shadow of a shame
Will fall upon thy name.
Stay, Frederic, stay!

FREDERIC:

Nay, Mabel, nay!
To-night I quit these walls,
The thought my soul appals,
But when stern Duty calls,
I must obey.

MABEL:

Ah, leave me not to pine
Alone and desolate;
No fate seemed fair as mine,
No happiness so great!
And nature, day by day,
Has sung, in accents clear,
This joyous roundelay,
'He loves thee—he is here.
Fal, la, la, la. Fal, la, la, la!'

FREDERIC:

Ah, must I leave thee here
In endless night to dream,
Where joy is dark and drear,
And sorrow all supreme!
Where nature, day by day,
Will sing, in altered tone,
This weary roundelay,
'He loves thee—he is gone.
Fal, la, la, la. Fal, la, la, la!'

Mabel swears to be true to him until he comes of age (!) and they sing together:

Oh, here is love, and here is truth,
And here is food for joyous laughter:
He/she will be faithful to his/her sooth
Till we are wed, and even after.

Frederic rushes away, the police march in, and Mabel informs the Sergeant that, as Frederic has, through a sense of duty, rejoined his old associates, the Police will have to attack the pirates without him. The Sergeant, in his famous song which put a quotation into the language, gives at any rate one reason for their lack of enthusiasm for the job:

When a felon's not engaged in his employment (His employ-
  ment)—
Or maturing his felonious little plans (Little plans)—
His capacity for innocent enjoyment ('Cent enjoyment)—
Is just as great as any honest man's (Honest man's)—
Our feelings we with difficulty smother ('Culty smother)—
When constabulary duty's to be done (To be done)—
Ah, take one consideration with another (With another)—
A policeman's lot is not a happy one.

When the enterprising burglar's not a-burgling (Not
  a-burgling)—
When the cut-throat isn't occupied in crime ('Pied in crime)—
He loves to hear the little brook a-gurgling (Brook a-gurgling)—
And listen to the merry village chime (Village chime)—
When the coster's finished jumping on his mother (On his
  mother)—
He loves to lie a-basking in the sun (In the sun)—
Ah, take one consideration with another (With another)—
A policeman's lot is not a happy one.

The Police hide themselves, as the Pirates are heard approaching,
and there is another skit on the absurdities of grand opera with the
Pirates singing at the tops of their voices:

> With cat-like tread,
> Upon our prey we steal,
> In silence dread
> Our cautious way we feel.
> No sound at all,
> We never speak a word,
> A fly's footfall
> Would be distinctly heard—
>
> POLICE: (*pianissimo*) Tarantara, tarantara!
>
> PIRATES
> So stealthily the pirate creeps,
> While all the houschold soundly sleeps.
> Come, friends, who plough the sea,
> Truce to navigation,
> Take another station;
> Let's vary piracee
> With a little burglaree!
>
> POLICE: (*pianissimo*) Tarantara, tarantara!

The Major-General enters in dressing-gown, carrying a light:

> Tormented with the anguish dread
> Of falsehood unatoned,
> I lay upon my sleepless bed,
> And tossed and turned and groaned.
> The man who finds his conscience ache
> No peace at all enjoys,
> And as I lay in bed awake
> I thought I heard a noise.

There is quite a noise, but the Major-General continues:

> No, all is still
> In dale, on hill;
> My mind is set at ease.
> So still the scene—
> It must have been
> The sighing of the breeze.

He waxes lyrical, to a rippling accompaniment:

> Sighing softly to the river
> Comes the loving breeze,
> Setting nature all a-quiver,
> Rustling through the trees—
>
> ALL:
> Through the trees.
>
> GENERAL:
> And the brook, in rippling measure,
> Laughs for very love,
> While the poplars, in their pleasure,
> Wave their arms above.
>
> POLICE and PIRATES:
> Yes, the trees, for very love,
> Wave their leafy arms above.
> River, river, little river,
> May thy loving prosper ever.
> Heaven speed thee, poplar tree,
> May thy wooing happy be.
>
> GENERAL:
> Yet, the breeze is but a rover;
> When he wings away,
> Brook and poplar mourn a lover!
> Sighing well-a-day!

ALL:
Well-a-day!

GENERAL:
Ah! the doing and undoing,
That the rogue could tell!
When the breeze is out a-wooing,
Who can woo so well?

POLICE and PIRATES:
Shocking tales the rogue could tell.
Nobody can woo so well.
Pretty brook, thy dream is over,
For thy love is but a rover!
Sad the lot of poplar trees,
Courted by a fickle breeze!

With Police and Pirates still in hiding, the General's daughters appear, night-capped and carrying lighted candles, and express their alarm:

Now what is this, and what is that, and why does father
  leave his rest
At such a time of night as this, so very incompletely dressed?
Dear father is, and always was, the most methodical of men!
It's his invariable rule to go to bed at half-past ten.
What strange occurrence can it be that calls dear father from
  his rest
At such a time of night as this, so very incompletely dressed?

Events move swiftly from now onwards. The Pirates rush out and seize the General, the Police give battle but are quickly defeated, the Pirates standing over them with drawn swords. Then the Sergeant plays his trump card: 'We charge you yield, in Queen Victoria's name!' This is too much for the Pirates. 'We yield at once, with humbled mien,' declares the King, 'Because, with all our faults, we love our Queen.'

The Police, in tears, prepare to lead the Pirates away, but Ruth bursts in with a convenient piece of information:

One moment! let me tell you who they are.
They are no members of the common throng;
They are all noblemen who have gone wrong!

GENERAL:
No Englishman unmoved that statement hears,
Because, with all our faults, we love our House of Peers.

He cheerfully hands over to the Pirates his daughters, 'all of whom are beauties,' and the opera closes to the strains of 'Poor wandering ones!'

Pirate King (PP) *Bass-baritone* Richard Temple was the original player in the London production.

Pish-Tush (M) *Baritone* A noble Lord, first played by Frederick Bovill.

Pitti-Sing (M) *Mezzo-soprano* One of the Three Little Maids, wards of Ko-Ko, originally played by Jessie Bond.

Plaintiff (J) *Soprano* The original was Nelly Bromley.

Plaza-Toro, Duchess of (G) *Contralto* The Duchess, who has the Duke well under control, was originally played by Rosina Brandram.

Plaza-Toro, Duke of (G) *Baritone* The Duke, who led his regiment from behind because 'he found it less exciting', was originally played by Frank Wyatt, his first appearance in Gilbert and Sullivan opera.

Poetry—Its Exquisite Anguish 'A hunting song? No, it is *not* a hunting song. It is the wail of the poet's heart on discovering that everything is commonplace. To understand it, cling passionately to one another and think of faint lilies.'—Reginald Bunthorne (P).

Point, Jack (Y) *Baritone* George Grossmith, the original player of the strolling jester, went for the comedy of the role, giving an amusing little twitch after swooning at the end, as though to assure the audience that he was still alive and kicking. But later, when on tour, Henry A. Lytton left no doubt in the audience's minds that Jack Point was dead, a reading of the part which met with Gilbert's approval: 'Jack Point should die and the end of the opera should be a tragedy.' By sheer coincidence and unknown to Lytton, another Jack Point touring with a different company at about the same time took the same view of the part. It is of course a wonderful role for an actor, making the point in its earlier stages that being consistently funny is very hard work and eventually underlining the old idea of the clown with a broken heart. 'A poor dull, heartbroken man, who must needs be merry, or he will be whipped;

who must rejoice, lest he starve; who must jest you, jibe you, quip you, crank you, wrack you, riddle you, from hour to hour, from day to day, from year to year, lest he dwindle, perish, starve, pine and die! Why, when there's naught else to laugh at, I laugh at myself till I ache for it!'

Pointdextre, Sir Marmaduke (S) *Bass-baritone* An elderly baronet, one of the leading residents in the village of Ploverleigh, originally played by Richard Temple.

Polonies 'Pretty polonies,' which are among the contents of Little Buttercup's basket (HMS), are partly-cooked pork sausages, called after Bologna, Italy, where they were first made.

Pooh-Bah (M) *Bass-baritone* Rutland Barrington was the original player of the Lord High Everything Else—First Lord of the Treasury, Lord Chief Justice, Commander-in-Chief, Lord High Admiral, Master of the Buckhounds, Groom of the Backstairs, Archbishop of Titipu, and Lord Mayor, both acting and elect, all rolled into one. 'And at a salary! A Pooh-Bah paid for his services! I a salaried minion! But I do it! It revolts me, but I do it!'

'Poor wandering one!' Mabel's song, complete with flourishes in the manner of an aria from Italian opera (PP).

Porter, Sir Joseph, KCB (HMS) *Baritone* First Lord of the Admiralty, first played by George Grossmith. Though it would seem that W. H. Smith, founder of the book-selling firm, was in fact an effective First Lord in Disraeli's government, it has always been accepted that Gilbert had him in mind when he created Sir Joseph Porter whose progress to the post of Ruler of the Queen's Navee was decidedly chairborne. Gilbert's all-too-innocent comment in a letter to Sullivan does nothing to shake this contention: 'The fact that the First Lord in the opera is a radical of the most pronounced type will do away with any suspicion that W. H. Smith is intended.' Sir Joseph's entrance in the opera, accompanied by his sisters and his cousins and his aunts, serves two purposes. It enables the female chorus to be brought on as individual people rather than just as a singing ensemble and, with their interruptions to his opening song, they indicate that, despite his self-importance, he is not the only pebble on the beach. Katisha with the Mikado and the Duchess with the Duke of Plaza-Toro (G) do much the same sort of thing in the later operas. On the W. H. Smith link,

Leslie Baily, in *The Gilbert and Sullivan Book*, has a story of a visit by the First Lord to launch a ship at Devonport. To avoid embarrassment, a message had been sent to the bandmaster of the Royal Marines Band not on any account to include music from *Pinafore*. But the message had become reversed in the course of transit—and the First Lord, not to his great amusement, was greeted by the ditty telling of Sir Joseph's progress to high office. The world fame of *Pinafore* is indicated by the fact that when, some three years after the first production, Sullivan visited the German port of Kiel as a guest of the Duke of Edinburgh, he was greeted by the Crown Prince, later the Kaiser, with a reference to Sir Joseph's song: 'I think you polished up the handle of the big front door, did you not, Mr Sullivan?'

Portraits There are paintings of both Gilbert and Sullivan in the National Portrait Gallery, London. That of Gilbert, painted by Frank Holl, RA, in 1886, shows him in knee breeches, leaning back at ease in a leather armchair, walking-stick in hand. Sullivan, painted by Millais in 1888, is sitting rather more formally, with hands clasped on the arm of his chair.

Posterity 'I fancy that posterity will know as little of me as I shall know of posterity,' said Gilbert. Yet he clearly had posterity in mind when, after the successful first night of *The Gondoliers*, he wrote to Sullivan in enthusiastic terms about his score and added: 'It gives one the chance of shining right through the twentieth century with a reflected light.'

Potter, Philip Joining the D'Oyly Carte Company in 1961, Philip Potter now sings Frederic (PP), Hilarion (PI), Nanki-Poo (M), Richard Dauntless (R), Fairfax (Y) and Luiz (G). Though not of Welsh origin, he found himself winning prizes as a boy treble, singing at Eisteddfods. He was born in Leicester but his father, a civil servant, moved to Wales to work on rockets during the war and young Philip was able to learn fluent Welsh. When he was ten the family moved to Kent and he joined the local church choir, but developing trouble with his vocal cords, had to give up singing for some time and only started again when he was sixteen. He studied at the Guildhall School of Music and Drama, where his successes included the Tenor Prize and, significantly, the Gilbert and Sullivan Prize. 'I got a teaching degree and taught for a while at Marylebone Grammar School,' he says. 'But I did not really care for teaching—I found the boys were so clever! I preferred singing to them instead.' Before being invited to join the D'Oyly Carte, he was in a number of musicals, including *Where's Charley?*, with Norman Wisdom, *Marigold*, a tour of *Chu Chin Chow* and *Flower Drum Song*. Favourite roles? 'From the singing point of view, I think Frederic and Hilarion, and, for a showy acting part, Dick Dauntless.'

Pounds, Courtice He was the original Colonel Fairfax (Y) and Marco Palmieri (G) and also sang many other leading tenor roles in the operas. His mother, Mary Courtice, was a well-known singer of the day. A Londoner, born in 1862, he was solo treble at St Stephens, South Kensington, and the Italian Church, Hatton Garden, before going on to study at the Royal Academy of Music. He made his first stage appearance in the chorus of *Patience* at the Savoy Theatre in 1881 and played his first principal part, Earl Tolloller (I), on tour. His sister, Louie Pounds, appeared in many musical shows and sang Iolanthe at the Savoy in 1901. In his later years Courtice Pounds played in many musicals and scored a great success as Ali Baba in the long run of *Chu Chin Chow* at His Majesty's Theatre. He died in 1927, aged sixty-five.

'Pour, oh, pour the pirate sherry' Opening chorus in which the pirates celebrate Frederic's completion of his indentures (PP).

Power, (Sir) George The original Ralph Rackstraw (HMS) and Frederic in the London production (PP), George Power was born in Dublin, son of Sir John Power, of Kilfane, Kilkenny. Educated at Trinity College, Dublin, he studied singing in Milan and Florence and sang tenor roles on the stage in Italy. In his later years he was a professor of voice production and singing. He died in 1928.

Pratt, Peter It cannot be said that Peter Pratt suddenly realised a burning ambition by joining D'Oyly Carte. He *did* realise an ambition to become a professional actor but he had never heard a Gilbert and Sullivan opera and, until a few weeks before he joined, had never even heard of the D'Oyly Carte Opera Company. Yet he fitted so neatly into the scheme of things that he remained with the company for fourteen years, eight of them officially as principal comedian in the direct succession from George Grossmith, Henry A. Lytton and Martyn Green. He is possibly unique in having sung the leading comedy part in *every* opera, those in *Utopia, Limited* and *The Grand Duke* being in performances broadcast in the BBC's

Third Programme. Like many of those who have found their way into the D'Oyly Carte Company, Peter Pratt, born in Eastbourne, had an early background of church choirs. He had little difficulty with the transition from treble to baritone and his father suggested that he should sing to an old friend of his. 'I sang to the old gentleman, who said, "I think the D'Oyly Carte would jump at him,"' recalls Peter Pratt. 'I had never heard of the D'Oyly Carte but I thought that anyone who would jump at me must be interesting.'

He joined the chorus in 1945 and three years later was singing such roles as Bouncer (C) and Bill Bobstay (HMS). The following year, when he was not yet official understudy to Martyn Green, both Green and the understudy fell ill and Peter Pratt sang half a dozen of the major comedy roles at Lewisham and Wood Green. In due course he became official understudy to Martyn Green and in 1951 took over the roles as the company's principal comedian. He is, by the way, one of the few Ko-Ko's—perhaps the only one—who have also sung the part of Go-To in the madrigal in *The Mikado*.

A man cannot play these roles for many years without encountering some amusing experiences and one of Peter Pratt's recollections concerns a performance of *The Mikado* when it had been decided that there would be only one encore for 'The flowers that bloom in the spring.' At the end of the encore, he was doing a quick change in the wings, ready for his scene with Katisha, when he heard the opening music for a *second* encore. 'By then,' he recalls, 'I was down to my vest. All I could do was to reach out and wave a little green sash from the wings!'

His favourite role? 'I used to have two stock answers to that question,' he says. 'One was: "If I had a favourite role, I would not reveal it." The other was: "The one in which I have the least work to do."' In the midst of an exhausting tour there may well have been some truth in that! But he does make the point: 'One of the most accurately and consistently *written* is that of Sir Joseph Porter (HMS). It does not deviate at all. Some of them have enormous deviations—Ko-Ko, for instance, is not consistent, but in the same opera Pooh-Bah is a completely consistent character.' Peter Pratt is married to actress Patience Sheffield, daughter of Leo Sheffield, the distinguished player of the 'Pooh-Bah roles' for many years.

Preposteros (T) Member of a travelling theatrical company, played by Henry Payne, well-known pantomime artist and brother of Frederick Payne.

Preston, Tatiana A principal of the D'Oyly Carte Company from 1952 until 1955, Tatiana Preston sang Phyllis (I), Yum-Yum (M), Rose Maybud (R) and Casilda (G).

Pretteia (T) Member of a travelling theatrical company, played by Miss Berend.

'Pretty Lisa, fair and tasty' Duet for Ludwig and Lisa (D).

PRINCESS IDA; or Castle Adamant First performed at the Savoy Theatre, London, on January 5, 1884, conducted by Sullivan. Initial run of 246 performances.

The original cast for the 'respectful Operatic Perversion of Tennyson's "Princess"' was:

KING HILDEBRAND	Mr Rutland Barrington
HILARION (*his Son*)	Mr Henry Bracy
CYRIL ⎫ (*Hilarion's Friends*)	Mr Durward Lely
FLORIAN ⎭	Mr Charles Ryley
KING GAMA	Mr George Grossmith
ARAC ⎫	Mr Richard Temple
GURON ⎬ (*His Sons*)	Mr Warwick Gray
SCYNTHIUS ⎭	Mr William Lugg
PRINCESS IDA (*Gama's Daughter*)	Miss Leonora Braham
LADY BLANCHE ⎫ (*Professors of Princess*	Miss Rosina Brandram
LADY PSYCHE ⎭ *Ida's College*)	Miss Kate Chard
MELISSA (*Lady Blanche's Daughter*)	Miss Jessie Bond
SACHARISSA ⎫	Miss Sybil Grey
CHLOE ⎬ (*Girl Graduates*)	Miss Heathcote
ADA ⎭	Miss Twyman

When she was one year old, Princess Ida, daughter of the ugly and misshapen King Gama, was betrothed to Hilarion, son of King Hildebrand. As the curtain rises on the opera King Hildebrand and his followers are gathered together, scanning the horizon as they await the arrival of Gama. But will he have his daughter with him? It will be either a happy occasion or one precipitating a war:

> Search throughout the panorama
> For a sign of royal Gama,
> Who to-day should cross the water
> With his fascinating daughter—
> Ida is her name.

Some misfortune evidently
Has detained them—consequently
Search throughout the panorama
For the daughter of King Gama,
Prince Hilarion's flame!

Florian, Hilarion's friend, discerns horsemen approaching and the crowd goes off, leaving Hilarion alone to ponder over his betrothal:

Ida was a twelvemonth old,
Twenty years ago!
I was twice her age, I'm told,
Twenty years ago!
Husband twice as old as wife
Argues ill for married life,
Baleful prophecies were rife,
Twenty years ago!

Still, I was a tiny prince
Twenty years ago.
She has gained upon me, since
Twenty years ago.
Though she's twenty-one, it's true,
I am barely twenty-two—
False and foolish prophets you,
Twenty years ago!

King Hildebrand returns with the news that King Gama is indeed in sight—but without Princess Ida. Hilarion reveals that he has heard that the Princess has forsworn the world and has shut herself in a lonely country house with a band of women, devoting themselves to study. On to the stage stride Arac, Guron and Scynthius, the ferocious-looking sons of King Gama.

ARAC:
We are warriors three,
Sons of Gama, Rex.
Like most sons are we,
Masculine in sex.

ALL:
Yes, yes, yes,
Masculine in sex.

ARAC:
Politics we bar,
They are not our bent;
On the whole we are
Not intelligent.

ALL:
No, no, no,
Not intelligent.

ARAC:
But with doughty heart,
And with trusty blade,
We can play our part—
Fighting is our trade.

ALL:
Yes, yes, yes,
Fighting is our trade.
Bold, and fierce, and strong, ha! ha!
For a war we burn,
With its right or wrong, ha! ha!
We have no concern.
Order comes to fight, ha! ha!
Order is obeyed.
We are men of might, ha! ha!
Fighting is our trade.
Yes, yes, yes,
Fighting is our trade, ha! ha!

They are followed by the ugly, twisted figure of King Gama, who
at once gives us an insight into his character:

If you give me your attention, I will tell you what I am:
I'm a genuine philanthropist—all other kinds are sham.
Each little fault of temper and each social defect
In my erring fellow-creatures I endeavour to correct.
To all their little weaknesses I open people's eyes;
And little plans to snub the self-sufficient I devise;
I love my fellow-creatures—I do all the good I can—
Yet everybody says I'm such a disagreeable man!
And I can't think why!

To compliments inflated I've a withering reply;
And vanity I always do my best to mortify;
A charitable action I can skilfully dissect;
And interested motives I'm delighted to detect;

I know everybody's income and what everybody earns;
And I carefully compare it with the income-tax returns;
But to benefit humanity however much I plan,
Yet everybody says I'm such a disagreeable man!
And I can't think why!

I'm sure I'm no ascetic; I'm as pleasant as can be;
You'll always find me ready with a crushing repartee;
I've an irritating chuckle, I've a celebrated sneer,
I've an entertaining snigger, I've a fascinating leer.
To everybody's prejudice I know a thing or two;
I can tell a woman's age in half a minute—and I do.
But although I try to make myself as pleasant as I can,
Yet everybody says I am a disagreeable man!
And I can't think why!

After a few ill-tempered personal exchanges, Gama confirms that
his daughter has established herself in Castle Adamant, one of his
country houses, where she rules over a university of a hundred girls.

GAMA:
Perhaps if you address the lady
Most politely, most politely—
Flatter and impress the lady,
Most politely, most politely—
Humbly beg and humbly sue—
She may deign to look on you,
But your doing you must do
Most politely, most politely, most politely!

HILDEBRAND:
Go you, and inform the lady,
Most politely, most politely,
If she don't, we'll storm the lady,
Most politely, most politely!
(*To* GAMA) You'll remain as hostage here;
Should Hilarion disappear,
We will hang you, never fear,
Most politely, most politely, most politely!

Hilarion calls his friends, Cyril and Florian, to his side and they
outline their plan of campaign in a trio:

HILARION:
Expressive glances
Shall be our lances,

And pops of Sillery
Our light artillery.
We'll storm their bowers
With scented showers
Of fairest flowers
That we can buy!

CHORUS:
Oh dainty triolet!
Oh fragrant violet!
Oh gentle heigho-let
(Or little sigh).
On sweet urbanity,
Though mere inanity,
To touch their vanity
We will rely!

CYRIL:
When day is fading,
With serenading
And such frivolity
We'll prove our quality.
A sweet profusion
Of soft allusion
This bold intrusion
Shall justify.

FLORIAN:
We'll charm their senses
With verbal fences,
With ballads amatory
And declamatory.
Little heeding
Their pretty pleading,
Our love exceeding
We'll justify!

King Hildebrand orders that Gama and his three sons shall in the meantime be thrust into prison.

ARAC, GURON and SCYNTHIUS:
For a month to dwell
In a dungeon cell;
Growing thin and wizen
In a solitary prison,

Is a poor look-out
For a soldier stout,
Who is longing for the rattle
Of a complicated battle—
For the rum-tum-tum
Of the military drum,
And the guns that go boom! boom!

HILDEBRAND:
When Hilarion's bride
Has at length complied
With the just conditions
Of our requisitions,
You may go in haste
And indulge your taste
For the fascinating rattle
Of a complicated battle—
For the rum-tum-tum
Of the military drum,
And the guns that go boom! boom!

But until that time they must remain in prison. They are marched off as the curtain falls on the first act.

The second act is set in the gardens of Castle Adamant, where the girl graduates sit at the feet of Lady Psyche, Professor of Humanities:

Towards the empyrean heights
Of every kind of lore,
We've taken several easy flights,
And mean to take some more.
In trying to achieve success
No envy racks our heart,
And all the knowledge we possess,
We mutually impart.

Lady Psyche advises them on the classics they must read:

If you'd climb the Helicon,
You should read Anacreon,
Ovid's *Metamorphoses*,
Likewise Aristophanes,
And the works of Juvenal:
These are worth attention, all;
But, if you will be advised,
You will get them Bowdlerised!

Pressed by Sacharissa, Lady Psyche explains to them the nature of the creature known as Man:

> Man will swear and Man will storm—
> Man is not at all good form—
> Man is of no kind of use—
> Man's a donkey—Man's a goose—
> Man is coarse and Man is plain—
> Man is more or less insane—
> Man's a ribald—Man's a rake,
> Man is Nature's sole mistake!

They all stand on the entrance of Lady Blanche, Professor of Abstract Science, who, being the contralto of the piece, is a lady of forbidding manner. She deals out various punishments—for instance to Sacharissa, who had brought in a set of chessmen ('They're men with which you give each other mate, and that's enough!'). They herald the arrival of Princess Ida:

> Mighty maiden with a mission,
> Paragon of common sense,
> Running fount of erudition,
> Miracle of eloquence,
> We are blind, and we would see;
> We are bound, and would be free;
> We are dumb, and we would talk;
> We are lame and we would walk.

Before treating them to a discourse on the superiority of Woman over Man, the Princess sings an aria to Minerva, the Roman goddess of wisdom:

> Oh, goddess wise
> That lovest light,
> Endow with sight
> Their unillumined eyes.
> At this my call,
> A fervent few
> Have come to woo
> The rays that from thee fall.
> Let fervent words and fervent thoughts be mine,
> That I may lead them to thy sacred shrine!

They go off, leaving Lady Blanche, who reveals that she has ambitions to rule the university and is only biding her time:

Come, mighty Must!
Inevitable Shall!
In thee I trust.
Time weaves my coronal!
Go, mocking Is!
Go, disappointing Was!
That I am this
Ye are the cursèd cause!
Yet humble second shall be first,
I ween;
And dead and buried by the curst
Has Been!
Oh, weak Might Be!
Oh, May, Might, Could, Would, Should!
How powerless ye
For evil or for good!
In every sense
Your moods I cheerless call,
Whate'er your tense
Ye are Imperfect, all!
Ye have deceived the trust I've shown
In ye!
Away! The Mighty Must alone
Shall be!

On her departure, Hilarion, Cyril and Florian appear, climbing over the wall and creeping cautiously around:

Gently, gently,
Evidently
We are safe so far,
After scaling
Fence and paling,
Here, at last, we are!
In this college
Useful knowledge
Everywhere one finds,
And already,
Growing steady,
We've enlarged our minds.

What they have learned so far is, in fact, that burglary is a science. They mock at the learned ambitions of the girls:

HILARION:
They intend to send a wire
To the moon—to the moon;
And they'll set the Thames on fire
Very soon—very soon;
Then they learn to make silk purses
With their rigs—with their rigs,
From the ears of Lady Circe's
Piggy-wigs—piggy-wigs.
And weasels at their slumbers
They trepan—they trepan;
To get sunbeams from cucucumbers,
They've a plan—they've a plan.
They've a firmly rooted notion
They can cross the Polar Ocean,
And they'll find Perpetual Motion,
If they can—if they can.

ALL:
These are the phenomena
That every pretty domina
Is hoping at her Universitee
We shall see!

CYRIL:
As for fashion, they forswear it,
So they say—so they say—
And the circle—they will square it
Some fine day—some fine day—
Then the little pigs they're teaching
For to fly—for to fly;
And the niggers they'll be bleaching,*
By and by—by and by!
Each newly-joined aspirant
To the clan—to the clan—
Must repudiate the tyrant
Known as Man—known as Man.
They mock at him and flout him,
For they do not care about him,
And they're 'going to do without him'
If they can—if they can!

Coming across some Collegiate robes, they decide to put them on:

*In 1954, the D'Oyly Carte Company amended this line to: 'And they'll
practise what they're preaching.'

HILARION:
I am a maiden, cold and stately,
Heartless I, with a face divine.
What do I want with a heart, innately?
Every heart I meet is mine!

ALL:
Haughty, humble, coy or free,
Little care I what maid may be.
So that a maid is fair to see,
Every maid is the maid for me!

CYRIL:
I am a maiden frank and simple,
Brimming with joyous roguery;
Merriment lurks in every dimple,
Nobody breaks more hearts than I!

ALL:
Haughty, humble, coy or free. . . .

FLORIAN:
I am a maiden coy and blushing,
Timid am I as a startled hind;
Every suitor sets me flushing:
I am the maid that wins mankind!

Princess Ida comes in and agrees to accept them into the university
—on their assurance that they will never marry men! They join
in a quartet:

PRINCESS:
The world is but a broken toy,
Its pleasure hollow—false its joy,
Unreal its loveliest hue,
Alas!
Its pains alone are true,
Alas!
Its pains alone are true.

HILARION:
The world is everything you say,
The world we think has had its day,
Its merriment is slow,
Alas!
We've tried it and we know,
Alas!
We've tried it and we know.

All is well until, the Princess having left them, Lady Psyche enters and is revealed to be Florian's sister. They confide in her and she treats them to her views on Man:

> A Lady fair, of lineage high,
> Was loved by an Ape, in the days gone by—
> The Maid was radiant as the sun,
> The Ape was a most unsightly one—
> So it would not do—
> His scheme fell through,
> For the Maid, when his love took formal shape,
> Expressed such terror
> At his monstrous error
> That he stammered his apology and made his 'scape,
> The picture of a disconcerted Ape.
>
> With a view to rise in the social scale,
> He shaved his bristles, and he docked his tail,
> He grew moustachios, and he took his tub,
> And he paid a guinea to a toilet club—
> But it would not do—
> The scheme fell through,
> For the Maid was Beauty's fairest Queen,
> With golden tresses,
> Like a real princess's,
> While the Ape, despite his razor keen,
> Was the apiest Ape that ever was seen!
>
> He bought white ties, and he bought dress suits,
> He crammed his feet into bright tight boots—
> And to start in life on a brand-new plan,
> He christened himself Darwinian man!
> But it would not do,
> The scheme fell through—
> For the Maiden fair, whom the monkey craved,
> Was a radiant Being,
> With a brain far-seeing—
> While a Man, however well-behaved,
> At best is only a monkey shaved!

Meanwhile Melissa, Lady Blanche's daughter, has entered and, decidedly thrilled to meet these forbidden creatures, agrees to keep the secret. They join in a lively quintet:

317

PSYCHE:
The woman of the wisest wit
May sometimes be mistaken, O!
In Ida's views, I must admit,
My faith is somewhat shaken, O!

CYRIL:
On every point than this,
Her learning is untainted, O!
But Man's a theme with which she is
Entirely unacquainted, O!
     —acquainted, O!
     —acquainted, O!
Entirely unacquainted, O!

ALL:
Then jump for joy and gaily bound,
The truth is found—the truth is found!
Set bells a-ringing through the air—
Ring here and there and everywhere—
And echo forth the joyous sound,
The truth is found, the truth is found!

MELISSA:
My natural instinct teaches me
(And instinct is important, O!)
You're everything you ought to be,
And nothing that you oughtn't, O!

HILARION:
That fact was seen at once by you
In casual conversation, O!
Which is most creditable to
Your powers of observation, O!
     —servation, O!
     —servation, O!
Your powers of observation, O!

As they are going off, Melissa encounters Lady Blanche, who agrees that the new 'girls' sing nicely, but points out that two are tenors and one a baritone! Melissa, however, persuades her to wink at the deception, arguing that, if Lady Blanche assists Hilarion to marry Princess Ida, *she* will become head of the university.

MELISSA:
Now wouldn't you like to rule the roast,
And guide this University?

BLANCHE:
I must agree
'Twould pleasant be.
(Sing hey, a Proper Pride!)

MELISSA:
And wouldn't you like to clear the coast
Of malice and perversity?

BLANCHE:
Without a doubt
I'll bundle 'em out,
(Sing hey, when I preside!)

BOTH:
Sing hey!
Sing, hoity, toity! Sorry for some!
Sing, marry come up and my/her day will come!
Sing, Proper Pride
Is the horse to ride,
And Happy-go-Lucky, my Lady, O!

BLANCHE:
For years I've writhed beneath her sneers,
Although a born Plantagenet!

MELISSA:
You're much too meek,
Or you would speak.
(Sing hey, I'll say no more!)

BLANCHE:
Her elder I by several years,
Although you'd ne'er imagine it.

MELISSA:
Sing, so I've heard
But never a word
Have I e'er believed before!

BOTH:
Sing hey!
Sing, hoity, toity! Sorry for some!
Sing, marry come up and my/her day will come!
Sing, she shall learn
That a worm will turn.
Sing Happy-go-Lucky, my Lady, O!

It is time for lunch and Princess Ida and the others enter. Unfortunately, Cyril indulges freely in the wine and, while his friends try to restrain him, bursts into song:

> Would you know the kind of maid
> Sets my heart a-flame-a?
> Eyes must be downcast and staid,
> Cheeks must flush for shame-a!
> She may neither dance nor sing,
> But, demure in everything,
> Hang her head in modest way,
> With pouting lips that seem to say,
> 'Oh, kiss me, kiss me, kiss me, kiss me,
> Though I die of shame-a!'
> Please you, that's the kind of maid
> Sets my heart a-flame-a!
>
> When a maid is bold and gay,
> With a tongue goes clang-a
> Flaunting it in brave array,
> Maiden may go hang-a!
> Sunflower gay and hollyhock
> Never shall my garden stock;
> Mine the blushing rose of May,
> With pouting lips that seem to say,
> 'Oh, kiss me, kiss me, kiss me, kiss me,
> Though I die of shame-a!'
> Please you, that's the kind of maid
> Sets my heart a-flame-a!

In the confusion that follows, Princess Ida runs to the bridge at the back of the garden, accidentally falls into the stream—and is rescued by Hilarion. Even so, the Princess promptly has the three men arrested. As they are bound and about to be led away, Hilarion declares himself:

> Whom thou has chained must wear his chain,
> Thou canst not set him free,
> He wrestles with his bonds in vain
> Who lives by loving thee!
> If heart of stone for heart of fire,
> Be all thou hast to give,
> If dead to me my heart's desire,
> Why should I wish to live?

No word of thine—no stern command
Can teach my heart to rove,
Then rather perish by thy hand,
Than live without thy love!
A loveless life apart from thee
Were hopeless slavery.
If kindly death will set me free,
Why should I fear to die?

No sooner have the three been taken away than King Hildebrand's
army launches its attack. The gates are battered down, soldiers
rush in—and with them are brought Arac, Guron and Scynthius,
handcuffed. King Hildebrand follows:

Some years ago
No doubt you know
(And if you don't I'll tell you so)
You gave your troth
Upon your oath
To Hilarion my son.
A vow you make
You must not break,
(If you think you may, it's a great mistake),
For a bride's a bride
Though the knot were tied
At the early age of one!
And I'm a peppery kind of King,
Who's indisposed for parleying
To fit the wit of a bit of a chit,
And that's the long and the short of it!

If you decide
To pocket your pride
And let Hilarion claim his bride,
Why, well and good,
It's understood
We'll let bygones go by—
But if you choose
To sulk in the blues
I'll make the whole of you shake in your shoes.
I'll storm your walls,
And level your halls,
In the twinkling of an eye!

For I'm a peppery Potentate,
Who's little inclined his claim to bate
To fit the wit of a bit of a chit,
And that's the long and the short of it!

Arac, Guron and Scynthius, Princess Ida's handcuffed brothers, make their point in a trio:

We may remark, though nothing can
Dismay us,
That if you thwart this gentleman,
He'll slay us.
We don't fear death, of course—we're taught
To shame it!
But still upon the whole we thought
We'd name it.
Yes, yes, yes, better perhaps to name it.

Our interests we would not press
With chatter,
Three hulking brothers more or less
Don't matter;
If you'd pooh-pooh this monarch's plan,
Pooh-pooh it,
But when he says he'll hang a man,
He'll do it.
Yes, yes, yes, devil doubt he'll do it.

But the Princess stands firm and, during the final ensemble, declares:

Though I am but a girl,
Defiance thus I hurl,
Our banners all
On outer wall
We fearlessly unfurl.

The third act—the only third act in the operas—finds Melissa, Sacharissa and the other girls, armed with battleaxes, in the courtyard of Castle Adamant:

Death to the invader!
Strike a deadly blow,
As an old Crusader
Struck his Paynim foe!

Let our martial thunder,
Fill his soul with wonder,
Tear his ranks asunder,
Lay the tyrant low!

But, despite their warlike manner, they are far from keen on battle. Sacharissa, the surgeon, cannot bear the thought of seeing real blood; the girls in the band, reports Ada, are too sick to play their martial music; and Psyche, in charge of the gunpowder, is more for talking things over. Princess Ida is in despair:

I built upon a rock,
But ere Destruction's hand
Dealt equal lot
To Court and cot,
My rock had turned to sand!
I leant upon an oak,
But in the hour of need,
Alack-a-day,
My trusted stay
Was but a bruisèd reed!
Ah, faithless rock,
My simple faith to mock!
Ah, trait'rous oak,
Thy worthlessness to cloak.

I drew a sword of steel,
But when to home and hearth
The battle's breath
Bore fire and death,
My sword was but a lath!
I lit a beacon fire,
But on a stormy day
Of frost and rime,
In wintertime,
My fire had died away!
Ah, coward steel,
That faith can unanneal!
False fire indeed,
To fail me in my need!

But she is surprised by the sudden appearance of her father, King Gama. He is pale and trembling, for he has been subjected to what, to him, is the most ghastly form of torture. Ill-tempered man that

he is, he has been given everything he desires and is in the awful
situation of having nothing at all to complain about:

> Whene'er I spoke
> Sarcastic joke
> Replete with malice spiteful,
> This people mild
> Politely smiled,
> And voted me delightful!
> Now when a wight
> Sits up all night
> Ill-natured jokes devising,
> And all his wiles
> Are met with smiles,
> It's hard, there's no disguising! . . . ah!
> Oh, don't the days seem lank and long
> When all goes right and nothing goes wrong,
> And isn't your life extremely flat
> With nothing whatever to grumble at!
>
> When German bands
> From music stands
> Played Wagner imper*fect*ly—
> I bade them go—
> They didn't say no,
> But off they went directly!
> The organ boys
> They stopped their noise
> With readiness surprising,
> And grinning herds
> Of hurdy-gurds
> Retired apologising!
>
> I offered gold
> In sums untold
> To all who'd contradict me—
> I said I'd pay
> A pound a day
> To anyone who kicked me—
> I bribed with toys
> Great vulgar boys
> To utter something spiteful,
> But, bless you, no!
> They *would* be so
> Confoundedly politeful . . . ah!

In short, these aggravating lads,
They tickle my tastes, they feed my fads,
They give me this and they give me that,
And I've nothing whatever to grumble at!

It is decided that, rather than that Hilarion should lower himself by setting his troops against an army of women, Gama's sons should fight it out with Hilarion and his friends. The chorus of soldiers contributes an appropriately warlike sound:

When anger spreads his wing,
And all seems dark as night for it,
There's nothing but to fight for it.
But ere you pitch your ring,
Select a pretty site for it,
(This spot is suited quite for it),
And then you gaily sing,
'Oh, I love the jolly rattle
Of an ordeal by battle,
There's an end of tittle-tattle
When your enemy is dead.
It's an arrant molly-coddle
Fears a crack upon his noddle,
And he's only fit to swaddle
In a downy feather-bed!'—
For a fight's a kind of thing
That I love to look upon,
So let us sing,
Long live the King,
And his son Hilarion!

Accoutred in heavy armour, Gama's three sons feel thoroughly uncomfortable. They could fight much better without it:

ARAC:
This helmet, I suppose,
Was meant to ward off blows,
It's very hot,
And weighs a lot,
As many a guardsman knows,
So off that helmet goes.

ALL:
Yes, yes, yes,
So off that helmet goes!

ARAC:
This tight-fitting cuirass
Is but a useless mass,
It's made of steel
And weighs a deal,
A man is but an ass
Who fights in a cuirass,
So off goes that cuirass.

ALL:
Yes, yes, yes,
So off goes that cuirass!

ARAC:
These brassets, truth to tell,
May look uncommon well,
But in a fight
They're much too tight,
They're like a lobster shell!

ALL:
Yes, yes, yes,
They're like a lobster shell!

ARAC:
These things I treat the same (*indicating leg-pieces*)
(I quite forget their name)
They turn one's legs
To cribbage pegs—
Their aid I thus disclaim,
Though I forget their name!

ALL:
Yes, yes, yes
Their aid we/they thus disclaim!

Hilarion, Florian and Cyril enter, and the two groups of three set upon each other, while the chorus give forth:

This is our duty plain towards
Our Princess all immaculate,
We ought to bless her brothers' swords
And piously ejaculate:
Oh, Hungary!
Oh, Hungary!
Oh, doughty sons of Hungary!

> May all success
> Attend and bless
> Your warlike ironmongery!
> Hilarion! Hilarion! Hilarion!

The clash does not last long. Arac, Guron and Scynthius are beaten to the ground and the victorious Hilarion, Cyril and Florian stand over them. Her brothers beaten, Princess Ida agrees to resign from her post as head of the university and to give up her cherished scheme by which 'at my exalted name Posterity would bow in gratitude.' But it is reasonably pointed out to her that if she had her way in the segregation of women, where would Posterity come from? The Princess appreciates the weight of the argument and cheerfully agrees to marry Hilarion, while Psyche pairs off with Cyril and Melissa with Florian.

> PRINCESS:
> With joy abiding,
> Together gliding
> Through life's variety,
> In sweet society,
> And thus enthroning
> The love I'm owning,
> On this atoning
> I will rely!
>
> CHORUS:
> It were profanity
> For poor humanity
> To treat as vanity
> The sway of Love.
> In no locality
> Or principality
> Is our mortality
> Its sway above!
>
> HILARION:
> When day is fading,
> With serenading
> And such frivolity
> Of tender quality—
> With scented showers
> Of fairest flowers,
> The happy hours
> Will gaily fly!

Princess Ida (PI) *Soprano* Leonora Braham was the original player.

Prince of Monte Carlo (D) *Bass-baritone* The role was first played by Scott Fishe.

Princess of Monte Carlo (D) *Soprano* The role was first played by Emmie Owen.

'Prithee, pretty maiden—prithee, tell me true' Duet for Patience and Archibald Grosvenor—'Hey willow waly O.' (P).

Promenade Concerts The first music from a Gilbert and Sullivan opera to be heard at a Promenade Concert in London was the selection from *HMS Pinafore* made by Hamilton Clarke for orchestra and military band and conducted by Sullivan at a Covent Garden 'Prom' in 1878—giving the box-office at the Opéra Comique a much-needed boost. Sir Malcolm Sargent conducted excerpts from the operas, by permission of Miss Bridget D'Oyly Carte, at a Royal Albert Hall 'Prom' in 1955, and in later seasons a Saturday evening programme devoted to Gilbert and Sullivan has been a highly popular feature.

Propriety 'We agreed that no lady of the company should be required to wear a dress that she could not wear with absolute propriety at a private fancy ball.'—Gilbert, looking back some years later on the partnership. Backstage, too, at the Savoy Theatre everything was conducted with the strictest eye to propriety.

For a lesson in the way in which a nicely brought-up English girl should behave when approached by a strange man, see Lady Sophy's song, 'Bold-faced ranger' (U).

Psyche, Lady (PI) *Soprano* Kate Chard was the original player of Lady Psyche, professor of humanities.

Punning During a break in rehearsal at the Savoy, a messenger was darting about the stage in the effort to find the person to whom his large package was addressed. 'He looks as though he might dance a *pas seul* any minute,' said somebody. 'Yes,' murmured Gilbert. 'A brown-paper *pas seul*!' Though he found it difficult to resist a pun in the course of private conversation, Gilbert did not make great use of the device in his libretti. But there are some examples, such as:

I love—and love, alas, above my station!
He loves—and loves a lass above his station! (HMS)

True, I lack birth.
You've a berth on board this very ship. (HMS)

For, adder-like, his sting lay in his tongue.
(His 'sting' is present, though his 'stung' is past)—
King Hildebrand (PI)

'How dare you bandy words with me?' snaps the misshapen King Gama.

'No need to bandy aught that appertains to you,' replies Cyril (PI).

FLORIAN:
Are there no males whatever in those walls?

KING GAMA:
None, gentlemen, excepting letter mails—
And they are driven (as males often are
In other large communities) by women.
Why, bless my heart, she's so particular
She'll scarcely suffer Dr Watt's hymns—
And all the animals she owns are 'hers'!

CYRIL:
Ah, then, they have male poultry?

KING GAMA:
Not at all.
The crowing's done by an accomplished hen! (PI)

I blushed and stammered so that she exclaimed,
'Can these be men?' Then, seeing this, 'Why these—'
'Are men,' she would have added, but 'are men'
Stuck in her throat!—Melissa (PI)
('Amen stuck in my throat.'—Shakespeare's *Macbeth*)

The only really tiresome bit of punning in which Gilbert engages occurs in the exchanges between Major-General Stanley and the Pirate King (PP) when they keep on ringing the changes between 'orphan' and 'often'. In later years, however, the text has been considerably cut here and, as arranged by Bridget D'Oyly Carte and played by Martyn Green and Darrell Fancourt, excessive repetition has been avoided.

'Quaff the nectar—cull the roses' Chorus on the first entrance of King Paramount (U).

Queen of the Fairies (I) *Contralto* In the first production the Queen of the Fairies, played by Alice Barnett, wore a Brunnhilde-type costume with the Valkyrie's winged helmet and spear. Wagner's *Der Ring des Nibelungen* had been presented for the first time in London at Her Majesty's Theatre in May 1882. *Iolanthe* had its first production in November of that year. The Queen of the Fairies, substantial in build and formidable in manner, is one of the succession of leading contralto parts of this nature in the Gilbert and Sullivan operas.

Queues The idea of forming a queue for seats was brought by Richard D'Oyly Carte from America and introduced for the production of *Iolanthe* at the Savoy Theatre.

Quotation Just as Mozart in *Don Giovanni* amusingly refers to his earlier opera *Figaro*, so does Gilbert tickle his audience by harking back to his own earlier successes. Major-General Stanley (PP) assures us that he can 'whistle all the airs from that infernal nonsense *Pinafore*' and when Captain Corcoran turns up in *Utopia, Limited* he repeats the 'What never? . . . Hardly ever!' gag from *Pinafore*. Also in *Utopia, Limited* King Paramount, in search of a punishment to suit a particular case, declares: 'I am in constant communication with the Mikado of Japan, who is a leading authority on such points.'

Rackstraw, Ralph (HMS) *Tenor* The smartest lad in all the fleet, who loved a lass above his station, was first played by George Power.

Ralland, Herbert The original Mr Blushington (U), Herbert Ralland sang also Fairfax (Y), Marco (G) and Captain Fitzbattleaxe (U).

Rands, Leslie Principal baritone with D'Oyly Carte for twenty-two years, Leslie Rands sang nineteen different roles with the company, among them being Dr Daly (S), Captain Corcoran (HMS), Pirate King (PP), Colonel Calverley and Archibald Grosvenor (P), Earl of Mountararat and Strephon (I), Florian (PI), Mikado and Pish-Tush (M) and Sir Richard Cholmondeley (Y). He was a boy chorister at Chichester Cathedral and later trained at the Royal College of Music. His first acquaintance with Gilbert and Sullivan came when, as a very young man, he was in Southern Rhodesia, as it then was, and was invited to sing Giuseppe in a production of *The Gondoliers* by Bulawayo Operatic Society. Returning to England, he was very soon a member of the D'Oyly Carte Company and he proudly recalls that he learned the acting side of the business from the celebrated J. M. Gordon, who had been stage manager under Gilbert. In 1926 he married soprano Marjorie Eyre and they were together throughout their D'Oyly Carte careers in Britain, America and Canada and with the Australia and New Zealand Gilbert and Sullivan Company in 1949, 1950 and 1951. Leslie Rands will not readily forget one performance of *Patience* in the provinces, during which somebody's cigarette dropped into a basket under the stage, causing the costumes to smoulder and fill the theatre with smoke. Firemen arrived and, ninety feet above the stage, opened up a ventilator so ancient that it fell to pieces, precipitating a heavy iron hoop to within inches from where Rands was standing. Still as enthusiastic as ever about the operas, Leslie Rands is to-day a busy producer of amateur societies.

Raphael 'I can tell undoubted Raphaels from Gerard Dows and Zoffanies.'—Major-General Stanley (PP). To distinguish the work of the great Italian painter (1483–1520) from that of the other two would not seem to involve any great intellectual strain.

Rapture (Modified!) The line 'Modified rapture!', which is so quaintly effective when spoken by Nanki-Poo to Yum-Yum (M), came about by an accident at rehearsal. The artist playing Nanki-Poo had spoken the word 'Rapture!' with more stress than Gilbert required. 'Modified "rapture," ' said Gilbert—and the artist repeated, 'Modified rapture!' Gilbert, who did not readily miss a theatrical point, kept it in just like that.

Ravelin 'When I know what is meant by "mamelon" and "ravelin." '—Major-General Stanley (PP). A ravelin was a detached outwork in fortification.

Rayner, Michael His principal baritone roles are Cox (C), Counsel (J), Captain Corcoran (HMS), Samuel (PP), Strephon (I) and Giuseppe (G). He was born and brought up in Derby, studied at Birmingham School of Music and appeared with Opera for All and the Welsh National Opera before joining D'Oyly Carte. He is married, with four children, and is a keen golfer and football enthusiast.

Recordings The first complete recording of a Gilbert and Sullivan opera, *The Mikado*, was made in 1917, since when there have been many. Recordings available at the time of writing include:

Cox and Box (Burnand & Sullivan) Complete recording with dialogue (1 side), coupled with *The Gondoliers* (3 sides). Cast: Box—Joseph Riordan; Cox—Alan Styler; Bouncer—Donald Adams. New Symphony Orchestra of London, conducted by Isidore Godfrey. Recorded under the supervision of Bridget D'Oyly Carte. Decca LK 4402–4; SKL 4138–40 (S).

Trial by Jury Complete recording (2 sides) by the D'Oyly Carte Opera Company, coupled with *Utopia Limited* (excerpts). Cast: Learned Judge—John Reed; Plaintiff—Ann Hood; Defendant—Thomas Round; Counsel for Plaintiff—Kenneth Sandford; Usher—Donald Adams; Foreman of the Jury—Anthony Raffell; with Royal

Opera House Orchestra, Covent Garden, conducted by Isidore Godfrey. Decca LK 4579; SKL 4579 (S).

Complete recording. Cast: Learned Judge—George Baker; Plaintiff—Elsie Morison; Defendant—Richard Lewis; Counsel for Plaintiff—John Cameron; Usher—Owen Brannigan; Foreman of the Jury—Bernard Turgeon. Pro Arte Orchestra and Glyndebourne Festival Chorus, conducted by Sir Malcolm Sargent. EMI SXLP 30089 (S).

The Sorcerer Musically complete recording (4 sides) by the D'Oyly Carte Opera Company. Cast: Sir Marmaduke Pointdextre—Donald Adams; Alexis—David Palmer; Dr Daly—Alan Styler; Notary—Riley; John Wellington Wells—John Reed; Lady Sangazure—Christene Palmer; Aline—Valerie Masterson; Mrs Partlet—Jean Allister; Constance—Ann Hood. Royal Philharmonic Orchestra, conducted by Isidore Godfrey. Decca LK 4825–6; SKL 4825–6 (S).

HMS Pinafore Complete recording, with dialogue, by the D'Oyly Carte Opera Company, under the direction of Bridget D'Oyly Carte (4 sides). Cast: Sir Joseph Porter—John Reed; Captain Corcoran—Jeffrey Skitch; Ralph Rackstraw—Thomas Round; Dick Deadeye—Donald Adams; Bill Bobstay—George Cook; Bob Becket—Wilson Hyde; Josephine—Jean Hindmarsh; Hebe—Joyce Wright; Little Buttercup—Gillian Knight. New Symphony Orchestra of London, conducted by Isidore Godfrey. Decca LK 4334–5; SKL 4081–2 (S).

Complete recording without dialogue, by the D'Oyly Carte Opera Company, under the direction of Bridget D'Oyly Carte (4 sides). Cast: Sir Joseph Porter—Martyn Green; Captain Corcoran—Leslie Rands; Ralph Rackstraw—Leonard Osborn; Dick Deadeye—Darrell Fancourt; Bill Bobstay—Richard Walker; Bob Becket—Radley Flynn; Josephine—Muriel Harding; Hebe—Joan Gillingham; Little Buttercup—Ella Halman. Chorus and Orchestra conducted by Isidore Godfrey. Decca ACL 104–5.

Musically complete recording, without dialogue. Cast: Sir Joseph Porter—George Baker; Captain Corcoran—John Cameron; Ralph Rackstraw—Richard Lewis; Dick Deadeye—Owen Brannigan; Boatswain—James Milligan; Boatswain's Mate—John Cameron; Josephine—Elsie Morison; Hebe—Marjorie Thomas; Little Buttercup—Monica Sinclair. Pro Arte Orchestra and Glyndebourne Festival Chorus, conducted by Sir Malcolm Sargent. EMI SXLP 30088–9 (S).

Highlights We sail the ocean blue; Hail, men-o'-war's men—I'm called Little Buttercup; A maiden fair to see; I am the Captain of the Pinafore; I am the monarch of the sea; When I was a lad; Never mind the why and wherefore; Pretty daughter of mine—He is an Englishman; Many years ago; Oh joy, oh rapture unforeseen. The D'Oyly Carte Opera Company: Ella Halman, Leonard Osborn, Leslie Rands, Martyn Green, Joan Gillingham, Muriel Harding, Richard Walker, with Chorus and Orchestra, conducted by Isidore Godfrey. Reverse side: *The Sorcerer*. Recorded under the direction of Bridget D'Oyly Carte. Decca LK 4078.

Highlights from the famed D'Oyly Carte recording of 1930. Cast: Sir Joseph Porter—Sir Henry Lytton; Captain Corcoran—George Baker; Ralph Rackstraw—Charles Goulding; Dick Deadeye—Darrell Fancourt; Boatswain—Sydney Granville; Boatswain's Mate—Stuart Robertson; Josephine—Elsie Griffin; Hebe—Nellie Briercliffe; Little Buttercup—Bertha Lewis. Conducted by Dr Malcolm Sargent. Contents: We sail the ocean blue; Hail, men-o'-war's men; I'm called Little Buttercup; My gallant crew, Good Morning . . . I am the Captain of the Pinafore; Over the bright blue sea . . . Sir Joseph's barge is seen . . . Now give three cheers; I am the Monarch of the sea . . . When I was a lad; For I hold that on the seas; A British tar is a soaring soul; Refrain, audacious tar; Can I survive this overbearing; This very night; Fair moon, to Thee I sing; Things are seldom what they seem; Never mind the why and wherefore; Kind Captain, I've important information; Carefully on tiptoe stealing; My pain and my distress; A many years ago; Oh joy, Oh rapture. Music for Pleasure 2070.

Excerpts My gallant crew, good morning—I am the Captain of the Pinafore; Over the bright blue sea—Sir Joseph's barge is seen; When I was a lad; Let's give three cheers; Never mind the why and wherefore; Oh joy, oh rapture unforeseen. The D'Oyly Carte Opera Company: Jeffrey Skitch, John Reed, Jean Hindmarsh, with Chorus and the New Symphony Orchestra of London, conducted by Isidore Godfrey. Recorded under the direction of Bridget D'Oyly Carte. Decca DFE 8632 (45 r.p.m.).

The Pirates of Penzance Complete recording, with dialogue, by the D'Oyly Carte Opera Company. Cast: Major-General Stanley—John Reed; Pirate King—Donald Adams; Samuel—George Cook; Frederic—Philip Potter; Sergeant of Police—Owen Brannigan; Mabel—Valerie Masterson; Edith—Jean Allister; Kate—Pauline Wales; Isabel—Susan Maisey; Ruth—Christene Palmer. Royal Philharmonic Orchestra, conducted by Isidore Godfrey. Recorded under the direction of Bridget D'Oyly Carte. Decca LK 4925–6; SKL 4925–6 (S).

Musically complete recording, without dialogue. Cast: Major-General Stanley—George Baker; Pirate King—James Milligan; Samuel—John Cameron; Frederic—Richard Lewis; Sergeant of Police—Owen Brannigan; Mabel—Elsie Morison; Edith—Heather Harper; Kate—Marjorie Thomas; Ruth—Monica Sinclair. Pro Arte Orchestra and Glyndebourne Festival Chorus, conducted by Sir Malcolm Sargent. EMI ALP 1801–2; ASD 381–2 (S).

Patience Complete recording, with dialogue, by the D'Oyly Carte Opera Company, under the direction of Bridget D'Oyly Carte. Cast: Colonel Calverley—Donald Adams; Major Murgatroyd—Cartier; Duke of Dunstable—Philip Potter; Reginald Bunthorne—John Reed; Archibald Grosvenor—Kenneth Sandford; Lady Angela—Yvonne Newman; Lady Saphir—Beti Lloyd-Jones; Lady Jane—Gillian Knight; Lady Ella—Jennifer Toye; Patience—Mary Sansom. D'Oyly Carte Opera Chorus and the New Symphony Orchestra of London, conducted by Isidore Godfrey. Decca LK 4414–5; SKL 4414–5 (S).

Musically complete recording by the D'Oyly Carte Opera Company. Cast: Colonel Calverley—Darrell Fancourt; Major Murgatroyd—Peter Pratt; Duke of Dunstable—Neville Griffiths; Reginald Bunthorne—Martyn Green; Archibald Grosvenor—Alan Styler; Lady Angela—Yvonne Dean; Lady Saphir—Ann Drummond-Grant; Lady Jane—Ella Halman; Lady Ella—Muriel Harding; Patience—Margaret Mitchell. Conducted by Isidore Godfrey. Recorded under the direction of Bridget D'Oyly Carte. Decca ACL 1174–5.

Iolanthe Complete recording, with dialogue, by the D'Oyly Carte Opera Company, under the direction of Bridget D'Oyly Carte. Cast: Lord Chancellor—John Reed; Earl of Mountararat—Donald Adams; Earl Tolloller—Thomas Round; Private Willis—Kenneth Sandford; Strephon—Alan Styler; Queen of the Fairies—Gillian Knight; Iolanthe—Yvonne Newman; Phyllis—Mary Sansom. Section of the Grenadier Guards Band and the New Symphony Orchestra of London, conducted by Isidore Godfrey. Decca LK 4378–9; SKL 4119–20 (S).

Complete recording without dialogue, under the direction of Bridget D'Oyly Carte. Cast: Lord Chancellor—Martyn Green; Earl of Mountararat—Eric Thornton; Earl Tolloller—Leonard Osborn; Private Willis—Fisher Morgan; Strephon—Alan Styler; Queen of the Fairies—Ella Halman; Iolanthe—Anne Drummond-Grant; Celia—Joyce Hill; Leila—Yvonne Dean; Phyllis— Margaret Mitchell. Chorus and orchestra conducted by Isidore Godfrey. Decca ACL 1128–9

Musically complete recording, without dialogue. Cast: Lord Chancellor—George Baker; Earl of Mountararat—Ian Wallace; Earl Tolloller—Alexander Young; Private Willis—Owen Brannigan; Strephon—John Cameron; Queen of the Fairies—Monica Sinclair; Iolanthe—Marjorie Thomas; Celia—April Cantelo; Leila —Heather Harper; Phyllis—Elsie Morison. Pro Arte Orchestra and Glyndebourne Festival Chorus, conducted by Sir Malcolm Sargent. EMI SXLP 30112-3 (S).

Highlights Entrance and march of the Peers; Such a susceptible Chancellor; When I went to the bar; Sentry's song; Love unrequited; When you're lying awake; If you go in; Soon as we may (Finale). The D'Oyly Carte Opera Company: Martyn Green, Fisher Morgan, Eric Thornton, Leonard Osborn, Margaret Mitchell, with Chorus and New Symphony Orchestra of London, conducted by Isidore Godfrey. Recorded under the direction of Bridget D'Oyly Carte. Reverse side: *The Gondoliers*. Decca LK 4073.

Highlights Cast: Lord Chancellor—Eric Shilling; Earl of Mountararat—Denis Dowling; Earl Tolloller—Stanley Bevan; Private Willis—Leon Greene; Strephon—Julian Moyle; Queen of the Fairies—Heather Begg; Iolanthe—Patricia Kern; Celia—Elizabeth Robson; Leila—Cynthia Morey; Phyllis—Elizabeth Harwood. Sadler's Wells Opera Chorus and Orchestra, conducted by Alexander Faris. EMI CLP 1567; CSD 1434 (S).

Excerpts Loudly let the trumpet bray; When I went to the bar; When Britain really ruled the waves; Tho' p'raps I may incur your blame; Soon as we may, off and away. The D'Oyly Carte Opera Company: John Reed, Donald Adams, Mary Sansom, Thomas Round, Kenneth Sandford, with a section of the Grenadier Guards Band and the New Symphony Orchestra of London, conducted by Isidore Godfrey. Recorded under the direction of Bridget D'Oyly Carte. Decca DFE 8631 (45 r.p.m.).

Princess Ida Musically complete recording by the D'Oyly Carte Opera Company. Cast: King Hildebrand—Kenneth Sandford; Hilarion—Philip Potter; Cyril—David Palmer; Florian—Jeffrey Skitch; King Gama—John Reed; Arac—Donald Adams; Guron—Anthony Raffell; Scynthius—George Cook; Princess Ida—Elizabeth Harwood; Lady Blanche—Christene Palmer; Lady Psyche—Ann Hood; Melissa & Sacharissa—Valerie Masterson. Royal Philharmonic Orchestra, conducted by Sir Malcolm Sargent. Recorded under the direction of Bridget D'Oyly Carte. Decca LK 4708-9; SKL 4708-9 (S).

Highlights Now harken to my strict command; To-day we meet; From the distant panorama . . . we are warriors three; If you give me your attention; Towards the empyrean heights; Minerva! oh, hear me; Gently, gently; I am a maiden; The world is but a broken toy; A lady fair of lineage high; The woman of the wisest wit; Would you know the kind maid?; Whene'er I spoke; When anger spreads his wing; This helmet, I suppose; With joy abiding. The D'Oyly Carte Opera Company: Kenneth Sandford, Philip Potter, Donald Adams, Anthony Raffell, George Cook, John Reed, Valerie Masterson, Ann Hood, Elizabeth Harwood, David Palmer, Jeffrey Skitch. The Royal Philharmonic Orchestra, conducted by Sir Malcolm Sargent. Recorded under the direction of Bridget D'Oyly Carte. Decca LK 4845; SKL 4845 (S).

The Mikado Complete recording, without dialogue, by the D'Oyly Carte Opera Company. Cast: The Mikado—Donald Adams; Nanki-Poo—Thomas Round; Ko-Ko—Peter Pratt; Pooh-Bah—Kenneth Sandford; Pish-Tush—Alan Styler; Go-To—Owen Grundy; Yum-Yum—Jean Hindmarsh; Pitti-Sing—Beryl Dixon; Peep-Bo—Jennifer Toye; Katisha—Ann Drummond-Grant. New Symphony Orchestra of London, conducted by Isidore Godfrey. Recorded under the supervision of Bridget D'Oyly Carte. Decca LK 4251-2; SKL 4006-7 (S).

Complete recording, without dialogue, by the D'Oyly Carte Opera Company. Cast: The Mikado—Darrell Fancourt; Nanki-Poo —Leonard Osborn; Ko-Ko—Martyn Green; Pooh-Bah—Richard Watson; Pish-Tush—Alan Styler; Go-To—Radley Flynn; Yum-Yum—Margaret Mitchell; Pitti-Sing—Joan Gillingham; Peep-Bo— Joyce Wright; Katisha—Ella Halman; Chorus and Orchestra conducted by Isidore Godfrey. Decca ACL 1014-5.

Complete vocal numbers, without dialogue. Cast: Nanki-Poo— John Wakefield; Yum-Yum—Marion Studholme; Mikado—John Holmes; Ko-Ko—Clive Revill; Pooh-Bah—Denis Dowling; Pish-Tush—John Heddle Nash; Pitti-Sing—Patricia Kern; Peep-Bo— Dorothy Nash; Katisha—Jean Allister. Sadler's Wells Opera Chorus and Orchestra, conducted by Alexander Faris. EMI CSD 1458-9 (S).

Musically complete recording, without dialogue. Cast: Nanki-Poo—Richard Lewis; Yum-Yum—Elsie Morison; Ko-Ko—Geraint Evans; Pooh-Bah—Ian Wallace; Mikado—Owen Brannigan; Pish-Tush—John Cameron; Pitti-Sing—Marjorie Thomas; Peep-Bo—Jeanette Sinclair; Katisha—Monica Sinclair. Pro Arte Orchestra and Glyndebourne Festival Chorus, conducted by Sir Malcolm Sargent. EMI ALP 1485-6; ASD 256-7 (S).

Excerpts Three little maids from school; A wandering minstrel; Behold the Lord High Executioner; The flowers that bloom in the spring. The D'Oyly Carte Opera Company: Jean Hindmarsh,

Beryl Dixon, Jennifer Toye, Thomas Round, Peter Pratt. Chorus and New Symphony Orchestra of London, conducted by Isidore Godfrey. Recorded under the direction of Bridget D'Oyly Carte. Decca DFE 6568; STO 116 (S) (45 r.p.m.).

Ruddigore Complete recording, without dialogue, by the D'Oyly Carte Opera Company, under the direction of Bridget D'Oyly Carte. Cast: Sir Ruthven Murgatroyd—John Reed; Richard Dauntless—Thomas Round; Sir Despard Murgatroyd—Kenneth Sandford; Rose Maybud—Jean Hindmarsh; Mad Margaret—Jean Allister; Dame Hannah—Gillian Knight; Sir Roderic Murgatroyd —Donald Adams; Old Adam—Riley; Zorah—Mary Sansom. Royal Opera House Orchestra, Covent Garden, conducted by Isidore Godfrey. Decca LK 4504-5; SKL 4504-5 (S).

Complete recording, without dialogue, by the D'Oyly Carte Opera Company. Cast: Sir Ruthven Murgatroyd—Martyn Green; Richard Dauntless—Leonard Osborn; Sir Despard Murgatroyd— Richard Watson; Old Adam—Radley Flynn; Sir Roderic Murgatroyd—Darrell Fancourt; Rose—Margaret Mitchell; Mad Margaret —Ann Drummond-Grant; Dame Hannah—Ella Halman; Zorah— Deidree Thurlow. Chorus and Orchestra, conducted by Isidore Godfrey. Decca ACL 1193-4.

Highlights Sir Rupert Murgatroyd; I know a youth; I shipped d'ye see; I once was as meek as a new-born lamb; Painted emblems of a race—When the night wind howls; I once was a very abandoned person; There grew a little flower. The D'Oyly Carte Opera Company: Ella Halman, Martyn Green, Margaret Mitchell, Leonard Osborn, Radley Flynn, Darrell Fancourt, Richard Watson, Ann Drummond-Grant, with Chorus and Orchestra conducted by Isidore Godfrey. Decca LK 4069. Reverse side: *The Yeomen of the Guard*.

The Yeomen of the Guard Musically complete recording by the D'Oyly Carte Opera Company. Cast: Sir Richard Cholmondeley— Anthony Raffell; Colonel Fairfax—Philip Potter; Sergeant Meryll —Donald Adams; Leonard Meryll—David Palmer; Jack Point— John Reed; Wilfred Shadbolt—Kenneth Sandford; First Yeoman— David Palmer; Second Yeoman—Thomas Lawlor; Elsie Maynard —Elizabeth Harwood; Phoebe Meryll—Ann Hood; Dame Carruthers—Gillian Knight; Kate—Eales. Royal Philharmonic Orchestra, conducted by Sir Malcolm Sargent. Recorded under the direction of Bridget D'Oyly Carte. Decca LK 4624-5; SKL 4624-5 (S).

Musically complete recording, without dialogue. Cast: Sir Richard Cholmondeley—Denis Dowling; Colonel Fairfax—

Richard Lewis; Sergeant Meryll—John Carol Case; Leonard Meryll
—Alexander Young; Jack Point—Geraint Evans; Wilfred Shadbolt
—Owen Brannigan; First Yeoman—Alexander Young; Second
Yeoman—John Cameron; Elsie Maynard—Elsie Morison; Phoebe
Meryll—Marjorie Thomas; Dame Carruthers—Monica Sinclair;
Kate—Doreen Hume. Pro Arte Orchestra and Glyndebourne
Festival Chorus, conducted by Sir Malcolm Sargent. EMI SXLP
30120–30121.

Highlights When maiden loves; Tower warders; Is life a boon?;
I have a song to sing, O; How say you, maiden, will you wed?;
I've jibe and joke and quip and crank; 'Tis done! I am a bride;
Were I thy bride; Night has spread her pall once more; Oh! A
private buffoon; Hereupon we're both agreed; Free from his
fetters grim; Strange adventure; Hark! What was that, sir? . . .
Like a ghost his vigil keeping; A man who would woo a fair maid.
The D'Oyly Carte Opera Company: Ann Hood, Thomas Lawlor,
Philip Potter, John Reed, Elizabeth Harwood, Anthony Raffell,
Gillian Knight, Kenneth Sandford, Donald Adams, Eales. Royal
Philharmonic Orchestra, conducted by Sir Malcolm Sargent.
Recorded under the direction of Bridget D'Oyly Carte. Decca LK
4809; SKL 4809 (S).

Highlights When maiden loves; Is life a boon?; I have a song to
sing, O; Were I thy bride; Oh! a private buffoon; Strange adventure; A man who would woo a fair maid; When a wooer goes a-
wooing; Oh, thoughtless crew. The D'Oyly Carte Opera Company:
Ann Drummond-Grant, Leonard Osborn, Martyn Green, Muriel
Harding, Darrell Fancourt, Ella Halman, Deidree Thurlow. Chorus
and Orchestra, conducted by Isidore Godfrey. Decca LK 4069.

Excerpts I have a song to sing, O!; 'Tis done! I am a bride; Were
I thy bride; Oh! a private buffoon; Free from his fetters grim. The
D'Oyly Carte Opera Company: Elizabeth Harwood, John Reed,
Ann Hood, Philip Potter. Royal Philharmonic Orchestra, conducted
by Sir Malcolm Sargent. Recorded under the direction of Bridget
D'Oyly Carte. Decca DFE 8630 (45 r.p.m.).

The Gondoliers Complete recording, with dialogue, by the D'Oyly
Carte Opera Company, coupled with *Cox and Box*. Cast: Duke of
Plaza-Toro—John Reed; Luiz—Jeffrey Skitch; Don Alhambra—
Kenneth Sandford; Marco Palmieri—Thomas Round; Giuseppe
Palmieri—Alan Styler; Antonio & Annibale—Michael Wakeham;
Francesco—Joseph Riordan; Giorgio—George Cook; Duchess of
Plaza-Toro—Gillian Knight; Casilda—Jennifer Toye; Gianetta—
Mary Sansom; Tessa—Joyce Wright; Fiametta—Dawn Bradshaw;
Vittoria—Ceinwen Jones; Giulia—Daphne Gill; Inez—Jeanette

Roach. New Symphony Orchestra of London, conducted by Isidore Godfrey. Recorded under the supervision of Bridget D'Oyly Carte. Decca LK 4402–4; SKL 4138–40 (S).

Musically complete recording by the D'Oyly Carte Opera Company. Cast: Duke of Plaza-Toro—Martyn Green; Luiz—Henry Goodier; Don Alhambra—Richard Watson; Marco Palmieri—Leonard Osborn; Giuseppe Palmieri—Alan Styler; Antonio—Geoffrey Sanders; Francesco—Thomas Hancock; Giorgio—Radley Flynn; Annibale—Stanley Youngman; Duchess of Plaza-Toro—Ella Halman; Casilda—Margaret Mitchell; Gianetta—Muriel Harding; Tessa—Yvonne Dean; Fiametta—Enid Walsh; Vittoria—Yvonne Dean; Giulia—Joyce Wright; Inez—Caryl Fane. Chorus and Orchestra, conducted by Isidore Godfrey. Recorded under the supervision of Bridget D'Oyly Carte. Decca ACL 1151–2.

Musically complete recording, without dialogue. Cast: Duke of Plaza-Toro—Geraint Evans; Luiz—Alexander Young; Don Alhambra—Owen Brannigan; Marco—Richard Lewis; Giuseppe—John Cameron; Francesco—Alexander Young; Giorgio—James Milligan; Duchess of Plaza-Toro—Monica Sinclair; Casilda—Edna Graham; Gianetta—Elsie Morison; Tessa—Marjorie Thomas; Fiametta—Stella Hitchens; Vittoria—Lavinia Renton; Giulia—Helen Watts; Inez—Helen Watts. Pro Arte Orchestra and Glyndebourne Festival Chorus, conducted by Sir Malcolm Sargent. EMI ALP 1504–5; 265–6 (S).

Highlights We're called Gondolieri; And now to choose our brides; In enterprise of martial kind; I stole the Prince; When a merry maiden marries; Then one of us will be Queen; For everyone who feels inclined; Rising early in the morning; Here we are at the risk of our lives; There lived a King; Small titles and orders. Cast as in complete recording ACL 1151–2. Decca LK 4073. Reverse side: *Iolanthe.*

Excerpts The merriest fellows are we; We're called Gondolieri; From the sunny Spanish shore; I stole the Prince; When a merry maiden marries; Take a pair of sparkling eyes; Dance a cachucha. The D'Oyly Carte Opera Company: Michael Wakeham, Thomas Round, Alan Styler, John Reed, Gillian Knight, Jennifer Toye, Jeffrey Skitch, Kenneth Sandford, Joyce Wright. New Symphony Orchestra of London, conducted by Isidore Godfrey. Recorded under the direction of Bridget D'Oyly Carte. Decca DFE 8633 (45 r.p.m.).

Utopia, Limited Excerpts: O make way for the wise men; Oh, maiden, rich in Girton lore; Oh, Zara, my beloved one; Words of love too loudly spoken; Eagle high in cloudland soaring. Preceded by *Trial by Jury*. The D'Oyly Carte Opera Company: John Reed, Kenneth Sandford, Ann Hood, Thomas Round, Jean Allister, Donald Adams, Anthony Raffell. Royal Opera House Orchestra, Covent Garden, conducted by Isidore Godfrey. Decca LK 4579; SKL 4579 (S).

Gilbert & Sullivan Highlights No. 1 Excerpts from *The Mikado, The Gondoliers, H.M.S. Pinafore*. Pro Arte Orchestra and Glyndebourne Festival Chorus, conducted by Sir Malcolm Sargent. EMI ALP 1904; ASD 472 (S).

Gilbert & Sullivan Highlights No. 2 Excerpts from *The Mikado, The Gondoliers, H.M.S. Pinafore, The Pirates of Penzance*. Pro Arte Orchestra and Glyndebourne Festival Chorus, conducted by Sir Malcolm Sargent. EMI ALP 1922; ASD 487 (S).

Gilbert & Sullivan Highlights No. 3 Excerpts from *The Pirates of Penzance, The Yeomen of the Guard, Iolanthe, Trial by Jury*. Pro Arte Orchestra and Glyndebourne Festival Chorus, conducted by Sir Malcolm Sargent. EMI ALP 1932; ASD 495 (S).

Gilbert & Sullivan Overtures Pro Arte Orchestra, conducted by Sir Malcolm Sargent. EMI XLP 20003; SXLP 20003 (S).

More Gilbert & Sullivan Overtures Pro Arte Orchestra, conducted by Sir Malcolm Sargent. EMI XLP 20032; SXLP 20032 (S).

Redmond, Tom The original First Citizen (Y).

Reed, John Principal comedian of the D'Oyly Carte Company, John Reed plays John Wellington Wells (S), Sir Joseph Porter (HMS), Major-General Stanley (PP), Bunthorne (P), Lord Chancellor (I), King Gama (PI), Ko-Ko (M), Robin Oakapple (R), Jack Point (Y) and the Duke of Plaza-Toro (G). Nimbleness of foot as well as of voice is of course essential for these wonderful roles and in his young days John Reed won many medals both for elocution and dancing. He was born in Bishop Auckland, played as a straight actor in repertory, joined Darlington Operatic Society, produced for many amateur societies, and was for a time producer and dancing instructor for Darlington Education Committee. He went for an audition with the D'Oyly Carte Company 'as an experiment', joined them in 1951, playing small parts and understudying Peter Pratt in the leading comedy roles. He officially succeeded to those roles in 1959. 'I enjoy them all for different reasons,' he will tell you. 'There is a lot of me in some of the characters—Jack Point and Ko-Ko, for instance. But I keep Jack Point quite separate from the others. After all, every comedian wants to make people cry as well as laugh. I play Ko-Ko as a "mischief". I think he is ageless. He can be any age. I do not think King Gama is a bit like me. When I first played him, I felt sorry for him but later I thought, "All right, if you want it nasty you shall have it that way!" Of course, one must play all these parts seriously. They are all characters and, if you play them straight, the lines are there and the laughs will come. An encore is a different thing—a bit of fun between me and the audience—then I come right back into character again.' Like many of those artists who appear completely at ease and unworried on the stage, John Reed confesses that he is 'always nervous' before going on.

'Refrain, audacious tar' Duet for Josephine and Ralph Rackstraw (HMS).

Rehearsals Though Gilbert drove his cast hard—and possibly near to distraction at times—they must at any rate have had the satisfaction of realising that he did know exactly what he wanted. Few experiences can be more frustrating and infuriating to an artist than to be saddled with a producer who is, so to speak, 'playing it by ear', changing his mind as he goes along and generally working to a system—or non-system—of trial and error. When he met the cast for the start of rehearsals Gilbert had already done his homework. Possibly he made some minor change when a new idea struck him but he had already worked out the full plan of the production down to every detail of position, grouping and move-ment. All this had evolved on the model stage at his home, each character being represented by a wooden block, differently coloured for each voice, the men three inches high and the women two and a half inches. The artists did not always take kindly to Gilbert's placing of them on the stage, those with a sense of 'stardom' feeling that they ought to occupy the most prominent position, as, for instance, the woman who pointed out that she was always centre-stage when she sang in Italian Opera. 'Unfortunately, madam,' said Gilbert, 'this is not Italian Opera but only a low burlesque of the worst possible kind.'

Sullivan's usual method was to go through his music with the cast, either he or one of his colleagues, Cellier perhaps, vamping an accompaniment, and it was only later, when they all knew their parts, that he set about the task of orchestration. He composed rapidly and when someone, impressed by his facility, remarked that it was like writing shorthand, he merely replied: 'But it's quicker.' There was an occasion when Gilbert's attention to detail jangled Sullivan's nerves and he wrote to D'Oyly Carte, complaining about the manner in which the stage rehearsals were conducted by Gilbert, 'wasting everybody's time and ruining my music.' But this was at the period of their bitterest quarrel.

D'Oyly Carte was wise enough never to interfere with the actual productions, leaving them entirely to Gilbert and Sullivan. But the stage manager was always there, notebook in hand, taking down Gilbert's detailed directions, ready for reference in the event of any deviations in later performances. Gilbert absolutely forbade spontaneous 'gagging' by any of his artists, though he was prepared to consider ideas they might put up to him. These, however, must never be used in performance without preliminary authorisation by him.

This complete authority set its stamp on the operas right from the start. As Gilbert said in later years: 'I attribute our success in our particular craft to the fact that Arthur Sullivan and I were in a commanding position. We controlled the stage altogether and were able to do as we wished, so far as the limitations of our actors would allow of it.'

On the lighter side of rehearsals, Hesketh Pearson in *Gilbert and Sullivan* mentions an occasion when the male chorus were required to raise their right hands. One of them, however, always managed to raise his left hand, bringing from Gilbert the chiding comment: 'My good fellow, if you don't know your right, ask the gentleman on your left.'

Undoubtedly there were bitterer exchanges with some of the artists who passed across the stage at the Savoy but there was built up a team which had immense loyalty towards Gilbert and Sullivan. That this was appreciated was made clear by Gilbert in an interview in the old *Pall Mall Gazette*: 'For twenty years I was in command of the Savoy stage and in all that time I never had a material difference with one of them. They were always most anxious to carry out my ideas in every way.'

Rehearsals were distinctly private affairs, though in the case of the penultimate opera, *Utopia, Limited*, Gilbert did agree that the dress rehearsal should be public so that the critics might have a better opportunity of assessing the work.

Réné, Louie Spanning twenty-one years with the D'Oyly Carte Company, Louie Réné played Lady Sophy (U) in her first season, 1894, and went on to play every leading contralto role with the exception of Dame Hannah (R). She left the company in 1915.

Residences Gilbert was born at No. 17 Southampton Street, Strand, London. From 1873 until 1882 he lived at No. 24 The

Bolton's, Kensington, and from then until 1890 at No. 39 Harrington Gardens, South Kensington, though he also had a place at Uxbridge. His last home was at Grim's Dyke (originally called Graeme's Dyke), a spacious mansion at Harrow Weald designed in Tudor style by Norman Shaw, with beautiful lawns, gardens and a lake—the lake in which he was drowned in 1911.

Sullivan was born at No. 8 Bolwell Terrace, Lambeth. He spent a great deal of time on the Continent but his main centre was his flat, No. 1 Queen's Mansions, 58 Victoria Street, London. It was there that he died in 1900, after having been working for some time at a house he had taken at Wokingham, Bedfordshire.

Respectability 'I don't think much of our profession but, contrasted with respectability, it is comparatively honest.'—Pirate King (PP).

Rhyming It would seem that Gilbert was rarely at a loss for a rhyme, however outrageous his solution might prove to be. A few examples:

> We shall quickly be parsonified,
> Conjugally matrimonified.
>> (PP)

> In short, when I've a smattering of elemental strategy,
> You'll say a better Major-General has never *sat* a gee.
>> Major-General Stanley (PP)

> Gentle, simple-minded Usher,
> Get you, if you like, to Russ*her*.
>> Learned Judge (J)

> Though if proper excuse you can trump any,
> You may wind up a Limited Company.
>> King Paramount (U)

> Two tender babes I nussed;
> One was of low condition,
> The other, upper crust,
> A regular patrician.
>> Little Buttercup (HMS)

> We're smart and sober men,
> And quite devoid of fe-ar.
> In all the Royal N.
> None are so smart as we are.
>> Chorus of sailors (HMS)

In that case unprecedented,
Single I must live and die—
I shall have to be contented
With a tulip or li*ly*!
Reginald Bunthorne (P)

The consequence was he was lost tot*ally*
And married a girl in the *corps de bally*!
Archibald Grosvenor (P)

I'm sorry to be of your pleasure a diminutioner . . .
so *you* shun her!

Pooh-Bah (M)

Jack Point (Y) offers a generous range: 'We can rhyme you
couplet, triolet, quatrain, sonnet, rondolet, ballade, what you will.'

Rialto 'Scramble money on the Rialto among the gondoliers.'—
Marco Palmieri (G). The Rialto Bridge is probably the most famous
in Europe and the district was once the commercial centre of Venice.

Richardson's Show Colonel Calverley throws in a reference
to this travelling show in his patter song (P). It is described by
Dickens in *Sketches by Boz*: 'This immense booth, with the large
stage in front, so brightly illuminated with variegated lamps, and
pots of burning fat, is "Richardson's", where you have a melodrama
(with three murders and a ghost), a pantomime, a comic song, an
overture, and some incidental music, all done in five-and-twenty
minutes.'

'Ring forth, ye Bells' Opening chorus of *The Sorcerer*.

Riordan, Joseph He joined the D'Oyly Carte chorus in 1956, was
with the company until 1963, his roles including Box (C), Defendant (J), Duke of Dunstable (P), Earl Tolloller (I), Richard Dauntless
(R), Leonard Meryll and Fairfax (Y).

'Rising early in the morning' Song by Giuseppe, with chorus,
about the daily 'chores' of Marco and himself as joint King (G).

Roberts, Helen First appearing with the D'Oyly Carte Company
under the name of Betty Roberts, Helen Roberts sang in her first
season in 1938 Josephine (HMS), Mabel (PP), Princess Ida, Elsie
Maynard (Y) and Gianetta (G). She later added Phyllis (I), Patience
and Yum-Yum (M). She married D'Oyly Carte baritone Richard

Walker and went with him to Australia. They spend much time in concert tours of Gilbert and Sullivan in America, where they are attached to the Gilbert and Sullivan Society in New York.

Roderick 'Swagger of Roderick, heading his clan.'—Colonel Calverley (P). It seems most likely that Gilbert had in mind the central figure in Sir Walter Scott's poem, *The Vision of Don Roderick*, founded on a Spanish legend and full of martial excitements. Southey also wrote a poem, *Roderick, the Last of the Goths*, with the same hero.

Rose, Jessie The original Bertha (D), Jessie Rose went on to play a great number of other roles—Plaintiff (J), Hebe (HMS), Edith (PP), Angela and Ella (P), Iolanthe and Leila (I), Psyche and Melissa (PI), Pitti-Sing and Peep-Bo (M), Phoebe (Y), Tessa and Gianetta (G).

Rosherville 'I spend the day at Rosherville!'—John Wellington Wells (S). Mr Wells is insisting that he is merely one of the *hoi polloi*. Rosherville Gardens, between Gravesend and Northfleet, were a place of popular resort for Londoners. Named after Jeremiah Rosher, they were opened to the public in 1837.

Rothschild 'The shares are a penny, and ever so many are taken by Rothschild and Baring.'—Lord Chancellor (I). The English house of the German banking family was founded by Nathan Meyer Rothschild (1777–1836).

Round, Thomas It was by decidedly unorthodox means that Thomas Round, principal tenor for several years, became a member of the D'Oyly Carte Company. Still in the RAF in 1945 and stationed near Basingstoke (of Gilbertian significance!) he spent a weekend's leave in London and saw that the company were playing at the King's Theatre, Hammersmith. Never having seen Gilbert and Sullivan opera on the stage, he went to a matinee of *The Mikado* and, thoroughly charmed by the first act, asked on the spur of the moment if he might see the D'Oyly Carte manager at the interval. 'I little dreamed that I had already set foot on the first rung of the ladder of my future career,' he recalls. 'I was confronted by a very big man with a shock of white hair and bristling white eyebrows— Hugh Jones. I told him that I was a tenor at present engaged in flying aeroplanes and would like an audition. He replied that the usual procedure was to write to the Savoy office but—perhaps, because of my uniform, he felt he couldn't turn me away—he asked me to see him after the performance. He had arranged for Mr Isidore Godfrey to hear me sing in one of the rehearsal rooms at the back of the theatre. Richard Walker was there to play the piano but, as I had no music with me, we spent the first few minutes trying to find a song we both knew. Eventually I sang "O Maiden, my Maiden" from *Frederica*.' In due course he was asked to go to the Savoy Theatre and sing for Rupert D'Oyly Carte, and was offered a contract to join the company on release from the RAF. Born at Barrow-in-Furness, Thomas Round was for a time a policeman in Lancaster before becoming a fighter pilot in the RAF. Stationed for a while in Texas, he took singing lessons and later studied in London with Joseph Hislop, Dino Borgioli and Roy Henderson. After his first period of three and a half years with D'Oyly Carte, he left to appear in a number of musical plays before spending five years as principal tenor with Sadler's Wells Opera, playing a wide variety of roles and scoring an outstanding success as Danilo in *The Merry Widow*. In 1953 he was chosen by Beecham for the Delius opera *Irmelin*, presented at Oxford. From 1958 he returned to the D'Oyly Carte Company for six years, singing Ralph Rackstraw (HMS), Frederic (PP), Nanki-Poo (M) and Marco (G). He sang Colonel Fairfax in the City of London Festival productions of the *Yeomen* at the Tower of London and is to-day a director and principal tenor of the Gilbert and Sullivan for All organisation. He appeared in the film, *The Story of Gilbert and Sullivan* (1953).

Royal Festival Hall For the first time in their career, the D'Oyly Carte Company gave a season at the Royal Festival Hall in July–August 1971. Because of fire regulations and the absence of a safety curtain, the usual scenery could not be employed but the conditions called forth much ingenuity in the way of basic settings and the use of lighting and back-projections. The works given were *Princess Ida*, *The Mikado*, *The Yeomen of the Guard* and *The Gondoliers* and the performances attracted audiences of about 2,500 a night.

Royal Gallery of Illustration Headquarters of the entertainments presented by Thomas German Reed, the Royal Gallery of Illustration, which was in the lower part of Regent Street, has its place in history as the scene of the first meeting of Gilbert and Sullivan. Both Gilbert and Sullivan had work presented by German Reed but never together.

'Royal Prince was by the King entrusted, The' Inez' recitative, in which she reveals that Luiz is the real King of Barataria (G).

Rubicon 'Having passed the Rubicon, take a pair of rosy lips.'—Marco Palmieri (G). Marco suggests that, having taken 'a pair of sparkling eyes,' you have reached the point of no return. The Rubicon was a stream forming the boundary between Italy and Cisalpine Gaul, Julius Caesar's own province. When he crossed it in 49 BC he invaded Italy and precipitated the Roman civil war.

RUDDIGORE; or The Witch's Curse First performed at the Savoy Theatre, London, on January 22, 1887, conducted by Sullivan. Initial run of 288 performances.

The original cast for the 'Supernatural Opera' was:

ROBIN OAKAPPLE (*a Young Farmer*)	Mr George Grossmith
RICHARD DAUNTLESS (*his Foster-Brother—a Man-o'-war's-man*)	Mr Durward Lely
SIR DESPARD MURGATROYD of Ruddigore (*a Wicked Baronet*)	Mr Rutland Barrington
OLD ADAM GOODHEART (*Robin's Faithful Servant*)	Mr Rudolph Lewis
ROSE MAYBUD (*a Village Maiden*)	Miss Leonora Braham
MAD MARGARET	Miss Jessie Bond
DAME HANNAH (*Rose's Aunt*)	Miss Rosina Brandram
ZORAH	Miss Josephine Findlay
RUTH	Miss Lindsay

Ghosts

SIR RUPERT MURGATROYD (*the First Baronet*)	Mr Price
SIR JASPER MURGATROYD (*the Third Baronet*)	Mr Charles
SIR LIONEL MURGATROYD (*the Sixth Baronet*)	Mr Trevor
SIR CONRAD MURGATROYD (*the Twelfth Baronet*)	Mr Burbank
SIR DESMOND MURGATROYD (*the Sixteenth Baronet*)	Mr Tuer
SIR GILBERT MURGATROYD (*the Eighteenth Baronet*)	Mr Wilbraham
SIR MERVYN MURGATROYD (*the Twentieth Baronet*)	Mr Cox
SIR RODERICK MURGATROYD (*the Twenty-First Baronet*)	Mr Richard Temple

Outside the cottage of Rose Maybud in the fishing village of Rederring, Cornwall, are gathered the professional bridesmaids. But they are feeling frustrated—and no wonder:

> Fair is Rose as bright May-day;
> Soft is Rose as warm west-wind;
> Sweet is Rose as new-mown hay—
> Rose is queen of maiden-kind!
> Rose, all glowing
> With virgin blushes, say—
> Is anybody going
> To marry you to-day?
>
> ZORAH:
> Every day, as the days roll on,
> Bridesmaids' garb we gaily don,
> Sure that a maid so fairly famed
> Can't long remain unclaimed.
> Hour by hour and day by day,
> Several months have passed away.
> Though she's the fairest flower that blows,
> No one has married Rose!

The girls bemoan the fact that, though Rederring is the only village in the world with a corps of professional bridesmaids, their services have not been required for six months. The ageing Dame Hannah appears and, in desperation, they suggest that *she* should marry. But she reveals that, many years ago, she was to have married a handsome youth who, she discovered on the day fixed for their wedding, was really Sir Roderic Murgatroyd, one of the bad Baronets of Ruddigore. She never saw him again and he died ten years ago. She recounts the legend of Sir Rupert Murgatroyd, the first Baronet:

> Sir Rupert Murgatroyd
> His leisure and his riches
> He ruthlessly employed
> In persecuting witches.
> With fear he'd make them quake—
> He'd duck them in his lake—
> He'd break their bones
> With sticks and stones,
> And burn them at the stake!

CHORUS:

This sport he much enjoyed,
Did Rupert Murgatroyd—
No sense of shame
Or pity came
To Rupert Murgatroyd!

DAME HANNAH:

Once, on the village green,
A palsied hag he roasted,
And what took place, I ween,
Shook his composure boasted;
For, as the torture grim
Seized on each withered limb,
The writhing dame
'Mid fire and flame
Yelled forth this curse on him:
'Each lord of Ruddigore,
Despite his best endeavour,
Shall do one crime, or more,
Once, every day, for ever!
This doom he can't defy,
However he may try,
For should he stay
His hand, that day
In torture he shall die!'

The prophecy came true:
Each heir who held the title
Had, every day, to do
Some crime of import vital;
Until, with guilt o'erplied,
'I'll sin no more!' he cried,
And on the day
He said that say,
In agony he died!

CHORUS:

And thus, with sinning cloyed,
Has died each Murgatroyd,
And so shall fall,
Both one and all,
Each coming Murgatroyd!

Rose comes out of the cottage and, asked by Dame Hannah why she does not marry, she explains that her life is governed by the little book of etiquette which she always carries:

If somebody there chanced to be
Who loved me in a manner true,
My heart would point him out to me,
And I would point him out to you.
But here it says of those who point,
Their manners must be out of joint—
You *may* not point—
You *must* not point—
It's manners out of joint, to point!
Had I the love of such as he,
Some quiet spot he'd take me to,
Then he could whisper it to me,
And I could whisper it to you.
But whispering, I've somewhere met,
Is contrary to etiquette:
Where can it be? (*Searching book*)
Now let me see—
Yes, yes!
It's contrary to etiquette!

If any well-bred youth I knew,
Polite and gentle, neat and trim,
Then I would hint as much to you,
And you could hint as much to him.
But here it says, in plainest print,
'It's most unladylike to hint'—
You *may* not hint—
You *must* not hint—
It says you mustn't hint, in print!
And if I loved him through and through—
(True love and not a passing whim),
Then I could speak of it to you,
And you could speak of it to him.
But here I find it doesn't do
To speak until your spoken to.
Where can it be? (*Searching book*).
Now let me see—
Yes, yes!
'Don't speak until you're spoken to!'

Left alone, Rose is about to go when young Robin Oakapple comes along. They shyly exchange politenesses about the weather and then each expresses the wish to consult the other concerning 'a friend':

ROBIN:
I know a youth who loves a little maid—
(Hey, but his face is a sight for to see!)
Silent is he, for he's modest and afraid—
(Hey, but he's timid as a youth can be!)

ROSE:
I know a maid who loves a gallant youth—
(Hey, but she sickens as the days go by!)
She cannot tell him all the sad, sad truth—
(Hey, but I think that little maid will die!)

ROBIN:
Poor little man!

ROSE:
Poor little maid!

BOTH:
Now tell me pray and tell me true,
What in the world should the maiden/young man do?

ROBIN:
He cannot eat and he cannot sleep—
(Hey, but his face is a sight for to see!)
Daily he goes for to wail—for to weep—
(Hey, but he's wretched as a youth can be!)

ROSE:
She's very thin and she's very pale—
(Hey, but she sickens as the days go by!)
Daily she goes for to weep—for to wail—
(Hey, but I think that little maid will die!)

ROBIN:
Poor little maid!

ROSE:
Poor little man!

BOTH:
Now tell me pray, and tell me true,
What in the world should that maiden/young
    man do?

ROSE:

If I were the youth I should offer her my name—
(Hey, but her face is a sight for to see!)

ROBIN:

If I were the maid I should fan his honest flame—
(Hey, but he's bashful as a youth can be!)

ROSE:

If I were the youth I should speak to her to-day—
(Hey, but she sickens as the days go by!)

ROBIN:

If I were this maid I should meet the lad half way—
(For I really do believe that timid youth will die!)

ROSE:

Poor little man!

ROBIN:

Poor little maid!

BOTH:

I thank you, miss/sir, for your counsel true;
I'll tell that youth/maid what he/she ought to do!

Rose leaves Robin sitting despondently. Old Adam Goodheart comes in and reveals a secret with his first words: 'My kind master is sad! Dear Sir Ruthven Murgatroyd—'. Says Robin: 'As you love me, breathe not that hated name. Twenty years ago, in horror at the prospect of inheriting that hideous title, and with it the ban that compels all who succeed to the baronetcy to commit at least one deadly crime per day, for life, I fled my home, and concealed myself in this innocent village under the name of Robin Oakapple. My younger brother, Despard, believing me to be dead, succeeded to the title and its attendant curse. For twenty years I have been dead and buried. Don't dig me up now.'

But Robin brightens at the news that his foster-brother Richard has arrived home from the sea. The bridesmaids welcome the returning sailor:

From the briny sea
Comes young Richard, all victorious!
Valorous is he—
His achievements all are glorious!
Let the welkin ring
With the news we bring—

Sing it—shout it—
Tell about it—
Safe and sound returneth he,
All victorious from the sea!

And the ebullient Richard Dauntless bounds on to the scene and gives an account of his adventures:

I shipped, d'ye see, in a Revenue sloop,
And, off Cape Finisterre,
A merchantman we see,
A Frenchman, going free,
So we made for the bold Mounseer,
D'ye see?
We made for the bold Mounseer.
But she proved to be a Frigate—and she up with her ports,
And fires with a thirty-two!
It come uncommon near,
But we answered with a cheer,
Which paralysed the Parley-voo,
D'ye see?
Which paralysed the Parley-voo!

Then our Captain he up and he says, says he,
'That chap we need not fear,—
We can take her, if we like,
She is sartin for to strike,
For she's only a darned Mounseer,
D'ye see?
She's only a darned Mounseer!
But to fight a French fal-lal—it's like hittin' of a gal—
It's a lubberly thing for to do;
For we, with all our faults,
Why, we're sturdy British salts,
While she's only a poor Parley-voo,
D'ye see?
While she's only a poor Parley-voo!'

So we up with our helm, and we scuds before the breeze
As we gives a compassionating cheer;
Froggee answers with a shout
As he sees us go about,
Which was grateful of the poor Mounseer,
D'ye see?
Which was grateful of the poor Mounseer!

And I'll wager in their joy they kissed each other's cheek
(Which is what them furriners do),
And they blessed their lucky stars
We were hardy British tars
Who had pity on a poor Parley-voo,
D'ye see?
Who had pity on a poor Parley-voo!

Richard executes a lively hornpipe and there are warm exchanges
between the two foster-brothers during which Robin confesses that
he loves Rose but is too shy to approach her. The self-assured
Richard agrees to plead his case for him, while Robin deplores his
own modest nature:

My boy, you may take it from me,
That of all the afflictions accurst
With which a man's saddled
And hampered and addled,
A diffident nature's the worst.
Though clever as clever can be—
A Crichton of early romance—
You must stir it and stump it,
And blow your own trumpet,
Or, trust me, you haven't a chance!
If you wish in the world to advance,
Your merits you're bound to enhance,
You must stir it and stump it,
And blow your own trumpet,
Or, trust me, you haven't a chance!

Now take, for example, *my* case:
I've a bright intellectual brain—
In all London city
There's no one so witty—
I've thought so again and again.
I've a highly intelligent face—
My features cannot be denied—
But, whatever I try, sir,
I fail in—and why, sir?
I'm modesty personified!

As a poet, I'm tender and quaint—
I've passion and fervour and grace—
From Ovid and Horace
To Swinburne and Morris,

They all of them take a back place.
Then I sing and I play and I paint:
Though none are accomplished as I,
To say so were treason:
You ask me the reason?
I'm diffident, modest, and shy!

Richard sets about his task with enthusiasm but, finding himself
attracted by Rose's charms, decides to follow his rule that his
conduct should be guided by his heart. Rose, after the correct
measure of hesitation prompted by her etiquette book, permits him
one kiss.

RICHARD:
The battle's roar is over,
O my love!
Embrace thy tender lover,
O my love!
From tempests welter,
From war's alarms,
O give me shelter
Within those arms!
Thy smile alluring,
All heart-ache curing,
Gives peace enduring,
O my love!

ROSE:
If heart both true and tender,
O my love!
A life-love can engender,
O my love!
A truce to sighing
And tears of brine,
For joy undying
Shall aye be mine,
And thou and I, love,
Shall live and die, love,
Without a sigh, love—
My own, my love!

Distressed though he is, Robin accepts his brother's dictum that
the heart must rule. They all express their points of view:

In sailing o'er life's ocean wide
Your heart should be your only guide;
With summer sea and favouring wind,
Yourself in port you'll surely find.

RICHARD:

My heart says, 'To this maiden strike—
She's captured you.
She's just the sort of girl you like—
You know you do.
If other man her heart should gain,
I shall resign.'
That's what it says to me quite plain,
This heart of mine.

ROBIN:

My heart says, 'You've a prosperous lot,
With acres wide;
You mean to settle all you've got
Upon your bride.'
It don't pretend to shape my acts
By word or sign;
It merely states these simple facts,
This heart of mine.

ROSE:

Ten minutes since my heart said 'white'—
It now says 'black.'
It then said 'left'—it now says 'right'—
Hearts often tack.
I must obey its latest strain—
You tell me so. (*To* RICHARD)
But should it change its mind again,
I'll let you know.

She turns from Richard to Robin, who embraces her, and they all
comment upon the dilemma:

In sailing o'er life's ocean wide
No doubt the heart should be your guide;
But it is awkward when you find
A heart that does not know its mind!

Robin and Rose go off together, and Richard departs, weeping.
There comes upon the scene the wild and tattered figure of Mad
Margaret:

Cheerily carols the lark
Over the cot.
Merrily whistles the clerk
Scratching a blot.
But the lark
And the Clerk,
I remark,
Comfort me not!

Over the ripening peach
Buzzes the bee.
Splash on the billowy beach
Tumbles the sea.
But the peach
And the beach
They are each
Nothing to me!

And why?
Who am I?
Daft Madge! Crazy Meg!
Mad Margaret! Poor Peg!
He! he! he!

Mad, I?
Yes, very!
But why?
Mystery!
Don't call!
Whisht! whisht!

No crime—
'Tis only
That I'm
Love—lonely!
That's all!

To a garden full of posies
Cometh one to gather flowers,
And he wanders through its bowers
Toying with the wanton roses,
Who, uprising from their beds,
Hold on high their shameless heads
With their pretty lips a-pouting,
Never doubting—never doubting
That for Cytherean posies
He would gather aught but roses!

In a nest of weeds and nettles
Lay a violet, half-hidden,
Hoping that his glance unbidden
Yet might fall upon her petals.
Though she lived alone, apart,
Hope lay nestling at her heart,
But, alas, the cruel awaking
Set her little heart a-breaking,
For he gathered for his posies
Only roses—only roses!

Poor Margaret is in tears when Rose encounters her. Rose is both
surprised and alarmed to hear that she is in love with the wicked
Sir Despard Murgatroyd and is determined to kill Rose for being
in love with him too! But Rose assures her that this is not the case
and they go off together on tiptoe. There arrives the chorus of
Bucks and Blades, who exchange compliments with the chorus of
bridesmaids, and then the sinister figure of Sir Despard Murgatroyd
strides in:

Oh, why am I moody and sad?
(CHORUS: Can't guess!)
And why am I guiltily mad?
(Confess!)
Because I am thoroughly bad!
(Oh yes.)
You'll see it at once in my face.
Oh, why am I husky and hoarse?
(Ah, why?)
It's the workings of conscience, of course.
(Fie, fie!)
And huskiness stands for remorse,
(Oh my!)
At least it does so in my case!
When in crime one is fully employed—
(Like you.)
Your expression gets warped and destroyed:
(It do.)
It's a penalty none can avoid;
(How true!)
I once was a nice-looking youth;
But like stone from a strong catapult—
(A trice—)

I rushed at my terrible cult—
(That's vice—)
Observe the unpleasant result!
(Not nice.)
Indeed I am telling the truth!
Oh, innocent, happy though poor!
(That's we—)
If I had been virtuous, I'm sure—
(Like me—)
I should be as nice-looking as you're!
(May be.)
You are very nice-looking indeed!
Oh, innocents, listen in time—
(We *doe*,)
Avoid an existence of crime—
(Just so—)
Or you'll be as ugly as I'm—
(No! No!)
And now, if you please, we'll proceed.

The girls flee from Sir Despard in horror and he proceeds to reveal to the audience that, though he is doomed to commit a crime every day, he makes a practice of getting it over early in the morning and spending the rest of the day in doing good. Meanwhile Richard Dauntless is not content to let Robin take Rose Maybud from him. He informs Sir Despard that, far from being dead, his elder brother Sir Ruthven is very much alive and is masquerading as Robin Oakapple. This means that Sir Despard can be free to lead a blameless life:·

RICHARD:
You understand?

SIR DESPARD:
I think I do;
With vigour unshaken
This step shall be taken.
It's neatly planned.

RICHARD:
I think so too;
I'll readily bet it
You'll never regret it!

BOTH:

For duty, duty must be done;
The rule applies to every one,
And painful though that duty be,
To shirk the task were fiddle-de-dee!

DESPARD:

The bridegroom comes—

RICHARD:

Likewise the bride—
The maidens are very
Elated and merry;
They are her chums.

DESPARD:

To lash their pride
Were almost a pity,
The pretty committee!

BOTH:

But duty, duty must be done;
The rule applies to every one,
And painful though that duty be,
To shirk the task were fiddle-de-dee!

Blissfully unaware of what is being planned, Rose and Robin are
greeted by the chorus as bride and bridegroom and there follows a
happy madrigal with much 'Fal lal la':

When the buds are blossoming,
Smiling welcome to the spring,
Lovers choose a wedding day—
Life is love in merry May!

Leaves in autumn fade and fall,
Winter is the end of all.
Spring and summer teem with glee:
Spring and summer, then, for me!

In the spring-time seed is sown:
In the summer grass is mown:
In the autumn you may reap:
Winter is the time for sleep.

Spring and summer pleasure you,
Autumn, aye, and winter too—
Every season has its cheer,
Life is lovely all the year!

The gaiety continues with a gavotte—until Sir Despard bursts in and declares that Robin is really Sir Ruthven Murgatroyd. Rose declares that she cannot now be Robin's and says she is prepared to marry Sir Despard. But he, on his part, points out that he is now a virtuous person and has vowed to marry Margaret. The act closes with two happy pairings-off—and misery for Robin:

ROSE and RICHARD:
Oh, happy the lily
When kissed by the bee;
And, sipping tranquilly,
Quite happy is he;
And happy the filly
That neighs in her pride;
But happier than any,
A pound to a penny,
A lover is, when he
Embraces his bride!

SIR DESPARD and MARGARET:
Oh, happy the flowers
That blossom in June,
And happy the bowers
That gain by the boon,
But happier by hours
The man of descent,
Who, folly regretting,
Is bent on forgetting
His bad baronetting,
And means to repent!

HANNAH, ADAM and ZORAH:
Oh, happy the blossom
That blooms on the lea,
Likewise the opossum
That sits on a tree,
When you come across 'em,
They cannot compare
With those who are treading
The dance at a wedding,
While people are spreading
The best of good fare!

ROBIN:

Oh, wretched the debtor
Who's signing a deed!
And wretched the letter
That no one can read!
But very much better
Their lot it must be
Than that of the person
I'm making this verse on,
Whose head there's a curse on—
Alluding to me!

Robin collapses as the curtain falls.

On the walls of the Picture Gallery are full-length portraits of the
Baronets of Ruddigore from the time of James I onwards. As the
curtain rises on the second act Robin and Old Adam enter. Their
appearances are transformed and they move melodramatically—
Robin a guilty-looking roué and Adam his wicked henchman:

ROBIN:

I once was as meek as a new-born lamb,
I'm now Sir Murgatroyd—ha! ha!
With greater precision
(Without the elision),
Sir Ruthven Murgatroyd—ha! ha!

ADAM:

And I, who was once his *valley-de-sham,*
As steward I'm now employed—ha! ha!
The dickens may take him—
I'll never forsake him!
As steward I'm now employed—ha! ha!

BOTH:

How dreadful when an innocent heart
Becomes, perforce, a bad young Bart,
And still more hard on Old A*dam,*
His former faithful *valley-de-sham!*

They move into the background and Richard Dauntless and Rose
Maybud enter, preceded by the chorus of bridesmaids.

RICHARD:

Happily coupled are we,
You see—
I am a jolly Jack Tar,
My star,

And you are the fairest,
The richest and rarest
Of innocent lasses you are,
By far—
Of innocent lasses you are!
Fanned by a favouring gale,
You'll sail
Over life's treacherous sea
With me,
And as for bad weather,
We'll brave it together,
And you shall creep under my lee,
My wee!
And you shall creep under my lee!

For you are such a smart little craft—
Such a neat little, sweet little craft,
Such a bright little, tight little,
Slight little, light little,
Trim little, prim little craft!

ROSE:
My hopes will be blighted, I fear,
My dear;
In a month you'll be going to sea,
Quite free,
And all of my wishes
You'll throw to the fishes
As though they were never to be;
Poor me!
As though they were never to be.
And I shall be left all alone
To moan,
And weep at your cruel deceit,
Complete;
While you'll be asserting
Your freedom by flirting
With every woman you meet!

Though I am such a smart little craft—
Such a neat little, sweet little craft,
Such a bright little, tight little,
Slight little, light little,
Trim little, prim little craft!

The couple have come to the castle to ask Robin's consent, as lord of the manor, to their marriage. He threatens imprisonment but Richard produces a Union Jack and they all kneel. 'Foiled—and by a Union Jack!' mutters Robin, in heavy melodramatic style. Rose pleads with him:

> In bygone days I had thy love—
> Thou hadst my heart.
> But Fate, all human vows above,
> Our lives did part!
> By the old love thou hadst for me—
> By the fond heart that beat for thee—
> By joys that never now can be,
> Grant thou my prayer!

Robin yields and they go off joyously, leaving him to brood upon the curse that condemns him to commit a crime every day. He begs his ancestors to have mercy on him—and the portraits suddenly come to life:

> Painted emblems of a race,
> All accurst in days of yore,
> Each from his accustomed place
> Steps into the world once more!

They step from their frames and march round the Gallery:

> Baronet of Ruddigore,
> Last of our accursèd line,
> Down upon the oaken floor—
> Down upon those knees of thine.
> Coward, poltroon, shaker, squeamer,
> Blockhead, sluggard, dullard, dreamer,
> Shirker, shuffler, wailer, weeper,
> Earthworm, maggot, tadpole, weevil!
> Set upon thy course of evil,
> Lest the King of Spectre-Land
> Set on thee his grisly hand!

Sir Roderic Murgatroyd, the most recently deceased, is the spokesman for all of them:

> SIR RODERIC:
> When the night wind howls in the chimney cowls, and
>   the bat in the moonlight flies,
> And inky clouds, like funeral shrouds, sail over the
>   midnight skies—
> When the footpads quail at the night-bird's wail, and black
>   dogs bay at the moon,

Then is the spectres' holiday—then is the ghosts' high-noon!

CHORUS:
Ha! Ha!
Then is the ghosts' high-noon!

SIR RODERIC:
As the sob of the breeze sweeps over the trees, and the
    mists lie low on the fen,
From grey tomb-stones are gathered the bones that once were
    women and men,
And away they go, with a mop and a mow, to the revel that
    ends too soon,
For cockcrow limits our holiday—the dead of the night's
    high-noon!

CHORUS:
Ha! ha!
The dead of the night's high-noon!

SIR RODERIC:
And then each ghost with his ladye-toast to their
    churchyard beds takes flight,
With a kiss, perhaps, on her lantern chaps, and a grisly
    grim 'good-night'!
Till the welcome knell of the midnight bell rings forth its
    jolliest tune,
And ushers in our next high holiday—the dead of the night's
    high-noon!

CHORUS:
Ha! ha!
The dead of the night's high-noon!

At Sir Roderic's command, Robin details his 'crimes' of the week.
But the list is unimpressive and the ghosts are far from satisfied. He
is ordered to commit the crime of carrying off a lady without delay.
The ancestors return to their frames, and Adam comes in and is
despatched to the village to seize a maiden. Robin launches into a
patter-song about the price of being a baronet:

> Away, Remorse!
> Compunction, hence!
> Go, Moral Force!
> Go, Penitence!
> To Virtue's plea
> A long farewell—

Propriety,
I ring your knell!
Come, Guiltiness of deadliest hue!
Come, desperate deeds of derring-do!

Henceforth all the crimes that I find in the *Times*,
I've promised to perpetrate daily;
To-morrow I start, with a petrified heart,
On a regular course of Old Bailey.
There's confidence tricking, bad coin, pocket-picking,
And several other disgraces—
There's postage-stamp prigging, and then, thimble-rigging,
The three-card delusion at races!
Oh! a baronet's rank is exceedingly nice,
But the title's uncommonly dear at the price!

Ye well-to-do squires who live in the shires,
Where petty distinctions are vital,
Who found Anthenæums and local museums,
With views to a baronet's title—
Ye butchers and bakers and candlestick-makers
Who sneer at all things that are tradey—
Whose middle-class lives are embarrassed by wives
Who long to parade as 'My Lady',
Oh! allow me to offer a word of advice,
The title's uncommonly dear at the price!

Ye supple MP's, who go down on your knees,
Your precious identity sinking,
And vote black or white as your leaders indite
(Which saves you the trouble of thinking),
For your country's good fame, her repute, or her shame,
You don't care the snuff of a candle—
But you're paid for your game when you're told that
     your name
Will be graced by a baronet's handle—
Oh! allow me to give *you* a word of advice—
The title's uncommonly dear at the price!

With Robin's departure, we are confronted by two other much-changed people—Despard, now freed from the witch's curse, and Margaret. They are dressed in sober black, he carrying an umbrella as the final mark of respectability, and together they present a perfect picture of solemn conformity:

DESPARD:
I once was a very abandoned person—

MARGARET:
Making the most of evil chances.

DESPARD:
Nobody could conceive a worse 'un—

MARGARET:
Even in all the old romances.

DESPARD
I blush for my wild extravagances,
But be so kind
To bear in mind,

MARGARET:
We were the victims of circumstances!
             (*Dance*)
That is one of our blameless dances.

MARGARET:
I was once an exceedingly odd young lady—

DESPARD:
Suffering much from spleen and vapours.

MARGARET:
Clergymen thought my conduct shady—

DESPARD:
She didn't spend much upon linen-drapers.

MARGARET:
It certainly entertained the gapers.
My ways were strange
Beyond all range—

DESPARD:
Paragraphs got into all the papers.
             (*Dance*)
We only cut respectable capers.

DESPARD:
I've given up all my wild proceedings.

MARGARET:
My taste for a wandering life is waning.

DESPARD:
Now I'm a dab at penny readings.

MARGARET:
They are not remarkably entertaining.

DESPARD:
A moderate livelihood we're gaining.

MARGARET:
In fact we rule
A National School.

DESPARD:
The duties are dull, but I'm not complaining.
(*Dance*)
This sort of thing takes a deal of training!

They have been married for a week. Margaret is still subject to occasional outbursts of hysteria but they have hit upon a word which, when uttered by Despard, immediately calms her, a word that 'teems with hidden meaning'—Basingstoke! On Robin's return Despard points out to him that, as Robin is the rightful baronet, his is the guilt for all the crimes committed in his name during the past ten years. Desperate, Robin decides to defy his ancestors, even if it means facing death:

ROBIN:
My eyes are fully open to my awful situation—
I shall go at once to Roderic and make him an oration.
I shall tell him I've recovered my forgotten moral senses,
And I don't care twopence-halfpenny for any consequences.
Now I do not want to perish by the sword or by the dagger,
But a martyr may indulge a little pardonable swagger,
And a word or two of compliment my vanity would flatter,
But I've got to die to-morrow, so it really doesn't matter!

DESPARD:
So it really doesn't matter—

MARGARET:
So it really doesn't matter—

ALL:
So it really doesn't matter, matter, matter, matter, matter!

MARGARET:
If I were not a little mad and generally silly
I should give you my advice upon the subject, willy-nilly;
I should show you in a moment how to grapple with the question,
And you'd really be astonished at the force of my suggestion.

On the subject I shall write you a most valuable letter,
Full of excellent suggestions, when I feel a little better,
But at present I'm afraid I am as mad as any hatter,
So I'll keep 'em to myself, for my opinion doesn't matter!

DESPARD:
Her opinion doesn't matter—

ROBIN:
Her opinion doesn't matter—

ALL:
My/Her opinion doesn't matter, matter, matter, matter, matter!

DESPARD:
If I had been so lucky as to have a steady brother
Who could talk to me as we are talking now to one another—
Who would give me good advice when he discovered I was erring
(Which is just the very favour which on you I am conferring),
My existence would have made a rather interesting idyll,
And I might have lived and died a very decent indiwiddle.
This particularly rapid, unintelligible patter
Isn't generally heard, and if it is it doesn't matter!

ROBIN:
If it is it doesn't matter—

MARGARET:
If it is it doesn't matter—

ALL:
If it is it doesn't matter, matter, matter, matter, matter!

At this moment Adam bursts in. He has carried out his master's daily crime by seizing a village maiden and, after a considerable tussle, has brought her along. Far from being a weak and wilting young maid, she is well capable of looking after herself. She is in fact Dame Hannah! She throws a small dagger to Robin and, seizing another from one of the armed figures, is about to do battle when Robin appeals to the portrait of Sir Roderic to save him. Sir Roderic steps from the frame and there is mutual recognition. 'Little Nannikin!' he exclaims. 'Roddy-doddy!' They were engaged to be married many years ago! Robin leaves them alone together.

HANNAH:
There grew a little flower
'Neath a great oak tree:
When the tempest 'gan to lower
Little heeded she:

No need had she to cower,
For she dreaded not its power—
She was happy in the bower
Of her great oak tree!
Sing hey,
Lackaday!
Let the tears fall free
For the pretty little flower and the great oak tree!

When she found that he was fickle,
Was that great oak tree,
She was in a pretty pickle,
As she well might be—
But his gallantries were mickle,
For Death followed with his sickle,
And her tears began to trickle
For her great oak tree!
Said she, 'He loved me never,
Did that great oak tree,
But I'm neither rich nor clever,
And so why should he?
But though fate our fortunes sever,
To be constant I'll endeavour,
Aye, for ever and for ever,
To my great oak tree!'

Meanwhile Robin has had an inspiration. With Rose and all the others he returns to point out to Sir Roderic that a baronet of Ruddigore can die only by refusing to commit his daily crime and that such a refusal is tantamount to suicide—which is in itself a crime. So that Sir Roderic should never have died at all! 'Then I'm practically alive!' he exclaims. Robin embraces Rose and there follows the lively finale:

ALL:
Oh, happy the lily
When kissed by the bee;
And, sipping tranquilly,
Quite happy is he;
And happy the filly
That neighs in her pride;
But happier than any,
A pound to a penny,
A lover is, when he
Embraces his bride!

Rudolph (D) *Baritone* Walter Passmore was the first artist to play Rudolph, Grand Duke of Pfennig-Halbpfennig.

Russell, Scott The original Lord Dramaleigh (U) and Dr Tannhäuser (D), Scott Russell was born at Malvern in 1868 and studied singing under Garcia at the Royal Academy of Music. He sang in America early in his career and made his first London appearance in the première of *Utopia, Limited* in 1893. He later sang many other roles in the operas—Leonard Meryll (Y), Cyril (PI), Mr Goldbury (U), Frederic (PP), Duke of Dunstable (P), Earl Tolloller (I), Nanki-Poo (M), Ralph Rackstraw (HMS), Fairfax (Y) and Marco (G).

Ruth (PP) *Contralto* In the London production, Emily Cross was the first to play Ruth, the pirate maid-of-work who, in her early days as a nursemaid, mistakenly apprenticed Frederic to a pirate instead of to a pilot.

Ruth (R) *Mezzo-soprano* Ruth, one of the professional bridesmaids, was first played by Miss Lindsay.

Ryley, Charles The first artist to play Florian (PI).

Sacharissa (PI) *Soprano* The role was first played by Sybil Grey.

Sacheverell, Doctor Colonel Calverley (P) refers to Henry Sacheverell (1674–1724), an English cleric who was impeached and tried in Westminster Hall for having preached an inflammatory sermon in St Paul's Cathedral. He was suspended from preaching for three years but later became rector of St Andrew's, Holborn.

Sadler's Wells Opera Immediately after the operas became free from copyright on January 1, 1962, Sadler's Wells Opera put on their own production of *Iolanthe* at Stratford-upon-Avon, bringing it to London later the same month. The cast included Patricia Kern (Iolanthe), Elizabeth Harwood (Phyllis), Heather Begg (Queen of the Fairies), Julian Moyle (Strephon), Eric Shilling (Lord Chancellor), Denis Dowling (Earl of Mountararat), Stanley Bevan (Earl Tolloller), Leon Greene (Private Willis), Elizabeth Robson (Celia), Cynthia Morey (Leila) and Marjorie Ward (Fleta). The producer, Frank Hauser, solved the problem of the fairies 'tripping lightly' by deliberately making them a somewhat ungainly lot, to the amusement of the audience. The designer was Desmond Heeley and the conductor Alexander Faris.

In the same year Sadler's Wells Opera presented *The Mikado* in a production by Douglas Craig with designs by Peter Rice. An outstanding success was scored by Clive Revill as Ko-Ko, whose performance was enormously funny, though it could not perhaps be called 'traditional'—at one moment he swung across the stage on a rope! The cast included John Holmes (Mikado), John Wakefield (Nanki-Poo), Denis Dowling (Pooh-Bah), John Heddle Nash (Pish-Tush), Marion Studholme (Yum-Yum), Patricia Kern (Pitti-Sing), Dorothy Nash (Peep-Bo) and Jean Allister (Katisha). Alexander Faris conducted.

373

At the London Coliseum in 1969 Sadler's Wells Opera presented *Patience*, conducted by Kenneth Montgomery and produced by John Cox, with designs by John Stoddart. The principal artists were Derek Hammond Stroud (Reginald Bunthorne), Emile Belcourt (Archibald Grosvenor), Eric Shilling (Colonel Calverley), Alan Charles (Major Murgatroyd), John Delaney (Duke of Dunstable), Shirley Chapman (Lady Angela), Pamela Fasso (Lady Saphir), Dorothy Nash (Lady Ella), Heather Begg (Lady Jane) and Wendy Baldwin (Patience).

Salata (U) *Soprano* Edith Johnston was the first artist to play the Utopian maiden.

Salesmanship Apart from his highly coloured patter-song, John Wellington Wells (S) has a strong line in sales talk for his great variety of wares: 'We've a choice assortment of wishing-caps, divining-rods, amulets, charms and counter-charms. We can cast you a divinity at a low figure, and we have a horoscope at three-and-six that we can guarantee. Our Abudah chests, each containing a patent Hag who comes out and prophesies disasters, with spring complete, are strongly recommended. Our Aladdin lamps are very chaste, and our Prophetic Tablets, foretelling everything—from a change of Ministry down to a rise in Unified—are much enquired for. Our penny Curse—one of the cheapest things in the trade—is considered infallible. We have some very superior Blessings, too, but they're very little asked for. We've only sold one since Christmas—to a gentleman who bought it to send to his mother-in-law—but it turned out that he was afflicted in the head, and it's been returned on our hands. But our sale of penny Curses, especially on Saturday nights, is tremendous. We can't turn 'em out fast enough.'

Sally Lunn 'Now for the gay Sally Lunn!' (S). A Sally Lunn is a teacake, called after a pastrycook who used to sell her wares in the streets of Bath in the late 1700's.

Samuel (PP) *Baritone* The Pirate King's lieutenant, first played in the London production by George Temple.

Sandford, Kenneth Though he has sung the Sergeant of Police (PP) in the past, Kenneth Sandford's roles with the D'Oyly Carte Company to-day—he joined in 1957—include Dr Daly (S), Grosvenor (P), Private Willis (I), King Hildebrand (PI), Pooh-Bah (M), Sir Despard Murgatroyd (R), Wilfred Shadbolt (Y) and Don

Alhambra (G). He originally set out to make painting his career. Born at Godalming, Surrey, but brought up in Sheffield, he studied at the College of Arts and Crafts there and won a scholarship to the Royal College of Art in London. After the interruption of the war, he took up his scholarship and, though he became an Associate of the Royal College of Art, he did not quite feel his former urge for painting. But he had been taking singing lessons and was attracted by the 'colour' of the theatre. Before joining the D'Oyly Carte Company, he had decidedly varied experience, in *Carousel*, *King's Rhapsody*, *Paint Your Wagon*, 800 performances as principal singer with the Crazy Gang, and in *Kismet*, as well as on the concert platform. 'I had six months at the Opera School and then somebody recommended me to Miss Bridget D'Oyly Carte,' he recalls. 'To my amazement I was selected and began singing principal roles with the company—straight in at the deep end!' In the City of London Festival production of the *Yeomen* at the Tower of London in 1962 Kenneth Sandford sang the role of Wilfred Shadbolt.

Sangazure, Lady (S) *Contralto* As her name indicates there is no doubt about the blue blood of Lady Sangazure. Even Sir Marmaduke Pointdextre is well satisfied about her lineage. Lady Sangazure, first in the line of Gilbert's ageing females, was originally played by Mrs Howard Paul.

Sansom, Mary Joining D'Oyly Carte in 1956, Mary Sansom sang Celia (I), Zorah (R), and Fiametta (G) in her first year with the company, adding soon afterwards Lady Ella (P), Phyllis (I), Yum-Yum (M) and Rose Maybud (R). Her later roles included Josephine (HMS), Mabel (PP), Lady Psyche (PI), Elsia Maynard (Y) and Casilda (G). She left the company in 1964.

Saphir, The Lady (P) *Mezzo-soprano* This 'rapturous maiden' was originally played by Julia Gwynne.

Sargent, Sir (Harold) Malcolm (Watts) Few people knew the scores of the operas more intimately. He never tired of them and to the end of his days he used to say, 'When I conduct Gilbert and Sullivan I feel forty years younger.' His acquaintance with them began at a very early age. In Stamford, Lincolnshire, where he spent his boyhood and youth, he studied the piano with Mrs Frances Tinkler and almost as early as he could remember he used to play and sing tunes from the operas. He used to act as programme boy in amateur productions in Stamford and at the age of thirteen walked on as Go-To, sword bearer to Ko-Ko. Only a year later he conducted for the first time in his life, stepping in on the instructions of Mrs Tinkler to conduct the local society in a rehearsal of *The Yeomen of the Guard* when the regular conductor was unable to get over to Stamford. Immediately after World War I, he founded and became musical director of the amateur operatic society at Melton Mowbray and also conductor of the revived Stamford society, specialising in Gilbert and Sullivan.

Sargent's association with the D'Oyly Carte Company began when Rupert D'Oyly Carte chose him to succeed Geoffrey Toye as principal conductor for the 1926 season at the Princes Theatre, Shaftesbury Avenue, and it was during *The Mikado* in this season that the BBC first broadcast excerpts from a D'Oyly Carte performance direct from the theatre. Sargent exercised considerable influence on the presentation of the operas. As Charles Reid has pointed out in his exhaustive biography, *Malcolm Sargent*, he was attacked by some of the critics for 'tampering' with the scores and by members of the company, notably Henry Lytton, Bertha Lewis and stage-director J. M. Gordon, for what they regarded as his unduly brisk speeds for some of the numbers. Sargent replied to his critics by pointing out that his performances were modelled on a study of Sullivan's original manuscripts and, with D'Oyly Carte's support, he won his way against criticism within the company. Through the years he made a number of complete recordings of the operas and also with great gusto conducted Saturday evenings of excerpts in several seasons of Promenade Concerts at the Royal Albert Hall. When conducting the operas, Sargent preferred an orchestra of 37 players—the same number as Sullivan used—though he sometimes added a few more when recording. He last conducted the D'Oyly Carte Company at the Savoy Theatre in the 1962–3 season. He died on October 3, 1967, at the age of seventy-two.

Savoy Hotel Six reception rooms in the Savoy Hotel are named after the operas: *Pinafore, Patience, Iolanthe, Princess Ida, Mikado* and *Gondoliers*. The hotel, adjoining the Savoy Theatre, was opened on August 6, 1889, and later extended. The offices of the D'Oyly Carte Opera Company are within the hotel building.

Savoy Theatre See under 'Theatres.'

Scaphio (U) *Baritone* One of the judges of the Utopian Supreme Court, Scaphio was first played by W. H. Denny.

Scots 'This comes of engaging a detective with a keen sense of the ridiculous! For the future I'll employ none but Scotchmen.'— Rudolph (D).

Scottish Opera In December 1968, Scottish Opera presented at the King's Theatre, Edinburgh, the first professional production of *The Gondoliers*, other than by the D'Oyly Carte Company, since the copyright expired. The cast was a strong one, including John Wakefield (Marco), Ronald Morrison (Giuseppe), Janet Coster (Tessa), Anne Pashley (Gianetta), Ian Wallace (Duke of Plaza-Toro), Johanna Peters (Duchess), Jill Gomez (Casilda), John Robertson (Luiz) and William McCue (Don Alhambra). Joan Cross's straightforwardly effective production presented the work for what it is, first-class operetta and neither musical comedy on the one hand nor oratorio on the other. The designer was Jack Notman and James Loughran conducted the BBC Scottish Symphony Orchestra and Scottish Opera Chorus. Ian Wallace's Duke of Plaza-Toro was dryly amusing without pushing for laughs and, as an encore to his duet with the Duchess on the advantages of a title, he added a topical verse written by himself. It seemed to the present writer to be legitimately in character and the sort of thing that Gilbert himself might well have included to-day. It is reproduced with Mr Wallace's permission:

> I am perfectly willing
> To earn the odd shilling
> As guide to the ducal apartments.
> There are guard-dogs to baffle
> All those who would snaffle
> A cannonball from the escarpments.
> I give cheques to pools winners
> Turn Saints into Sinners—
> It substantially adds to my budget.
> My fee for promotion
> Of after-shave lotion
> Is huge and they really don't grudge it.

When the Queen, the Duke of Edinburgh and Princess Anne attended one of the performances, Ian Wallace had prepared special verses for the occasion:

> DUKE:
> We're all of a flutter—
> Our knees turn to butter

When we're entertaining the Monarch.
We must organise banquets,
Air monogrammed blankets,
And polish the spare room with Ronuk.
I've read books on polo
And how to fly solo:
I pore over each publication—
Large tomes on race horses
And show-jumping courses,
So I can make bright conversation.

DUCHESS:
I'm thrilled to the marrow—
Pick flowers by the barrow.
As hostess I'll never be beaten.
My husband's a spartan—
He'll be kilted in tartan—
His school was at Moray, not Eton.

DUKE:
I couldn't make Eton.

DUCHESS:
We're very embarrassed—
We're visibly harassed—
We can't drive them out to the city.

DUKE:
Why not to the city?

DUCHESS:
Another great failing—
We can't offer sailing.
There's just not enough in the kitty.

DUKE:
Damn all in the kitty!
We'll stand close together
And pray for fine weather
When they disembark from Britannia.

DUCHESS:
The staff up at Toro
At most numbers fouro—
Their motto is firmly mañana.

DUKE:
It's always mañana.

BOTH:
> But if simple pleasure
> Enriches their leisure,
> A fiesta we'll get off our chesta.
> And what could be smarter—
> We'll be called to the Palace—
> The Duke and his Alice—
> And festooned with a Bath or a Garter,
> A Bath or a Garter.

Scynthius (PI) *Bass-baritone* Scynthius, one of King Gama's three sons, was first played by William Lugg.

'Search throughout the panorama' Opening chorus of the opera (PI).

'See how the fates their gifts allot' Glee for Pitti-Sing, Katisha, Ko-Ko, Pooh-Bah and the Mikado about the injustice of Fate (M).

Selvagee 'I can hand, reef and steer, and ship a selvagee.'—Captain Corcoran (HMS). In nautical language a selvagee is a coil formed by winding rope yarn.

Sergeant of Police (PP) *Bass* In the London production, Rutland Barrington was the first artist to play the Sergeant of Police, whose 'lot is not a happy one'.

Sessions, Anne Born in Birmingham, where she appeared in musical comedy and light opera for various amateur companies, Anne Sessions sings the Plaintiff (J), Lady Psyche (PI) and Fiametta (G) with the D'Oyly Carte Company, which she joined in 1956. After seven years, she left with her husband, tenor Ralph Mason, to go into the cast of *My Fair Lady* at Drury Lane, where she understudied the role of Eliza Doolittle. She later rejoined D'Oyly Carte, remaining until August 1969, when she left to start a family.

Seven Dials 'As in the lowly air of Seven Dials.' (I). The one-time rowdy district, where seven narrow streets meet near Shaftesbury Avenue in the centre of London, was the subject of one of Dickens's *Sketches by Boz*.

Sewell and Cross 'A Sewell and Cross young man.'—Archibald Grosvenor (P). A well-known firm of London drapers.

Shadbolt, Wilfred (Y) *Bass-baritone* W. H. Denny was the first artist to play the lugubrious Head Jailor and Assistant Tormentor of the Tower of London. The reverse of the clown who wants to play Hamlet, Shadbolt hankers after emulating Jack Point as a jester: 'I have a pretty wit—a light, airy, joysome wit, spiced with anecdotes of prison cells and the torture chamber. Oh, a very delicate wit! I have tried it on many a prisoner and there have been some who smiled. Now it is not easy to make a prisoner smile, and it should not be difficult to be a good jester, seeing that thou art one.' Rather surprisingly Henry A. Lytton at one time played Shadbolt but, being small in stature, he changed the characterisation, making him a cringing Uriah Heep type. It is, however, the custom for the part to be played as a middle-aged or older man by the artist who plays Pooh-Bah, a custom which is reasonably challenged by Audrey Williamson in *Gilbert and Sullivan Opera* who points out that not only would a younger portrayal make Wilfred a more credible suitor for Phoebe but also that he is only an *Assistant* Tormentor after all.

Shaw, Captain It is not recorded whether Captain Eyre Massey Shaw felt embarrassed when Alice Barnett as the Fairy Queen sang 'Oh, Captain Shaw!' on the first night of *Iolanthe*, but certainly he was sitting in the audience. He was chief of London Fire Brigade and, having remodelled the whole service, was knighted on his retirement. The Thames fire-float 'Massey Shaw', which took part in the Dunkirk evacuation, was named after him.

Sheffield, Leo Distinguished player of the 'Pooh-Bah roles' for many years, Leo Sheffield was born at Malton, Yorkshire, in 1873 and made his first stage appearance as Second Yeoman at the Savoy Theatre in 1906. His first principal role was Luiz (G) in 1907, adding Private Willis (I), Samuel (PP), Cholmondeley and Sergeant Meryll (Y) in the next two years. He appeared in a great number of other shows but was back with D'Oyly Carte for the 1919–20 Princes Theatre season as the Judge (T), Dr Daly (S), Captain Corcoran (HMS), Sergeant of Police (PP), Archibald Grosvenor (P), Private Willis (I), King Hildebrand (PI), Pooh-Bah (M), Wilfred Shadbolt (Y) and Don Alhambra (G). After many performances in London and on tour, he temporarily left D'Oyly Carte in 1928 in order to appear in other productions but was back at the Savoy for the 1929–30 season. He had one unusual and somewhat disturbing experience in a provincial theatre. During the performance he had made a few whispered comments to one of the other artists; at the end a group of girls came round from the audience and told him exactly what he had said. It turned out that they were workers in the cotton mills and, because of the noise, had learned to lip-read! For a time towards the end of World War II Leo Sheffield was with the BBC Drama Repertory Company. He died in 1951.

Shirley, W. R. The original Leonard Meryll (Y), he also sang other roles on tour, including Nanki-Poo (M), Fairfax (Y) and Marco (G).

'Sighing softly to the river' Major-General Stanley's ballad (PP).

Sillery 'Pops of Sillery our light artillery.'—Hilarion (PI). The reference is to the popping of champagne corks, Sillery being one of the champagne districts of France.

Sillimon (T) Stage manager to a travelling theatrical company, played by J. G. Taylor, who later took over the part of the Judge in *Trial by Jury*.

'Silvered is the raven hair' Lady Jane's song, at the opening of the second act, about a women's fading charms (P). Gilbert never wrote anything in worse taste than this unpleasant lyric. But it is interesting to note that Sullivan's tune, with a different lyric, was published as a separate ballad and became very popular.

Simmery Axe John Wellington Wells' pronunciation of St Mary Axe, the address of his firm of family sorcerers in the City of London (S).

Singers The Mikado has a fitting punishment for 'the amateur tenor whose vocal villainies all desire to shirk' and Gilbert himself seems to have viewed singers with a good deal of suspicion, especially tenors: 'They never can act and they are more trouble than all the other members of the company put together.' Sopranos, too. When it was suggested that Gilbert should write a libretto for a Sullivan 'grand' opera, he wrote to Sullivan: 'Where in God's name is your grand opera soprano who can act to be found?' Singers, he felt, tended to get in the way of his words. Durward Lely, the original Nanki-Poo, is quoted by Leslie Baily (*The Gilbert and Sullivan Book*) as recalling Gilbert saying to him at a rehearsal:

'Very good, Lely, very good indeed. But I have just come down from the back seat in the gallery and there were two or three words which failed to reach me quite distinctly. Sullivan's music, is of course, very beautiful, and I heard every note without difficulty, but I think my words are not altogether without merit and ought also to be heard without undue effort. Please pay particular attention to the consonants, the M's, the N's and especially the S's.'

One cannot help feeling that, if he were alive now, Gilbert would be vastly interested in the situation to-day, when producers from the straight theatre, full of exciting ideas, tend to forget that an opera singer likes to get a glimpse of the conductor at critical moments and when the leading singing roles in musicals are as often as not taken by actors who can't sing.

Sullivan, too, had his own particular difficulties with Gilbert's actor-singers. 'Bravo,' he said to one of them. 'That is really a very good air of yours. Now, if you have no objection, I will ask you to sing mine.' And to another he suggested that it might be a good idea if the artist would let him have his (the artist's) tune before he started composing the piece.

Of the early days when *Thespis* was written, Sullivan recalled some years later: 'In those days there were comparatively few actors and actresses who could sing and, of those who pretended to, hardly any could be said to compass more than six notes. Naturally I found myself rather restricted as a composer in having to write vocal music for people without voices! Notwithstanding all this, *Thespis* was fairly successful and ran a good many nights.' Many an amateur—and professional, too—will be quick to point out, however, that a good deal of the music that Sullivan later wrote is not by any means easy to sing.

'Sir Joseph's barge is seen' Chorus of sailors welcoming the arrival of Sir Joseph Porter aboard the *Pinafore* (HMS).

'Sir Rupert Murgatroyd his leisure and his riches' Dame Hannah relates the story of the Witch's Curse (R).

Sizars and Servitors 'You'll find no sizars here, or servitors.'—Princess Ida. Sizars (Cambridge or Dublin) and servitors (Oxford) were undergraduates partly supported from college funds and expected to assist by waiting at table.

Skitch, Jeffrey A principal artist with D'Oyly Carte for thirteen years, he sang Luiz (G) in his first season, 1952, moving on to

Grosvenor (P), Strephon (I), Pish-Tush (M), Giuseppe (G), Captain Corcoran and Samuel (HMS). His later roles included Florian (PI) and Learned Judge (J). He was with the company until 1965.

Slave of Duty, the   Alternative title of *The Pirates of Penzance*.

Slyboots   'The slyboots, how she wheedled him!'—Sergeant Meryll on Phoebe's handling of Wilfred, the jailer. (Y). The term, meaning someone who appears to be dull but is in fact very much alive, occurs in a work of 1729, *Adventures of Abdalla*: 'The frog called the lazy one several times, but in vain; there was no such thing as stirring him, though the sly-boots heard well enough all the while.'

'Small titles and orders'   Duet for the Duke and Duchess of Plaza-Toro (G).

Snickersnee   'I drew my snickersnee!'—Ko-Ko (M). Snickersnee, meaning a long knife, is not Japanese in origin but Scandinavian.

'Society has quite forsaken all her wicked courses'   King Paramount's song, with chorus (U).

Sodor and Man   'Style of the Bishop of Sodor and Man.'—Colonel Calverley (P). Created in the 11th century, the diocese of Sodor and Man originally embraced the Isle of Man, the Hebrides and other islands west of Scotland. Since the 14th century it has consisted only of the Isle of Man.

'So go to him and say to him, with compliment ironical'   Duet for Bunthorne and Lady Jane (P).

Somerset House   'A Somerset House young man.'—Archibald Grosvenor (P). Somerset House, in the Strand near the end of Waterloo Bridge, was built in the late 18th century on the site of the palace of Edward Seymour, Duke of Somerset, known as the Protector Somerset.

'Some seven men form an Association'   Mr Goldbury's song on the subtleties of company promotion (U).

'Some years ago no doubt you know'   King Hildebrand's song (PI).

'Song of birds in ivied towers, The' Phylla's solo at the opening of the opera (U).

'Soon as we may, off and away!' Phyllis introduces the finale to the opera (I).

Sophy, Lady (U) *Contralto* Rosina Brandram was the first artist to play the English governess to King Paramount's daughters.

'So please you, sir, we much regret' Quartet for Yum-Yum, Peep-Bo, Pitti-Sing and Pooh-Bah (M).

Sopranos Principal soprano roles in the operas are: Plaintiff (J); Aline and Constance (S); Josephine (HMS); Mabel and Edith (PP); Patience and Lady Ella (P); Phyllis and Celia (I); Princess Ida, Lady Psyche and Sacharissa (PI); Yum-Yum and Peep-Bo (M); Rose Maybud and Zorah (R); Elsie Maynard and Kate (Y); Casilda, Gianetta, Fiametta and Giulia (G); Princess Zara, Princess Nekaya, Princess Kalyba and Phylla (U); Princess of Monte Carlo, Julia Jellicoe, Lisa and Olga (D).

SORCERER, THE First performed at the Opéra Comique, London, on November 17, 1877, conducted by Sullivan. Initial run of 178 performances.

The cast for the 'entirely New and Original Modern Comic Opera' in its first performance at the Opéra Comique was:

LADY SANGAZURE	Mrs Howard Paul
ALINE (*her Daughter*)	Miss Alice May
CONSTANCE (*a Pupil Teacher*)	Miss Giulia Warwick
MRS PARTLET (*a Pew Opener*)	Miss Helen Everard
SIR MARMADUKE POINTDEXTRE	Mr Richard Temple
ALEXIS (*his Son*)	Mr George Bentham
DOCTOR DALY (*Vicar of Ploverleigh*)	Mr Rutland Barrington
NOTARY	Mr Fred Clifton
MR WELLS (*of the firm of J. W. Wells &* *Co., Family Sorcerers*)	Mr George Grossmith, Jnr

It is a lively scene outside the mansion of Sir Marmaduke Pointdextre. Sir Marmaduke's son Alexis, an officer in the Grenadier Guards, is to be officially betrothed to Lady Sangazure's daughter Aline and the villagers catch the spirit of the occasion:

Ring forth, ye bells,
With clarion sound—
Forget your knells,
For joys abound.
Forget your notes
Of mournful lay,
And from your throats
Pour joy to-day.

But not everyone is happy, as we learn when Mrs Partlet enters with her daughter Constance:

When he is here,
I sigh with pleasure—
When he is gone,
I sigh with grief.
My hopeless fear
No soul can measure—
His love alone
Can give my aching heart relief!
When he is cold,
I weep for sorrow—
When he is kind,
I weep for joy.
My grief untold
Knows no to-morrow—
My woe can find
No hope, no solace, no alloy!

To her mother's considerable surprise, Constance confesses that the man for whom she yearns is none other than Dr Daly, the elderly Vicar of Ploverleigh, who at that precise moment appears and, not seeing the others, meditates upon the passing of the years:

Time was, when Love and I were well acquainted.
Time was, when we walked ever hand in hand.
A saintly youth, with worldly thoughts untainted—
None better-loved than I in all the land!
Time was, when maidens of the noblest station,
Forsaking even military men,
Would gaze upon me, rapt in adoration—
Ah me, I was a fair young curate then!

Had I a headache? sigh'd the maids assembled;
Had I a cold? welled forth the silent tear;
Did I look pale? then half a parish trembled;
And when I coughed all thought the end was near!
I had no care—no jealous doubts hung o'er me,
For I was loved beyond all other men.
Fled gilded dukes and belted earls before me—
Ah me, I was a pale young curate then!

Mrs Partlet comes forward with Constance and puts out a few feelers on her daughter's behalf but Dr Daly professes himself resigned to bachelordom. After their departure there is a brief scene between Sir Marmaduke and Alexis in which it is revealed that, fifty years ago, Sir Marmaduke was in love with his son's future mother-in-law, Lady Sangazure.

The mood changes when a chorus of girls ushers in Aline, who gives forth in waltz-time:

Oh, happy young heart!
Comes thy young lord a-wooing
With joy in his eyes,
And pride in his breast—
Make much of thy prize,
For he is the best
That ever came a-suing.
Yet—yet we must part,
Young heart!
Yet—yet we must part!

Oh, merry young heart,
Bright are the days of wooing!
But happier far
The days untried—
No sorrow can mar,
When Love has tied
The knot there's no undoing.
Then, never to part,
Young heart!
Then, never to part!

She is warmly greeted by her mother and rapturously by Alexis with whom she immediately becomes preoccupied. Lady Sangazure and Sir Marmaduke, finding themselves alone together, indulge in one of those duets, much favoured by Gilbert, in which each speaks out boldly and then, in an aside, reveals inner feelings:

SIR MARMADUKE:

Welcome joy, adieu to sadness!
As Aurora gilds the day,
So those eyes, twin orbs of gladness,
Chase the clouds of care away.
Irresistible incentive
Bids me humbly kiss your hand;
I'm your servant most attentive—
Most attentive to command!
(*Aside*)
Wild with adoration!
Mad with fascination!
To indulge my lamentation
No occasion do I miss!
Goaded to distraction
By maddening inaction,
I find some satisfaction
In apostrophe like this:
'Sangazure immortal,
Sangazure divine,
Welcome to my portal,
Angel, oh, be mine!'
(*Aloud*)
Irresistible incentive
Bids me humbly kiss your hand;
I'm your servant most attentive—
Most attentive to command!

LADY SANGAZURE:

Sir, I thank you most politely
For your graceful courtesee;
Compliment more true and knightly
Never yet was paid to me!
Chivalry is an ingredient
Sadly lacking in our land—
Sir, I am your most obedient,
Most obedient to command!
(*Aside*)
Wild with adoration!
Mad with fascination!
To indulge my lamentation
No occasion do I miss!
Goaded to distraction

By maddening inaction,
I find some satisfaction
In apostrophe like this:
'Marmaduke immortal,
Marmaduke divine,
Take me to thy portal,
Loved one, oh, be mine!'
(*Aloud*)
Chivalry is an ingredient
Sadly lacking in our land;
Sir, I am your most obedient,
Most obedient to command!

But the time has come for the signing of the marriage contract and, this completed, Aline and Alexis are left alone. He sings a charming ballad:

Love feeds on many kinds of food, I know,
Some love for rank, and some for duty:
Some give their hearts away for empty show,
And others love for youth and beauty.
To love for money all the world is prone:
Some love themselves, and live all lonely:
Give me the love that loves for love alone—
I love that love—I love it only!

What man for any other joy can thirst,
Whose loving wife adores him duly?
Want, misery, and care may do their worst,
If loving woman loves you truly.
A lover's thoughts are ever with his own—
None truly loved is ever lonely:
Give me the love that loves for love alone—
I love that love—I love it only!

So carried away is Alexis by his own prospects of happiness that he decides that everyone in the village must share it. He will distribute a love-philtre from J. W. Wells & Co., the old-established firm of family sorcerers. Conveniently Mr Wells himself is in the refreshment tent and, coming at once at Alexis's call, runs through his firm's wares in a patter-song that is a model for many that were to follow in other operas:

My name is John Wellington Wells,
I'm a dealer in magic and spells,

In blessings and curses,
And ever-fill'd purses,
In prophecies, witches, and knells.

If you want a proud foe to 'make tracks',
If you'd melt a rich uncle in wax,
You've but to look in
On our resident Djinn,
Number seventy, Simmery Axe!

We've a first-rate assortment of magic;
And for raising a posthumous shade,
With effects that are comic or tragic,
There's no cheaper house in the trade.
Love-philtre, we've quantities of it;
And for knowledge if anyone burns,
We're keeping a very small prophet, a prophet
Who brings us unbounded returns.
For he can prophesy
With a wink *of* his eye,
Peep with security
Into futurity,
Sum up your history,
Clear up a mystery,
Humour proclivity
For a nativity, for a nativity;
He has answers oracular,
Bogies spectacular,
Tetrapods tragical,
Mirrors so magical,
Facts astronomical,
Solemn or comical,
And, if you want it, he
Makes a reduction on taking a quantity!

Oh!
If anyone anything lacks,
He'll find it all ready in stacks,
If he'll only look in
On the resident Djinn,
Number seventy, Simmery Axe!
He can raise you hosts
Of ghosts,
And that without reflectors;

And creepy things
With wings,
And gaunt and grisly spectres;
He can fill you crowds
Of shrouds,
And horrify you vastly;
He can rack your brains
With chains,
And gibberings grim and ghastly!

Then, if you plan it, he
Changes organity,
With an urbanity
Full of Satanity,
Vexes humanity
With an inanity
Fatal to vanity,
Driving your foes to the verge of insanity!

Barring tautology,
In demonology,
'Lectro biology,
Mystic nosology,
Spirit philology,
High-class astrology,
Such is his knowledge, he
Isn't the man to require an apology!

Oh!
My name is John Wellington Wells,
I'm a dealer in magic and spells,
In blessings and curses,
And ever-fill'd purses,
In prophecies, witches, and knells.
If anyone anything lacks,
He'll find it all ready in stacks,
If he'll only look in
On the resident Djinn,
Number seventy, Simmery Axe!

At Alexis' bidding, Aline fetches a large teapot which Mr Wells
fills up with the love-philtre, explaining that it has no effect on
married people. There is a violent flash from the teapot as he indulges in strange incantations, accompanied by a chorus of spirits.
The villagers are in gay mood as the cups are passed round:

Now to the banquet we press;
Now for the eggs, the ham.
Now for the mustard and cress,
Now for the strawberry jam!
Now for the tea of our host,
Now for the rollicking bun,
Now for the muffin and toast,
Now for the gay Sally Lunn!

During the ensemble which closes the first act, all are seen to be feeling the effects of the philtre, staggering about, rubbing their eyes, and eventually collapsing on the ground.

It is midnight when the second act opens, with all the peasants asleep in the moonlight. Mr Wells explains to Alexis and Aline:

I did not think it meet to see
A dame of lengthy pedigree,
A Baronet and KCB,
A Doctor of Divinity
And that respectable QC,
All fast asleep, al-fresco-ly,
And so I had them carried home
And put to bed respectably!

The first shock occurs when Constance arrives in tears and leading on the deaf old lawyer who had presided at the betrothal ceremony:

Dear friends, take pity on my lot,
My cup is not of nectar!
I long have loved—as who would not?—
Our kind and reverend rector.
Long years ago my love began
So sweetly—yet so sadly—
But when I saw this plain old man,
Away my old affection ran—
I found I loved him madly.

I know not why I love him so;
It is enchantment, surely!
He's dry and snuffy, deaf and slow,
Ill-tempered, weak, and poorly!
He's ugly and absurdly dressed,
And sixty-seven nearly.
He's everything that I detest,
But if the truth must be confessed,
I love him very dearly!

Alexis makes a wrong tactical move when he suggests to Aline that they, too, ought to drink the philtre so that he might be assured of her love for ever. But she sharply refuses—'If you cannot trust me, you have no right to love me—no right to be loved *by* me.' He sings the sad ballad:

> Thou hast the power thy vaunted love
> To sanctify, all doubt above,
> Despite the gathering shade:
> To make that love of thine so sure
> That, come what may, it must endure
> Till time itself shall fade.
> Thy love is but a flower
> That fades within the hour!
> If such thy love, oh, shame!
> Call it by other name—
> It is not love!
>
> Thine is the power and thine alone,
> To place me on so proud a throne
> That kings might envy me!
> A priceless throne of love untold,
> More rare than orient pearl and gold.
> But no, no! Thou wouldst be free!
> Such love is like the ray
> That dies within the day:
> If such thy love, oh, shame!
> Call it by other name—
> It is not love!

Sir Marmaduke *has*, however, taken the philtre and, to everyone's astonishment, he enters arm-in-arm with Mrs Partlet! There is a lively quintet:

> ALEXIS:
> I rejoice that it's decided,
> Happy now will be his life,
> For my father is provided
> With a true and tender wife.
>
> ALL:
> She will tend him, nurse him, mend him,
> Air his linen, dry his tears;
> Bless the thoughtful fates that send him
> Such a wife to soothe his years!

ALINE:

No young giddy thoughtless maiden,
Full of graces, airs, and jeers—
But a sober widow, laden
With the weight of fifty years!

SIR MARMADUKE:

No high-born exacting beauty,
Blazing like a jewelled sun—
But a wife who'll do her duty,
As that duty should be done!

MRS PARTLET:

I'm no saucy minx and giddy—
Hussies such as them abound—
But a clean and tidy widdy
Well be-known for miles around!

DR DALY:

All the village now have mated.
All are happy as can be—
I to live alone am fated:
No one's left to marry me!

Mr John Wellington Wells is by now getting worried about the
wholesale and unexpected effects of his drug—even more so when
the veteran Lady Sangazure catches sight of him, is instantly
fascinated, and swoops down upon him. He protests vigorously,
while she becomes more tenderly insistent:

Hate me! I drop my H's—have through life!
Love me! I'll drop them too!
Hate me! I always eat peas with a knife!
Love me! I'll eat like you!
Hate me! I often roll down One Tree Hill!
Love me! I'll meet you there!
Hate me! I sometimes go to Rosherville!
Love me! that joy I'll share!
Love me! my prejudices I'll drop!
Hate me! that's not enough!
Love me! I'll come and help you in the shop!
Hate me! the life is rough!
Love me! my grammar I will all forswear!
Hate me! abjure my lot!
Love me! I'll stick sunflowers in my hair!
Hate me! they'll suit you not!

In order to disentangle himself, Mr Wells protests that he is already engaged to a maiden on a South Pacific isle. After further exchanges in which Lady Sangazure insists that it will be all his fault if she goes to her family vault to bury her life-long woe, they depart.

Aline has by now changed her mind and decided to abide by Alexis' wishes. She drinks the love philtre but, as she is going off, she sees Dr Daly and is clearly fascinated by him. He plays upon a flageolet and sings:

> Oh, my voice is sad and low,
> And with timid step I go—
> For with load of love o'erladen
> I inquire of every maiden,
> 'Will you wed me, little lady?
> Will you share my cottage shady?'
> Little lady answers 'No!
> Thank you for your kindly proffer—
> Good your heart, and full your coffer;
> Yet I must decline your offer—
> I'm engaged to so-and-so!'
> So-and-so! So-and-so!
> So-and-so! So-and-so!
> She's engaged to so-and-so!
>
> What a rogue young hearts to pillage!
> What a worker on Love's tillage!
> Every maiden in the village
> Is engaged to so-and-so!
> So-and-so! So-and-so!
> So-and-so! So-and-so!
> All engaged to so-and-so!

They meet, with the now-familiar result, and burst into a rapturous duet:

> Oh, joyous boon! Oh, mad delight!
> Oh, sun and moon! Oh, day and night!
> Rejoice, rejoice with me!
> Proclaim our joy, ye birds above—
> Ye brooklets, murmur forth our love
> In choral ecstasy:
> Oh, joyous boon!
> Oh, mad delight!
> Oh, sun and moon!
> Oh, day and night!
> Rejoice, rejoice with me!

Alexis arrives, embraces Aline, and is amazed when she rejects him. Aline and Dr Daly explain the situation:

ALINE:

Alas! that lovers thus should meet:
Oh pity, pity me!
Oh, charge me not with cold deceit;
Oh pity, pity me!
You bade me drink—with trembling awe
I drank and, by the potion's law,
I loved the very first I saw!
Oh pity, pity me!

DR DALY:

My dear young friend, consolèd be—
We pity, pity you.
In this I'm not an agent free—
We pity, pity you.
Some most extraordinary spell
O'er us has cast its magic fell—
The consequence I need not tell.
We pity, pity you.

Dr Daly makes a magnanimous offer: 'I will be no man's rival. I shall quit the country at once and bury my sorrow in the congenial gloom of a Colonial Bishopric.' But his sacrifice is not required, for Mr Wells turns up and explains that the spell can be broken if he (Wells) or Alexis yields up his life. 'I should have no hesitation in sacrificing my own life to spare yours,' says Mr Wells. 'But we take stock next week, and it would not be fair on the Co.' Aline, however, protests that if Alexis dies she will be left out in the cold, with no love to be restored to! The problem is put to the general vote. Mr Wells must be the victim:

So be it! I submit! My fate is sealed.
To public execration thus I yield!
Be happy all—leave me to my despair—
I go—it matters not with whom—or where!

All of them rejoin their true loves and, as Mr Wells disappears through a trapdoor in a burst of red fire, things are clearly back to normal:

Now for the tea of our host—
Now for the rollicking bun—
Now for the muffin and toast—
Now for the gay Sally Lunn!

'Sorry her lot who loves too well' Josephine's ballad (HMS).

Sparkeion (T) Member of a travelling theatrical company, played by Mlle Clary.

'Sprites of earth and air' Incantation by Aline, Alexis, Mr Wells and Chorus (S).

'Spurn not the nobly born' Earl Tolloller's ballad—'Blue blood! Blue blood!' (I).

Statutory Duel, The Alternative title of *The Grand Duke*.

'Stay, Frederic, stay!' Duet for Mabel and Frederic (PP).

Steward, Frank First appearing as the Foreman (J) in 1907, Frank Steward was associated with D'Oyly Carte for twenty-nine years, during which he played many of the leading baritone roles.

'Strange adventure' Quartet for Fairfax, Sergeant Meryll, Dame Carruthers and Kate (Y).

Stranger, The 'The Stranger, a touch of him.'—Colonel Calverley (P). One of the most successful plays by the German dramatist Kotzebue (1761–1819) was *Menschenhass und Reue*, which enjoyed long popularity in England, translated by Benjamin Thompson under the title *The Stranger*. The central figure was Count Waldbourg, who left his wife and home and wandered round the world.

'Strange the views some people hold!' Quintet for Ludwig, Lisa, Notary, Ernest and Julia (D).

Strephon (I) *Baritone* The Arcadian shepherd who becomes a Member of Parliament was first played by Richard Temple. Son of Iolanthe, Strephon is a fairy down to the waist and a mortal beyond that.

'Strephon's a Member of Parliament!' Chorus of fairies (I).

Stupidas (T) Member of a travelling theatrical company, played by Frederick Payne, well-known pantomime artist and brother of Henry Payne.

Styler, Alan Born in Redditch, Worcestershire, he studied singing before joining the Grenadier Guards at the age of seventeen. After demobilisation in 1946 he turned to singing professionally, joined the D'Oyly Carte Company the following year and was soon taking principal baritone parts, his roles including Cox (C), Captain Corcoran (HMS), Samuel (PP), Florian (PI), Lieutenant of the Tower (Y) and Giuseppe (G). Alan Styler, who is married to ex-D'Oyly Carte singer Vera Ryan, left the company in 1968.

'Subjected to your heavenly gaze' Duet for King Paramount and Lady Sophy (U).

Sullivan, Frederic Brother of the composer, Frederic Sullivan was born in 1840, two years before Arthur. He showed early talent as an entertaining performer and, when Arthur was a chorister at the Chapel Royal, would sometimes go along and amuse the boys with comic songs. The two brothers were at one time members of the Pimlico Dramatic Society. But from the professional point of view Fred was originally an architect. Later in life, when he was giving evidence in a court case, he was asked: 'You are an architect, Mr Sullivan?' 'I have been an architect but am now on the stage,' replied Fred. 'I am still drawing big houses.' He was the original Apollo in *Thespis* and, as a member of the Dolaro company, was in the cast of *La Périchole* at the Royalty Theatre when it was decided to add *Trial by Jury* to the bill. This gave Fred his great chance. He was a good musician as well as a lively actor and his creation of the role of the Judge was the big hit of the show. Indeed, Gilbert said afterwards that the success of the piece was due in no small measure to Fred Sullivan's 'admirable performance'. The role of John Wellington Wells in the next opera, *The Sorcerer*, was specifically written with Fred in mind but he did not live to play it. During his last illness, his devoted younger brother sat by his bedside reading verses by Adelaide Anne Procter, his setting of one of which was published a few years later and became enormously popular, 'The Lost Chord'. Indeed, it became so familiar that it attracted a parody, provoking Sullivan to write to the perpetrator, 'I wrote "The Lost Chord" in sorrow at my brother's death. Don't burlesque it.' Fred Sullivan died in January 1877, aged thirty-six.

Sir Francis Burnand (1836–1917), who wrote the libretto of *Cox and Box* for Arthur Sullivan, said of his brother (*Records and Reminiscences*, 1903): 'Fred Sullivan, Arthur's brother, was one of the most naturally comic little men I ever came across. He, too, was a first-rate practical musician, and Arthur always found him employment in any orchestra that he had to conduct. As he was the most absurd person, so was he the very kindliest. The brothers were devoted to each other, but Arthur went up, and poor little Fred went under.'

Sumner, William Joining the D'Oyly Carte chorus in 1932, William Sumner played Bob Becket (HMS), Guron (PI), Cox (C), Major Murgatroyd (P) and the Learned Judge (J) in the years preceding World War II.

'Sun whose rays are all ablaze, The' Song for Yum-Yum, far from blind to her own charms (M).

Swan and Edgar 'Let Swan secede from Edgar.'—Princess Ida. The reference is to the big store in the west end of London.

Swearing The sudden 'Damme, it's too bad!' from the sorely-tried and exasperated Captain Corcoran precipitates a comically dramatic twist in *Pinafore*. And Robin Oakapple, 'praising' his foster-brother Richard to Rose Maybud, assures her, not particularly helpfully: 'When he's excited he uses language fit to make your hair curl.' (R). For that matter Gilbert himself was said to be an expert practitioner of the art, so fluent that, when roused, he could swear at length with impressive imagination and without ever repeating himself.

Swears and Wells 'We're Swears and Wells young girls.' (P). The firm of furriers has establishments in several parts of London to-day.

Swinburne 'To Swinburne and Morris.'—Robin Oakapple (R). Algernon Charles Swinburne, the English writer of romantic and sensuous verse, was born in London in 1837 and died in 1909.

'Take a Pair of Sparkling Eyes' Marco's song, one of the best-known in the operas (G).

'Take care of him—he's much too good to live' Lisa's song (D).

'Taken from the county jail' Ko-Ko's song about the curious start to his career as Lord High Executioner (M).

Tannhäuser, Dr (D) *Tenor* Scott Russell was the first artist to play Dr Tannhäuser, the notary.

Tarara (U) *Baritone* Walter Passmore was the first artist to play Tarara, Public Exploder at the Court of King Paramount.

Telephone 'No telephone communicates with his cell.'—(HMS). There had been invented in 1860 an instrument which could transmit musical sounds. But it was not until 1876 that Graham Bell produced a device which could transmit speech. Gilbert's reference in *Pinafore* (1878) was highly topical. During the rehearsals of *Iolanthe* Gilbert established a direct telephone link between the Savoy Theatre and his home and persuaded Sullivan to do the same. Thus it was that, when the Prince of Wales was a guest at a party at Sullivan's flat, he and the other guests were able to listen to a rehearsal of *Iolanthe* —probably the first 'broadcast' of an opera.

Temple, George The first artist to sing the role of Samuel (PP) in the London production.

Temple, Richard His real name was Richard Cobb. He originated a long list of the leading roles in the operas—Sir Marmaduke

Pointdextre (S), Dick Deadeye (HMS), Pirate King, in the London production (PP), Colonel Calverley (P), Strephon (I), Arac (PI), Mikado, Sir Roderick Murgatroyd (R) and Sergeant Meryll (Y). He was born in London in 1847, son of a stockbroker, and made his first professional stage appearance in Bellini's opera *La Sonnambula* at Crystal Palace in 1869. He died in 1912.

'Ten minutes since I met a chap' Ludwig's song, with chorus (D).

Tennyson Alfred, Lord Tennyson (1809–92), Poet Laureate, would probably not be greatly flattered to be linked with the minor poet Martin Tupper in Colonel Calverley's patter song (P).

'Tenor, all singers above, A' Captain Fitzbattleaxe's song about the difficulties of singing under stress of emotion (U).

Tenors The principal tenor roles in the operas are: Defendant (J); Alexis (S); Ralph Rackstraw (HMS); Frederic (PP); Duke of Dunstable (P); Earl Tolloller (I); Hilarion and Cyril (PI); Nanki-Poo (M); Richard Dauntless (R); Colonel Fairfax, Leonard Meryll and First Yeoman (Y); Marco Palmieri, Luiz and Francesco (G); Captain Fitzbattleaxe (U); Ernest Dummkopf and Dr Tannhäuser (D).

Tessa (G) *Mezzo-soprano* Jessie Bond was the first to play Tessa, a contadina (Italian peasant).

Thackeray There are two references to William Makepeace Thackeray, author of *Vanity Fair*: 'Narrative powers of Dickens and Thackeray'—Colonel Calverley (P); 'An Earl of Thackeray and p'r'aps a Duke of Dickens'—King Paramount (U).

Theatres The London theatres which saw the birth of the operas were:

The Gaiety, where the first Gilbert and Sullivan piece, *Thespis*, was presented. This was not the Gaiety which many will remember on the corner of Aldwych and the Strand and demolished in the 1950's to make way for English Electric's headquarters. The old Gaiety was between Wellington Street and Catherine Street and started life as the Strand Music Hall in 1864. It was completely reconstructed and opened as the Gaiety in 1868 with John Hollingshead, formerly stage director at the Alhambra, as manager. One of the opening pieces was by F. C. Burnand, who had collaborated with Sullivan in *Cox and Box*, and another was a burlesque on Meyerbeer's opera called *Robert the Devil* and written by none other than W. S. Gilbert. Hollingshead built up a team of regular players who became favourites with the public. The old Gaiety was pulled down early in the present century in the LCC's Aldwych scheme.

The Royalty, in Dean Street, Soho, where *Trial by Jury* was first given in March 1875, when Richard D'Oyly Carte was manager for Mme Selina Dolaro. The theatre was opened in 1840 as Miss Kelly's Theatre and Dramatic School and underwent many re-constructions and changes of name before settling down as the Royalty. It was closed shortly before World War II and demolished in the 1950's.

The Opera Comique, where *The Sorcerer*, *HMS Pinafore*, *The Pirates of Penzance* and *Patience* were produced. Approached from the Strand and other streets by underground tunnels and backing on to the old Globe Theatre in one-time Wych Street, it must have been a decidedly curious place, understandably earning the nicknames of the 'Op. Com.' and the 'Theatre Royal Tunnels'. It is even said that people sometimes found themselves in the wrong theatre. It was opened in 1870 and one of its early presentations was a piece based on Molière's comedy, *Le Médecin Malgré Lui*, called *The Doctor in Spite of Himself*, with music by Richard D'Oyly Carte, who later became manager. The theatre was closed in 1899.

The Savoy Theatre, built by Richard D'Oyly Carte with great consideration for the comfort of his patrons, was opened on October 10, 1881, with *Patience*, transferred from the Opera Comique where it had been running since April. In an early programme one finds the notice: 'Although great care is taken by the management to prevent draughts in the auditorium, it is impossible to avoid their occasional occurrence; it is earnestly requested, therefore, that any person inconvenienced by a draught should communicate with the attendant, who will at once endeavour to remedy the evil.' There were no cloakroom fees and programmes were free: 'Any attendant detected in accepting money from visitors will be instantly dismissed. The public is therefore requested not to tempt the attendants by offering them gratuities.' For his new theatre Carte chose a historic site, close to that on which had stood the Savoy Palace, where John of Gaunt and the Dukes of Lancaster had lived. But he was thoroughly up to date in his approach to his task. His theatre was the first in the world to be lit throughout by electricity—and, to prove to his audience that there was no danger of fire from the newfangled lighting, he stood on the stage and smashed an electric-light bulb on the floor. But he also took the precaution of having a stand-by gas-lighting system. The theatre was built to the plans of C. J. Phipps, who was later concerned in designing Queen's Hall, and originally had its main frontage on the Thames Embankment side. Later, however, after the completion of the Savoy Hotel, the theatre entrance was moved to the Strand. In 1929 an extraordinarily rapid job of reconstruction was carried out to the plans of Frank A. Tugwell. Only the outer shell was left standing and, within a few months, the building was given an entirely new interior, decorated by Basil Ionides and with Sir (then Dr) Malcolm Sargent advising on the design of the orchestra pit. The theatre reopened with a revival of *The Gondoliers*.

The Princes Theatre (now called the Shaftesbury), the Saville, Sadler's Wells and the Scala are other London theatres in which several seasons have been presented by the D'Oyly Carte Opera Company, which spends the greater part of the year touring.

'**Then away we go to an island fair**' Finale to the first act (G).

'**Then I may sing and play?**' Quartet for Nekaya, Lord Drama-leigh, Kalyba and Mr Goldbury (U).

'**Then one of us will be a queen**' Quartet for Marco, Giuseppe, Gianetta and Tessa (G).

'**There grew a little flower 'neath a great oak tree**' Dame Hannah's ballad, with Sir Roderic Murgatroyd (R).

'**There is beauty in the bellow of the blast**' Duet for Katisha and Ko-Ko (M).

'**There lived a King, as I've been told**' Don Alhambra's song, with Marco and Giuseppe (G)—'When every one is somebodee, then no one's anybody!'

'**There's a little group of isles beyond the wave**' Princess Zara's solo in the finale to the opera (U).

'**There was a time**' Duet for Casilda and Luiz (G).

THESPIS; or The Gods Grown Old First performed at the Gaiety Theatre, London, on December 26, 1871, conducted by Sullivan. 64 performances given.

The cast for the 'entirely original Grotesque Opera' was:

JUPITER	Mr John Maclean
APOLLO	Mr Frederic Sullivan
MARS	Mr Frank Wood
DIANA	Mrs H. Leigh
MERCURY	Miss Ellen Farren
VENUS	Miss Jolly
THESPIS (*Manager of a travelling theatrical company*)	Mr J. L. Toole
SILLIMON (*his stage manager*)	Mr J. G. Taylor
TIMIDON	Mr Marshall
TIPSCION	Mr Robert Soutar
PREPOSTEROS	Mr Henry Payne
STUPIDAS	Mr Fred Payne
SPARKEION	Mlle Clary
NICEMIS	Miss Constance Loseby
PRETTEIA	Miss Rose Berend
DAPHNE	Miss Annie Tremaine
CYMON	Miss L. Wilson

On Mount Olympus, the abode of the gods, the temple has fallen into ruin and the gods themselves are looking old and decrepit. Mercury has been down on the earth, stealing such things as pills and hair dye for the ageing gods, but he complains that he never gets any thanks for his efforts: 'I'm the celestial drudge.' Jupiter bemoans the fact that the standard of sacrifices from earth has fallen off terribly and is now down to preserved Australian beef. Something must be done.

Upon the scene come the members of a theatrical troupe, led by Sparkeion and Nicemis, who are newly married—or, at any rate, half married, for the ceremony takes all day. Thespis, manager of the company, has celebrated the occasion by giving them all a picnic on the mountain-top. The other members of the company arrive and there follows the chorus which was later re-used in *The Pirates of Penzance*:

> Climbing over rocky mountain,
> Skipping rivulet and fountain,
> Passing where the willows quiver,
> By the ever rolling river,

Swollen with the summer rain.
Threading long and leafy mazes,
Dotted with unnumbered daisies,
Scaling rough and rugged passes,
Climb the hardy lads and lasses,
Till the mountain-top they gain.

DAPHNE:
Fill the cup and tread the measure,
Make the most of fleeting leisure,
Hail it as a true ally,
Though it perish bye and bye!
Every moment brings a treasure
Of its own especial pleasure;
Though the moments quickly die,
Greet them gaily as they fly!

NICEMIS:
Far away from grief and care,
High up in the mountain air,
Let us live and reign alone,
In a world that's all our own.
Here enthroned in the sky,
Far away from mortal eye,
We'll be gods and make decrees,
Those may honour them who please.

They are bickering about who shall sit next to whom during the picnic when Thespis treats them to a song about a man who undermined his influence by associating with his inferiors:

I once knew a chap who discharged a function
On the North South East West Diddlesex junction.
He was conspicuous exceeding
For his affable ways and his easy breeding.
Although a Chairman of Directors,
He was hand in glove with the ticket inspectors.
He tipped the guards with bran-new fivers,
And sang little songs to the engine drivers.

But it has a sad ending:

He followed out his whim with vigour,
The shares went down to a nominal figure.
These are the sad results proceeding
From his affable ways and his easy breeding!

The line, with its rails and guards and peelers,
Was sold for a song to marine store dealers.
The shareholders are all in the work'us,
And he sells pipe-lights in the Regent Circus.

The gods show themselves and at first demand that the mortals
shall depart at once. But they realise that their visitors might have
something to teach them and Thespis suggests that the gods should
disguise themselves and spend a year on earth, while the actors and
actresses stand in for them on Mount Olympus. Jupiter accepts the
idea and the gods depart, leaving Thespis as Jupiter, Sparkeion as
Apollo, Nicemis as Diana, Timidon as Mars and Daphne as Calliope.

When the curtain rises on the second act, the ruins have disappeared and in their place stands a magnificent new temple. But
difficulties have arisen among the pseudo-gods, mainly because
mythology requires different pairings-off of lovers. Sparkeion,
however, points out the impermanence of love affairs in a song,
the only one in the operetta, apart from the 'rocky mountain'
chorus, for which Sullivan's music still exists:

Little maid of Arcadee
Sat on Cousin Robin's knee,
Thought in form and face and limb,
Nobody could rival him.
He was brave and she was fair.
Truth, they made a pretty pair.
Happy little maiden, she—
Happy maid of Arcadee!

Moments fled as moments will,
Happily enough, until,
After, say, a month or two,
Robin did as Robins do.
Weary of his lover's play,
Jilted her and went away.
Wretched little maiden, she—
Wretched maid of Arcadee!

To her little home she crept,
There she sat her down and wept,
Maiden wept as maidens will—
Grew so thin and pale—until
Cousin Richard came to woo!
Then again the roses grew!
Happy little maiden, she—
Happy maid of Arcadee!

The real Mercury appears and, much amused by the muddle the actors have made of things, sings a song ending with the words:

> A premier in Downing Street, forming a Cabinet,
> Couldn't find people less fit for their work!

There is more wrangling among the Thespian-gods about who is now married to whom until eventually the real gods, their year's sojourn on earth having been completed, reappear and there is a full assessment of the state of affairs. At the end of it, Jupiter pronounces an awful curse:

> Away to earth, contemptible comedians,
> And hear our curse before we set you free;
> You shall all be eminent tragedians,
> Whom no one ever goes to see!

Thespis (T) Manager of a travelling theatrical company, played by J. L. Toole, one of the most distinguished comedy actors of his day. After being leading comedian at the Adelphi, he was at the Gaiety for five years and later became proprietor of the Folly Theatre, which was renamed 'Toole's'. Toole, who died at Brighton in 1906, does not seem to have been profoundly impressed by *Thespis*, although he played the title role in it. In his *Reminiscences* (Routledge, 1892) he dismisses it in a single sentence: '*Thespis*, in two acts, was Gilbert and Sullivan's first effort in the way of opera-bouffe or comic English opera.' In the piece he had at least one good song, a patter number about the chairman of directors of the North South East West Diddlesex Junction Railway, who 'tipped the guards with bran-new fivers and sang little songs to the engine drivers.'

'They intend to send a wire to the moon' Hilarion's song about the aims of the girl graduates (PI).

'Things are seldom what they seem' Duet for Little Buttercup and Captain Corcoran, full of mysterious allusions and mixed-up proverbs (HMS).

'This helmet, I suppose, was meant to ward off blows' Arac's song (PI).

Thorne, George His name is remembered to-day as that of the artist who, at the same time as Lytton but in a different touring company, made Jack Point 'die', giving the *Yeomen* a tragic ending. His first leading role was that of Bunthorne in a tour shortly after the première of *Patience* in 1881 and he played many of the chief comedy roles through the years up to 1899.

Thornton, Eric He played Bouncer (C) in his first season with D'Oyly Carte in 1950 and later the Learned Judge (J), Captain Corcoran (HMS), Lord Mountararat (I) and Luiz (G). He also made some appearances as the Pirate King (PP) and Sir Roderic (R) before going out to Australia in 1952.

Thornton, Frank The original Major Murgatroyd (P), he also played Bunthorne (P) and Samuel and Major-General Stanley (PP) in the original productions. He later played the Lord Chancellor (I).

'Though I am but a girl' Princess Ida's song at the close of the second act (PI).

'Though p'r'aps I may incur your blame' Quartet for Earl of Mountararat, Earl Tolloller, Phyllis, and Private Willis—'In Friendship's name.' (I).

'Though the views of the House have diverged' Earl of Mountararat's solo (I).

'Thou hast the power thy vaunted love to sanctify' Ballad for Alexis (R), ending with the words 'It is not love!'

'Threatened cloud has passed away, The' Ensemble for Nanki-Poo, Pooh-Bah, Yum-Yum, Pitti-Sing and Peep-Bo in the finale to the first act (M).

'Three little maids from school are we' Trio for Yum-Yum, Peep-Bo and Pitti-Sing (M).

'Time was, when Love and I were well acquainted' Dr Daly's ballad (S), ending with the well-known words 'Ah me, I was a pale young curate then.'

Timidon (T) Member of a travelling theatrical company, played by Mr Marshall.

Timoneer 'Teach him the trade of a timoneer.'—Don Alhambra (G). A timoneer is one who handles a boat.

Tipscion (T) Member of a travelling theatrical company, played by Robert Soutar, stage manager at the Gaiety. He was married to Nellie Farren, one of the theatre's stars, who played Mercury in *Thespis*.

''Tis done! I am a bride!' Elsie Maynard's dramatic recitative and song after she has been married, blindfolded, to Colonel Fairfax (Y).

''Tis said that joy in full perfection' Trio for Phoebe, Elsie Maynard and Dame Carruthers in the finale of the opera (Y).

''Tis twelve, I think, and at this mystic hour' Trio for Aline, Alexis and Mr Wells, with chorus, opening the second act (R).

Titles After Gilbert had been knighted in 1907, twenty-four years after Sullivan, he said in a speech at Harrow School:

'I am not an agricultural labourer, but I have this in common with a certain type of ploughman who in bygone days was awarded by the squire with a pair of corduroy breeches and a crown piece in each pocket, in consideration of his having brought up a family of fifteen children without extraneous assistance. I have been rewarded for having brought up a family of sixty-three plays without ever having to apply to the relieving officer for parochial assistance. This knighthood I take to be a sort of commuted old-age pension. . . .'

Of the same event, he wrote to a friend: 'I found myself politely described in the official list as Mr William Gilbert, *playwright*, suggesting that my work was analogical to that of a wheelwright, or a millwright, or a wainwright, or a shipwright, as regards the mechanical character of the process by which our respective results are achieved. There is an excellent word, "dramatist", which seems to fit the situation, but it is not applied until we are dead, and then we become dramatists, as oxen, sheep and pigs are transfigured into beef, mutton and pork on their demise. You never hear of a novel-wright or a picture-wright or a poem-wright, and why a play-wright?'

In the early *Thespis*, Gilbert gives Mercury these lines:

> Well, well, it's the way of the world,
> And will be through all its futurity;
> Though noodles are baroned and earled,
> There's nothing for clever obscurity!

'All baronets are bad.'—Ruth (R).

Tolloller, Earl (I) *Tenor* Durward Lely was the first artist to play Earl Tolloller ('Blue blood! Blue blood!').

Tommy Among the wares in her basket Little Buttercup (HMS) has 'soft tommy'—soft bread.

'To thy fraternal care' Trio for Wilfred Shadbolt, Fairfax and Phoebe (Y).

'Towards the empyrean heights' Girl graduates' opening chorus to the second act (PI).

'Tower Warders, under orders' Chorus as the Yeomen make their first entrance (Y).

Town of Titipu, The Alternative title of *The Mikado*.

Toye, Jennifer She joined the D'Oyly Carte chorus in 1953 and in the following year was singing the small part of Ada (PI). In 1956 she went to Florence to study with her uncle, Francis Toye, and on her return sang Plaintiff (J), Sacharissa (PI) and Kate (Y). In the years before she left the company in 1965 her roles included Casilda (G), Isabel and Mabel (PP), Josephine (HMS), Patience, Elsie Maynard (Y), Yum-Yum (M) and Gianetta (G).

Transvestism 'We resolved that, on artistic principles, no man should play a woman's part and no woman a man's.'—Gilbert, looking back some years later on his partnership with Sullivan. There was an exception to this rule in *Thespis*, their first collaboration, in which Nelly Farren, a great favourite at the Gaiety Theatre, showed off her legs as the god Mercury. But in this early work Gilbert and Sullivan followed to a great extent the Gaiety tradition, employing mainly players who were already well-known at that theatre. Later, however, they carefully chose their own regular players and indeed roles were written with specific artists in mind. In *Princess Ida*, Hilarion, Cyril and Florian do don women's collegiate robes for the purposes of the plot but this is rather different from men playing women's *roles*.

TRIAL BY JURY First performed at the Royalty Theatre, London, on March 25, 1875, conducted by Sullivan. Initial run of 131 performances.

Described as 'a novel and entirely original Dramatic Cantata', the piece had this cast for its first performance:

THE LEARNED JUDGE	Mr Frederic Sullivan
COUNSEL FOR THE PLAINTIFF	Mr J. Hollingsworth
THE DEFENDANT	Mr Walter H. Fisher
FOREMAN OF THE JURY	Mr C. Kelleher
USHER	Mr B. R. Pepper
THE PLAINTIFF	Miss Nellie Bromley
BRIDESMAIDS	Mesdames Verner, Sassalle, Grahame, Durrant, Palmer, Beverley, Clifford, Villers, etc.
GENTLEMEN OF THE JURY	Messrs Campbell, Husk, etc.

The scene is set in a court of law, the original setting being based by Gilbert on the Clerkenwell court in which he had appeared during his early, brief and unremunerative career as a lawyer. The case to be heard is a breach-of-promise action, as the chorus of barristers, attorneys, jurymen and public at once make clear in the opening chorus:

> Hark, the hour of ten is sounding;
> Hearts with anxious fears are bounding,
> Hall of Justice crowds surrounding,
> Breathing hope and fear—
> For to-day in this arena,
> Summoned by a stern subpoena,
> Edwin, sued by Angelina,
> Shortly will appear.

The Usher, punctuating the proceedings with stentorian cries of 'Silence in Court!' points out that the case must be tried 'from bias free of every kind'—though his references to 'the broken-hearted bride' and 'the ruffianly defendant' suggest that this is the last thing to be expected. Indeed, the defendant, on his appearance, points out that they are at present quite in the dark about the merits of his pleadings, and then reviews his situation:

> When first my old, old love I knew,
> My bosom welled with joy;
> My riches at her feet I threw—
> I was a love-sick boy!

No terms seemed too extravagant
Upon her to employ—
I used to mope, and sigh, and pant,
Just like a love-sick boy.
Tink-a-Tank—Tink-a-Tank.

But joy incessant palls the sense;
And love, unchanged will cloy,
And she became a bore intense
Unto her love-sick boy!
With fitful glimmer burnt my flame,
And I grew cold and coy,
At last, one morning, I became
Another's love-sick boy.
Tink-a-Tank—Tink-a-Tank.

The jurymen, entering their box, show that from experience they have a measure of sympathy but are determined to point out that they are now reformed characters:

Oh, I was like that when a lad!
A shocking young scamp of a rover,
I behaved like a regular cad;
But that sort of thing is all over.
I'm now a respectable chap
And shine with a virtue resplendent,
And, therefore, I haven't a scrap
Of sympathy with the defendant!
He shall treat us with awe,
If there isn't a flaw,
Singing so merrily—Trial-la-law!
Trial-la-law—Trial-la-law!
Singing so merrily—Trial-la-law!

The Usher calls in his bass voice for 'Silence in court' and the Judge enters, to be greeted by the jurymen, clearly determined to be in with the right people:

All hail great Judge!
To your bright rays
We never grudge ecstatic praise.
All hail!
May each decree
As statute rank,
And never be reversed in banc.
All hail!

On his part, the Judge, like many of Gilbert's later creations on their first entrance, at once obliges with an account of his career up to date:

When I, good friends, was called to the bar,
I'd an appetite fresh and hearty,
But I was, as many young barristers are,
An impecunious party.
I'd a swallow-tail coat of a beautiful blue—
A brief which I bought of a booby—
A couple of shirts and a collar or two,
And a ring that looked like a ruby!

In Westminster Hall I danced a dance,
Like a semi-despondent fury;
For I thought I never should hit on a chance
Of addressing a British Jury.—
But I soon got tired of third-class journeys,
And dinners of bread and water;
So I fell in love with a rich attorney's
Elderly, ugly daughter.

The rich attorney, he jumped with joy,
And replied to my fond professions:
'You shall reap the reward of your pluck, my boy,
At the Bailey and Middlesex Sessions.
You'll soon get used to her looks,' said he.
'And a very nice girl you'll find her!
She may very well pass for forty-three
In the dusk, with a light behind her!'

The rich attorney was good as his word;
The briefs came trooping gaily,
And every day my voice was heard
At the Sessions or Ancient Bailey.
All thieves who could my fees afford
Relied on my orations,
And many a burglar I've restored
To his friends and his relations.

At length I became as rich as the Gurneys—
An incubus then I thought her,
So I threw over that rich attorney's
Elderly, ugly daughter.

The rich attorney my character high
Tried vainly to disparage—
And now, if you please, I'm ready to try
This Breach of Promise of Marriage!

A comical touch is achieved in the swearing of the jurymen who, kneeling for that purpose, entirely disappear in the jury-box, only their raised hands being visible. The build-up to the Plaintiff's entrance is admirably stage-managed so as to have the maximum effect both on the audience and on the jurymen—she is preceded by her bridesmaids in their full get-up. They sing:

Comes the broken flower—
Comes the cheated maid—
Though the tempest lower,
Rain and cloud will fade!
Take, oh maid, these posies:
Though thy beauty rare
Shame the blushing roses—
They are passing fair!
Wear the flowers till they fade;
Happy be thy life, oh maid!

The Judge, who has a decidedly roving eye, has already been smitten by the first bridesmaid, to whom he despatches the Usher with a note which she kisses and places in her bosom. But he at once transfers his affections when the Plaintiff appears on the scene. The Usher is instructed to retrieve the note and hand it to Angelina, who receives it with appropriate demonstrations of rapture. She sings:

O'er the season vernal,
Time may cast a shade;
Sunshine, if eternal,
Makes the roses fade:
Time may do his duty;
Let the thief alone—
Winter hath a beauty
That is all his own.
Fairest days are sun and shade:
I am no unhappy maid!

Counsel for the Plaintiff launches into an account of the dastardly behaviour of the Defendant, rounding off with:

413

> Picture, then, my client naming,
> And insisting on the day:
> Picture him excuses framing—
> Going from her far away;
> Doubly criminal to do so,
> For the maid had bought her *trousseau*!

Amidst general expressions of sympathy, the Judge suggests that perhaps she might like to recline on him—an invitation which she briskly accepts, jumping on to the Bench and falling sobbing on his breast. The Defendant is clearly on the losing side as he explains his wayward behaviour:

> Oh, gentlemen, listen, I pray,
> Though I own that my heart has been ranging,
> Of nature the laws I obey,
> For nature is constantly changing.
> The moon in her phases is found,
> The time and the wind and the weather,
> The months in succession come round,
> And you don't find two Mondays together.
> Ah! Consider the moral, I pray,
> Nor bring a young fellow to sorrow,
> Who loves this young lady to-day,
> And loves that young lady to-morrow!
>
> You cannot eat breakfast all day,
> Nor is it the act of a sinner,
> When breakfast is taken away,
> To turn his attention to dinner;
> And it's not in the range of belief,
> To look upon him as a glutton,
> Who, when he is tired of beef,
> Determines to tackle the mutton.
> Ah! But this I am willing to say,
> If it will appease her sorrow,
> I'll marry this lady to-day,
> And I'll marry the other to-morrow!

The Judge is inclined to think that this is a reasonable proposition. Counsel, however, bursts in with:

> But I submit, m'lud, with all submission,
> To marry two at once is Burglaree!

And, referring to a law book, he continues impressively:

> In the reign of James the Second,
> It was generally reckoned
> As a rather serious crime
> To marry two wives at a time.

The Plaintiff, with an eye to heavy damages, embraces the Defendant and stresses what a heavy loss she has suffered through being jilted:

> I love him—I love him—with fervour unceasing,
> I worship and madly adore;
> My blind adoration is always increasing,
> My loss I shall ever deplore.
> Oh, see what a blessing, what love and caressing
> I've lost, and remember it, pray,
> When you I'm addressing are busy assessing
> The damages Edwin must pay!

Edwin, however, is not to be outdone. He points out that he is far from being a good catch:

> I smoke like a furnace—I'm always in liquor,
> A ruffian—a bully—a sot:
> I'm sure I should thrash her, perhaps I should kick her,
> I am such a very bad lot!
> I'm not prepossessing, as you may be guessing,
> She couldn't endure me a day;
> Recall my professing, when you are assessing
> The damages Edwin must pay!

The Judge has a bright idea:

> The question, gentlemen, is one of liquor;
> You ask for guidance—this is my reply:
> He says, when tipsy, he would thrash and kick her,
> Let's make him tipsy, gentlemen, and try!

There are general objections—except from the Defendant, who does not at all mind the idea. But the Judge is becoming impatient and, flinging his books and papers around, he announces a somewhat surprising solution:

> All the legal furies seize you!
> No proposal seems to please you.
> I can't sit up here all day.
> I must shortly get away.

Barristers, and you, attorneys,
Set out on your homeward journeys;
Gentle, simple-minded Usher,
Get you, if you like, to Russ*her*;
Put your briefs upon the shelf,
I will marry her myself!

Springing down from the Bench, he embraces Angelina and pronounces:

Though homeward as you trudge
You declare my law is fudge,
Yet of beauty I'm a judge.

ALL:
And a good Judge, too!

'Tripping hither, tripping thither' Entrance of the fairies at the opening of the opera (I).

Trollope Anthony Trollope (1815–82), the prolific novelist to whom Colonel Calverley refers (P), had completed his notable series of 'Barsetshire' novels only a few years before the Gilbert and Sullivan partnership began.

'True love must single-hearted be' Song for Patience, with Bunthorne's interspersed 'Exactly so!' (P).

'Try we life-long, we can never straighten out life's tangled skein' Quintet for Duke and Duchess of Plaza-Toro, Casilda, Luiz and Don Alhambra (G).

Tucker, Tom (HMS) The midshipmite was first played by 'Mr Fitzaltamont', a stage name probably given to several different young artists.

Tunks, Leicester Prominent D'Oyly Carte baritone, Leicester Tunks sang Captain Corcoran (HMS), Samuel (PP), Colonel Calverley (P), Lord Mountararat (I), Florian (PI), Pish-Tush (M), Lieutenant of the Tower (Y) and Luiz (G) in his first season, 1905. In the period until he left the company in 1917, he added many other roles, among them Dick Deadeye (HMS), Pirate King (PP), Strephon (I), Grosvenor (P), Mikado, Sergeant Meryll (Y) and Giuseppe (G).

Tupper Colonel Calverley links Tupper with Tennyson in his patter song (P). Martin Farquhar Tupper (1810–89), born in London, was a minor poet whose *Proverbial Philosophy* enjoyed a big sale in Britain and America.

'Turn, oh, turn in this direction' Chorus of maidens as they group round Archibald Grosvenor (P).

Tussaud, Madame Gilbert makes two references to Marie Tussaud the Swiss woman who brought her waxwork museum from Paris to London in 1802, installing it in turn at the Lyceum Theatre, at Blackheath, in Baker Street and finally in Marylebone Road. She died in 1850, aged ninety.

Colonel Calverley (P) refers to her in his Heavy Dragoon song. The Mikado includes among his list of punishments that of the amateur tenor who 'shall, during off-hours, exhibit his powers to Madame Tussaud's waxwork.'

'Twenty love-sick maidens we' Opening chorus of the aesthetic young ladies (P).

'Jack Point' — Mr George Grossmith   'Elsie Maynard' — Miss Geraldine Ulmar

Ulmar, Geraldine Having sung some performances (though not originating the role) as Rose Maybud in the original production of *Ruddigore* at the Savoy Theatre, Geraldine Ulmar, whom Sullivan had first met in New York, created the parts of Elsie Maynard (Y) and Gianetta (G). She later sang Josephine (HMS), Yum-Yum (M) and Rose Maybud in New York. She married Ivan Caryll, who became musical director for George Edwardes at the Gaiety Theatre, London, in 1894, and who wrote a series of successful musical comedies, among them *The Shop Girl*, *The Toreador* and *The Duchess of Dantzic*. In her later years Geraldine Ulmar became a well-known teacher of singing, her pupils including Jose Collins and Evelyn Laye.

'Upon our sea-girt land' Chorus in the second act (U).

Usher (J) *Bass* The original was B. R. Pepper.

UTOPIA LIMITED; or The Flowers of Progress First performed at the Savoy Theatre, London, on October 7, 1893, conducted by Sullivan. Initial run of 245 performances.
 The cast of the original production was:

KING PARAMOUNT THE FIRST (*King of Utopia*)	Mr Rutland Barrington
SCAPHIO ⎱ (*Judges of the Utopian*	Mr W. H. Denny
PHANTIS ⎰ *Supreme Court*)	Mr John Le Hay
TARARA (*the Public Exploder*)	Mr Walter Passmore
CALYNX (*the Utopian Vice-Chamberlain*)	Mr Bowden Haswell
LORD DRAMALEIGH (*a British Lord Chamberlain*)	Mr Scott Russell
CAPTAIN FITZBATTLEAXE (*First Life Guards*)	Mr Charles Kenningham

CAPTAIN SIR EDWARD CORCORAN, KCB (*Royal Navy*)	Mr Lawrence Gridley
MR GOLDBURY (*a Company Promoter*)	Mr Scott Fishe
SIR BAILEY BARRE, QC	Mr Enes Blackmore
MR BLUSHINGTON (*of the County Council*)	Mr Herbert Ralland
THE PRINCESS ZARA (*King Paramount's Eldest Daughter*)	Miss Nancy McIntosh
THE PRINCESS NEKAYA \(*her Younger*	Miss Emmie Owen
THE PRINCESS KALYBA |*Sisters*)	Miss Florence Perry
THE LADY SOPHY (*their English Gouvernante*)	Miss Rosina Brandram
SALATA \	Miss Edith Johnston
MELENE \}(*Utopian Maidens*)	Miss May Bell
PHYLLA |	Miss Florence Easton

The curtain rises on a palm grove in the gardens of King Paramount, with the sea in the distance. Salata, Melene, Phylla and other Utopian maidens laze luxuriously:

> In lazy languor—motionless,
> We lie and dream of nothingness;
> For visions come
> From Poppydom
> Direct at our command:
> Or, delicate alternative,
> In open idleness we live,
> With lyre and lute
> And silver flute,
> The life of Lazyland!

> PHYLLA:
> The song of birds
> In ivied towers;
> The rippling play
> Of waterway;
> The lowing herds;
> The breath of flowers;
> The languid loves
> Of turtle doves—
> These simple joys are all at hand
> Upon thy shores, O lazyland!

In comes Calynx, the Vice-Chamberlain, with the news that Princess Zara, the King's eldest daughter, is returning to Utopia after five years' study at Girton College in England. Soon Utopia will be completely anglicised. The group is interrupted by the arrival of a curious character called Tarara, who explains that he has been appointed to the office of Public Exploder, with the duty of blowing up whatever might be denounced by the two wise men, Scaphio and Phantis. This duty extends even to blowing up the King, should the wise men so decree—and, having come across a scandal-sheet called the *Palace Peeper*, which accuses the King of a variety of disgraceful practices, Tarara is bewildered and enraged that he has not already been called upon to blow him up! He departs in a temper, and the chorus greet Scaphio and Phantis:

O make way for the Wise Men!
They are prizemen—
Double-first in the world's university!
For though lovely this island
(Which is *my* land),
She has no one to match them in *her* city.

They're the pride of Utopia—
Cornucopia
Is each in his mental fertility.
O they never make blunder,
And no wonder,
For they're triumphs of infallibility.

SCAPHIO and PHANTIS:
In every mental lore
(The statement smacks of vanity)
We claim to rank before
The wisest of humanity.
As gifts of head and heart
We're wasted on 'utility',
We're 'cast' to play a part
Of great responsibility.

Our duty is to spy
Upon our King's illicities,
And keep a watchful eye
On all his eccentricities.
If ever a trick he tries
That savours of rascality,
At our decree he dies
Without the least formality!

We fear no rude rebuff,
Or newspaper publicity;
Our word is quite enough,
The rest is electricity.
A pound of dynamite
Explodes in his auriculars;
It's not a pleasant sight—
We'll spare you the particulars.

Its force all men confess,
The King needs no admonishing—
We may say its success
Is something quite astonishing.
Our despot it imbues
With virtues quite delectable:
He minds his P's and Q's
And keeps himself respectable.

Of a tyrant polite
He's a paragon quite.
He's as modest and mild
In his ways as a child;
And no one ever met
With an autocrat, yet,
So delightfully bland
To the least in the land!

The two are left alone together on the stage. Phantis confesses
that, though fifty-five, he passionately loves Princess Zara, while
Scaphio, at sixty-six, says that he has never known what love is.

SCAPHIO:
Let all your doubts take wing—
Our influence is great.
If Paramount our King
Presume to hesitate,
Put on the screw,
And caution him
That he will rue
Disaster grim
That must ensue
To life and limb,
Should he pooh-pooh
This harmless whim.

BOTH:
This harmless whim—this harmless whim,
It is, as I/you say, a harmless whim.

PHANTIS (*dancing*):
Observe this dance
Which I employ
When I, by chance,
Go mad with joy.
What sentiment
Does this express?
Supreme content and happiness!

BOTH:
Of course it does! Of course it does!
Supreme content and happiness!

PHANTIS:
Your friendly aid conferred,
I need no longer pine.
I've but to speak the word,
And lo! the maid is mine!
I do not choose
To be denied,
Or wish to lose
A lovely bride—
If to refuse
The King decide,
The Royal shoes
Then woe betide!

BOTH:
Then woe betide—then woe betide!
The Royal shoes then woe betide!

SCAPHIO (*dancing*):
This step to use
I condescend
Whene'er I choose
To serve a friend.
What it implies
Now try to guess:
It typifies
Unselfishness!

BOTH:
Of course it does! Of course it does!
It typifies unselfishness!

They go off and, with the chorus singing 'Quaff the nectar—cull the roses,' the King enters, attended by guards and nobles.

KING PARAMOUNT:
A King of autocratic power, we—
A despot whose tyrannic will is law—
Whose rule is paramount o'er land and sea,
A Presence of unutterable awe!
But though the awe that I inspire
Must shrivel with imperial fire
All foes whom it may chance to touch,
To judge by what I see and hear,
It does not seem to interfere
With popular enjoyment, much.

The King announces that as it is the public wish that Utopia shall be modelled upon Great Britain, his two younger daughters, Nekaya and Kalyba, who have been 'finished' by an English lady, shall be exhibited daily as examples of maidenly perfection. As the girls enter at the King's bidding, the chorus express their admiration:

How fair! How modest! How discreet!
How bashfully demure!
See how they blush, as they've been taught,
At this publicity unsought!
How English and how pure!

NEKAYA and KALYBA:
Although of native maids the cream,
We're brought up on the English scheme—
The best of all
For great and small
Who modesty adore.

NEKAYA:
For English girls are good as gold,
Extremely honest (so we're told),
Demurely coy—divinely cold—

KALYBA:
And we are that—and more.
To please papa, who argues thus—
All girls should mould themselves on us
Because we are
By furlongs far
The best of all the bunch.
We show ourselves to loud applause
From ten to four without a pause—

NEKAYA:
Which is an awkward time because
It cuts into our lunch.

BOTH:
Oh, maids of low and high degree,
Whose social code is rather free,
Please look at us and you will see
What good young ladies ought to be!

NEKAYA:
And as we stand, like clockwork toys,
A lecturer whom papa employs
Proceeds to praise
Our modest ways
And guileless character—

KALYBA:
Our well-known blush—our downcast eyes—
Our famous look of mild surprise

NEKAYA:
(Which competition still defies)—

KALYBA:
Our celebrated 'Sir!!!'
Then all the crowd take down our looks
In pocket memorandum books.
To diagnose
Our modest pose
The Kodaks do their best:

NEKAYA:
If evidence you would possess
Of what is maiden bashfulness,
You only need a button press—

KALYBA:
And *we* will do the rest.

Lady Sophy, 'an English lady of mature years and extreme gravity
of demeanour and dress', is led in most deferentially by the King
and proceeds to give a lecture on proper behaviour, with the girls
illustrating by gestures:

Bold-faced ranger
(Perfect stranger)
Meets two well-behaved young ladies.
He's attractive,

Young and active—
Each a little bit afraid is.
Youth advances,
At his glances
To their danger they awaken;
They repel him
As they tell him
He is very much mistaken—
Very, very much mistaken.
Though they speak to him politely,
Please observe they're sneering slightly,
Just to show he's acting vainly.
This is Virtue saying plainly,
'Go away, young bachelor,
We are not what you take us for!'
When addressed impertinently,
English ladies answer gently,
'Go away, young bachelor,
We are not what you take us for!'

As he gazes,
Hat he raises,
Enters into conversation.
Makes excuses—
This produces
Interesting agitation.
He, with daring,
Undespairing,
Gives his card—his rank discloses.
Little heeding
This proceeding,
They turn up their little noses—
Yes, their little, little noses.

Pray observe this lesson vital—
When a man of rank and title
His position first discloses,
Always cock your little noses.
When at home, let all the class
Try this in the looking-glass.
English girls of well-bred notions
Shun all unrehearsed emotions.
English girls of highest class
Practise them before the glass.

His intentions
Then he mentions.
Something definite to go on—
Makes recitals
Of his titles,
Hints at settlements, and so on.
Smiling sweetly,
They, discreetly,
Ask for further evidences:
Thus invited,
He, delighted,
Gives the usual references.
(Don't forget the references.)

This is business. Each is fluttered
When the offer's fairly uttered.
'Which of them has his affection?'
He declines to make selection.
Do they quarrel for his dross?
Not a bit of it—they toss!
Ah! Please observe this cogent moral—
English ladies never quarrel.
When a doubt they come across,
English ladies always toss.

All go off except the King, who is joined by Scaphio and Phantis, and it is revealed that all the scandal in the *Palace Peeper* is written by the King himself at the command of the two wise men. Further, he has written a comic opera called 'King Tuppence—or A Good Deal Less than Half a Crown.' But the King reflects that, properly considered, life is a farce anyway:

First you're born—and I'll be bound you
Find a dozen strangers round you.
'Hallo,' cries the new-born baby,
'Where's my parents? Which may they be?'
Awkward silence—no reply—
Puzzled baby wonders why!
Father rises, bows politely—
Mother smiles (but not too brightly)—
Doctor mumbles like a dumb thing—
Nurse is busy mixing something.
Every symptom tends to show
You're decidedly *de trop*.

ALL:

Ho! Ho! Ho! Ho! Ho! Ho! Ho!
Time's teetotum,
If you spin it,
Gives its quotum
Once a minute.
I'll go bail
You hit the nail,
And if you fail
The deuce is in it!

KING:

You grow up, and you discover
What it is to be a lover.
Some young lady is selected—
Poor, perhaps, but well-connected,
Whom you hail (for Love is blind)
As the Queen of fairy kind.
Though she's plain—perhaps unsightly,
Makes her face up—laces tightly,
In her form your fancy traces
All the gifts of all the graces.
Rivals none the maiden woo,
So you take her and she takes you!

ALL:

Ho! Ho! Ho! Ho! Ho! Ho! Ho!
Joke beginning,
Never ceases
Till your inning
Time releases,
On your way
You blindly stray,
And day by day
The joke increases!

KING:

Ten years later—Time progresses—
Sours your temper—thins your tresses;
Fancy, then, her chain relaxes;
Rates are facts and so are taxes.
Fairy Queen's no longer young—
Fairy Queen has got a tongue.
Twins have probably intruded—
Quite unbidden—just as you did—

They're a source of care and trouble—
Just as you were—only double.
Comes at last the final stroke—
Time has had his little joke!

ALL:
Ho! Ho! Ho! Ho! Ho! Ho! Ho!
Daily driven
(Wife as drover)
Ill you've thriven—
Ne'er in clover;
Lastly, when
Three-score and ten
(And not till then),
The joke is over!

There follows an encounter between Lady Sophy, the girls' English governess, and the King who is clearly fond of her. But she upbraids him about the scandal that appears in the *Palace Peeper* and cannot understand why he does not seek out and punish the writer. The King plays for time by telling her he is waiting to discover a suitably drastic punishment.

KING:
Subjected to your heavenly gaze
(Poetical phrase),
My brain is turned completely.
Observe me now,
No Monarch, I vow,
Was ever so far afflicted!

LADY SOPHY:
I'm pleased with that poetical phrase,
'A heavenly gaze',
But though you put it neatly,
Say what you will,
Those paragraphs still
Remain uncontradicted.
Come, crush me this contemptible worm
(A forcible term),
If he's assailed you wrongly.
The rage display,
Which, as you say,
Has moved your Majesty lately.

KING:
Though I admit that forcible term,
'Contemptible worm',
Appeals to me most strongly,
To treat this pest
As you suggest
Would pain my Majesty greatly!

LADY SOPHY:
This writer lies!

KING:
Yes, bother his eyes!

LADY SOPHY:
He lives, you say?

KING:
In a sort of a way.

LADY SOPHY:
Then have him shot.

KING:
Decidedly not.

LADY SOPHY:
Or crush him flat.

KING:
I cannot do that.

BOTH:
O royal Rex,
My/her blameless sex
Abhors such conduct shady.
You/I plead in vain,
You/I never will gain
Respectable English lady!

They go off and, to the strains of a march, the stage fills as the Court heralds the arrival of Princess Zara, escorted by Captain Fitzbattle-axe and four troopers in full uniform of the 1st Life Guards.

CHORUS:
Oh, maiden, rich in Girton lore,
That wisdom which
We prized before,
We do confess
Is nothingness,
And rather less,
Perhaps, than more.

On each of us
Thy learning shed.
On calculus
May we be fed.
And teach us, please,
To speak with ease
All languages,
Alive and dead!
On each of us thy learning shed.

ZARA:

Five years have flown since I took wing—
Time flies and his footstep ne'er retards—
I'm the eldest daughter of your king.

TROOPERS:

And we are the escort—First Life Guards!
On the royal yacht,
When the waves were white,
In a helmet hot
And a tunic tight,
And our great big boots,
We defied the storm:
For we're not recruits,
And his uniform
A well-drilled trooper ne'er discards—
And we are the escort—First Life Guards!

ZARA:

These gentlemen I present to you,
The pride and boast of their barrack-yards;
They've taken, O! such care of me!

TROOPERS:

For we are the escort—First Life Guards!
When the tempest rose,
And the ship went *so*—
Do you suppose
We were ill? No, no!
Though a qualmish lot
In a tunic tight,
And a helmet hot,
And a breastplate bright
(Which a well-drilled trooper ne'er discards),
We stood as the escort—First Life Guards!

CHORUS:
Knightsbridge nursemaids—serving fairies—
Stars of proud Belgravian airies;
At stern duty's call you leave them,
Though you know how that must grieve them!

ZARA:
Tantantarara-rara-rara!

FITZBATTLEAXE:
Trumpet-call of Princess Zara!

CHORUS:
That's trump-call, and they're all trump cards—

FITZ. and TROOPERS:
And we are the escort—First Life Guards!

ZARA:
Ah! gallant captain, brave and true
In tented field and tourney,
I grieve to have occasioned you
So very long a journey.

FITZBATTLEAXE:
When soldier seeks Utopian glades
In charge of Youth and Beauty,
Then pleasure merely masquerades
As Regimental Duty!

During the ensuing ensemble, they sing together, aside:

Oh! the hours are gold
And the joys untold,
When your/my eyes behold
Your/my beloved Princess;
And the years will seem
But a brief day-dream,
In our happiness,
And the years will seem
But a brief day-dream,
In the joy extreme
Of our happiness!

As the crowd disperses, Scaphio and Phantis emerge and it becomes clear that Scaphio, who had promised his colleague full support in regard to Zara, has fallen passionately in love with her himself. Their discourse is interrupted by Zara and Captain Fitzbattleaxe, who convincingly quotes an English 'law' which provides that, when two gentlemen are in love with the same lady and until it is settled which of them is to blow out the brains of the other, the lady shall be entrusted to an officer of the Household Cavalry as stakeholder. The Captain launches into what becomes a lively quartet:

> It's understood, I think, all round
> That, by the English custom bound,
> I hold the lady safe and sound
> In trust for either rival,
> Until you clearly testify
> By sword or pistol, by and by,
> Which gentleman prefers to die,
> And which prefers survival.

With the departure of Scaphio and Phantis, the lovers indulge in a duet:

> Oh admirable art!
> Oh neatly-planned invention!
> Oh happy intervention—
> Oh well-constructed plot!
> When sages try to part
> Two loving hearts in fusion,
> Their wisdom's a delusion,
> And learning serves them not!

> FITZBATTLEAXE:
> Until quite plain
> Is their intent,
> These sages twain
> I represent.
> Now please infer
> That, nothing loth,
> You're henceforth, as it were,
> Engaged to marry both—
> Then take it that I represent the two—
> On that hypothesis, what would you do?

> ZARA:
> What would I do? What would I do?
> In such a case,
> Upon your breast,
> My blushing face
> I think I'd rest—(she does so)

Then perhaps I might
Demurely say—
'I find this breastplate bright
Is sorely in the way!'

FITZBATTLEAXE:
Our mortal race
Is never blest—
There's no such case
As perfect rest;
Some petty blight
Asserts its sway—
Some crumpled roseleaf light
Is always in the way!

There follows a short scene between Zara and the King in which the Princess reveals that she, too, has seen the *Palace Peeper*. The King breaks down and tells her that, far from being an absolute monarch, he is completely controlled by Scaphio and Phantis. Conveniently, the Princess has brought with her 'six representatives of the principal causes that have tended to make England the powerful, happy and blameless country which the consensus of European opinion has declared it to be'. All he needs to do is to place his country in their hands.

PRINCESS ZARA (*presenting* CAPTAIN FITZBATTLEAXE):
When Britain sounds the trump of war
(And Europe trembles),
The army of the conqueror
In serried ranks assembles;
'Tis then this warrior's eyes and sabre gleam
For our protection—
He represents a military scheme
In all its proud perfection!

PRINCESS ZARA (*presenting* SIR BAILEY BARRE, QC, MP):
A complicated gentleman allow me to present,
Of all the arts and faculties the terse embodiment,
He's a great Arithmetician who can demonstrate with ease
That two and two are three, or five, or anything you please;
An eminent Logician who can make it clear to you
That black is white—when looked at from the proper point
    of view;
A marvellous Philologist who'll undertake to show
That 'yes' is but another and a neater form of 'no.'

SIR BAILEY:
Yes—yes—yes—
'Yes' is but another and a neater form of 'no'.
All preconceived ideas on any subject I can scout,
And demonstrate beyond all possibility of doubt,
That whether you're an honest man or whether you're a thief
Depends on whose solicitor has given me my brief.

PRINCESS ZARA (*presenting* LORD DRAMALEIGH *and* MR BLUSH-
    INGTON *of the County Council*):
What these may be, Utopians all,
Perhaps you'll hardly guess—
They're types of England's physical
And moral cleanliness.
This is a Lord High Chamberlain,
Of purity the gauge—
He'll cleanse our Court from moral stain
And purify our Stage.

LORD DRAMALEIGH:
Yes—yes—yes—
Court reputations I revise,
And presentations scrutinize,
New plays I read with jealous eyes
And purify the Stage.

PRINCESS ZARA:
This County Councillor acclaim,
Great Britain's latest toy—
On anything you like to name
His talents he'll employ—
All streets and squares he'll purify
Within your city walls,
And keep meanwhile a modest eye
On wicked music halls.

MR BLUSHINGTON:
Yes—yes—yes—
In towns I make improvements great,
Which go to swell the County Rate—
I dwelling-houses sanitate,
And purify the Halls!

PRINCESS ZARA (*presenting* MR GOLDBURY):
A Company Promoter this, with special education,
Which teaches what Contango means and also Backwarda-
    tion—

To speculators he supplies a grand financial leaven,
Time was when *two* were company—but now it must be
   seven.

MR GOLDBURY:
Yes—yes—yes—
Stupendous loans to foreign thrones
I've largely advocated;
In ginger-pops and peppermint-drops
I've freely speculated;
Then mines of gold, of wealth untold,
Successfully I've floated,
And sudden falls in apple-stalls
Occasionally quoted:
And soon or late I always call
For Stock Exchange quotation—   ·
No schemes too great and none too small
For Companification!

PRINCESS ZARA (*presenting* CAPTAIN SIR EDWARD CORCORAN, RN):
And lastly I present
Great Britain's proudest boast,
Who from the blows
Of foreign foes
Protects her sea-girt coast—
And if you ask him in respectful tone,
He'll show you how you may protect your own!

CAPTAIN CORCORAN:
I'm Captain Corcoran, KCB,
I'll teach you how we rule the sea,
And terrify the simple Gauls;
And how the Saxon and the Celt
Their Europe-shaking blows have dealt
With Maxim gun and Nordenfeldt
(Or will, when the occasion calls).
If sailor-like you'd play your cards,
Unbend your sails and lower your yards,
Unstep your masts—you'll never want 'em more.
Though we're no longer hearts of oak,
Yet we can steer and we can stoke,
And, thanks to coal, and thanks to coke,
We never run a ship ashore!

(CHORUS: 'What never?' . . . CAPTAIN: 'Hardly ever!')

The 'experts' all start offering advice but it is Mr Goldbury, the company promoter, who makes himself most effectively heard:

Some seven men form an Association
(If possible, all Peers and Baronets)
They start off with a public declaration
To what extent they mean to pay their debts.
That's called their Capital; if they are wary
They will not quote it at a sum immense.
The figure's immaterial—it may vary
From eighteen million down to eighteenpence.
I should put it rather low;
The good sense of doing so
Will be evident at once to any debtor.
When it's left to you to say
What amount you mean to pay,
Why, the lower you can put it at, the better.

They then proceed to trade with all who'll trust 'em,
Quite irrespective of their capital
(It's shady, but it's sanctified by custom);
Bank, Railway, Loan, or Panama Canal.
You can't embark on trading too tremendous—
It's strictly fair, and based on common sense—
If you succeed, your profits are stupendous—
And if you fail, pop goes your eighteenpence.
Make the money-spinner spin!
For you only stand to win,
And you'll never with dishonesty be twitted.
For nobody can know,
To a million or so,
To what extent your capital's committed!

If you come to grief, and creditors are craving,
(For nothing that is planned by mortal head
Is certain in this Vale of Sorrow—saving
That one's Liability is Limited),—
Do you suppose that signifies perdition?
If so you're but a monetary dunce—
You merely file a Winding-Up Petition,
And start another Company at once!
Though a Rothschild you may be
In your own capacity,

As a Company you've come to utter sorrow—
But the Liquidators say,
'Never mind—you needn't pay'
So you start another Company to-morrow!

Mr Goldbury admits that Britain has not yet quite come to being governed on the Joint Stock principle—'but we're tending rapidly in that direction. The date's not far distant.' The King enthusiastically decides to be the first sovereign in Christendom to register his Crown and Country under the Joint Stock Company's Act of Sixty-Two.

The second act opens in the Throne Room of the Palace, with Captain Fitzbattleaxe singing to Zara:

Oh, Zara, my beloved one, bear with me!
Ah, do not laugh at my attempted C!
Repent not, mocking maid, thy girlhood's choice—
The fervour of my love affects my voice!

A tenor, all singers above
(This doesn't admit of a question),
Should keep himself quiet,
Attend to his diet
And carefully nurse his digestion;
But when he is madly in love
It's certain to tell on his singing—
You can't do chromatics
With proper emphatics
When anguish your bosom is wringing!
When distracted with worries in plenty,
And his pulse is a hundred and twenty,
And his fluttering bosom the slave of mistrust is,
A tenor can't do himself justice.
Now observe—(*Sings a high note*) Ah!
You see, I can't do myself justice!

I could sing if my fervour were mock,
It's easy enough if you're acting—
But when one's emotion
Is born of devotion
You mustn't be over-exacting.
One ought to be firm as a rock
To venture a shake in *vibrato*.
When fervour's expected
Keep cool and collected
Or never attempt *agitato*.

But, of course, when his tongue is of leather,
And his lips appear pasted together,
And his sensitive palate as dry as a crust is,
A tenor can't do himself justice.
Now observe—(*sings a cadence*) Ah!
It's no use—I can't do myself justice!

Unworried about the higher notes of the voice, Princess Zara is more concerned about the higher qualities of the heart—and of the splendours of the Anglicisation of Utopia. Mr Goldbury has even gone so far as to turn every man, woman and child into a limited liability company. Zara and the Captain sing a soft love-duet.

ZARA:
Words of love too loudly spoken
Ring their own untimely knell;
Noisy vows are rudely broken,
Soft the song of Philomel.
Whisper sweetly, whisper slowly,
Hour by hour and day by day;
Sweet and low as accents holy
Are the notes of lover's lay!

FITZBATTLEAXE:
Let the conqueror, flushed with glory,
Bid his noisy clarions bray;
Lovers tell their artless story
In a whispered virelay.
False is he whose vows alluring
Make the listening echoes ring;
Sweet and low when all-enduring
Are the songs that lovers sing!

But it is time for the King, dressed as a Field-Marshal, to hold his first cabinet meeting.

KING:
Society has quite forsaken all her wicked courses,
Which empties our police courts, and abolishes divorces.

CHORUS:
Divorce is nearly obsolete in England.

KING:
No tolerance we show to undeserving rank and splendour;
For the higher his position is, the greater the offender.

CHORUS:

That's a maxim that is prevalent in England.

KING:

No peeress at our Drawing-Room before the Presence passes
Who wouldn't be accepted by the lower-middle classes.
Each shady dame, whatever be her rank, is bowed out neatly.

CHORUS:

In short, this happy country has been Anglicized completely!
It really is surprising
What a thorough Anglicizing
We have brought about—Utopia's quite another land;
In her enterprising movements,
She is England—with improvements,
Which we dutifully offer to our mother-land!

KING:

Our city we have beautified—we've done it willy-nilly—
And all that isn't Belgrave Square is Strand and Piccadilly.

CHORUS:

We haven't any slummeries in England!

KING:

We have solved the labour question with discrimination
    polished
So poverty is obsolete and hunger is abolished—

CHORUS:

We are going to abolish it in England.

KING:

The Chamberlain our native stage has purged, beyond a
    question,
Of 'risky' situation and indelicate suggestion;
No piece is tolerated if it's costumed indiscreetly—

CHORUS:

In short, this happy country has been Anglicized completely!

KING:

Our Peerage we've remodelled on an intellectual basis,
Which certainly is rough on our hereditary races—

CHORUS:

We are going to remodel it in England.

KING:

The Brewers and the Cotton Lords no longer seek admission,
And Literary Merit meets with proper recognition—

CHORUS:

As Literary Merit does in England.

KING:

Who knows but we may count among our intellectual
   chickens,
Like you, an Earl of Thackeray and p'r'aps a Duke of Dickens—
Lord Fildes and Viscount Millais (when they come) we'll
   welcome sweetly—

CHORUS:

In short, this happy country has been Anglicized completely!

There follows a representation of a Royal Drawing-Room, with
all the paraphernalia of titles and uniforms, the King pointing out
that, in following Great Britain's courtly ways 'we'll gloriously
succeed or nobly fail.' The Chorus, unaccompanied, catch the
spirit:

> Eagle high in cloudland soaring—
> Sparrow twittering on a reed—
> Tiger in the jungle roaring—
> Frightened fawn in grassy mead—
> Let the eagle, not the sparrow,
> Be the object of your arrow—
> Fix the tiger with your eye—
> Pass the fawn in pity by.
> Glory then will crown the day—
> Glory, glory, anyway!

The stage having emptied, Scaphio and Phantis, now dressed in the
red and ermine robes of judges, express a different view:

SCAPHIO:

With fury deep we burn—

PHANTIS:

We do—

SCAPHIO:

We fume with smothered rage—

PHANTIS:

We do—

SCAPHIO:

These Englishmen who rule supreme,
Their undertaking they redeem
By stifling every harmless scheme
In which we both engage—

PHANTIS:
They do—

SCAPHIO
In which we both engage.

PHANTIS:
We think it is our turn—

SCAPHIO:
We do—

PHANTIS:
We think our turn has come—

SCAPHIO:
We do—

PHANTIS:
These Englishmen, they must prepare
To seek at once their native air.
The King as heretofore, we swear,
Shall be beneath our thumb—

SCAPHIO:
He shall—

PHANTIS:
Shall be beneath our thumb—

SCAPHIO:
He shall.

BOTH:
For this mustn't be, and this won't do,
If you'll back me, then I'll back you,
No, this won't do,
No, this mustn't be.
No, this mustn't be, and this won't do.

With the arrival of the King, Scaphio and Phantis complain bitterly that the innovations of the new regime have meant that all their private schemes are ruined. But the King defies them.

SCAPHIO:
If you think that when banded in unity,
We may both be defied with impunity,
You are sadly misled of a verity!

PHANTIS:
If you value repose and tranquillity,
You'll revert to a state of docility,
Or prepare to regret your temerity!

KING:
If my speech is unduly refractory,
You will find it a course satisfactory
At an early Board meeting to show it up.
Though if proper excuse you can trump any,
You may *wind* up a Limited Company,
You cannot conveniently *blow* it up!
(*He dances quietly*)
Whene'er I chance to baffle you,
I, also, dance a step or two—
Of this now guess the hidden sense:
It means complete indifference.

SCAPHIO and PHANTIS:
Of course it does—
It means complete indifference—

KING:
Indifference, indifference, indifference!

The King continues to dance quietly, while Scaphio and Phantis
dance furiously.

SCAPHIO and PHANTIS:
As we've a dance for every mood
With *pas de trois* we will conclude.
What this may mean you all may guess—
It typifies remorselessness!

KING:
It means unruffled cheerfulness!

The two Wise Men realise that, as the King is now a Corporation,
they are helpless. But they call in the aid of Tarara.

TRIO:
With wily brain upon the spot
A private plot we'll plan,
The most ingenious private plot
Since private plots began.
That's understood. So far we've got
And, striking while the iron's hot,
We'll now determine like a shot
The details of this private plot.

They get involved in elaborate argument and eventually address
the audience:

At last a capital plan we've got;
We won't say how and we won't say what:
It's safe in my noddle—
Now off we will toddle,
And slyly develop this capital plot!

The timid young Princesses Nekaya and Kalyba, modelled by
Lady Sophy on the English pattern, have an encounter with Lord
Dramaleigh and Mr Goldbury, in which the latter points out that
English girls are not really so ridiculously demure:

A wonderful joy our eyes to bless,
In her magnificent comeliness,
Is an English girl of eleven stone two,
And five foot ten in her dancing shoe!
She follows the hounds, and on she pounds—
The 'field' tails off and the muffs diminish—
Over the hedges and brooks she bounds
Straight as a crow, from find to finish.
At cricket, her kin will lose or win—
She and her maids, on grass or clover,
Eleven maids out—eleven maids in—
And perhaps an occasional 'maiden over'!

Oh! Go search the world and search the sea,
Then come you home and sing with me
There's no such gold and no such pearl
As a bright and beautiful English girl!

With a ten-mile spin she stretches her limbs,
She golfs, she punts, she rows, she swims—
She plays, she sings, she dances, too,
From ten or eleven till all is blue!
At ball or drum, till small hours come
(Chaperone's fan conceals her yawning)
She'll waltz away like a teetotum,
And never go home till daylight's dawning.
Lawn-tennis may share her favours fair—
Her eyes a-dance and her cheeks a-glowing—
Down comes her hair, but what does she care?
It's all her own and it's worth the showing!

Her soul is sweet as the ocean air,
For prudery knows no haven there;
To find mock-modesty, please apply
To the conscious blush and the downcast eye.

Rich in the things contentment brings,
In every pure enjoyment wealthy,
Blithe as a beautiful bird she sings,
For body and mind are hale and healthy.
Her eyes they thrill with right goodwill—
Her heart is light as a floating feather—
As pure and bright as the mountain rill
That leaps and laughs in the Highland heather!

The four join in a quartet, in which the girls express their delight that the rules of English behaviour permit them to be much more relaxed. As Mr Goldbury puts it:

Whatever you are—be that:
Whatever you say—be true:
Straightforwardly act—
Be honest—in fact,
Be nobody else but *you*.

The quartet sums up:

Oh, sweet surprise. Oh, dear delight
To find it undisputed quite—
All musty, fusty rules despite—
That Art is wrong and Nature right!

They dance off and Lady Sophy enters, in thoughtful mood:

When but a maid of fifteen year,
Unsought—unplighted—
Short-petticoated—and, I fear,
Still shorter-sighted—
I made a vow, one early spring,
That only to a spotless King
Who proof of blameless life could bring
I'd be united.
For I had read, not long before,
Of blameless Kings in fairy lore,
And thought the race still flourished here—
I was a maid of fifteen year!
Well, well—well, well,
I was a maid of fifteen year!

Each morning I pursued my game
(An early riser);
For spotless monarchs I became
An advertiser:

But all in vain I searched each land,
So, kingless, to my native strand
Returned, a little older, and
A good deal wiser!
I learnt that spotless King and Prince
Have disappeared some ages since—
Even Paramount's angelic grace—
Is but a mask on Nature's face!
Ah, me! Ah, me! Is but a mask on Nature's face!

The King, who has entered and overheard, rushes forward and tells her the truth about the *Palace Pepper* and the machinations of Scaphio and Phantis.

LADY SOPHY:
Oh, the rapture unrestrained
Of a candid retractation!
For my sovereign has deigned
A convincing explanation—
And the clouds that gathered o'er,
All have vanished in the distance,
And of Kings of fairy lore
One, at least, is in existence!

KING:
Oh, the skies are blue above,
And the earth is red and rosal,
Now the lady of my love
Has accepted my proposal!
For that *asinorum pons*
I have crossed without assistance,
And of prudish paragons
One, at least, is in existence!

As the King kisses Lady Sophy, three other couples enter—Lord Dramaleigh with Nekaya, Mr Goldbury with Kalyba, and Zara with Captain Fitzbattleaxe. They all dance an exuberant tarantella before going off. The stage fills with Scaphio, Phantis, Tarara and the Chorus:

Upon our sea-girt land
At our enforced command
Reform has laid her hand
Like some remorseless ogress—
And made us darkly rue
The deeds she dared to do—

And all is owing to
Those hated Flowers of Progress!
So down with them . . .!
Down with the Flowers of Progress!

Indeed, under the new administration, the Army and Navy are so
strong that war is impossible, the doctors are out of work because
there is no disease, and so are the lawyers through the absence of
crime. But the King has a brainwave. They have omitted one
feature of the English system—Government by Party. All will yet
be well—'No political measures will endure, because one Party
will assuredly undo all that the other Party has done.' Scaphio and
Phantis are taken away to jail and there is general celebration:

ZARA:
There's a little group of isles beyond the wave—
So tiny, you might almost wonder where it is—
That nation is the bravest of the brave,
And cowards are the rarest of all rarities.
The proudest nations kneel at her command;
She terrifies all foreign-born rapscallions;
And holds the peace of Europe in her hand
With half a score invincible battalions!

PRINCIPALS and CHORUS:
Such, at least, is the tale
Which is borne on the gale,
From the island which dwells in the sea.
Let us hope, for her sake,
That she makes no mistake—
That she's all she professes to be!

KING:
Oh, may we copy all her maxims wise,
And imitate her virtues and her charities;
And may we, by degrees, acclimatize
Her Parliamentary peculiarities!
By doing so, we shall, in course of time,
Regenerate completely our entire land—
Great Britain is that monarchy sublime,
To which some add (but others do not) Ireland.
Such at least is the tale. . . .

Valley-de-Sham This is the nearest Old Adam Goodheart (R) can get to *valet de chambre*.

Victor Emmanuel Colonel Calverley's reference (P) is to the man (1820–78) who, formerly Victor Emmanuel II of Sardinia, became Victor Emmanuel I of a united Italy. His monument is the massive and elaborate marble edifice which dominates the Piazza de Venezia in Rome and is known to visitors as the 'wedding cake'.

Vincent, Ruth Though she later concentrated on 'grand' opera, Ruth Vincent, who was born in Yarmouth, made her first stage appearance at the Savoy Theatre, creating the role of Gretchen in *The Grand Duke* in March 1896. She also sang Kate (Y), Elsie Maynard (Y), Josephine (HMS) and Casilda (G). At Covent Garden in 1910 she created the leading role of Vrenchen in the première of Delius's opera *A Village Romeo and Juliet*, conducted by Beecham.

Virelay 'In a whispered virelay.'—Captain Fitzbattleaxe (U). An ancient form of French verse.

Vittoria (G) *Mezzo-soprano* A contadina (Italian peasant), first played by Annie Cole.

Von Palmay, Ilka In 1893 it became known that in a projected production of *The Mikado* in Berlin it was proposed to have a *woman* Nanki-Poo—Ilka von Palmay. An injunction put a stop to the plan but the episode does not seem to have left any ill-feelings. Three years later, Ilka von Palmay originated the role of Julia Jellicoe in *The Grand Duke*, and, in the first revival of *The Yeomen of the Guard* the following year, she played Elsie Maynard.

Wagner King Gama (PI) has a reference to German bands playing Wagner. The composer had died in Venice only a year before the first production of *Princess Ida* in 1884.

Wales, Pauline It was by no means accidental that Pauline Wales became a member of the D'Oyly Carte Company. She was born at Stockton-on-Tees of a musical family, and started her musical studies at an early age. The Gilbert and Sullivan roles fascinated her from the age of sixteen, when she began writing frequently to the D'Oyly Carte office asking if she could join the company, and receiving a letter from Miss Bridget D'Oyly Carte, suggesting that she should wait until she was a little older. She was a keen member of a local amateur society, playing soubrette roles in a number of productions such as *The New Moon, The Maid of the Mountains, The Student Prince* and *The Vagabond King*. In due course, when she was twenty, she was granted an audition and joined the D'Oyly Carte chorus the following year. Her leading mezzo-soprano roles now include Hebe (HMS), Kate (PP), Lady Saphir (P), Leila (I), Melissa (PI), Peep-Bo (M) and Tessa (G). She is married to Thomas Lawlor, lately principal baritone with the company.

Walker, James After being associate conductor of D'Oyly Carte for seven years, James Walker succeeded Isidore Godfrey and was musical director from 1968 until 1971. An Australian, he was educated there and at the Royal Academy of Music, London. He began his professional career in British film studios and, after wartime service in the RNVR, was musical director of the International Ballet from 1947 until 1954. Before joining D'Oyly Carte, he was recording supervisor of the Decca Record Company in London.

Walker, Richard Baritone Richard Walker was a member of the D'Oyly Carte Company for twenty-four years, starting in the chorus in 1924. He was singing the smaller roles of Antonio and Giorgio (G) three years later and went on to add several other parts, including Guron (PI), and Major Murgatroyd (P). In the war years he was singing Sergeant of Police (PP), Pooh-Bah (M), Wilfred Shadbolt (Y) and Don Alhambra (G). Private Willis (I) and Gorsvenor (P) followed later. Richard Walker married soprano Helen Roberts and together they went to Australia, where he played Doolittle in the musical *My Fair Lady* for more than four years. They have made many concert tours in Gilbert and Sullivan in America, where they are attached to the Gilbert and Sullivan Society, New York.

'Wandering minstrel I, A' Nanki-Poo's song on his first entrance (M).

'Warders are ye?' Dame Carruthers' tirade against the Yeomen after the escape of Fairfax (Y).

Warwick, Giulia The first artist to play the part of Constance (S), Giulia Warwick also played Aline in some performances of the original production. She was with the Carl Rosa Opera Company.

Waterloo House 'A Waterloo House young man!'—Archibald Grosvenor (P). In London's Cockspur Street, in which are now concentrated the offices of various shipping lines, there formerly stood the Nash building called Waterloo House, occupied by the fashionable drapery establishment of White, Pearce and Stone, later merged with Swan and Edgar, in Piccadilly Circus.

Watson, Richard Private Willis (I) and King Hildebrand (PI) were among the roles sung by Richard Watson with the D'Oyly Carte Company in the period from 1932 until he went out to Australia in 1935. Returning in 1947, he sang a number of roles, including Bouncer (C), Learned Judge (J), Captain Corcoran (HMS), Pooh-Bah (M) and Don Alhambra (G). Before going out to become professor of music in a Canadian university in 1951, he had added Grosvenor (P), Pish-Tush (M), Giuseppe (G), Sergeant of Police (PP), Sir Despard (R) and Wilfred Shadbolt (Y). Back in Australia, he died in Adelaide in August 1968.

Watteau 'An existence à la Watteau.'—Counsel for Plaintiff (J). The French painter, Antoine Watteau (1684–1721), specialised in idyllic pastoral subjects.

Watts, Dr 'She'll scarcely suffer Dr Watts's hymns.'—King Gama (PI). Dr Isaac Watts (1674–1748) was a noted English preacher and hymn-writer, his best-known being 'O God, our help in ages past' and 'When I survey the wondrous cross'.

'We are dainty little fairies' Celia's solo after the fairies have entered at the start of the opera (I).

'We are warriors three' Arac's song, with Guron and Scynthius —'Fighting is our trade.' (PI).

Webley, John This young baritone was singing the roles of Counsel (J), Captain Corcoran (HMS), Pish-Tush (M), Lieutenant of the Tower (Y) and Giuseppe (G) with the D'Oyly Carte Company when his promising career was cut short by his death in 1971 at the age of twenty-four. Like many artists who join D'Oyly Carte, he had been a boy chorister, singing for eight years in the Cathedral at Portsmouth, where he was born. After leaving school, he had voice-training in London and joined D'Oyly Carte in 1966.

'Welcome, joy! adieu to sadness!' Duet for Lady Sangazure and Sir Marmaduke Pointdextre (S).

'Welcome to our hearts again' Chorus after Iolanthe has returned from banishment (I).

Wellington Lord Mountararat (I) has a reference to the Iron Duke: 'When Wellington thrashed Bonaparte. . . .'

Wells, John Wellington (S) *Baritone* Principal of the firm of J. W. Wells & Co., Family Sorcerers, St Mary Axe. Fred Sullivan, the composer's brother, for whom the part was written, had died before the production of the opera and the role went to George Grossmith, who thus made his first appearance on the dramatic stage and began his long association with the 'little men' roles in the operas. Mr Wells's final exit, a highly dramatic affair in which he disappears amid flames through a trapdoor into the depths, came adrift one night when Lytton was playing the part. The trapdoor stuck and Lytton was obliged to disappear rather less dramatically—by walking off the stage. 'Hell's full!' shouted a voice from the audience.

'We may remark, though nothing can dismay us' Trio for Arac, Guron and Scynthius (PI).

'We're called gondolieri' Duet for Marco and Giuseppe Palmieri (G).

'Were I king in very truth' Song by Ernest Dummkopf, the theatrical manager (D).

'Were I thy bride' Phoebe's teasing song to Wilfred, the jailer (Y).

'We're rigged out in magnificent array' Duet for the Prince and Princess of Monte Carlo (D).

'Were you not to Ko-Ko plighted' Duet for Nanki-Poo and Yum-Yum (M).

'We sail the ocean blue' Opening chorus of sailors (HMS).

Westminster Hall 'In Westminster Hall I danced a dance, like a semi-despondent fury.'—Learned Judge (J). High court cases were heard in Westminster Hall before the opening of the Royal Courts of Justice, in the Strand, by Queen Victoria in 1882.

'What these may be, Utopians all, perhaps you'll hardly guess' Princess Zara's solo, introducing Lord Dramaleigh (the Lord Chamberlain) and the County Councillor (U).

'When a felon's not engaged in his employment' The Sergeant of Police's song—'The policeman's lot is not a happy one.' (PP).

'When all night long a chap remains' Private Willis's song at the opening of the second act—'Either a little Liberal or else a little Conservative.' (I).

'When a merry maiden marries' Tessa's song (G). It was brought to Sullivan's notice that this tune resembled that of J. L. Molloy's 'Love's Sweet Song.' To which Sullivan replied: 'I do not happen to have heard the song but, even if I had, you must remember that Molloy and I had only seven notes on which to work between us.'

'When anger spreads his wing' Chorus of soldiers (PI).

'When a wooer goes a-wooing' Quartet for Elsie Maynard, Phoebe, Fairfax and Jack Point (Y).

'When Britain really ruled the waves' Earl of Mountararat's song—'As in King George's glorious days.' (I).

'When Britain sounds the trump of war' Princess Zara's solo about Captain Fitzbattleaxe (U).

'When but a maid of fifteen year' Lady Sophy's song (U).

'When darkly looms the day' Strephon's opening to the finale of the first act—with the eavesdropping Peers misinterpreting what is said (I).

'Whene'er I poke sarcastic Joke' King Gama's song—'And I've nothing whatever to grumble at.' (PI).

'When first my old, old love I knew' Defendant's song, with 'Tink-a-tank' impression of a guitar (J).

'When Frederic was a little lad' Ruth's song in which she reveals that in error she apprenticed Frederic to a pirate instead of to a pilot (PP).

'When he is here, I sigh with pleasure' Constance's aria (S).

'When I first put this uniform on' Colonel Calverley's song about his self-satisfaction when he donned the uniform of an officer in the Heavy Dragoons (P).

'When I, good friends, was called to the bar' The Learned Judge's song, in which he gives an account of his career to date (J).

'When I go out of door' Duet for Bunthorne and Grosvenor—'A greenery-yallery, Grosvenor Gallery, foot-in-the-grave young man.' (P).

'When I was a lad I served a term' Sir Joseph Porter's account of the steps by which he became Ruler of the Queen's Navee (HMS).

'When I went to the Bar as a very young man' Lord Chancellor's song about his resolutions at the start of his career—'Said I to myself—said I.' (I).

'When maiden loves, she sits and sighs' There is no opening chorus to the *Yeomen*. On the rise of the curtain Phoebe, at her spinning-wheel, sings this song.

'When our gallant Norman foes' Dame Carruthers' song about the Tower of London—'I keep my silent watch and ward.' (Y).

'When the buds are blossoming' Madrigal (R).

'When the foeman bares his steel, Tarantara! tarantara!' Song by the Sergeant of Police as the gallant members of the Force march in single file (PP).

'When the night wind howls' Sir Roderic Murgatroyd's song in the big scene of the opera—'The Ghosts' High-Noon.' (R).

'When you find you're a broken-down critter' Rudolph's song (D).

'When you had left our pirate fold' Trio for Ruth, Pirate King and Frederic—'a most ingenious paradox'. (PP).

'When you're lying awake with a dismal headache' The Lord Chancellor recounts the details of his nightmare in one of the most brilliant of the patter songs (I).

'Whom thou hast chained must wear his chain' Hilarion's song (PI).

Wilbraham, J. The first artist to play Sir Gilbert Murgatroyd (R), First Yeoman (Y) and Annibale (G).

Williamson, Howard This Manchester-born member of the D'Oyly Carte Company cherished a boyhood ambition to work in the theatre and, while concentrating on the study of languages, appeared in amateur dramatic productions, including Gilbert and Sullivan. After studies at the Marchesi Singing Academy and at the London Academy of Music and Dramatic Art for five years, he joined D'Oyly Carte in 1966. His principal baritone roles include the Judge (J), Major-General Stanley (PP), Major Murgatroyd (P) and Antonio and Annibale (G).

Willis, Private (I) *Bass-baritone* The Grenadier Guards sentry on duty outside the Houses of Parliament ('Either a little Liberal or else a little Conservative') was first played by Charles Manners.

Wilson, Ethel The original Elsa (D).

Wilson, Robert He was with D'Oyly Carte from 1930 until 1937, starting in the chorus and going on to sing the Defendant (J), Ralph Rackstraw (HMS), Frederic (PP), Nanki-Poo (M) and Leonard Meryll (Y).

Wit 'An accepted wit has but to say "Pass the mustard," and they roar their ribs out!'—Jack Point (Y).
'I will teach thee all my original songs, my self-constructed riddles, my own ingenious paradoxes; nay, more, I will reveal to thee the source whence I get them.'—Jack Point.
Gilbert was, of course, an adept at bringing out the apt comment on the spur of the moment, as many lively anecdotes testify.
Standing impressively in the theatre foyer, he was mistaken for a commissionaire by a member of the audience. 'Call me a cab!' ordered the man. 'You are a four-wheeler, sir,' retorted Gilbert. 'I'm afraid I cannot call you hansom.'
He was asked by an acquaintance: 'Do you happen to know a fellow with one eye, called Michael?' 'I don't know,' said Gilbert. 'What's the other eye called!'
Approached with a request to give a certain actor the first refusal of a part, he immediately agreed. 'With pleasure,' he said. 'I refuse him at once.'
In his club one day, Gilbert was talking about his play *Gretchen*, based on the *Faust* idea, when a man on the fringe of the group burst in to ask how the piece ended. 'It ended in a fortnight,' retorted Gilbert sharply.
As the forthright man of words, Gilbert was productive of a fuller flow of anecdotes than Sullivan, the more reticent man of music. Nevertheless Sullivan had his own turn of wit on occasion. There was the time, for instance, when a member of the wealthy Sassoon family, one of Sullivan's circle of friends, approached him and, pointing out that every seat was taken for one of the Savoy's fashionable first nights, begged him to find a place somewhere. 'It's quite impossible,' Sullivan apologised. 'But, if you change the first letter of your name to B, I might find room for you in the orchestra!'

Witch's Curse, The Alternative title of *Ruddigore*.

'**With a sense of deep emotion**' Song by Counsel for the Plaintiff, in which he opens his case for breach of promise of marriage (J).

'**With aspect stern and gloomy stride**' Chorus opening the finale to the first act (M).

'**With cat-like tread, upon our prey we steal**' Chorus of pirates—sung very loudly! (PP).

'**With ducal pomp and ducal pride**' Chorus, with the Duke and Duchess of Plaza-Toro (G).

'**With fury deep we burn**' Duet for Scaphio and Phantis (U).

'**With fury indescribable I burn**' Baroness von Krakenfeldt's song (D).

'**With Heart and with Voice**' Chorus, first for the girls and later for the men (S).

'**Within this breast there beats a heart**' Richard Dauntless's solo (R).

'**With joy abiding**' Princess Ida's opening to the finale of the opera (PI).

'**With wily brain upon the spot**' Trio for Scaphio, Phantis and Tarara (U).

'**Woman of the wisest wit, The**' Quintet for Psyche, Melissa, Hilarion, Cyril and Florian (PI).

Women Gilbert's women—the women of the operas—fall into three main categories: the nice girls, the pert little minxes who have a very good opinion of themselves, and the forbidding, ageing spinsters.

One might put, for instance, Elsie Maynard, Gianetta and Ida in the first category. The present writer fell in love with Elsie at a very tender age, though it may well be that his youthful judgment was considerably influenced by the fact that the role was then played by the delightful Winifred Lawson. True, Elsie is prepared to accept a hundred crowns to marry a man whom she has never seen and who is about to be executed—but that is only in order to buy medicine for her ailing mother.

The pert and saucy ones have undoubted charm but they are in no way shy in letting us know about it. 'I am indeed beautiful!' says Yum-Yum (M), complacently. 'Sometimes I sit and wonder, in my artless Japanese way, why it is that I am so much more attractive than anybody else in the world.' And she goes on to compare herself, on equal terms, with the sun and the moon. Pitti-Sing, during the colourful account of the imaginary 'execution', is at pains to point out how the victim was soothed by the sight of *her*.

Strephon (I) bids his sweetheart look in a mirror and ask herself if it is rational to expect him to wait two years to marry her. 'No,' says Phyllis calmly. 'You're quite right—it's asking too much.'

As to the middle-aged women, Gilbert, himself blessed by a long and happy marriage, seemed to take it as a positive affront on their part that they should look less blooming than in their young days. He never missed an opportunity of ridiculing them in the operas and, perhaps even more cruelly, of insisting on them making *themselves* ridiculous. Right at the start, the Learned Judge (J) relates with relish how, at the beginning of his career, he fell in love with a rich attorney's elderly ugly daughter, who might 'very well pass for forty-three in the dusk with a light behind her'. Lady Sangazure (S) is described in the cast-line as 'a Lady of Ancient Lineage'. To Ko-Ko (M), Katisha is 'a most unattractive old thing, with a caricature of a face'. Sergeant Meryll (Y) harps on about being pursued by Dame Carruthers.

The substantially-built Queen of the Fairies (I) is made to say: 'Who taught me to curl myself inside a buttercup? Iolanthe. Who taught me to swing upon a cobweb? Iolanthe! Who taught me to dive into a dewdrop—to nestle in a nutshell—to gambol upon gossamer? Iolanthe!' 'She certainly did surprising things,' comments Leila. Lady Jane (P) declares: 'If you but knew what a wealth of golden love is stored up in this rugged old bosom of mine.' 'And a pretty damozel *you* are!' says Bunthorne. 'No, not pretty,' replies Lady Jane. 'Massive.' And she has that rather unpleasant song, 'Silvered is the raven hair,' though, by her comic business with the cello, the artist more often than not persuades us to laugh *with* her and not *at* her. At Sullivan's request Gilbert did make Lady Sophy (U) less forbidding than he had originally intended.

In the course of conversation, Gilbert was on one occasion making some comments about the Crimean War when a woman listener said, 'Of course *I* can't remember the Crimean War.' 'Oh, I'm sure you could if you tried,' murmured Gilbert. In the theatre one day he asked where a certain artist was. 'She's round behind,' he was told, meaning backstage. 'I know *that*,' he retorted. 'But *where* is she?'

Women's Education

'A Woman's college! maddest folly going!
What can girls learn within its walls worth knowing?
I'll lay a crown (the Princess shall decide it)
I'll teach them twice as much in half-an-hour outside it.'
—Florian (PI).

'Wonderful joy for our eyes to bless, A' Mr Goldbury's song about the sporting English girl (U).

'Won't it be a pretty wedding?' Opening chorus by members of Dummkopf's theatrical company (D).

Wood, (Sir) Henry J. Co-founder of the Promenade Concerts at Queen's Hall in 1895, he played the piano for the rehearsals of *The Yeomen of the Guard* at the Savoy Theatre in 1888, when he was nineteen. Three years later he assisted in the preparation of Sullivan's opera *Ivanhoe* at the Royal English Opera House.

Wooing by Proxy When Richard Dauntless woos Rose Maybud on behalf of his foster-brother, Robin Oakapple, he quickly changes his mind and pleads his own case (R). Colonel Fairfax generously agrees to show Jack Point how to woo Elsie Maynard—and the result is Jack's tragic discomfiture (Y). And Sir Joseph Porter, pointing out to Josephine that difference in rank does not debar her from marrying him, little realises that he is arguing the case for her to marry an ordinary seaman! (HMS).

'Words of love too loudly spoken' Duet for Princess Zara and Captain Fitzbattleaxe (U).

Workman, C. Herbert Workman, who was born in Bootle, Lancs, became a distinguished player of the 'little men' parts in the operas—the Grossmith parts. He made his first stage appearance as Calynx, the Utopian vice-chamberlain (U) at the Memorial Theatre, Stratford-upon-Avon, in 1894, and two years later he created the role of Ben Hashbaz in *The Grand Duke* at the Savoy. In the course of his career—he was only 49 when he died in 1923—he played a part in every Gilbert and Sullivan opera except *Ruddigore*.

'World is but a broken toy, The' Quartet for Princess Ida, Hilarion, Cyril and Florian (PI).

'Would you know the kind of maid sets my heart a-flame-a?' Cyril's song when slightly tipsy (PI).

Wright, Colin Principal tenor roles sung by him now include those of the Defendant (J), Frederic (PP), Nanki-Poo (M), Colonel Fairfax (Y) and Luiz (G). Born in Scunthorpe, he originally trained as a pianist at the Royal Academy of Music. Turning to singing, he was with the Welsh National Opera, then spent two years with the Black and White Minstrels and a year with Opera for All before joining D'Oyly Carte as a chorister.

Wright, Joyce Starting in the chorus in 1947, mezzo-soprano Joyce Wright was with the D'Oyly Carte Company for fifteen years. Her early principal roles included Peep-Bo (M), followed by several others, and in 1951 she took over Hebe (HMS), Angela (P), Iolanthe, Pitti-Sing (M), Mad Margaret (R), Phoebe (Y) and Tessa (G). She left the company in June 1962.

Wyatt, Frank As George Grossmith had then left the company, Frank Wyatt was brought in to create the part of the Duke of Plaza-Toro (G), the only part he played in the operas. He married Violet Melnotte and together they built and ran the Trafalgar Theatre which was opened in 1892. Three years later its name was changed to the Duke of York's. After Wyatt's death Violet Melnotte continued to run the theatre and became an influential and colourful figure in London's West End.

Xebeque The boat in which Marco and Giuseppe set out for Barataria (G) is a xebeque, sometimes spelt xebec, a small three-masted craft formerly used in the Mediterranean.

YEOMEN OF THE GUARD, The; or The Merryman and His Maid First performed at the Savoy Theatre, London on October 3, 1888, conducted by Sullivan. Initial run of 423 performances.

The cast in the first performance was:

SIR RICHARD CHOLMONDELEY (*Lieutenant of the Tower*)	Mr Wallace Brownlow
COLONEL FAIRFAX (*under sentence of death*)	Mr Courtice Pounds
SERGEANT MERYLL (*of the Yeomen of the Guard*)	Mr Richard Temple
LEONARD MERYLL (*his son*)	Mr W. R. Shirley
JACK POINT (*a strolling Jester*)	Mr George Grossmith
WILFRED SHADBOLT (*Head Jailor and Assistant Tormentor*)	Mr W. H. Denny
THE HEADSMAN	Mr Richards
FIRST YEOMAN	Mr J. Wilbraham
SECOND YEOMAN	Mr A. Medcalf
THIRD YEOMAN	Mr Murton
FOURTH YEOMAN	Mr Rudolph Lewis
FIRST CITIZEN	Mr Tom Redmond
SECOND CITIZEN	Mr Boyd
ELSIE MAYNARD (*a strolling Singer*)	Miss Geraldine Ulmar
PHOEBE MERYLL (*Sergeant Meryll's daughter*)	Miss Jessie Bond
DAME CARRUTHERS (*Housekeeper to the Tower*)	Miss Rosina Brandram
KATE (*her Niece*)	Miss Rose Hervey

After the overture the curtain opens on Tower Green, revealing Phoebe, Sergeant Meryll's daughter, sitting at her spinning-wheel. For the first time in the Savoy operas, there is no opening chorus. Phoebe is alone, singing:

When maiden loves, she sits and sighs,
She wanders to and fro;
Unbidden tear-drops fill her eyes,
And to all questions she replies
With a sad 'heigho!'
'Tis but a little word—'heigho!'
So soft, tis scarcely heard—'heigho!'
An idle breath—
Yet life and death
May hang upon a maid's 'heigho!'

When maiden loves, she mopes apart,
As owl mopes on a tree;
Although she keenly feels the smart,
She cannot tell what ails her heart,
With its sad 'Ah me!'
'Tis but a foolish sigh—'Ah me!'
Born but to droop and die—'Ah me!'
Yet all the sense
Of eloquence
Lies hidden in a maid's 'Ah me!'

She is shedding a tear as the Head Jailer and Assistant Tormentor'
Wilfred Shadbolt, enters, to be mocked by her about his gruesome
profession. Their conversation reveals that Phoebe has been attracted
by the good looks of the young prisoner, Colonel Fairfax, who is
to be beheaded that day on a charge of sorcery. Wilfred departs,
grumbling jealously, and the Green is filled by a crowd of townsfolk, followed by the Yeomen of the Guard. 'Tower Warders,
Under orders, Gallant pikemen, valiant sworders!' sing the crowd,
with the Yeomen joining in:

In the autumn of our life,
Here at rest in ample clover,
We rejoice in telling over
Our impetuous May and June.
In the evening of our day,
With the sun of life declining,
We recall without repining
All the heat of bygone noon. . .

In an outburst to Dame Carruthers, housekeeper of the Tower,
Phoebe insists that Fairfax is no sorcerer but an innocent student of
alchemy. Her tirade against the bloodthirstiness of the Tower brings
Dame Carruthers at once to its defence:

When our gallant Norman foes
Made our merry land their own,
And the Saxons from the Conqueror were flying,
At his bidding it arose,
In its panoply of stone,
A sentinel unliving and undying.
Insensible, I trow,
As a sentinel should be,
Though a queen to save her head should come a-suing.
There's a legend on it's brow
That is eloquent to me,
And it tells of duty done and duty doing.
'The screw may twist and the rack may turn,
And men may bleed and men may burn,
O'er London town and its golden hoard
I keep my silent watch and ward!'

Within its wall of rock
The flower of the brave
Have perished with a constancy unshaken.
From the dungeon to the block,
From the scaffold to the grave,
Is a journey many gallant hearts have taken.
And the wicked flames may hiss
Round the heroes who have fought
For conscience and for home in all its beauty;
But the grim old fortalice
Takes little heed of aught
That comes not in the measure of its duty.
'The screw may twist and the rack may turn,
And men may bleed and men may burn,
O'er London town and its golden hoard
I keep my silent watch and ward!'

Sergeant Meryll, with Phoebe, awaits the arrival of his son Leonard who, after gallant service, has been appointed a Yeoman of the Guard. But he brings only a despatch for the Lieutenant of the Tower—no reprieve for Fairfax. Meryll, who reveals that Fairfax had twice saved his life, suggests that, as no one has seen or would recognise Leonard, he shall go into hiding while Fairfax, with beard removed, is taken from his cell and presented as the returned son. (It seems odd that, just because Fairfax shaves off his beard, none of the warders will recognise him! The trio: 'Alas! I waver to and fro! Dark danger hangs upon the deed!' is well justified).

Fairfax, out on exercise under guard, greets his old friend Meryll and, in a much-admired ballad, muses philosophically upon his fate:

> Is life a boon?
> If so, it must befall
> That Death, whene'er he call,
> Must call too soon.
> Though fourscore years he give,
> Yet one would pray to live
> Another moon!
> What kind of plaint have I,
> Who perish in July?
> I might have had to die,
> Perchance, in June!
>
> Is life a thorn?
> Then count it not a whit!
> Man is well done with it;
> Soon as he's born
> He should all means essay
> To put the plague away;
> And I, war-worn,
> Poor captured fugitive,
> My life most gladly give—
> I might have had to live
> Another morn!

Fairfax has a last request to make of the Lieutenant of the Tower. The charge of sorcery has been laid against him by a kinsman who will succeed to his estates if he dies unmarried. Can a bride, any bride, be found for him? The Lieutenant's hesitancy is overcome by Fairfax's comment: 'There never was a marriage fraught with so little of evil for the contracting parties. In an hour she'll be a widow, and I—a bachelor again for aught I know!'

As they go off the mood changes into one of excitement as Jack Point, the strolling jester, rushes in with his companion, Elsie Maynard, both of them alarmed by the shouting crowd which pursues them:

> Here's a man of jollity,
> Jibe, joke, jollify!
> Give us of your quality,
> Come fool, follify!
>
> If you vapour vapidily,
> River runneth rapidly,

Into it we fling
Bird who doesn't sing!
Give us an experiment
In the art of merriment;
Into it we throw
Cock who doesn't crow!
Banish your timidity,
And with all rapidity
Give us quip and quiddity—
Willy-nilly, O!
River none can mollify;—
Into it we throw
Fool who doesn't follify,
Cock who doesn't crow!

Jack has a good deal of trouble with some of the more boisterous citizens who try to embrace the attractive Elsie but, to satisfy the crowd, the two of them oblige with 'the singing farce of the Merryman and His Maid', which gives the opera its sub-title:

POINT:
I have a song to sing, O!

ELSIE:
Sing me that song, O!

POINT:
It is sung to the moon
By a love-lorn loon,
Who fled from the mocking throng, O!
It's a song of a merryman, moping mum,
Whose soul was sad, and whose glance was glum,
Who sipped no sup, and who craved no crumb,
As he sighed for the love of a ladye.
Heighdy! heighdy!
Misery me, lackadaydee!
He sipped no sup, and he craved no crumb,
As he sighed for the love of a ladye.

ELSIE:
I have a song to sing, O!

POINT:
What is your song, O!

ELSIE:
It is sung with the ring
Of the songs maids sing

Who love with a love life-long, O!
It's the song of a merrymaid, peerly proud,
Who loved a lord, and who laughed aloud
At the moan of the merryman, moping mum,
Whose soul was sad, and whose glance was glum,
Who sipped no sup, and who craved no crumb,
As he sighed for the love of a ladye!
Heighdy! heighdy!
Misery me, lackadaydee!
He sipped no sup. . . .

POINT
I have a song to sing, O!

ELSIE:
Sing me your song, O!

POINT:
It is sung to the knell
Of a churchyard bell,
And a doleful dirge, ding dong, O!
It's a song of a popinjay, bravely born,
Who turned up his noble nose with scorn
At the humble merrymaid, peerly proud,
Who loved a lord and who laughed aloud
At the moan of the merryman, moping mum,
Whose soul was sad, and whose glance was glum,
Who sipped no sup, and who craved no crumb,
As he sighed for the love of a laydye!
Heighdy! heighdy!
Misery me, lackadaydee!
He sipped no sup. . . .

ELSIE:
I have a song to sing, O!

POINT:
Sing me your song, O!

ELSIE:
It is sung with a sigh
And a tear in the eye,
For it tells of a righted wrong, O!
It's a song of the merrymaid, once so gay,
Who turned on her heel and tripped away
From the peacock popinjay, bravely born,
Who turned up his noble nose in scorn

At the humble heart that he did not prize:
So she begged on her knees, with downcast eyes,
For the love of the merryman, moping mum,
Whose soul was sad, and whose glance was glum,
Who sipped no sup, and who craved no crumb,
As he sighed for the love of a ladye!

ALL:
Heighdy! heighdy!
Misery me, lackadaydee!
His pains were o'er, and he sighed no more,
For he lived in the love of a ladye!

Amid the applause, one of the citizens tries to kiss Elsie who draws a dagger, just as the Lieutenant arrives on the scene, inquiring what all the row is about. He ascertains that Jack and Elsie are not man and wife—though Jack says meaningly that 'Time works wonders' —and makes the offer of a hundred crowns if Elsie will marry Fairfax. As they are there to pick up some silver to buy an electuary (a sweetened medicine) for Elsie's sick mother, and as they are assured that Fairfax is to die, Jack agrees to the plan. They express their points of view in a trio:

LIEUT.:
How say you, maiden, will you wed
A man about to lose his head?
For half an hour
You'll be a wife,
And then the dower
Is yours for life.
A headless bridegroom why refuse?
If truth the poets tell,
Most bridegrooms, ere they marry, lose
Both head and heart as well!

ELSIE:
A strange proposal you reveal,
It almost makes my senses reel.
Alas! I'm very poor indeed,
And such a sum I sorely need.
My mother, sir, is like to die,
This money life may bring.
Bear this in mind, I pray, if I
Consent to do this thing!

POINT:

Though as a general rule of life
I don't allow my promised wife,
My lovely bride that is to be,
To marry anyone but me,
Yet if the fee is promptly paid,
And he, in well-earned grave
Within the hour is duly laid,
Objection I will waive!
Yes, objection I will waive!

ALL:

Temptation, oh, temptation,
Were we, I pray, intended
To shun, whate'er our station,
Your fascinations splendid;
Or fall, whene'er we view you,
Head over heels into you!

Blindfolded, Elsie is led away into the Cold Harbour Tower, while the Lieutenant questions Jack about his profession as jester. Jack explains:

I've jibe and joke
And quip and crank,
For lowly folk
And men of rank.
I ply my craft
And know no fear,
But aim my shaft
At prince or peer.
At peer or prince—at prince or peer,
I aim my shaft and know no fear!

I've wisdom from the East and from the West,
That's subject to no academic rule;
You may find it in the jeering of a jest,
Or distil it from the folly of a fool.
I can teach you with a quip, if I've a mind;
I can trick you into learning with a laugh;
Oh winnow all my folly, and you'll find
A grain or two of truth among the chaff!

I can set a braggart quailing with a quip,
The upstart I can wither with a whim;
He may wear a merry laugh upon his lip,
But his laughter has an echo that is grim!

467

When they're offered to the world in merry guise,
Unpleasant truths are swallowed with a will—
For he who'd make his fellow creatures wise
Should always gild the philosophic pill!

On the Lieutenant suggesting that he might be able to offer a
permanent job, Jack runs through some samples of his jokes and
they go off together, as Wilfred brings back Elsie and removes the
bandage from her eyes. She pours forth her feelings after being
married to a man she has never seen:

'Tis done! I am a bride! Oh, little ring,
That bearest in thy circlet all the gladness
That lovers hope for, and that poets sing,
What bringest thou to me but gold and sadness?
A bridegroom all unknown, save in this wise,
To-day he dies! To-day, alas, he dies!

Though tear and long-drawn sigh
Ill fit a bride,
No sadder wife than I
The whole world wide!
Ah me! Ah me!
Yet maids there be
Who would consent to lose
The very rose of youth,
The flower of life,
To be, in honest truth,
A wedded wife,
No matter whose!

Ah me! what profit we,
O maids that sigh,
Though gold, should live
If wedded love must die?

Ere half an hour has rung,
A widow I!
Ah heaven, he is too young,
Too brave to die!
Ah me! Ah me!
Yet wives there be
So weary worn, I trow,
That they would scarce complain,

So that they could
In half an hour attain
To widowhood,
No matter how!

O weary wives
Who widowhood would win,
Rejoice that ye have time
To weary in.

It is now time for Phoebe to play her part in the scheme. Wilfred re-enters after Elsie's departure and is pondering over what can have taken place in Fairfax's cell—his own special keyhole had been blocked up!—when Phoebe brings her charms to play upon him, watched from the background by her father. As she soothes him with smooth flattery and the vaguest hints that there might be a future for them together, she quietly takes the bunch of keys from his belt and passes it to her father. Her song continues to hold the attention of the bemused Wilfred:

Were I thy bride,
Then the whole world beside
Were not too wide
To hold my wealth of love—
Were I thy bride!

Upon thy breast
My loving head would rest,
As on her nest
The tender turtle dove—
Were I thy bride!

This heart of mine
Would be one heart with thine,
And in that shrine
Our happiness would dwell—
Were I thy bride!

And all day long
Our lives should be a song:
No grief, no wrong
Should make my heart rebel—
Were I thy bride!

The silvery flute,
The melancholy lute,

Were night owl's hoot
To my love-whispered coo—
Were I thy bride!

The skylark's trill
Were but discordance shrill
To the soft thrill
Of wooing as I'd woo
Were I thy bride!

Meryll re-enters, gives the keys to Phoebe who replaces them at Wilfred's girdle. Meryll departs and Phoebe continues:

The rose's sigh
Were as a carrion's cry
To lullaby
Such as I'd sing to thee,
Were I thy bride!

A feather's press
Were leaden heaviness
To my caress.
But then, of course, you see
I'm not thy bride!

No wonder Wilfred is in a bewildered frame of mind as he follows Phoebe off the stage. Meryll comes forward as Colonel Fairfax arrives, minus beard and moustache and wearing Yeoman's uniform —a quick change indeed!

The Yeomen arrive and greet the man they believe to be Leonard Meryll, with praise for his gallant deeds:

Didst thou not, oh, Leonard Meryll,
Standard lost in last campaign,
Rescue it at deadly peril—
Bear it safely back again?
Leonard Meryll, at his peril,
Bore it safely back again!
Didst thou not, when prisoner taken,
And debarred from all escape,
Face, with gallant heart unshaken,
Death in most appalling shape?
Leonard Meryll faced his peril,
Death in most appalling shape!

FAIRFAX (*aside*):
Truly I was to be pitied,
Having but an hour to live,
I reluctantly submitted,
I had no alternative!
(*aloud*)
Oh! the tales that are narrated
Of my deeds of derring-do
Have been much exaggerated,
Very much exaggerated,
Scarce a word of them is true!

Phoebe rushes forward and embraces Fairfax, much to his puzzlement until he realises that she is his 'sister'. The jealous Wilfred points out that he and Phoebe are betrothed. 'Or more or less,' adds Phoebe. 'But rather less than more.' Wilfred, satisfied that, as they are brother and sister, it must be all right for them to embrace each other, adjures Fairfax always to watch over her—to which Phoebe agrees with the greatest warmth!

WILFRED:
To thy fraternal care
Thy sister I commend;
From every lurking snare
Thy lovely charge defend:
And to achieve this end,
Oh! grant, I pray, this boon—
She shall not quit thy sight:
From morn to afternoon—
From afternoon to night—
From seven o'clock to two—
From two to eventide—
From dim twilight to 'leven at night
She shall not quit thy side!

PHOEBE:
So amiable I've grown,
So innocent as well,
That if I'm left alone
The consequences fell
No mortal can foretell.
So grant, I pray, this boon—
I shall not quit thy sight;
From morn to afternoon—
From afternoon to night—

From seven o'clock to two—
From two to eventide—
From dim twilight to 'leven at night
I shall not quit thy side!

FAIRFAX:

With brotherly readiness,
For my fair sister's sake,
At once I answer 'Yes'—
That task I undertake—
My word I never break.
I freely grant that boon,
And I'll repeat my plight.
From morn to afternoon—(*kiss*)
From afternoon to night—(*kiss*)
From seven o'clock to two—(*kiss*)
From two to evening meal—(*kiss*)
From dim twilight to 'leven at night—(*kiss*)
That compact I will seal.

But it is time for the execution of Fairfax. The bell tolls, a funeral
march is played, the crowd pours in, the block is put in position and
the headsman stands ready. The Lieutenant orders Fairfax (!) and
two others to bring in the prisoner. Elsie, with the chorus sings:

Oh, Mercy, thou whose smile has shone
So many a captive heart upon;
Of all immured within these walls,
To-day the very worthiest falls!

Suddenly all is turmoil. The prisoner's cell is empty! Poor Wilfred
is arrested, protesting: 'My lord, I did not set him free. I hate
the man—my rival he!' Elsie turns to Jack Point: 'What have I
done! Oh, woe is me! I am his wife, and he is free!' But Jack is
thinking of what it means to *him*:

Oh, woe is *you*? Your anguish sink!
Oh, woe is *me*, I rather think!
Oh, woe is *me*, I rather think!
Yes, woe is *me*, I rather think!
Whate'er betide
You are his bride,
And I am left
Alone—bereft!
Yes, woe is *me*, I rather think!
Yes, woe is *me*, I rather think!

The Lieutenant offers a reward of a thousand crowns to anyone who brings back the prisoner dead or alive, Yeomen and citizens rush away on the chase, Elsie faints in Fairfax's arms, and the thwarted headsman is still standing beside the block as the curtain falls.

It is moonlight on the same scene when the curtain rises on the second act. The chorus cry shame on the 'loutish jailer-folk' and, arriving with her niece Kate, Dame Carruthers, that devoted housekeeper of the Tower, gives the warders the length of her tongue:

> Warders are ye?
> Whom do you ward?
> Bolt, bar, and key,
> Shackle and cord,
> Fetter and chain,
> Dungeon of stone,
> All are in vain—
> Prisoner's flown!
> Spite of ye all—he is free!
> Whom do ye ward? Pretty warders are ye!

The Yeomen break in:

> Up and down, and in and out,
> Here and there, and round about;
> Every chamber, every house,
> Every chink that holds a mouse,
> Every crevice in the keep,
> Where a beetle black could creep,
> Every outlet, every drain,
> Have we searched, but all in vain.

They go off to resume their search, making way for a depressed Jack Point, reading from a large volume, 'The Merrie Jests of Hugh Ambrose'. He meets an equally depressed Wilfred Shadbolt and, with a show of high spirits, rallies Wilfred on his lack of success as a jailer. Wilfred confides that he has often thought that the profession of jesting would suit him. Jack gives him some advice on the hazards of the job:

> Oh! a private buffoon is a light-hearted loon,
> If you listen to popular rumour;
> From the morn to the night he's so joyous and bright,
> And he bubbles with wit and good humour!
> He's so quaint and so terse both in prose and in verse;

Yet though people forgive his transgression,
There are one or two rules that all family fools
Must observe, if they love their profession.
There are one or two rules,
Half a dozen, maybe,
That all family fools,
Of whatever degree,
Must observe, if they love their profession.

If you wish to succeed as a jester, you'll need
To consider each person's auricular:
What is all right for B would quite scandalize C
(For C is so very particular);
And D may be dull, and E's very thick skull
Is as empty of brains as a ladle;
While F is F sharp, and will cry with a carp
That he's known your best jokes from his cradle!
When your humour they flout,
You can't let yourself go;
And it *does* put you out
When a person says, 'Oh,
I have known that old joke from my cradle!'

If your master is surly, from getting up early
(And tempers are short in the morning),
An inopportune joke is enough to provoke
Him to give you, at once, a month's warning.
Then if you refrain, he is at you again,
For he likes to get value for money;
He'll ask then and there, with an insolent stare,
'If you know that you're paid to be funny?'
It adds to the tasks
Of a merryman's place,
When your principal asks,
With a scowl on his face,
If you know that you're paid to be funny?

Comes a Bishop, maybe, or a solemn DD—
Oh, beware of his anger provoking!
Better not pull his hair—don't stick pins in his chair;
He don't understand practical joking.
If the jests that you crack have an orthodox smack,
You may get a bland smile from these sages;
But should they, by chance, be imported from France,
Half-a-crown is stopped out of your wages!

It's a general rule,
Though your zeal it may quench,
If the family fool
Tells a joke that's too French,
Half-a-crown is stopped out of his wages!

Though your head it may rack with a bilious attack,
And your senses with toothache you're losing,
Don't be mopy and flat—they don't fine you for that,
If you're properly quaint and amusing!
Though your wife ran away with a soldier that day,
And took with her your trifle of money;
Bless your heart, they don't mind—they're exceedingly
  kind—
They don't blame you—as long as you're funny!
It's a comfort to feel,
If your partner should flit,
Though *you* suffer a deal,
They don't mind it a bit—
They don't blame you—so long as you're funny!

Jack thinks of a scheme whereby his sweetheart Elsie, though she
has been married to Fairfax, will appear to be free. He makes a
bargain. In return for lessons in jesting, Wilfred will swear that he
shot Fairfax while he was trying to swim across the river and he
(Jack) will back up the story:

> BOTH:
> Hereupon we're both agreed,
> All that we two
> Do agree to
> We'll secure by solemn deed,
> To prevent all
> Error mental.
>
> POINT:
> You on Elsie are to call
> With a story
> Grim and gory;
>
> WILFRED:
> How this Fairfax died, and all
> I declare to
> You're to swear to.

BOTH:
Tell a tale of cock and bull,
Of convincing detail full,
Tale tremendous,
Heaven defend us!
What a tale of cock and bull!

BOTH:
In return for your/my own part
You are/I am making
Undertaking
To instruct me/you in the art
(Art amazing,
 Wonder raising)

POINT:
Of a jester, jesting free.
Proud position—
High ambition!

WILFRED:
And a lively one I'll be,
Wag-a-wagging,
Never flagging!

BOTH:
Tell a tale of cock and bull. . . . .

They depart to work out their plan and Fairfax enters, pondering on his situation in an appealing ballad:

Free from his fetters grim—
Free to depart;
Free both in life and limb—
In all but heart!
Bound to an unknown bride
For good and ill;
Ah, is not one so tied
A prisoner still?

Free, yet in fetters held
Till his last hour,
Gyves that no smith can weld,
No rust devour!
Although a monarch's hand
Had set him free,
Of all the captive band
The saddest he!

Fairfax is joined by Sergeant Meryll and Dame Carruthers, who has been nursing the distraught Elsie Maynard. She reveals that her niece Kate, while sitting by the bedside, had heard Elsie moaning, 'How shall I marry one I have never seen?' and 'I love him not, and yet I am his wife.' Fairfax, Meryll, Dame Carruthers and Kate join in a solemn quartet:

> Strange adventure! Maiden wedded
> To a groom she's never seen—
> Never, never, never seen!
> Groom about to be beheaded,
> In an hour on Tower Green!
> Tower, Tower, Tower Green!
> Groom in dreary dungeon lying,
> Groom as good as dead, or dying,
> For a pretty maiden sighing—
> Pretty maid of seventeen!
> Seven—seven—seventeen!
>
> Strange adventure that we're trolling:
> Modest maid and gallant groom—
> Gallant, gallant, gallant groom!
> While the funeral bell is tolling,
> Tolling, tolling, Bim-a-boom!
> Bim-a, Bim-a, Bim-a-boom!
> Modest maiden will not tarry;
> Though but sixteen year she carry,
> She must marry, she must marry,
> Though the altar be a tomb—
> Tower—Tower—Tower tomb!

So the charming Elsie is his unknown bride! muses Fairfax—and, as she enters, he decides to woo her, not very kindly it might be thought, in the guise of Leonard Meryll. But she resists him and, just when he is about to reveal himself as her husband, there comes the sound of an arquebus being fired from the wharf. The crowd rush in impatiently, and Wilfred and Jack Point, rather in the manner of the imaginary execution in *The Mikado*, tell their tale:

> WILFRED:
> Like a ghost his vigil keeping—
>
> POINT:
> Or a spectre all-appalling—
>
> WILFRED:
> I beheld a figure creeping—

POINT:
I should rather call it crawling—

WILFRED:
He was creeping—

POINT:
He was crawling—

WILFRED:
He was creeping, creeping—

POINT:
Crawling!

WILFRED:
He was creeping—

POINT:
He was crawling—

WILFRED:
He was creeping, creeping—

POINT:
Crawling!

WILFRED:
Not a moment's hesitation—
I myself upon him flung,
With a hurried exclamation
To his draperies I hung;
Then we closed with one another
In a rough-and-tumble smother;
Colonel Fairfax and no other
Was the man to whom I clung!

ALL:
Colonel Fairfax and no other
Was the man to whom he clung!

WILFRED:
After mighty tug and tustle—

POINT:
It resembled more a struggle—

WILFRED:
He, by dint of stronger muscle—

POINT:
Or by some infernal juggle—

WILFRED:
From my clutches quickly sliding—

POINT:
I should rather call it slipping—

WILFRED:
With a view, no doubt, of hiding—

POINT:
Or escaping to the shipping—

WILFRED:
With a gasp and with a quiver—

POINT:
I'd describe it as a shiver—

WILFRED:
Down he dived into the river,
And, alas, I cannot swim.

ALL:
It's enough to make one shiver—
With a gasp and with a quiver,
Down he dived into the river;
It was very brave of him!

WILFRED:
Ingenuity is catching;
With the view my king of pleasing,
Arquebus from sentry snatching—

POINT:
I should rather call it seizing—

WILFRED:
With an ounce or two of lead
I despatched him through the head!

ALL:
With an ounce or two of lead
He despatched him through the head!

WILFRED:
I discharged it without winking,
Little time I lost in thinking,
Like a stone I saw him sinking—

POINT:
I should say a lump of lead.

ALL:
He discharged it without winking,
Little time he lost in thinking.

WILFRED:

Like a stone I saw him sinking—

POINT:

I should say a lump of lead.

WILFRED:

Like a stone, my boy, I said—

POINT:

Like a heavy lump of lead.

WILFRED:

Anyhow, the man is dead,
Whether stone or lump of lead!

ALL:

Anyhow, the man is dead,
Whether stone or lump of lead!
Arquebus from sentry seizing,
With the view his king of pleasing,
Wilfred shot him through the head,
And he's very, very dead.
And it matters very little whether stone or lump
    of lead;
It is very, very certain that he's very, very dead!

The 'heroic' Wilfred is carried off shoulder-high. Jack Point reminds Elsie that she is now free to choose her husband and is just starting to put forward his own claims when Fairfax points out that wooing is an art in itself. Fairfax, Elsie and Phoebe give their advice on the subject in a delightful trio:

FAIRFAX:

A man who would woo a fair maid
Should 'prentice himself to the trade,
And study all day,
In methodical way,
How to flatter, cajole and persuade.
He should 'prentice himself at fourteen,
And practice from morning to e'en;
And when he's of age,
If he will, I'll engage
He may capture the heart of a queen!

ALL:

It is purely a matter of skill,
Which all may attain if they will:

But every Jack,
He must study the knack
If he wants to make sure of his Jill!

ELSIE:
If he's made the best use of his time,
His twig he'll so carefully lime
That every bird
Will come down at his word,
Whatever its plumage and clime.
He must learn that the thrill of a touch
May mean little, or nothing, or much;
It's an instrument rare,
To be handled with care,
And ought to be treated as such.

ALL:
It is purely a matter of skill. . . .

PHOEBE:
Then a glance may be timid or free,
It will vary in mighty degree,
From an impudent stare
To a look of despair
That no maid without pity can see!
And a glance of despair is no guide—
It may have its ridiculous side;
It may draw you a tear
Or a box on the ear;
You can never be sure till you've tried!

ALL:
It is purely a matter of skill. . . .

Fairfax demonstrates how he would accomplish the wooing of Elsie, and Jack Point, believing that all this is done on his behalf, is at first full of approval. But it gradually becomes clear that Fairfax is avowing his own love, to the alarm of Jack, and of Phoebe, who bursts into tears.

ELSIE and FAIRFAX:
When a wooer
Goes a wooing,
Naught is truer
Than his joy.

481

Maiden blushing
All his suing—
Boldly blushing—
Bravely coy!

ALL:
Oh, the happy days of doing!
Oh, the sighing and the suing!
When a wooer goes a wooing,
Oh, the sweets that never cloy!

PHOEBE (*weeping*):
When a brother
Leaves his sister
For another,
Sister weeps.
Tears that trickle,
Tears that blister—
'Tis but mickle
Sister reaps!

ALL:
Oh, the doing and undoing,
Oh, the sighing and the suing,
When a brother goes a-wooing,
And a sobbing sister weeps!

POINT:
When a jester
Is outwitted,
Feelings fester,
Heart is lead!
Food for fishes
Only fitted,
Jester wishes
He was dead!

ALL:
Oh, the doing and undoing,
Oh, the sighing and the suing,
When a jester goes a-wooing,
And he wishes he was dead!

They leave Phoebe alone. She is discovered weeping by Wilfred, to whom she unwittingly reveals that the man supposed to be Leonard Meryll is *not* her brother—and Wilfred guesses the truth. He is starting to vow vengeance when she reminds him that he has already sworn to having killed Fairfax! But, having lost Fairfax, she agrees to marry Wilfred, but with no great show of enthusiasm.

The real Leonard Meryll arrives, with the news that Fairfax has been reprieved, the message having been held back by the Colonel's malicious kinsman. Phoebe tells her father that she had accidentally revealed to Wilfred the truth about Fairfax—and the eavesdropping Dame Carruthers seizes her advantage: 'So this is a plot to shield this arch-fiend, and I have detected it. A word from me and three heads besides his would roll from their shoulders!' Reluctantly, Sergeant Meryll agrees to marry her.

The opera moves swiftly to its close, with Elsie at last realising that the man she loves is the man to whom she is married. But all is not joyful. Jack Point enters, dejectedly:

> Oh, thoughtless crew!
> Ye know not what ye do!
> Attend to me, and shed a tear or two—
> For I have a song to sing, O!

He is joined by Elsie in the song they have sung so often together, though her words are now significantly different:

> It is sung with the ring
> Of the songs maids sing
> Who love with a love life-long, O!
> It's the song of a merrymaid, nestling near,
> Who loved her lord—but who dropped a tear
> At the moan of the merryman, moping mum,
> Whose soul was sad, and whose glance was glum,
> Who sipped no sup, and who craved no crumb,
> As he sighed for the love of a ladye!

As Fairfax and Elsie embrace, Jack Point falls insensible at their feet.

'Yes—yes—yes—Stupendous loans to foreign thrones' Solo by Mr Goldbury, the company promoter (U).

'Ye torrents roar! Ye tempests howl!' Katisha's part in the ensemble which closes the first act (M).

'Ye wanderers from a foreign State' Quartet for Zara, Lady Sophy, Captain Fitzbattleaxe and the King in the first act finale (U).

Young, David He had appeared in *The Yeomen of the Guard* at the Tower of London during the City Festival in 1962 and had then been with Sadler's Wells Opera before joining D'Oyly Carte in 1968. He was born in Ayrshire and joined the local police force, studying singing while serving with them and making several guest appearances as a tenor on Scottish television. He became a professional singer in 1961.

'Young man, despair' Pooh-Bah's song, with Nanki-Poo and Pish-Tush—'And the brass will crash.' (M).

'Your maiden hearts, ah, do not steel' Duke of Dunstable's song, accompanied by sighing and weeping from his fellow dragoons (P).

'You told me you were fair as gold!' Duet for Frederic and Ruth (PP).

'You understand?' Duet for Sir Despard Murgatroyd and Richard Dauntless—'For duty, duty must be done' (R).

Yum-Yum (M) *Soprano* One of the Three Little Maids, wards of Ko-Ko, Yum-Yum does not by any means underrate her own charms—'We really know our worth, the sun and I.' The role was originally played by Leonora Braham.

Zara, Princess (U) *Soprano* Nancy McIntosh was the first artist to play King Paramount's eldest daughter.

Zoffany 'I can tell undoubted Raphaels from Gerald Dows and Zoffanies.'—Major-General Stanley (PP). Johann Zoffany (1734–1810), was born in Germany, studied in Italy and painted mainly in England, specialising in portraits and theatrical scenes. He was a founder-member of the Royal Academy in London in 1768.

Zorah (R) *Soprano* Josephine Findlay was the first artist to play Zorah, one of the professional bridesmaids.

782.81 A
AYRE
    THE GILBERT AND SULLIVAN
COMPANION   12.50

DATE DUE

JAN 2 6 1994	
JAN 2 0 1996	
SEP 2 6 1996	
FEB 1 1997	
JAN 2 9 2001	
FEB 2 7 2001	
11/26/04	
1/29/15 5/7/13 14c	

GAYLORD   PRINTED IN U.S.A.